Insert within front
cover of book

From Union to Union

Nationalism, Democracy and Religion in Ireland — Act of Union to EU

From Union to Union

Nationalism, Democracy and Religion in Ireland — Act of Union to EU

Brian Girvin

Gill & Macmillan

This is for Rona

Thanks for staying the distance

Gill & Macmillan Ltd
Hume Avenue, Park West, Dublin 12
with associated companies throughout the world
www.gillmacmillan.ie

0 7171 3336 2
Index compiled by Helen Litton
Design and print origination by Carole Lynch
Printed by ColourBooks Ltd, Dublin

This book is typeset in New Baskerville 10 on 12pt.

The paper used in this book comes from the wood pulp of managed forests. For every tree felled, at least one tree is planted, thereby renewing natural resources.

A CIP catalogue record for this book is available from the British Library.

1 3 5 4 2

Contents

Preface

The idea for this book came to me shortly after I was invited to write a chapter for the seventh volume of the Royal Irish Academy's *New History of Ireland*. While doing the original research, I realised that the Irish experience of nationalism, democracy and religion has many lessons for the contemporary world. Not least of these lessons is how deeply ingrained ethnic identity is and how it contributes to nationalist conflict and instability. In more positive light, there is the evidence that democracy is not incompatible with a society that has strong nationalist and religious values. But it also demonstrated to me how central nationalism is to modern political life, not only when a nation is demanding self-determination but even when an independent state is well established and stable. Ireland, north and south, remains an important case study for both the positive and negative aspects of nationalism, and its experience may, as a consequence, be of general interest and application.

On a more personal note, my maternal grandfather, Ned Hegarty, fought in the War of Independence and opposed the Treaty in 1922. He remained a Fianna Fáil supporter throughout his life. My father grew up in Northern Ireland of Scots-Ulster parentage and became a militant republican as a young man. He was an active supporter of the Provisional IRA in later life. Despite being brought up in a strong republican tradition, I ceased to be a nationalist in my twenties. There are complex reasons for this, including the conflict in Northern Ireland and the recognition that Ulster unionists have a right to self-determination as well as Irish nationalists. However, the most important reason is that I find nationalism limiting and the attractions of liberal universalism more appealing. I'm afraid I can never accept Decatur's maxim 'our country, right or wrong'. I now recognise that there are values which transcend any loyalty to a nation or state.

Writing a book may be an individual endeavour, but the author accumulates considerable debts in the process. I would like to take this opportunity to thank those who have helped me while I was working on this book. Librarians and archivists in University College Cork, the University of Glasgow, the National Library of Ireland, the National Archives of Ireland, University College Dublin Archives Department, the Public Record Office, London, and the National Archives, Washington DC, gave me considerable help while carrying out the research. A special word of thanks to Philip Hannon at Fianna Fáil, for his help with the party archives. Ivan Doherty gave me permission to consult the Fine Gael party minutes in UCD. My postgraduate students in University College Cork, in particular Tracey Connolly, Maureen Hartigan,

Michael Harte, Brian McCarthy, Seán Kelly and Fiona Wallace, provided me with numerous insights into various aspects of twentieth-century Ireland.

My good friend Gary Murphy not only read much of the book and offered insightful comments on a whole range of issues, but also shared his own research work with me. Roy Foster kindly invited me to deliver an early version of chapter 3 to the seminar on Irish history at Hertford College, the University of Oxford. Roy also alerted me to the wartime activities of Elizabeth Bowen and made available to me copies of her despatches to London. Patrick Maume read draft versions of the first two chapters and generously provided me with extensive comments and suggestions. Celia Weston read an earlier version of the text and commented incisively on style and content. While working on the book I was also engaged in a joint project on the Irish volunteers who fought for the Allies in the Second World War with my friend and colleague Geoff Roberts. Geoff could not have been more helpful, both in the intellectual sense and in giving me encouragement when I was at low ebb. I continue to owe an intellectual debt to Joe Lee. He has been my teacher, supervisor and colleague for over twenty-five years now and, though I no longer work with him, his influence on my thinking remains one of the most enduring. My colleague James Kellas in Glasgow has been generous with his time and experience both in respect of Scotland and more generally on nationalism.

I received financial assistance from the John Robertson Bequest at the University of Glasgow while carrying out research for this book. I would like to thank the University for this support.

I am delighted that this book has given me the opportunity to work again with Fergal Tobin at Gill & Macmillan. His advice on earlier versions has always been apt and the current version owes much to him.

My father died while I was writing this book. I am sorry that he could not have read it. He might not have agreed with everything I have to say here, but what it does contain owes much to my engagement with him over the years and my attempt to understand his view of the world. A special word of thanks to my brother Kevin for checking a number of references for me at short notice.

The most important influence on this book has been that of Rona Fitzgerald. She has read and re-read successive versions with patience, good humour and acute insight. My interaction with her has been intellectually creative, providing a balanced view when my thinking was wayward. She has always given me the emotional support to continue this research, even when it means that I disappear into an archive or my office for extended periods of time. All this while she has been developing a new area of expertise and research herself. For all of this and for putting up with me for so long, the book is dedicated to her. In all other respects I am responsible for the ideas contained in this book.

Brian Girvin
Glasgow, April 2002

Abbreviations

ACC	Agricultural Credit Corporation
AFIL	All for Ireland League
CIU	Congress of Irish Unions
EEC	European Economic Community
EFTA	European Free Trade Area
FIM	Federation of Irish Manufacturers
GAA	Gaelic Athletic Association
GATT	General Agreement on Tariffs and Trade
IDA	Industrial Development Authority
IMA	Irish Medical Association
INTO	Irish National Teachers' Organisation
IPP	Irish Parliamentary Party
IRA	Irish Republican Army
IRB	Irish Republican Brotherhood
ITGWU	Irish Transport and General Workers' Union
ITUC	Irish Trades Union Congress
MP	Member of Parliament
NLP	National Labour Party
OEEC	Organisation for European Economic Co-operation
TCD	Trinity College Dublin
TD	Teachta Dála (member of Irish parliament)
UCC	University College Cork
UCD	University College Dublin
UN	United Nations
UVF	Ulster Volunteer Force

1

Why the Irish did not become British!

Introduction: Ireland and nationalism

Between the Act of Union in 1800 and the decision by an independent Irish government to apply for membership of the European Economic Community (EEC) in 1961, nationalism was at the centre of Irish political life. During that time Irish nationalism emerged, developed and quickly became the political expression of the majority of those who lived on the island. Britain reluctantly acknowledged its claim to self-determination in 1922, but the Irish Free State quickly set about extending and institutionalising its distinctive form of nationalism in the new state through its laws and constitution. Though successful in achieving many of its objectives, Irish nationalism had become exhausted by 1961. The decision to apply for EEC membership was a decisive one for Ireland, as crucial perhaps as the original Act of Union or the achievement of independence in 1922. This decision concluded the phase of Irish nationalist history which began in 1800. While there were some discontinuities between 1800 and 1961, Irish nationalism during this period shared basic assumptions and values which allowed for continuity. This was broken in 1961 and a new phase began.

To suggest that a new phase of Irish history began in 1961 is not to claim that nationalism ceased to be important. Partition remained an open sore for public opinion, while renewed conflict at the end of the 1960s increased tension between nationalists and unionists on the island. Rather, the focus for nationalism in the Irish Republic turned to economic development, European integration and the consequences of social and political change. There is a tension between this new nationalism and the more inward-looking, irredentist and at times violent traditional form associated with the Provisional IRA. The consequences of the 1961 decision are still being felt in Ireland, north and south, but there has been a serious modification of the form and content of Irish nationalism. This is probably best expressed in the 1998 Belfast Agreement and the decision to amend Articles 2 and 3 of the constitution.

Without the shift in emphasis in 1961 and subsequently, these changes would have been more difficult for public opinion to accept.[1]

As a consequence of Ireland's long association with nationalism, it provides an early example of how nationalist mobilisation can both unify and divide people in a specific territory. It also shows how successful nationalism can be when it challenges the state and commands legitimacy. Developments in Ireland also highlight the role of religion in contributing to identity and the central role that ethnicity plays in securing loyalty. Ireland provides evidence that political integration can fail when ethnic and religious loyalties are ignored or dismissed by the state, even a liberal state such as the United Kingdom. The British state became increasingly liberal during the nineteenth century, but not in the sense demanded by John Stuart Mill in his classic statement *On Liberty*, published in 1859. The state became more tolerant and plural and increasingly withdrew from the micro-management of religious and social affairs, for example atheists were permitted to sit in the House of Commons by the late 1880s. The state may have been tolerant, but it was neither a neutral nor a secular state, as the influence of religion, especially non-conformism, on liberalism gave the polity a decidedly Protestant aspect. Despite this, the British state was changing its nature in an attempt to accommodate the complex issues associated with mass politics. In other respects Ireland is a forerunner for subsequent developments in the twentieth century. Conflict between nationalism and unionism demonstrated the difficulties associated with resolving secessionist claims. Furthermore, the devolution of government to Northern Ireland in 1920 did not provide a solution to this long-running conflict, but in fact built the divisions into the institutional structure of the polity. In contrast, the experience of the Irish Free State and the Irish Republic established that there could be a democratic basis to a nationalist political system. Ireland, then, is not an anomaly in the modern world, but in some respects provides an early archetype of nationalist experience which became generalised in the course of the twentieth century. While Ireland's experience cannot be generalised in every respect, developments there between 1800 and 1961, though uniquely Irish, are also examples of how nationalism appears and develops in other regions of the world. In this context, Ireland provides a laboratory case at the heart of the modern world for the way in which nationalism spread out of Europe to command the loyalty of most people in most places. Nationalism as a political movement has its origin in the crisis that transformed Europe after 1760. Prior to this, specific communities often had a strong sense of cultural or linguistic distinctiveness (the Germans and Italians for example) but such distinctiveness was rarely given political meaning. As nationalism emerged as a mass political movement, its demands went well beyond cultural or linguistic recognition and struck at the existing traditional state system itself. Political nationalism demanded a state where the national community could decide its own destiny. Traditional states were normally multinational, but the individual communities often had considerable internal autonomy or were largely ignored by the rulers. Once the mass of the population entered politics during the modern age, shared identity came to be a political denominator in many cases. Modernisation was essentially about mass politics, if not democracy, and nationalism claimed to express most adequately the will of the people. Nationalism thus made a successful political appeal to a national community, normally demanding a state for the nation as its main political objective. The success of nationalism in appealing for support provides evidence that large numbers of individuals could share in a political community with others who they might never meet. Nationalism implies that each individual in a community shares at least a minimum set of values and that these can be transmitted to the next generation.[2]

Ireland participated at the birth of this modern world due to its location at the heart of the British state. More than most, Ireland faced the strain accompanying the changes that undermined much of traditional Europe. By the end of the eighteenth century, Ireland had already been savaged by the conflicts of the Reformation and the Counter-Reformation, while its traditional social structure had been destroyed during the wars of the seventeenth century. This, in turn, led to subjugation and the imposition of an alien ruling class over most of the society. Furthermore, the successful plantation of the north-east by a predominantly Presbyterian population weakened traditional Irish society. During the eighteenth century the Anglican elite, which dominated land and politics, secured its power by the political and social exclusion of Catholics (and Presbyterians), through its control of the means of violence and as the representative of the English church and state in Ireland. As a consequence Ireland was quite unlike Scotland prior to or immediately after its union with England. Scotland negotiated a treaty with England, one which deprived it of a parliament but retained most of its other civic institutions. The union may not at first have been popular in Scotland, but it became so. Scotland and Wales contributed to and benefited from their association with British identity. Being British remained compatible with Scottish, Welsh and English identity.[3]

Daniel O'Connell and the emergence of Irish nationalism

In Ireland, the context and outcome are different. The extension of the British state into Ireland after 1690 is divisive rather than unifying. The Protestant nature of the state alienated the defeated Catholic majority in Ireland while, outside the north-east, the Anglican ruling elite acted as the repressive apparatus of this alien culture. Church, state and property were controlled by this elite. In Ireland ethnicity and religion converged even before the beginning of the modern age. After the Reformation, the intrusion of the English (later the British) state into Ireland had a decidedly denominational character. Catholics by virtue of their religion were considered to be disloyal by the state, while Protestants were condemned as heretics by the papacy and by Catholic opinion. This ideological clash between Catholic and Protestant in Ireland echoes similar divisions elsewhere in Europe, where a continental-wide conflict eventually exhausted the competing forces by the end of the seventeenth century. By the beginning of the eighteenth century, religion in Ireland reflected denomination and oppression. Catholics were the oppressed majority within the island, while Protestants acted as the dominant force in the society. At every level of Irish society, religion reflected difference, domination and oppression, cutting across and subordinating other possible differences, such as class or language, to this fundamental reality.[4] This new order not only excluded Catholics from power but also actively repressed them through the Penal Laws. Even at the end of the eighteenth century, at a time when relations between Anglicans, Presbyterians and Catholics had improved, John Fitzgibbon, the Irish Lord Chancellor, admitted that 'When we speak of the people of Ireland it is a melancholy truth that we do not speak of the great body of the people.'[5] Though the Presbyterian majority in the north-east were politically more radical than either the Anglican elite or the Catholic majority, their historic hostility to Catholicism and the papacy weakened the prospect of an alliance between the two. Despite this, many Presbyterians supported reform of the Dublin parliament and more advanced thinkers also advocated the extension of civil rights to Catholics. The reforms of the late eighteenth century met some of the complaints frequently made by Catholics, but did not resolve the question of identity in Ireland. Among the possible options available between 1760 and 1850, a number stand out as more realistic than others. One possibility was that the three Irish religious subcultures would become British, as happened in England, Scotland and Wales. This would allow each subgroup to retain traditional features unique to itself (language, law or religion), while accepting a notion of Britishness which would provide a common identity.

In *Britons*, Linda Colley excludes Ireland from her analysis, on the grounds that the notion of Britishness as a useful concept is limited to the island of Britain. However, the fact that the Irish did not become British does not mean that they could not have. In fact a significant proportion of those living in Ireland did become British after the Union in a fashion similar to that of Scotland and Wales. At the very least, accommodation was possible between the Catholic aristocracy, the Catholic Church in Ireland, sections of the Catholic middle class and more inclusive concepts of Britishness. The moderate and constitutional reformism of mainstream Catholic opinion was maintained into the first decade of the nineteenth century. This was noted by the Irish Chief Secretary, Viscount Castlereagh, in 1801 and reinforced by the public statements and actions of the Catholic hierarchy throughout the period. It is possible that if the British political establishment had acted to relieve Catholic grievances after the Act of Union, as was expected by most Catholics, this would have generated a quite different situation.[6] King George III's refusal to concede Catholic Emancipation in 1801 led to the resignation of the Prime Minister, William Pitt, the Lord Lieutenant, Charles Cornwallis, and Castlereagh in protest. In the short term, Catholic opinion remained optimistic that a British government would in the near future concede the political demands. Nor can the King's behaviour be taken in isolation from the popular basis of anti-Catholicism in Britain. If opposition had been restricted to the King and his immediate circle, it would have been possible for a politician with Pitt's ability to overcome these reservations.[7] The quarter century after 1800 was crucial because during this time new identities were employed to give force to new forms of mobilisation in Ireland, with long-term consequences. Nor was this confined to Ireland: similar developments occurred throughout Europe.[8] If, and it is a big if, Pitt, Cornwallis and Castlereagh had continued to emphasise a conservative, Christian (but not anti-Catholic) anti-republican alliance in defence of king, religion and empire, which is what Edmund Burke had in mind, a closer relationship could have been forged between the Catholic Irish and Protestant Britain. Such a relationship could have provided the political glue for reworking the basic notion of Britishness. While this is speculative, I would suggest that at the opening of the modern age in Ireland there were more opportunities available than might appear to be the case retrospectively. The poet Tom Moore certainly believed that this was a possibility as late as 1810.[9]

If the Protestant nature of the British state in 1800 undermined the possibility of a British identity imprinting itself among the Catholic Irish, the appeal to a new Irish identity also failed. Theobald Wolfe Tone gave the best-known expression of this view. In 1791 he argued that Catholic, Protestant and Dissenter had the means to forge a new national identity in Ireland, one which excluded both the British state and British identity from Ireland. Tone assumed that Enlightenment principles were spreading among the Irish, especially among middle-class Catholics. He concluded that the Pope would have little influence on Catholic behaviour, and that the intolerant nature of Catholicism would not undermine the unity of the three denominations. His argument was based on liberal and republican principles:

> But if all barriers between the two religions [Protestant and Catholic] were beaten down, so far as civil matters are concerned, if the odious distinction of Protestant and Presbyterian, and Catholic, were abolished, and the three great sects blended together, under the common and sacred title of Irishman, what interest could a Catholic member of Parliament have, distinct from his Protestant brother sitting on the same bench, exercising the same function, bound by the same ties? Would liberty be less dear to him, justice less sacred, property less valuable, infamy less dreadful?

While there may have been some hope of such a blend, it was based on weak foundations. The type of secular republican nationalism promoted by Tone was weak in Ireland, restricted to fairly unrepresentative groups within each religion.[10] This is not to deny the possibility that a revolutionary breakthrough could have occurred. However, it remained only a possibility without substantial French assistance to the United Irishmen and while tensions between the denominations continued to be so central to Irish politics. Presbyterians and Catholics could share their hostility to the Anglican ascendancy, but even this, as Nancy Curtin has suggested, could not be guaranteed. Defeat may not have been inevitable, but a successful transformation of Irish political culture in the 1790s remained a long shot.[11]

Anglicans were profoundly hostile to any changes in the status quo which guaranteed their ascendancy. They believed that their minority tyranny over Catholics would be replaced by a majority tyranny exercised by Catholics. With notable exceptions, Anglicans chose to commit themselves to the British state in the belief that its armed apparatus would secure their privileged position. The record of the Anglican political class was generally oppressive in respect of Catholics of all categories. Most Catholics despised the Anglican political class which controlled the Dublin parliament, and many welcomed the imposition of direct rule from London. A leading Catholic representative, Denys Scully, wrote in 1803 that:

> You see that the Faction, whom you dread, have changed sides, and are become the most discontented party in the country; that they are become the most clamorous against the British connection, because it has clipped their monopoly; that they are incensed by the late Union, which has demolished not our Parliament (for we had no share in it), but their club house.[12]

Scully adopted an optimistic view of the Union. This view was shared by many educated middle-class Catholics in the first decade after the Union and also by the Catholic Church and aristocracy. However, the British state disappointed them; Catholics expected more and were critical when they did not get it. In the first decade after the Union, Catholics often expressed pro-government sentiments, though this was not the same as being British. There was considerable hostility to the French Revolution among the Irish hierarchy, a view shared by many lay Catholics because of its anti-religious campaigns.

Nor, despite earlier indications, were Presbyterians attracted to an alliance with Catholics to forge a new identity. Though this alliance had more potential than one including Anglicans, it foundered on the political weakness of the United Irishmen, sectarian rural politics in Ulster and the reservations which the Presbyterian (and Catholic) middle class had concerning the French Revolution.[13] It is possible that a revolutionary elite could have broken the British link with French aid, thus establishing an independent republic. Such an outcome, however, was dependent on French military strength and would have suffered the same reversal as other radical alternatives in Europe once Britain and its allies had defeated the French. By the 1820s, the United States and some Latin American states were the only republics left intact from the Revolutionary Wars. It is unlikely that political control by republicans in Ireland would have survived the fall of Napoleon. However, what needs stressing is that various opportunities were available, if in weak form, but were not realised by those advocating them. The fiasco of 1798 demonstrated the inherent instability of political unity in Ireland. Moreover, the influence of 1798 on Presbyterianism was limited. Within a relatively short period of time that community accepted the Union, internalising further its historical connections with Scotland and Britain. This east–west channel of communication was of long standing in any event, surviving the north–south possibilities of the 1790s and reinforced by the new economics and politics of the early nineteenth century.[14] Presbyterians remained a puzzle for Irish nationalists throughout the nineteenth century. Their identification with the Union and rejection of Repeal, Home Rule and a united Ireland undermined the Irish nationalist claim to represent all those who lived in Ireland. Irish Presbyterians had been close to Scotland prior to the Union and shared in the identification with the nineteenth-century reforming British state. Irish Presbyterians became British alongside their Scottish counterparts. Anglicans outside of Ulster remained dependent on British power to secure their privileged position, and consequently remained weak and fearful. Both Anglicans and Presbyterians in Ulster developed a British identity during the nineteenth century. This established a distinct frame of reference for them, providing the basis for a separate political evolution from both Irish Catholics and southern Irish Protestants.[15]

Presbyterians accepted the Union because it weakened the hold of the ascendancy over Ireland generally and political life in Ulster particularly. The Union addressed some of the demands that had been made for reform in the 1790s. A union with Britain placed Irish Presbyterians on an equal footing with their Scottish co-religionists within the state. A more inclusive notion of individual citizenship was developed as a consequence, and it was one that Irish Presbyterians enthusiastically embraced during the nineteenth century. The Union also resolved the question of what to do with Catholic Ireland in a democratising world. Protestants generally feared that Catholic political power would be used in an oppressive fashion, but the Union secured a Protestant majority within the British state under virtually any representative system. Thus conservative as well as moderate Presbyterians could be satisfied by the Union.

Therefore, in the fluid politics of the late eighteenth century various options were formulated, but some paths were explored more successfully than others. Following the Act of Union, Catholic Ireland faced a crucial dilemma concerning its future. Its political leadership, both clerical and lay, eschewed the secular republican nationalism of Tone, the United Irishmen and Robert Emmet. Catholic opinion remained cautious and in the main loyal throughout the Napoleonic Wars.[16] In 1803, for example, Daniel O'Connell condemned the insurrection organised by Emmet and supported his execution: 'he merits and will suffer the severest punishment'. This loyalty, however, was not evidence of the emergence of Britishness among Irish Catholics, though there was some potential for this development. If Irish Catholics had continued to accept the Union, the possibilities for political integration would have been enhanced. The opportunity to copper-fasten Irish Catholics to the Union was quickly lost by the prevarication of the British government and by the behaviour of the Anglican ruling class in Ireland, which took the opportunity of war to enhance its political control and to exclude Catholics from influence and power. Catholics, even aristocrats, were suspect in the eyes of the Irish ascendancy because of their Catholicism. Lord Fingal, perhaps the most loyal of the Catholic aristocracy, had to defend himself against charges of disloyalty when he was appointed a justice of the peace in 1803, while O'Connell highlighted the partisan nature of the Protestant judiciary on numerous occasions.[17]

The failure to realise a united Irish identity or the accommodation of Irish

Catholics with a British multinational identity led the search for a distinct political identity in another direction. Nationalist mobilisation is often prompted by a belief that a dominant and alien majority in control of the state rejects the community. This is reinforced by a conviction that the community can run its own affairs separate from the majority and by a fear that the community's distinctiveness would be eroded if it remained in the larger union.[18] Indeed by the first decade of the nineteenth century each of the religious subcultures in Ireland was edging towards redefining its identity in terms of historic cultural attachments. The crucial event is the transformation of Irish Catholic politics between 1800 and 1829 from that of a demand for civil rights within the United Kingdom to the mass mobilisation of Catholics around a set of political demands which, though couched in terms of equality and tolerance, actually reflected the assertion of a distinct Irish identity. At the heart of this change stands Daniel O'Connell, a deeply ambivalent figure. He was simultaneously a child of the Enlightenment, a successful self-made professional, and a chieftain and Catholic democrat. O'Connell rejected the radical republicanism of the French Revolution and the violence of the terror, yet he remained attached to the ideals of the Enlightenment. Though a moderate in political terms, he was committed to undoing the Union and in that sense can be considered an institutional separatist. This can be seen in O'Connell's first public speech at the age of twenty-five, when he condemned the proposed Union at a meeting of Catholics in Dublin. In this speech he raised various themes he was to return to over the next forty-seven years. O'Connell stressed the need for Catholics and Protestants to co-operate:

> The enlightened mind of the Catholics had taught them the impolicy, the illiberality, and the injustice of separating themselves on any occasion from the rest of the people of Ireland. The Catholics had therefore resolved, and they had wisely resolved, never more to appear before the public as a distinct and separate body.

Yet this was a Catholic meeting addressed by Catholics. The reason for this was that the administration was claiming that Catholics were favourable to the Union. O'Connell firmly rejected this view and asserted openly:

> that if the alternative were offered him of union, or the re-enactment of the penal code in all its pristine horrors, that he would prefer without hesitation the latter, as the lesser and more sufferable evil; that he would rather confide in the justice of his brethren, the Protestants of Ireland, who have already liberated him, than lay his country at the feet of foreigners.[19]

It is reported that those in attendance warmly received O'Connell's speech. It is unlikely that O'Connell really intended his listeners to take him seriously on the Penal Laws. What his speech reflects, however, are some characteristic features of nationalism. There is a belief that government by Irishmen was better than that by a foreign power. This was the case even when, as in Ireland, the local political elite was often hostile to the majority. O'Connell had a profound belief in the essential unity of all Ireland and its separateness from Britain. His opposition to the Union was based on his belief in a shared Irish nationality and not merely on arguments for better government.

O'Connell maintained this belief in a common Irish nationality throughout his life. As late as 1810 he could still express a political philosophy echoing that of Tone: 'The Protestant alone could not expect to liberate his country — the Roman Catholic alone could not do it — neither can the Presbyterian — but amalgamate the three in the Irishman, and the Union is repealed.'[20] He believed that the British government was the cause of Ireland's problems. He insisted that once the Union was repealed Irish freedom would be assured. He was genuine in emphasising the primacy of Repeal over Catholic objectives, as he was already a nationalist. Yet O'Connell was instrumental in creating a political movement acceptable to only one section of the Irish people, the Catholics. Despite O'Connell's commitment to a politics of inclusion, the consequences of his political intervention were to provide a denominational basis for Irish politics in the nineteenth century. O'Connell's most successful campaigns all had a denominational focus. The campaign against the proposed veto by the state on the appointment of Catholic bishops mobilised middle-class Catholics against any interference in the church by the state. In turn Catholic Emancipation removed the obstacles preventing Catholics from sitting in parliament, while the mass movement against tithes sought to prevent the Church of Ireland from receiving support from those not its members. All of these issues were reformist, addressing real issues of concern, but they also inflamed religious animosity. They were denominational in character, emphasising in each case the rights of Catholics and what they were deprived of. The aim was to gain concessions for Catholics, but also to give Irish Catholics political leverage and independence. The mobilisation of Catholic opinion sustained during these three campaigns, and later in the Repeal movement, had a number of consequences for Irish politics. The appeal to democratic participation in the campaigns undermined the influence of the Catholic aristocracy on Catholic politics, and replaced it with a new middle-class leadership. It also brought the Catholic Church to the centre of Irish politics. This may have been unintended, but the outcome was that the institutional and organisational influence of the church was harnessed to democratic mass mobilisation and gave the movement a Catholic character, which was unusual in the politics of the time. It likewise associated denomination quite strongly with the emergence of national identity. While democracy and Catholicism proved incompatible during the nineteenth century in continental Europe, in Ireland and the United States a successful accommodation was achieved.[21]

Irish national identity was established during the first half of the nineteenth century. It coincided with the growth of a democratic political culture, which had a powerful nationalist content. The strength of Irish democracy and the depth of its national identity drew its power from the emotional response of Irish Catholics to their oppression. O'Connell also imposed discipline on mass politics, turning the 'mob' into a coherent political movement with a specific set of objectives. This sense of order was most successful among the middle classes and property owners, but extended well beyond these groups. It is not an exaggeration to claim that O'Connell was one of the first politicians to recognise the importance of an oppressed people establishing its moral authority over its oppressor through well-organised, disciplined and peaceful agitation. O'Connell recognised that Protestant power in Ireland could be effectively countered by peaceful means rather than through violence, because the British state was not absolutist and there was a limit to its intolerance. Commenting on O'Connell's political success after a visit to Ireland in 1835, Alexis de Tocqueville observed that 'when one allows the forms of liberty to subsist, sooner or later they will kill tyranny'. By recognising the tolerant strain in British political culture, O'Connell and his supporters were able to achieve most of their objectives by peaceful means.[22] This is not to claim that violence was absent from these campaigns, but O'Connell insisted that discipline was a prerequisite to political victory in the Repeal movement as well as in his earlier campaigns. O'Connell's achievement in reducing violence while orchestrating mass campaigns is extraordinary when one considers the weak transport infrastructure, the levels of literacy and the excitement generated by political mobilisation and sectarian animosity. The growth of the temperance movement and the decline in faction fighting also contributed to and affected this pacification of Irish opinion.[23] The only comparable achievement that I am familiar with is that of Gandhi in the context of the Indian independence movement. Both figures recognised the need for the nation to be self-disciplined and both succeeded to a remarkable degree. Within a fairly short period of time, Irish Catholics had been transformed into a powerful political movement, well organised and with a purposeful political programme. It had coherent objectives expressed by a disciplined mass movement under the control of a self-conscious political elite.[24]

It is unlikely that O'Connell or those close to him had sectarian intentions, but in the context of mass mobilisation it is the denominational character of Irish life which is most pronounced. Henry Inglis, travelling in Ireland in 1834, observed that the main divisions were along religious lines: 'There is a Protestant and a Catholic inn — known by these names; the Protestant and Catholic coach, driven by, and supported by, persons of different persuasions; and the very children, playing or squabbling in the street are divided into sects.' He found this represented throughout the island, in urban as well as rural areas. In Wicklow, a riot followed when 'Protestant Boy' beat 'Daniel O'Connell' in a horse race, while in the same county Inglis was able to identify specific Catholic and Protestant breweries.[25] O'Connell sometimes slipped into identifying Irishness with Catholicism:

> The combination of national action — all Catholic Ireland acting as one man — must necessarily have a powerful effect on the minds of the ministry and of the entire British nation. A people who can thus be brought together and by one impulse are too powerful to be neglected and too formidable to be long opposed.[26]

One of the by-products of this mass mobilisation was the alienation of non-Catholics from Irish nationalism. As the character of Irish nationalism emerged in the 1820s and 1830s, its most pronounced feature to non-Catholics in Ireland and to outside observers was the close identity between Catholics and nationalism. But this does not entail that Irish nationalism was theocratic or controlled by the church. The Catholic Church in Ireland became an explicitly Irish church and acquired nationalist sympathies. While retaining its institutional links with the universal church and the papacy, the Irish Catholic Church recognised earlier than most national hierarchies that the continuing influence of Catholicism with the Irish people depended upon maintaining and cementing links with the popular forces. This was quite unusual in nineteenth-century Europe. That the alliance was maintained for so long without serious instability attested to the intelligence and sophistication of both nationalist leaders and the Catholic hierarchy.[27]

Catholic nationalism in nineteenth-century Ireland

By the 1840s, the reach of Irish nationalism as a political movement coincided with Catholicism in Ireland. The Repeal movement failed to attract any significant body of Protestant support in Ireland, being especially weak in Ulster. Ulster Protestant opinion was divided on many issues, but its opposition to Repeal was consistent and widespread. Nor was this an isolated incident. In electoral terms, Protestant Ulster expressed its British identity and its opposition to Irish nationalism throughout the century.[28] Moreover, O'Connell seems to have become more devotedly Catholic by the later stages of his life, at times conflating his personal, political and religious views on issues. This should not be treated in isolation, as it is impossible to ignore the nature of the British state in Ireland, its sectarian nature and its unmitigated suspicion of any Catholic politician. If for no other reason, this pushed O'Connell closer to the church and his co-religionists. During the last decade of his life it is more difficult to find evidence for O'Connell's belief that all Irish people could co-operate under Repeal and his hostility to Young Ireland reflected some of these tensions. His parliamentary activities, though supportive of the Liberal wing of British politics, had an inevitable denominational character to it. His correspondence contains considerable exchanges with members of the hierarchy covering the need for action on Catholic issues in parliament. This reflected the reality of power and influence in Ireland, though O'Connell's relationship with the Catholic Church remained a complex one. The priest could provide the institutional means to extend O'Connell's movement into the countryside, where urban residents had little influence. But it was also a reciprocal relationship, because the priests were also nationalists.

In a letter to Paul Cullen in 1842 O'Connell provides a fascinating insight into his mature political mind. He probably recognised the need to appeal to Cullen, Rector of the Irish College in Rome, to secure himself with the Pope and his advisers. The concerns in the letter are those of a working nationalist politician who recognised the delicacy of his position in respect of the church. O'Connell's fear, and it is one which recurs regularly among Irish nationalists until 1922, was that the papacy would take decisions based on universalistic considerations, but which would have consequences for Irish nationalism. In this case O'Connell feared that the proclamation of Charles Acton as Cardinal for England and Wales would have political implications for Ireland. O'Connell condemned Acton's reference to the English, Irish and Scots as British, denying that Ireland could be included under the British rubric, 'For we are, thank Heaven, a separate nation still and have preserved through ages of persecution — English persecution, political as well as religious — our separate existence.' O'Connell insisted on the distinctiveness of the Irish, but in a way which identified denomination with nationality:

> British!!! I am not British. You are not British. When the British north and south fell away and dissipated amongst the profligate and the renegades of Protestantism and of every species of infidelity, the inheritance of the Lord amidst the land, the Irish Nation and the Irish Church were the victims of and not the participators in these crimes. ... I do not wish to have the relations of Ireland with the Holy See relaxed or diminished. On the contrary, my anxious desire is that nothing should arise to injure those relations which I most cordially wish to see strengthened and increased and confirmed for all ages. No man can be more attached to the centre of unity than I am. No man can be more entirely convinced that the stability of the faith depends on the submission to and union with the Holy See.

O'Connell then argued that the Irish church should define its relationship with the papacy independent of any changes in the English Catholic Church. He commended Repeal to Cullen on the grounds that it 'would be an event of the most magnificent importance to Catholicity'. He could not do so publicly as such an open statement would increase British hostility to that project, he added. However, he did provide sixteen reasons why the Catholic Church should support Repeal. If Repeal was achieved, the consequences of the Reformation in Ireland would have been reversed. O'Connell believed that the property confiscated from the Catholic Church at the time of the Reformation should be returned to its original owners. Likewise, his view of Protestantism, perhaps reflecting his interaction with Protestants, was decidedly unflattering. Protestantism in Ireland was, he affirmed, political rather than religious. Protestants' involvement in religion was a mask for controlling resources and power:

> If the Union were repealed and the exclusive system abolished, the great mass of the Protestant community would with little delay melt into the overwhelming majority of the Irish nation. Protestantism would not survive the Repeal ten years. Nothing but persecution would keep it alive and the Irish Catholics are too wise and too good to persecute.[29]

Given the contents of this letter, it was wise that O'Connell kept his thoughts private, because what he claimed within it was what concerned many Protestants in Ireland, not all of them bigots.

By the time O'Connell died his movement had effectively subsumed nationalism and religion under the one heading. This was to remain a characteristic of Irish nationalism for one hundred and fifty years. The political imperatives of mass mobilisation facilitated this, as did the policy demands of his clerical supporters. But it also responded to the growing identification of religion and nationality among Irish Catholics, especially when Protestants were overwhelmingly hostile to O'Connell's movement and frequently took punitive action against his supporters. During his travels in Ireland de Tocqueville was informed that landlords reorganised their estates to replace Catholic tenants with loyal Protestants in response to the political support given to O'Connell's movement. He also recounted the intense hostility to O'Connell and to Catholics generally on the part of Protestant opinion as well as the reciprocal hostility of Catholics to Protestants. While travelling in County Clare a fellow coach passenger recounted in detail the persecutions and confiscations that had taken place in the past. On another occasion particular Catholics were identified to de Tocqueville as members of families which had been deprived of their lands. Although sympathetic to the Catholic cause, de Tocqueville was not an uncritical observer. He reported the views that the church did not wish to be part of the state, but wondered if the church might come to the view that the 'State would do well enough as part of the Church'. De Tocqueville's snapshot account is borne out by many other observers. What they report is a society deeply segmented along denominational lines and a Catholic Church reviving after repression and becoming increasingly self-confident in respect of the Protestant church in Ireland and the British state. What is also discernible is a people mobilised along democratic lines for the first time, while also identifying with the church as a national movement.[30]

The growing overlap between religion and nationalism was a consequence of the nature of O'Connell's political campaigns, but it also reflected the growing polarisation of politics in Ireland. Although Protestant Ulster evolved separately from the rest of Ireland in the nineteenth century, it shared in this polarisation for similar reasons. In contrast with Britain, liberal politics never dominated either side of the denominational divide in Ireland, though liberalism had some political success and influence between 1850 and 1870. The primary reason for this was the growth of democratic politics, the heightened sense of national identity based on religion on both sides and the mutual incomprehension expressed by Catholics and Protestants alike. Nor did the Famine change this: indeed it provided a profound basis for reinforcing it. After 1850 Irish nationalism was more cohesive and assertive than before, reflecting its more homogeneous nature. O'Connell's pacifism has often been criticised in the face of British government intransigence in the 1840s and again when faced with the Famine. Yet it was also realistic politics. There was no likelihood that a British government would concede major changes to existing constitutional arrangements. This applied as much to the Chartist demands for electoral reform as it did to Repeal. A consensus had emerged within Britain between conservatives and liberals. One feature of this was that reform was admissible in certain circumstances, while root and branch constitutional change was not. In analysing Ireland in the early nineteenth century it is possible to overlook the changing nature of British politics, which was also in considerable flux. The political compromise which was in place by the early 1840s, though immensely significant in contributing to the emergence of Liberal Britain, was based on a delicate balance between left and right in Britain. Not only did this preclude major constitutional innovation, but it intensified the focus of British governments on British issues. This consensus was maintained for over thirty years and only began to dissolve during the 1870s.[31]

The actions of Young Ireland in 1848 have often been cited in contrast to O'Connell's constitutionalism. The use of violence might have seemed noble, but in the light of political circumstances was fruitless. We have few enough examples at this time for successful secessions by national groups. A number of contrasts can be made in relation to secession in the nineteenth century. The secession of Belgium from the Netherlands in 1830 was not opposed by the major powers with an interest in the region, whereas attempts by Poland and Hungary to secede were savagely repressed by the imperial power on each occasion. Likewise the Greek independence movement was fortunate in that a number of factors favourable to its cause coincided with the interests of the major European powers. The point to be emphasised here is that Belgian and Greek independence were unusual in the nineteenth century.[32] Britain retained the capacity and the will to repress any secessionist movement, whether in India in 1857 or in Ireland at any time. Nor was this just a characteristic of British rule: it can be found in the United States at the time of the Civil War, all over Europe in 1848 and in the tensions within the Austrian Empire right up to 1914. In contrast to the physical force tradition in Irish politics, the constitutional alternative developed by O'Connell, and maintained by most nationalist politicians thereafter, was the strategy most likely to achieve the objectives of Irish nationalism. His emphasis on national unity, on the use of mass mobilisation to achieve constitutional aims peacefully and on the separateness of Ireland from Britain have been key motifs in Irish nationalism ever since. The behaviour of the Catholic Church and the Catholic middle classes provides little evidence that either favoured a revolutionary alternative, despite Young Ireland and the Fenians.

The Irish Famine consolidated these constitutional forces in Irish politics and provided the means for furthering the aims of Irish nationalism within the British state over the next seventy years. Two factors facilitated this. The first was the changing nature of the British state and the inclusion of Ireland in its liberalising process. In contrast to the colonies or the white dominions, Ireland was fully involved in the political modernisation of the United Kingdom of Britain and Ireland in the nineteenth century. It became increasingly possible to formulate nationalist political programmes and to express them in the imperial parliament. The second feature was that the Famine changed the nature of Irish nationalist politics. The death or emigration of a significant section of landless labourers and cottiers largely dissolved the pre-Famine tension between Catholics with property and those without. In its place a confrontation between a Catholic tenant-farming majority and a Protestant land-owning class — a less complex cleavage system than previously — came to define the politics of the second half of the century. In political terms, the Famine confirmed to Catholic Ireland that they were not British. It is not necessary to claim that the British state's intention during the Famine was malign or genocidal to accept that there was a degree of neglect on the part of the state. It is true that the crisis in Ireland was immense, but if such a crisis had been faced in Britain the response would have been more adequate. A state is more likely to be positive in response to famine or other disasters if those suffering share a common identity. When that is not the case the officials involved treat the issue as one of a number of pressing problems. Britain and Europe between 1845 and 1850 were in turmoil; consequently Ireland was just one, albeit an increasingly serious one, of a number of problems pressing on British officials.

What Irish nationalists could do subsequently was blame Britain for its lack of concern at the plight of the Irish and draw the logical nationalist conclusion. The comparison with the potato famine in the Scottish Highlands and Islands in 1846 is illustrative. The government here, as in Ireland, was inept and indecisive in response to the crop failure, but private charity and relief prevented the mass starvation in evidence in Ireland. In the Scottish Highlands and Islands many of the same conditions prevailed as in Ireland. Yet despite the spread of disease, the failure of the potato crop and increased mortality, Scotland did not suffer the devastation which occurred in Ireland. Tom Devine has noted that by 'the Summer of 1847, death rates had returned to normal levels and the threat of starvation had receded'. He attributes the different outcomes to a number of factors. These included the difference in scale and the restricted nature of the famine in Scotland, even in the Highlands. Furthermore, the Highlands were generally less dependent on the potato than was Ireland, while in many areas alternative economic activity and employment were available, which provided the means to purchase other foodstuffs. Private charity was well organised and efficient, while the churches played a pivotal role in responding to the crisis. Many landlords contributed to relief of famine, but the crisis also provided the opportunity to clear the estates of unwanted tenants. Scotland was spared the Irish experience by the relative wealth of Scotland, which was not as dependent on agriculture as was Ireland. Nor was the cottier or labouring class as widespread in Scotland, an economy that was becoming industrialised. The majority of those in Scotland, especially the churches, identified with the plight of those affected and had the resources to respond.[33]

O'Connell was never a separatist in a strict sense. He argued that Repeal of the Union would provide Ireland with enough power to negotiate a modified relationship with the Crown. This was certainly the case in institutional terms, and the influence of the Repeal movement continued to be seen in the main nationalist campaigns after the Famine.[34] Yet in another sense the movement for Repeal had separatist implications. Virtually all the arguments used by O'Connell in favour of Repeal assumed that the Irish people were a distinct nationality and that the case for Repeal rested on this, not simply on the reform of existing institutions or good government. O'Connell's legacy to the second half of the century was crucial not only in defining the objectives of Irish nationalism, but also in insisting on the distinctness of Ireland and Irish nationality. This was as much the case with the National Association as it was with the Home Rule Party, Cardinal Cullen or Parnell. By insisting on Ireland's distinctness, O'Connell and his successors not only prevented Catholic Ireland from becoming British, but also laid the basis for the disestablishment of British power in Ireland. Notwithstanding the fragmentation of nationalist politics after 1850, what remained important were the values shared by most Catholics in the political culture. By the time the Home Rule Party emerged in 1874, most sections of Catholic Ireland had embraced these political values. Throughout the second half of the century, nationality and religion remained fixed features of Irish political culture. In other respects, there were differences over tactics, for example in the argument over the use of violence against the state developed by the Fenians. But even here it can be said that Paul Cullen, the inveterate opponent of the revolutionaries, shared with the Fenians a common set of values in relation to nationalism. Moreover, this was a society which was fairly homogeneous, increasingly middle class and, as the century progressed, comparatively well educated.[35] This is not to claim that social or political divisions did not exist: it would have been an abnormal society if this were so. Conflict took place and was modified within an environment predicated on a common political culture, in this case nationalism. Such a community of interest placed a very high premium on internal unity and solidarity in the face of the British state and its Anglican army of occupation in Ireland.[36]

These features also allowed Irish nationalist politics to be expressed in representative forms. While the parliamentary tradition in Irish public life can be exaggerated, especially in the eighteenth century, Irish nationalism adopted it during the nineteenth century. The main current in Irish politics from the Union to 1916 was parliamentary rather than revolutionary.[37] The basis for this was O'Connell's insistence on non-violence and Cullen's reinforcement of this position during the 1850s and 1860s. The political legitimacy for this was provided by the evidence from the 1851 religious census, which showed that Catholics were in an overall majority on the island. Democracy in Ireland entailed the recognition that the majority of the electorate was both Catholic and nationalist. Ireland was the only predominantly Catholic region of the United Kingdom, but it had a population and territory which was cohesive. This allowed for electoral mobilisation on the basis of a specific religious and national identity. It put pressure on the British state, which was also liberalising to address the demands made by Catholic-nationalist Ireland. The emergence of the Liberal Party and the extension of the franchise in 1867 and 1884 provided the means to effect change in Ireland. The success of parliamentary politics in Ireland rested on the willingness of the British state to introduce reform, not on a dogmatic opposition to the use of violence. The electorate remained opposed to revolutionary politics because there was an alternative which delivered the objectives of Catholic nationalism. It also depended on the existence of a liberal state. While a liberal state might be tempted to ignore the democratic will of a people expressed electorally, doing so would undermine its liberalism.[38] It is no coincidence that the pressure for reform in Ireland increases as the franchise is extended and popular mobilisation occurs. There is, however, a major dilemma for the British state throughout the second half of the century. As a minority within the British state, Catholic nationalism could successfully appeal for reform and relief, while demonstrating that they had the support of a majority within Ireland for their objectives. This same minority status within the state prevented Catholic-nationalism from realising its ultimate objectives electorally, unless the state was prepared to recognise the nation as the basis for calculation. This it was never prepared to do. While the Irish nation insisted on its right to self-determination, both Protestant Ireland and the British state refused to concede this.[39]

The disestablishment of British power in Ireland

The problem of how to reconcile state and nation remained at the heart of the Irish question until 1922 and was probably always unresolvable short of secession. The British political elite (whether conservative or liberal) resisted nationalist claims to self-determination, as did all multinational states and empires. Most Irish Protestants accepted the Union, whereas nationalist mobilisation was aimed at dismantling this structure. In a manner which has been repeated in many places ever since, Catholic nationalist mobilisation led to counter-mobilisation by Protestant unionists, most successfully in what was to become Northern Ireland.[40] The electoral geography of the second half of the century reflected the dominance of each of the national communities. Catholic nationalism had a majority of the population on the island, but within the north-east Protestants and unionists were in the majority. The electoral consequence of this mobilisation was a form of partition predating its institutionalisation in the twentieth century. Two sets of problems are apparent. The first is the refusal of the state to recognise the Irish nation's right to self-determination. Arguments here rested on the unity of the empire, the integrity of the state and the will of the majority within the state. All of these arguments ignored the expressed will of the Catholic-nationalist population to renegotiate its status. However, Catholic nationalism was also remiss in ignoring or denying the consistent opposition of Protestant unionism to Repeal or Home Rule for the entire island. Northern unionists in particular have been as consistent in their determination to remain outside a state dominated by Catholic nationalism as Catholic nationalists were in their determination to leave a state dominated by Protestants. Once mobilisation and counter-mobilisation were complete around the time of the first Home Rule bill (1886), alternatives narrowed appreciably. In the short term, reform and the promise of devolution could conciliate Catholic nationalism, but in the longer term separatism could be prevented only by the use of force. In either case, the moral high ground was clearly occupied by Catholic nationalism. Likewise, Ulster unionism, though not Irish unionism as a whole, could not easily be persuaded to accept a government for the whole island without the use of coercion. Neither side accepted the legitimacy of the other's claim or the national basis of its support. The evidence we have suggests that by the beginning of the twentieth century, two well-established and self-contained political cultures existed in Ireland, inhabiting contiguous territories but without any real relationship with one another. When such a situation exists, ethno-religious conflict frequently erupts.[41]

Consequently, the Irish experience of democracy differed from that of Britain. Democratisation in Britain was inclusive, providing the basis for the political, economic and institutional integration of England, Scotland and Wales. This process enhanced political legitimacy, which in turn generated the conditions for stable change over time.[42] However, even in a European context, the British experience was unusual before 1945. Democracy in Ireland increased divisions between the two major denominations and communities. Within each community, majority rule became the acknowledged method of settling political differences. But democracy did not provide such a basis for reconciling political differences between nationalists and unionists. Nationalists invoked a majority within Ireland, while unionists pointed to their majority within the United Kingdom. Consequently, democracy secured majority consent within each community, but was denied when it came into conflict with each community's political objectives (secession or union).

Furthermore, liberal and democratic Britain emphasised toleration, pluralism and secularism, features noticeably absent in both Protestant and Catholic Ireland. Irish democratic development, because of its relationship to nationalism, reinforced the denominational basis for political conflict, weakening other possible political arrangements, and so too did unionism. While it is possible to exaggerate the extent of secularism and toleration in Britain, there was a strong and noticeable trend in the direction of a more tolerant state in fact if not in theory. Catholic nationalism successfully resisted these influences, becoming if anything more religious by the beginning of the twentieth century. A similar observation can be made in the case of Protestant unionism. What seems clear is that modernisation is an extremely complex phenomenon and the British experience is but one among many possible alternatives.[43] The importance of religion in Ireland does not make it an anomaly in a European context, especially during the nineteenth century. Sectarian tensions, sometimes leading to violence, were a feature of countries as diverse as the United States, Britain, the Netherlands and Germany well into the twentieth century.

Catholic-nationalist Ireland became democratic but it did not become liberal. Its anti-liberalism was a consequence of the Catholic Church's opposition to modernism and Irish nationalism's hostility to Britain. As a consequence, the nation's religious and political leadership could share in the rejection of the liberal version of modernity, especially its individualism and secularism. Because of the close identity between religion and nationalism in Ireland, the relationship between priest and people has been amicable. Notwithstanding the controversy over Parnell, Ireland remained relatively free of anti-clericalism as well as secularism and liberalism until the second half of the twentieth century. The complex relationship between church and nation was never a forgone conclusion, but depended on the skill and ability of both elites. Within a triangular power structure, composed of church, state and nation, symmetry was never possible. The British state was at an increasing disadvantage as the century progressed, while the relationship between church and nation became progressively more intimate. The church could not depend on the piety of nationalists in all circumstances, nor could nationalists take the church's support for granted. The very obvious piety of the Irish nation depended on the church responding to the needs of the nation. If it had not, anti-clericalism could have become a formidable force. In turn, however, nationalists had to preserve constitutionalism and not embrace revolutionary politics. The Fenians were condemned because of the conspiratorial and violent nature of their organisation, not because they were nationalists. In effect, a wide-ranging consensus existed between church and nation, which the controversy over Parnell threatened but did not undermine. The Irish hierarchy had at all times to balance the demands of Ireland with those of the Vatican. That it did so successfully can be attributed to the political skills and diplomatic sensitivity of Cardinal Cullen and his successors. In time, Irish piety took on even stronger form and expressed itself through the culture and identity of the nation. By the end of the nineteenth century religion had become an expression of Irishness itself. It is necessary to revise the conventional view of Cullen — that he was an opponent of nationalism in all its forms. His condemnation of the Fenians disguises the fact that his views were those of a moderate nationalist in a democratising society. That he could accommodate both democracy and nationalism in Ireland while actively supporting an anti-modern offensive on the part of the papacy is incongruous only if one concludes that opposition to the modern world is always reactionary. Cullen's moderate conservatism had much in common with conservatives in Britain or the United States who sought to use electoral and other modern means to control or harness modernisation, especially when it entailed liberalism.[44]

Catholicism provided Irish nationalism with a distinctive character within the United Kingdom. It set Irish Catholics apart from their Protestant counterparts, but it also provided the leverage to separate Ireland from the United Kingdom. Historical memory and a distinct cultural evolution reinforced this feature. George Boyce has asked why Irish MPs, even before the appearance of mass electoral politics in the 1880s, did not 'fulfil the same role as Scottish politicians and simply act as some sort of geographical expression of political representation'. In the first place, Scottish MPs acted together to represent the national interest in Westminster as was the case with the Irish. By the second half of the nineteenth century most Scots accepted the political compromise implicit in the Union and recognised the economic and political benefits of integration. In addition, the answer lies in the unique relationship that existed between religion and politics in Ireland, but even so Scotland's relationship with the British state was more problematic than this comparison suggests. The Scots maintained a distinct national identity, but between the Union and the last quarter of the twentieth century the assertion of this identity did not require a politics of separatism. Colley has identified a number of factors contributing to this outcome, including participation in the empire, Protestantism and foreign wars. Also, while Scotland lost its independent parliament in 1707, it retained institutions (including religious, educational and legal ones) that were products of Scottish traditions.[45]

In contrast to Ireland after 1800, Scotland had a high degree of autonomy, an autonomy accepted by the British state. The decision to appoint a Secretary for Scotland in 1885 and establish a Scottish Office, though located in London, recognised that Scotland was distinct within the Union. The decision to set up the Scottish Standing Committee in 1894 was a further recognition of this. In the circumstances, Scottish sensitivities were met by the British state to a degree not present in Ireland. Most importantly, the public perception of the Union differed radically. Whatever misgivings Scots had concerning the Union were eventually dispelled, while in Ireland, after a brief period of possibility, the Union became a symbol of oppression. It has been claimed that Scottish identity was reflected in the richness of its 'civil society', rather than through the state. Furthermore, the weight of the state was fairly light in nineteenth-century Scotland and its institutions were embodied within a Scottish context responding to Scottish requirements. London was not like Paris in Scotland, but it was in Ireland. It was then easier for Scottish MPs to represent Scotland as a nation because its identity was not threatened by the relationship. This proved to be much more difficult in Ireland, where the development of its civil society and separate institutions confronted the British state and conferred political legitimacy on the nation. This was considered seditious by much of the British political elite. In a United Kingdom context, the expression of Scottish national identity was compatible with the continuation of the territorial integrity of the state, whereas in Ireland it presented a challenge.[46]

Liberal thinkers in the nineteenth century also misunderstood the nature of substate nationalism. For many liberals Ireland's claims could be met within the United Kingdom by judicious reform. Liberals were often suspicious of both nationalism and Catholicism, especially when they were linked. The Italian nationalist Giuseppe Mazzini denied that the Irish had a legitimate case for demanding self-determination. While sympathetic to reform, he asserted (without very much evidence) that Ireland (unlike Italy!) did not possess the characteristic features of a nation. Better government for Ireland was a justified demand, Mazzini believed, but the Irish did not fulfil the criteria that Mazzini provided for full recognition of nationality. For Mazzini, this involved the Irish claiming that they had a 'distinct principle of life or system of legislation, derived from native peculiarities, and contrasting radically with English wants and wishes'. Could the Irish, he asked, claim any such 'high special function', and his reply was in the negative.[47] Nor was Mazzini an isolated voice in this respect. John Stuart Mill, perhaps the most influential liberal thinker in the nineteenth century and one who paid particular attention to Irish matters, also questioned the extent of Ireland's distinctness. Mill considered the Irish to be a nationality, but believed that they were so because of oppression rather than as a consequence of the spirit of nationalism:

> No Irishman is now less free than an Anglo-Saxon, nor has a less share of every benefit either to his country or to his individual fortunes than if he were sprung from any other portion of the British dominions. The only remaining real grievance of Ireland, that of the State Church, is one which half, or nearly half, the people of the larger island have in common with them. There is now next to nothing, except the memory of the past, and the difference in the predominant religion, to keep apart two races, perhaps the most fitted of any two in the world to be the complementing counterpart of one another.

Mill believed that the Irish would be foolish to give up the benefits of participating in the British state, that they would fare better as citizens of 'one of the freest, as well as most civilised and powerful, nations of the earth' than as foreigners.[48] Mazzini and Mill believed that 'big' nations had greater moral integrity than small ones, but this was a bias on their part and one shared by many critics of 'ethnic' or 'separatist' nationalism ever since. Yet in some respects the analysis had an impact on Irish thinking about nationalism, if for no other reason than that Mazzini and Mill were significant and influential figures during the nineteenth century. It has always proved important for separatists to claim that their nation was distinct from other peoples within the state. But distinctiveness must be more than mere cultural difference, which might be accommodated within multinational states.[49] A further consideration in the Irish case was that by the end of the nineteenth century there existed a concern that Catholic Ireland was being Anglicised by modernisation and that any residual distinctness would soon disappear.

It was with these considerations in mind that Douglas Hyde spoke to the National Literary Society in November 1892 'On The Necessity for De-Anglicising the Irish People'. There was a great fear among nationalists that the Irish nation was being submerged by the modern secular and industrial world and that it could be undermined. Was Ireland special, Hyde asked, and if so in what respect? This was the challenge posed by Mazzini and Mill. Hyde was addressing an English-speaking audience and his arguments recognised this. But his claim was not just to revive the Irish language, which had been largely lost, but to acquire a means to offset the influence of English in the new Ireland. There are two aspects to this criticism. The first concerns the role of the British state in Ireland, its control over the society and the belief among Irish nationalists that this had been generally if not universally negative. This was a criticism from the standpoint of nationalism, but there is also a fear of the modern associated with Britain and the English language. Hyde emphasised the dilemma for the Irish: 'the Irish race is at present in a most anomalous position, imitating England and yet apparently hating it'. According to this version of the relationship between the two islands, the outcome for the Irish would be serious if something could not be done, 'And yet this actual ideal of complete Anglicisation which I have here put before you in all its crudity, is and has been making silent inroads upon us for nearly a century.' This pessimism was shared by some Irish critics, such as D.P. Moran and Pádraic Pearse. Others such as Tom Kettle remained far more representative of educated and nationalist opinion than the more pessimistic voices in the cultural revival. Despite this, there was concern among the political and cultural elite that forces hostile to it might overwhelm Irish nationality.[50]

But was Ireland actually Anglicising during the nineteenth century? Those who set up the Gaelic League shortly after Hyde's prompting certainly thought so and associated the decline in the use of Gaelic with a process of Anglicisation. If the use of the English language in Ireland is an indicator of Anglicisation, then clearly this was the case. But the use of English and the decline of Gaelic should not be taken in isolation. In most other respects by 1914, Catholic-nationalist Ireland was more confident of itself, more self-sufficient and independent than at any time in the nineteenth century. While cultural nationalists complained about the loss of Gaelic, they failed to appreciate that the social basis for British rule in Ireland, outside of the north-east, had been undermined and nationalist Ireland had effectively disestablished the British state. By 1914 the British state could rule in Ireland only by coercion or in alliance with nationalism. As noted earlier, de Tocqueville had observed that Catholic Emancipation had been won because the British state had left enough liberty in Ireland to provide the basis for Catholics to undermine Protestant tyranny. If true in 1835, this remark had considerably more force by 1914. Many years later, John J. Horgan, the Cork Home Rule activist, argued that while Irish Catholics had achieved political emancipation in 1829, social emancipation had to wait until the beginning of the twentieth century.[51] The possession of the vote was a necessary condition for social progress, but in itself was not sufficient for the social emancipation of Catholic-nationalist Ireland. These conditions were met during the fifty years prior to 1914. The most public expression of this included the disestablishment of the Church of Ireland in 1869, which struck at the heart of the wealth and power of Protestantism outside the north-east. The electoral success of the Home Rule Party undermined any claim that there was electoral support for the Union within Catholic Ireland. Furthermore, the Land League campaign to transform the system of tenure, which led eventually to the Wyndham Land Act (1903), destroyed the economic and social power of the landed aristocracy in Ireland.[52]

These changes marked a radical shift in power within Ireland and were reinforced by the mobilisation of large sectors of the Catholic population into mass organisations. Membership of such bodies enhanced the links between elite, people and nationalism. Membership of these organisations was frequently more inclusive than the right to vote, which remained limited to men in any event. This inclusiveness led to the socialisation into nationalist life of those who could not participate by voting. Education in large part was under denominational and nationalist control, while the Catholic Church enhanced its social and institutional relationship with the society. This can be seen in the expansion of church building, in the increase in ordinations and in the way in which the church through its clergy proved to be the central institution in nationalist Ireland. Its involvement in politics might be criticised on liberal grounds, but its role was almost uniformly welcomed by and positive for the community. It reflected the strength of the links between church and nation, but also secured the constitutional aspects of nationalism in parliamentary fashion. The reorganisation of the Irish university system in 1908, with the establishment of the National University of Ireland, further enhanced the influence of Catholic-nationalist Ireland. Not only did it resolve another point of tension between state and nation, but did so in terms broadly acceptable to church and nation.[53] Furthermore, public opinion no longer accepted that Catholics should be excluded from public office, the professions or private companies because of their religion or nationality. D.P. Moran used the *Leader* as a vehicle to criticise the exclusive nature of Protestant Ireland with considerable effect. He demonstrated that Protestants were over-represented in many businesses and organised a campaign against what he believed was anti-Catholic bias on the part of Protestant businessmen. One of the most successful was the campaign to introduce public examination for administrative appointments in the railways. Moran confidently predicted that this would give Catholics a fair opportunity to compete for these posts. The campaign against the Great Southern Railway was particularly successful in this respect.[54] It is certainly the case that well-educated Irish Catholics were excluded from some professions and were underrepresented in many others, but in the decades prior to 1914 this was proving more difficult to maintain. By this time, Irish Catholics were increasingly angry and irritated by the petty restrictions that affected them, and were more assertive in proclaiming their religion and nationality publicly. This in itself was a reflection of the extent to which Catholic nationalism had broken with Britain and extended its influence within Ireland. At a political level, the reorganisation and democratisation of local government in 1898 effectively dismantled another obstacle to Catholic-nationalist power. In fact the political and social influence of Irish nationalism was continuously enhanced in the years preceding the First World War. Cultural nationalists and separatists often ignored these major advances and criticised Redmond and the Irish Parliamentary Party (IPP) for assisting the Anglicisation of Ireland. These critics ignored the widespread evidence for Irish distinctiveness in the face of British influence and drew attention to what were in most cases superficial borrowings from Britain.[55]

The argument here is that Irish nationality was not weakening in the decades before 1914. By 1914 Irish nationalism had met the challenge of Anglicisation and modernity by building a powerful movement within Catholic Ireland which challenged the authority of the state. A form of dual power existed uneasily in Ireland during these decades, expressly acknowledged by Britain during the Home Rule debates of 1912–14.[56] This was a process of de-Anglicisation but without Gaelicisation. Increasingly, Irish institutions were created to challenge those associated with Britain. The church was probably the most formidable obstacle to Anglicisation, but the IPP also provided a nationalist alternative to

Liberal, Conservative or Labour appeals in Ireland. The formation of the Irish Transport and General Workers' Union in 1909 sought to organise Irish workers on a distinct Irish basis and to challenge British-based unions in Ireland. Arthur Griffith recognised the importance of this departure but, while welcoming the union on nationalist grounds, criticised James Larkin because of his English origins.[57] The Gaelic Athletic Association (GAA) was remarkably successful in promoting a distinctive Irish sporting culture, but also had important political consequences. It provided a powerful counter-attraction to British sports, emphasising the masculine values associated with Irish traditions. Its political dimension was most overt when it decided to exclude police, soldiers and militiamen on active duty from participation in the association.[58] Likewise the Gaelic League was remarkably successful in promoting a renewed interest in, if not the actual revival of, the Gaelic language. By 1913, on one estimate, the Gaelic League had 1,000 branches with approximately 100,000 members. In addition to this, the number of schoolchildren learning Gaelic increased from less than 2,000 in 1899 to approximately 180,000 in 1911. The summer schools organised by the Gaelic League in Ballingeary, County Cork, attracted more students in 1908–9 than the Queen's Colleges in Cork and Galway. Furthermore, the Gaelic League successfully persuaded the authorities to accept Gaelic as a matriculation subject for university entry. What is impressive about both the GAA and the Gaelic League is the density of organisation in the period before 1914. While the GAA had a more extensive and nationwide network of clubs, the Gaelic League had by this stage established deep roots among nationalist activists. One estimate suggests that some 2.5 per cent of the adult male population in pre-war County Wexford were members of the GAA, while 1 per cent were members of the Gaelic League. While one should not extrapolate this figure to the country generally, it does provide evidence of the appeal of both organisations.[59]

What is also noticeable is the vigorous intellectual life which was sustained within Catholic-nationalist Ireland at this time. The importance of Yeats, Synge and Joyce cannot be overestimated, but there was also a burgeoning literary culture which, though not receiving international recognition, nevertheless provided a strong Irish contribution to the arts. Canon Sheehan, probably the best-selling novelist in Ireland at the time, sold over 100,000 copies of his novels by 1913. Though now neglected, his novels continued to be read in nationalist Ireland into the 1960s.[60] A lively nationalist and Catholic press supplemented this, as did weekly and monthly journals including, among others, the *Leader*, *Sinn Féin* and *Studies*. One of the most important aspects of this process was the dramatic success of the *Irish Independent* under the stewardship of its owner, William Martin Murphy, and his chief editor, T.R. Harrington. The *Independent* had many of the characteristics of English popular newspapers, but these were placed within a clear nationalist context. Murphy, despite the bad press he has received, was a more advanced nationalist than John Redmond, becoming a critic of the IPP because of its conservative stance on fiscal policy and the limited nature of Home Rule. By 1915 the *Independent* was selling 100,000 copies per issue, substantially more than any other newspaper sold in

Ireland. While the *Independent*'s success could be interpreted as an example of the Anglicisation of Irish popular culture, this would be mistaken. It is another example of de-Anglicisation by using the most modern means to generate a specifically Irish newspaper.[61]

If Ireland was, on this account, de-Anglicising, why did a significant proportion of cultural nationalists not appreciate this? One obvious reason is that the outcome is evident only retrospectively; another is that ideal situations are rarely if ever realisable, and consequently the real world will seem imperfect to the activist. In contrast to this, many nationalists did appreciate the importance of the changes, but were not always able to persuade their more radical counterparts of this. In different ways, John Redmond, Arthur Griffith and Pádraic Pearse recognised the political opportunity for Irish nationalism which had opened up between the 1880s and 1914. They believed that the British state had at last recognised the just claims of the Irish nation; indeed both Griffith and Pearse accepted this as late as 1913.[62] But Pearse and other more militant nationalists also had a cultural claim to make. For them, the loss of the Gaelic language removed a barrier to Anglicisation. The difficulty for cultural nationalists was their refusal to recognise that Irish nationalism had never been Gaelic speaking. Indeed, the progress of Irish nationalism in the nineteenth century had coincided with the decline of spoken Gaelic. What is of interest in the Irish case is that in two generations, most of Catholic-nationalist Ireland ceased to be Gaelic speaking and adopted English as the medium of communication. The reasons for doing so are complex. The change was undoubtedly a traumatic one and fairly rare in nineteenth-century European history. Does this entail that the Irish were less Irish because they no longer spoke Irish? There were some, certainly, who believed so, but the simplest explanation is that the society adopted a new language and discarded the previous one, and in the process of doing this also created a strong nationalist movement. Despite the concerns of nationalists then and since, Gaelic has been marginal to the development and success of Irish nationalism. There is no real contradiction between Irish nationalism and the 'loss' of the language as such.[63] Moreover, it also demonstrated that nationalism was overwhelmingly political in terms of its objectives. Repeal, Home Rule, the disestablishment of the Church of Ireland and land reform all required a political party in Westminster and mass mobilisation by the nationalist electorate. Irish nationalism was from the outset a political movement with a fairly clear programme (Repeal) and this involved negotiating with the state. The interesting outcome is that the Irish language, which might have been seen as intrinsic to that movement, was actually discarded by it. The movement to revive the Gaelic language comes *after* the consolidation of Irish nationalism as an English-speaking political movement. As a consequence, cultural nationalism would always be subordinate to the mainly political focus of Irish nationalism.

The most sustained and effective obstacle to Anglicisation came in fact from nationalism itself, and especially its close association with Catholicism. Nationalism by its nature emphasises distinct history, memories and identity while religion has frequently also been associated with this assertion. In this case Catholic Ireland already had a strong defence against the intrusion of the modern and the British in Ireland. Canon Sheehan appreciated the force of this relationship, while worrying that it could not indefinitely counter the insidious influence of materialism, secularism and nihilism. He concluded that Irish identity if linked to a religious sensibility would be strong enough to resist modern ways and influences. The Irish, he believed, had acquired a balance between healthy activity and religious commitment, in contrast to much of Europe. This led him to conclude that 'you cannot move in any circle here, or change your location, or stir hand or foot without coming bolt upright against God'. This Irish reality, he asserted, was increasingly rare in modern society. Sheehan believed that Irish history and the oppression of Catholics had prepared Ireland to resist the blandishments of modernity:

> But I know that the sturdy character of the people, after their eight hundred years of fight, and their religious instincts which nothing can uproot, and their power of adapting all that is best in life with all that is useful for eternity, and above all, their sense of humour, will help them after the first shock to vibrate back towards their traditional and historical ideals, and finally settle down into the perfect poise of reason and religion combined.[64]

Sheehan's assessment was confirmed by the French writer L. Paul-Dubois, who noted that while the English and the Irish interacted in many ways, the chief characteristic of the relationship between them was difference. He also observed that 'anti-English sentiment' was widespread when he visited Ireland, expressed frequently in suspicion of any action by the British government and the motives involved in this. Drawing similar conclusions to Horgan, Paul-Dubois noted that a process of emancipation was under way in Ireland, especially for middle- and upper-class Catholics. He believed that some Anglicisation had taken place but also concluded that 'the Irish cannot become English', though he did fear they could be 'denationalised' by the influence of England. Yet his description of Ireland is one which supports the view developed above that during the decades prior to 1914 Catholic nationalism was gaining in strength and confidence. Although he did not make as strong a connection between nationality and religion as did Sheehan, Paul-Dubois was struck with the central importance of this force: 'Her religion is in the blood of Ireland. It is a second nature, a hereditary and traditional instinct, which has no need to be reasoned in order to be profound.'[65] In contrast to Mazzini and Mill, Paul-Dubois, Sheehan and other observers at the beginning of the twentieth century realised that Irish nationalism was a complex political and cultural phenomenon and as such had the confidence and self-sufficiency to resist the threat from Anglicisation and modernisation. Though some Irish nationalists feared that Ireland was denationalising, in fact Irish nationalism contained all the attributes normally associated with nationality, with the exception of a state.

Conclusion and consequences

There was however a price to be paid for this success and that was the exclusion of Irish Protestants from the national community. Catholic nationalism did not intend to do this. But the unintended consequences of the way in which the political culture evolved after the Act of Union made it extremely unlikely that a united Ireland could be achieved. If Catholic nationalism resisted Anglicisation, Protestant unionists also resisted the appeal of Irish nationalism and reinforced their identity with Britain and Protestantism. Monk Gibbon recalled that his father considered himself to be both British and Irish, but was also a Protestant minister, a unionist and a member of the County Dublin branch of the Ulster Volunteer Force (UVF). For most Protestants in Ireland, their Irish identity was compatible with being British, as was the case with most Scots and Welsh. This complex sense of identity was alien to Catholic nationalism, which consequently failed to appreciate the nature of Protestant-unionist opposition to Home Rule and attributed base motives to it. Although Catholic nationalists would never admit it, there was never a place for Protestant unionists in a Home Rule Ireland.[66] This continued to be the dilemma for Irish nationalism in 1914. While Irish nationalism claimed to represent the entire population of Ireland, a significant section of this population rejected that assertion and denied Catholic nationalism any legitimacy over them. While the unionists in the south could do little in the face of overwhelming numbers on the part of Catholic nationalism, this was not the case with the self-contained, self-confident and cohesive Protestant-unionist population in the north-east. At the very moment when the strength of Catholic nationalism was to be tested, it failed to recognise that the real threat to Irish nationalism came not from Anglicisation or the British state, but instead from those within Ireland whom it claimed as its own. Notwithstanding the difficulties posed by unionist opposition to Home Rule, Irish nationalists were optimistic that their political claims would be met after the return of a Liberal government in 1906. What was not recognised was that in attempting to meet the demand for Home Rule, without accommodating the resistance of Ulster unionists, Ireland would draw perilously close to civil war.

The concern of this chapter has been to explain why the Irish did not become British. A number of conclusions can be drawn from this discussion. The first is that the assimilative draw of British identity was weaker in Ireland than in the neighbouring island; though it had some attraction in the early nineteenth century, Protestant hostility to Catholicism prevented Irish Catholics from sharing in British identity. Furthermore, the close link between Irish identity and religion presented a formidable barrier to this prospect. The most important factor was the political one. The Act of Union provided the institutional basis for Britishness in Ireland, as had also been the case earlier in Scotland. Opposition to the Union appeared early and by the 1830s had become widespread among Catholics. By this time a nationalist mass movement had appeared which reinforced the differences between Ireland and Britain.

The second conclusion, though not discussed in detail in this chapter, is nevertheless of considerable importance. This is the need to recognise that a significant minority of Irish people did become British during the nineteenth century. This group was overwhelmingly Protestant and concentrated in the north-east. The Union served the interests of this community more adequately than was the case with Irish Catholics. It allowed them to share in a common identity (British) and to benefit from the political, religious and cultural opportunities associated with the Union. A distinction should be drawn between the Protestant community in the north-east, which was a self-sustained nationality with deeply rooted links with Scotland, and the isolated enclaves of Protestants in the rest of Ireland, which acted effectively as a British garrison.

A third conclusion is that the evolution of democratic politics in Ireland contributed to the divisions which emerged over the Union. At quite an early stage the main political cleavages within Ireland were based on denomination, identity politics and the nature of the Union. Both Catholic nationalists and Protestant unionists were able to demonstrate that their respective claims had significant electoral support. This democratic mandate reinforced the demands made by both nations on the state, but was also invoked by the state itself. The British government could insist that the decision-making context should be the state and that democracy rested on majorities in Westminster. If it accepted this, Irish nationalism could never achieve its objectives because it could never achieve a majority in Westminster. To counter this, Irish nationalists argued that the island of Ireland should be the basis for providing democratic majorities. This in turn was rejected by Protestant unionists, who insisted that either the state or the north-east region be the electoral unit. The various counterclaims based on democratic arguments increased the prospect of instability in Ireland in the decade before 1914. It draws attention to the early difficulties associated with managing any multinational political entity in a democratic age. The decision in 1912 to introduce another Home Rule bill for Ireland brought these contradictions into the open once again.

2

Nationalism, Unionism and Violence

The Impact of the 1916 Rebellion on Irish Political Culture, 1910–1922

The failure to meet the challenge of Ulster unionism

By 1914 the prospect of Home Rule was close. Irish nationalism had successfully challenged the legitimacy of the British state, but Ulster unionism denied it was part of the Irish nation and organised effective resistance to Home Rule. Ireland provides an important test of what occurs when two distinct religious and ethnic communities disagree over political authority, self-determination and nationality. Irish nationalism remained optimistic about the future in 1912. By this time the limits of the British state in Ireland had been established. The 1912 Home Rule bill was a moderate enough reform, but it went to the heart of the Union and the British constitutional order. Less apparent, but far more significant for the future, was that the limits of Irish nationalism had also been established. Not only was this largely unnoticed, but the failure on the part of Irish nationalism to recognise the limits to its own legitimacy has been a major source of political instability in Ireland ever since. By 1912 both southern Irish unionism and the British state were seeking an accommodation with Irish nationalism. As a result most sections of Irish nationalism believed that Ulster unionism would also negotiate terms in much the same way that their southern counterparts were doing.

Writing in July 1913, Pádraic Pearse believed that Ireland had entered a momentous period: 'I said last month that this generation of Irishmen will be called upon in the near future to make a very passionate assertion of nationality and that the form which that assertion shall take must depend largely upon the passage or non-passage of the present Home Rule Bill.' Pearse thought that a Gaelic party would dominate a Home Rule Ireland, removing all 'foreign influence'. He warned, 'If the Home Rule Bill does not pass ... the assertion must be made in other ways.' Pearse was impatient with the IPP, arguing that its behaviour in parliament was not assisting the Irish nation and that it was doubtful 'whether their own countrymen will retain them in office sufficiently long to allow them to pass Home Rule'.[1] Although Pearse was still a fairly marginal figure in Irish nationalist circles, some of his sentiments were widely shared. The exception was his opinion about the IPP, whose political support remained strong as long as Home Rule remained the primary objective. An editorial in one nationalist newspaper in 1914 captured the continuing strength of the party's position: 'Until Irish self-government has been secured, subsidiary considerations must wait, and all the energy of nationalists must be dedicated to strengthening the hands of the Irish leaders in every way possible.'[2] Redmond benefited from this broad consensus within nationalist Ireland, but support for the IPP could not be guaranteed unless he delivered Home Rule.

However, Home Rule increased the divisions between nationalism and unionism in Ireland. Because this was reinforced by a denominational cleavage, it deepened the gap between Catholic nationalist and Protestant unionist. When Home Rule was reintroduced in 1912, few appreciated the extent of these divisions between nationalism and unionism. For British Liberals it was the realisation of their reform programme; for Irish nationalists it was a long overdue concession. For Irish unionists, however, it was a threat to their British political culture. In the northeast, Protestant unionism had already a well-developed historical community, which was politically self-confident and prepared to oppose Home Rule. The unionist counterclaim emphasised its willingness to remain within the state and its distinctiveness in contrast to Catholic nationalism.[3] Although unionist opposition to Home Rule was well documented, nationalists chose to ignore it. This was not new, having been a feature of nationalist politics since O'Connell. One of the most serious failings of Irish nationalists, even those of a moderate hue, was the tendency to speak of Ireland as if only nationalists inhabited it. When Ramsay MacDonald, the leader of the British Labour Party, contributed to the debate on Home Rule in April 1912, he commented that if north-east Ulster did not exist, there would be no opposition to the bill. John Horgan, then an influential nationalist in Cork, who was present in the House of Commons for the debate, made a speech to a Liberal rally in Birmingham the next day at which he asserted that Home Rule would be unanimously accepted in Ireland. Horgan included this in his memoirs, written over thirty years later, adding 'as indeed, with insignificant exceptions it was'. Yet, Ulster loomed much larger than this dismissive comment suggests. Tom Kettle, a close friend of Horgan, in his influential book *The Open Secret of Ireland* dismissed unionism as a 'hallucination', sneering at its traditions while promising that force would be used if necessary to implement a united Ireland under Home Rule. He thought that coercion would not be necessary and that proper education would suffice.[4]

Horgan's political enemy in Cork, William O'Brien, was one of the few nationalists who recognised the threat to Home Rule, believing that nationalists should conciliate Ulster unionism whenever possible. In a letter to a northern correspondent in 1914, he claimed that 'my friends and myself are prepared to go very much further than you in order to satisfy every reasonable apprehension in Ulster'. Indeed, O'Brien promised that Ulster unionists would have 'an absolute veto' over 'anything actually apprehensive being attempted' by the majority in a Home Rule Ireland. Likewise, another of O'Brien's correspondents, the writer Standish O'Grady, believed that 'Irish nationalists would pay that great price [equality of representation] for the Protestant alliance'.[5] Yet, neither O'Brien nor O'Grady was a unionist or partitionist. O'Brien was committed to an advanced form of nationalism, which embraced the traditional republican belief that all those who lived in Ireland were part of the Irish nation.[6] Arthur Clery, a contributor to the *Leader* and Professor of Law at University College Dublin, criticised O'Brien for his failure to recognise the differences between nationalism and unionism: 'You may win over the Southern Protestant by abandoning your principles one after the other. You can't win over the Northern Protestant on any terms.' Clery considered that the only way to respond to Ulster unionism was to partition Ireland, permitting the counties dominated by Protestants their self-determination. Clery's attitude may have been unusual for an Irish nationalist, but he could see through the illusion generated by the belief in a single Irish nation, whereas others, equally intelligent, could not. His analysis was realistic, emphasising that the 'Ulsterman' (Protestant) had little in common with nationalist Ireland. In effect Ulster Protestants constituted a separate nationality similar to that of Irish nationalism. Clery concluded:

> Now, in reality the chances of our absorbing Ulster under Home Rule, and of England absorbing us if we do not get it, are about equal. It may be done, but it will take some doing, and just men will prefer not to see that doing. ... that they are sincere in their opposition it is mere futility to deny. They have adopted precisely the same methods of propagating their opinions that we have ours. The press, the platform and the ballot box have all borne witness to their national faith, and it seems to me that if these persons demand their national independence, and if they are, in truth, distinct in nationality, it requires a strong reason not to prevent their getting it. ... If we can prove that Irish freedom causes bondage to no man we shall have done much to help our cause.[7]

It was inconceivable that Irish nationalism by 1912 would be prepared to accept Clery's view on unionism, as it was tantamount to accepting either partition or a veto on Home Rule.

Nationalism and partition

Irish nationalists were unwilling to compromise with Ulster unionism because they continued to believe that the Liberal government would deliver Home

Rule. This ignored the extent of opposition among Ulster unionists to the proposals. It also overestimated the extent to which the Liberals were prepared to coerce the unionists.[8] Redmond also recognised that any compromise on partition would provide an opportunity for opponents to challenge the dominance of the IPP. Redmond's political strength was real in 1914, though it may have also been deceptive. It was dependent on retaining the loyalty of Irish nationalists, which in turn was dependent on delivering Home Rule. Arthur Griffith warned Redmond as early as 1911 that Sinn Féin's attitude was dependent on Irish objectives being realised by the IPP:

> Mr Redmond may rest in peace. It will not play into the hands of any man who may hope hereafter to excuse the failure of his courage and the breaking of his rosy pledges on the aged plea that faction and disunity thwarted him. Mr Redmond holds a stronger hand in the British Parliament than Parnell held. How he plays it will be seen in the Bill of 1912. Sinn Féin will not interfere with his play. When the result is shown Sinn Féin will sit in judgement.[9]

Sinn Féin was not a large organisation in 1911, but it did have some influence. The dramatist Edward Martyn maintained that Sinn Féin's role should be educational on the grounds that if it entered competitive politics 'it would appear as only another faction in Ireland'.[10] Griffith's attitude to unionism rested on the view that 'The Ulster Unionists riot but he never goes to war.' He dismissed unionists in an offhand fashion: 'He fights on while there is a chance to win but he never fights against the inevitable. He accepts it and uses it all he can. He will riot against a Home Rule Bill. He will be the loyal supporter of a Home Rule Act.'[11] For Griffith, as for most Irish nationalists, Ulster unionists were part of the nation but at the same time bigots and British dupes. If somewhat misled by imperial inducements, they could be persuaded by education or coercion to accept Home Rule. What nationalists never conceded was that unionist identity was as strong as that of nationalists, and that there was no basis for their inclusion in a Home Rule Ireland. When, in early 1914, it became clear that some form of partition was under serious consideration not only by the government but also by Redmond, Sinn Féin was outraged. Griffith concluded that 'the time has now come to put the curb on his Irish pawn [Ulster unionism] — in English party interest also', on the grounds that the divisions in British politics, no less than in Ireland, had their basis in unionist opposition to Home Rule. He asserted that the solution to unionist opposition was to introduce Home Rule for all of Ireland, though he did not indicate how this could be achieved without coercion. The nationalist dogma that all those who lived in Ireland were members of the nation prevented Irish nationalism from adopting a more flexible strategy on Home Rule or from considering alternatives to accommodate unionism.[12]

Griffith was confronted by the hard realities of Ulster when Alice Milligan, a northern nationalist, wrote to *Sinn Féin* challenging the conventional view on unionism. She claimed that 'The partition of Ireland has been an accomplished fact for 300 years and the Plantation people are largely unabsorbed.' Milligan charged that nationalists living in Dublin did not appreciate the anti-Irish nature of Ulster unionism or its determination 'never to allow any pacification between English and Scottish people and the native population of Ireland'. She believed that it was necessary for the two peoples to develop separately for six to ten years, a period of time that would permit Irish nationalists to appreciate the seriousness of the division: 'You would then be in a position to undertake what has never been thoroughly attempted — a mission to convert the Planter people. The political parties have never been able to understand this but have concentrated their attention on English constituencies.' Griffith's reply was an exercise in denial, refusing to acknowledge the evidence marshalled by Milligan while reasserting a cosy view of a united people:

> The Protestant people of Ulster of English and Scottish blood formally and unanimously accepted Irish nationality in 1782, and the plantation chapter and the plantation claims were closed at Dungannon. The stern fact we have to look in the face is that Ireland cannot acquiesce in any partition of her territory without forfeiting *all* her rights as a nation.[13]

In an editorial in the same issue Griffith claimed that Ulster was an integral part of the country and that partition was 'logically untenable' and need not be even discussed. He asserted that 'modern Irish political nationalism has been based on the dogma that Ireland is one and indivisible'. He had previously criticised Redmond for undermining this dogma by considering partition, cautioning that 'This Home Rule Bill had one value for us — that it created a national centre in Ireland. The exclusion of Ulster deprives it of that value.' The O'Rahilly suggested to *Sinn Féin*'s readers that the balance of power could be restored if nationalists organised an effective volunteer force to meet unionism's challenge.[14]

Almost the entire political spectrum of Irish nationalism shared this hostility to Ulster unionism, while also demonstrating considerable ignorance about a section of Irish society it claimed to represent. The crisis which Ireland faced prior to August 1914 was that the island was already effectively partitioned in political, economic and social terms. The Ulster Volunteer Force and the Irish Volunteers were armed and appeared determined to secure their positions militarily if necessary, while the British state was wholly ineffective in the face of this. William O'Brien, former close associate of Parnell and leader of the dissident All for Ireland League (AFIL) believed that the threat from partition could be met by negotiations between nationalists and unionists. He criticised Redmond and the IPP for ignoring unionist objections and was prepared to postpone the introduction of Home Rule in order to achieve an amicable outcome. He, in turn, was criticised by the IPP and when he opposed the Home Rule Bill in the House of Commons in May 1914 on the grounds that it was partitionist, this had serious consequences for his party in Cork. At the 1911 local elections, the AFIL had had a plurality of seats; three years later it lost seven seats in the county council elections. At the municipal election in January and the county council election in May 1914, Redmond's supporters in Cork successfully linked the AFIL candidates with unionist opposition to Home Rule. While this caricatured the AFIL position, it proved to be electorally successful, as O'Brien's correspondence shows.[15] O'Brien's failure can, in large part, be attributed to his careful and reasoned response to unionism, yet unlike him neither Sinn Féin nor Redmond offered a realistic response to unionist leader Edward Carson or the UVF. It would be mistaken to claim that unionism could have been easily conciliated in 1912. Yet a more careful policy on the part of mainstream nationalism could have weakened Carson's position politically, something he was also aware of. It would have made it more difficult for the Conservative Party to continue its principled opposition to Home Rule and in practice would have provided a means to pressurise unionism.[16]

The nationalist reaction came from outside the constitutional arena, when Eoin MacNeill published 'The North Began' in November 1913 as a response to the organisation of the UVF. The article provided the intellectual catalyst for the formation of the Irish Volunteers, though military preparation was already under way among some nationalists. MacNeill highlighted the evidence that the UVF was not in danger of suppression by the British army and argued that nationalists should therefore establish a similar force. Though a northerner, MacNeill's article displayed a similar lack of familiarity with Protestant Ulster as his contemporaries. He did assert that 'The Ulster Volunteer movement is essentially and obviously a Home Rule movement', but failed to appreciate that this was equivalent to accepting partition. MacNeill emphasised the anti-British aspects of the UVF and its refusal to accept state authority, but then applied the model of 1782 to the circumstances of 1913. What MacNeill did not see was that Home Rule for Carson and the UVF was a fall-back position for northeast Ulster, should Home Rule be introduced. He concluded from this that 'Ireland is united' because 'Unionist as well as nationalist are determined to have their own way in Ireland.' The wish for unity leads to the conclusion that because the UVF and unionism professed aims hostile to the British government this is equivalent to agreement among the Irish, even though the aims of the two movements are incompatible.[17]

For most Irish nationalists the UVF was an enemy force, but MacNeill claimed that if the UVF marched on Cork, as had been threatened, nationalists would welcome them. When he spoke at a Volunteer rally in Cork, and called for three cheers for Carson, the platform was attacked and a riot followed. Frank Gallagher, who attended the meeting, claimed that the attack was a premeditated one organised by the Redmondites, though John J. Horgan considered it a spontaneous angry response by the crowd. John Muldoon MP wrote immediately after, asking, 'Then what in Heaven's name is the meaning of cheering for Carson who has organised an army to prevent Home Rule by force. Are the people of the world to laugh at us or pity us?'[18] MacNeill himself was a moderate in politics; indeed he claimed to be a supporter of Redmond, writing privately to Horgan: 'A new movement with new men in it is naturally suspect and may be a real danger. What I ask you to do is to allow Mr Redmond to know in the best way you can, that I pledge myself against any use of the Volunteer movement to weaken his party (which is also my party).'[19] The organisation of the Volunteers highlights the contradictions within nationalist Ireland. Home Rule could have been achieved in 1914 if partition had been accepted, but Home Rule could only have been achieved for the island as a whole if Protestant Ulster had been coerced. Irish nationalism's historic commitment to a united Ireland ruled out the partitionist option, but also weakened its commitment to parliamentary politics. Redmond recognised that the Volunteer movements struck at the heart of constitutional politics in Ireland, but never fully appreciated that coercion might be necessary to respond to unionism. The IPP feared that the Volunteer movement was outside the control of the party leadership, but in its early stages did not recognise the attractiveness of its militaristic appeal. Those who joined the Irish Volunteers after November 1913 did so to counter the armed threat to Home Rule for all of Ireland by the UVF, recognising that unionism in Ulster was not willing to be ruled by nationalist Ireland.[20] One anguished nationalist MP wrote: 'Anybody can see that it is one that adds powerful corroboration to what the Unionists have been saying — that there are two Irelands. Both are drilling! Why? Home Rule is not going to produce peace but war.'[21] The political reality of Volunteer success undermined Redmond's reluctance to work with the movement, though he imposed conditions in return for his active participation.

Writing at approximately the same time, Pearse reasserted the cult of the militarist in Irish political life — the alternative feared by Redmond:

> I am glad, then, that the North has 'begun.' I am glad that the Orangemen have armed, for it is a goodly thing to see arms in Irish hands. I should like to see the [Ancient Order of Hibernians] armed. I should like to see the Transport Workers armed. I should like to see any and every body of Irish citizens armed. We must accustom ourselves to the thought of arms, to the sight of arms, to the use of arms. We may make mistakes in the beginning and shoot the wrong people; but bloodshed is a cleansing and a sanctifying thing, and the nation which regards it as the final horror has lost its manhood. There are many things more horrible than bloodshed; and slavery is one of them.

What Pearse or his successors failed to address was whose blood would be shed. Because of the 1916 Rebellion and the subsequent executions, it is normally assumed that Pearse meant the blood of the British forces and the Irish Volunteers fighting them. Pearse assumed the only obstacle to Home Rule was the British presence in Ireland.[22] The reality was more prosaic: the real enemy was Irish unionism, especially the UVF. If blood was going to be spilt, it was likely to be Irish blood and lead to a nasty ethnic conflict, similar to that taking place in the Balkans at the same time. Indeed, MacNeill feared such an outcome and deplored it, though he blamed the unionists for generating an atmosphere where it might occur. That the Irish Volunteers were directed against Ulster was evident to one elderly Parnellite in 1914. M.J. Horgan (father of John J.) wrote to a Volunteer meeting apologising for his non-attendance, but forwarding a subscription. He added that if he had been younger he would certainly have been involved in the movement: 'Not for aggression, but to help in asserting the rights of Catholic Ireland which, so far, has never had Catholic Emancipation only in name. To perpetuate that state of affairs has been the one and only object of Carson and Co., in the interests of the castle gang.'[23] Likewise, Roger Casement recognised that Britain would not coerce Ulster unionists, because Ulster would fight the imposition of what it did not want. Casement was prepared to fight: 'If John Bull betrays Ireland again, as I am certain he means to do, then with the help of God and *some* Irishmen he'll learn that all Irishmen are not slaves and that there is some fight in us still.' Casement asserted that Irish nationalism placed religion above nationality and therefore would not kill to achieve its objectives, but that unionists were not restrained in this way and were consequently taken seriously. Casement echoed Pearse's sentiment that it was better to die than to accept dishonour.[24] While this evidence is not indisputable, it does provide some substance to the claim made here, that the push for militarisation comes from the existence of unionism as a serious obstacle to the achievement of a united Home Rule Ireland and its willingness to neutralise it.

The First World War and Irish nationalism

The British government's decision to declare war on Germany dramatically changed the political environment in Ireland. Though Home Rule was passed, it was suspended for the duration of the conflict. The really radical approach at this moment would have been to implement Home Rule and ask both parties to the Irish problem to co-operate for the duration of the war. While the grounds for such co-operation were weak in 1914, Redmond did persuade southern unionists that such arrangements were viable in a Home Rule Ireland. Again we would have to double guess the actions of the unionists, but it is unlikely that they would have taken up arms while the state was at war if a more vigorous approach had been taken in August 1914. However, the conservative position was adopted by the government and agreed to by Redmond, though at the time it did appear that this decision postponed the possibility of conflict within Ireland. Without the war, conflict on an extensive scale had been likely in Ireland. Two armed camps faced each other, with little prospect of compromise.[25] For those who dismiss this scenario, the alternatives require some elaboration. *If* Home Rule had been passed without a partitionist element, then Ulster unionism would have acted against the prospect of Dublin rule. If the Liberal Party had split and Home Rule had again failed to be realised, it is possible that nationalists would have sought to secure it by other means, as Pearse certainly believed. It is likely at the very minimum that the nature of Irish politics would have changed. Alternatively, if a compromise had been agreed, this would have had a partitionist component to it, a prospect that most nationalists continued to oppose. Perhaps constitutional politics could have been maintained, but it would have been difficult without discarding the commitment to a united Ireland.

Nor can the Irish situation be compared with the political instabilities present in pre-1914 Britain. The challenge from the suffragettes or the trade union movement could be accommodated within the pre-existing political culture, if at times with difficulty. This was not the case in Ireland, because neither nationalists nor unionists accepted the rules of the political game as established for Britain. Nationalists and unionists had established their own rules for their own people and these were not transferable between the two groups within Ireland. There is some truth, therefore, in Tom Garvin's observation that: 'The true tragedy of the 1912–21 period was the absence of a really consensual politics in British-ruled Ireland, essentially because the constitutional relationship between Britain and Ireland made such a democratic politics of reason and compromise impossible.'[26] Yet, this is only a partial answer to this issue, and seriously underestimates the extent of democratic politics in nationalist Ireland. It is not necessary to romanticise Redmond or the IPP (as Garvin claims Conor Cruise O'Brien does) to recognise that the parliamentary tradition had become embedded in the political culture by 1914 and remained influential even in the face of violence between 1919 and 1921.[27] At a deeper and comparative level, the British state could not impose a consensual politics on a region of a multinational state which was divided along nationalist lines. Within Britain consensual politics was possible because national differences had not become the key source of political identity, cleavage or mobilisation. Compromise and reason are only possible when there is a shared political culture to facilitate agreement. When ethno-national identity is at stake, the limits of compromise and reason are established by each nationalist community, and while internally coherent cannot be applied universally. Despite all the failings of the British state in Ireland, and they were many, the key to understanding the crisis in Ireland between 1912 and 1922 remains within Ireland. By 1912 nationalist identity and division had achieved a dynamic independent of Britain, reflected in the two Volunteer movements primed to prevent their opponents' objectives from being realised. Now it is a moot point whether the British state could have acted differently than it did. At one level, the Liberal government failed to appreciate the extent of unionist opposition to Home Rule, but it also failed to understand that loyalty to the state in Ireland was limited by the appeal of each nationalist community.[28] The nature of the international order further obscured the dynamics of conflict in Ireland. It was assumed by most if not all liberals that Home Rule was not a first instalment of secession and that the empire would remain intact. Home Rule was a reform *within* the British state and the empire. What was not clearly recognised in 1914 was that multinational states and empires were extremely fragile in a democratic age. Irish nationalists failed to recognise that the main obstacle to Home Rule was Ulster unionism not the British state. There was a particular reluctance to engage with the possibility that Ulster unionism also had national rights, similar to those demanded by Irish nationalists.[29]

Though it would be excessive to argue that the British state is irrelevant to the outcome — clearly it is a significant player — it is possible to overemphasise the state in nationalist conflicts. Unless the state adopts a policy of exercising massive force (as in Yugoslavia or India for example) against secessionist demands, the power to decide outcomes rests with the actors within the nationalist communities. To provide an answer to 1916, the War of Independence and the Civil War, it is necessary to assess the choices available and taken, the agency involved, the mistakes made and the consequences of these actions cumulatively. What many writers on this period will not accept is that Ulster Protestants constitute, to all intents and purposes, a separate nationality within Ireland. That Ulster Protestants wished to remain within the Union, as was the case with the Scots and Welsh, does not diminish their right to self-determination. Self-determination may normally be concerned with separatism, but this need not always be the case. The key to the breakdown of order in Ireland after 1912 can only partly be attributed to the actions of the British state; the main contributory factor was the effective mobilisation of Ulster unionism against Home Rule and the counter-mobilisation by Irish nationalism against Ulster unionism. Parliamentary and constitutional politics become a game played out by nationalists and unionists, but the reality of Irish politics by 1914 was the presence of two armed camps within Ireland, each claiming to uphold a set of nationalist certainties which the other rejected.

The nationalist complaint against Carson, Ulster unionism and the opposition to Home Rule was in one respect correct. Ulster unionist behaviour was disloyal (though not traitorous) in that it rejected the British government's right to impose on its community a political settlement to which it had not given consent.[30] This is exactly what Irish nationalists maintained when their opinion was ignored by the Westminster parliament. If Carson was a traitor, then so were Pearse, Connolly and those who fought in 1916, but neither Garvin nor other writers are generally prepared to draw this conclusion. The reason for this is that Irish nationalism is given a superior moral authority which is denied to *both* the British state *and* Ulster unionism. The denial of British authority is understandable and justifiable in the context of national self-assertion, whether in Ireland or India; what is less understandable is why Irish nationalism (and a large part of the British liberal establishment) also refused to concede Ulster unionism an equal place as a distinct nation within Ireland, the legacy of which is still being fought out now. The main reason for this between 1912 and 1921 was based on the lack of knowledge and a refusal to face the political reality of a divided Ireland. Another contributory factor was the continuing assertion that Ireland constituted a single nation, despite unionism's rejection of this claim. The reason why consensus did not exist in Ireland between 1912 and 1914 is that two incompatible political objectives were in conflict with one another. The behaviour of both sides at this time lends no support to the view that compromise was possible: indeed by 1914 hostility had deepened appreciably. One possible outcome of this confrontation was an inter-communal war between nationalists and unionists. Paradoxically, it was the existence of the British state in Ireland which prevented this in 1914 and again in 1921–2. In comparison with inter-ethnic conflicts elsewhere in Europe at the end of the First World War and subsequently, inter-communal violence has been mercifully low key in Ireland, but it has not been absent. The British presence in

Ireland throughout the crisis of 1912 to 1921 was a major contributory factor to this, as was the influence of constitutional politics and the Catholic Church. Similar pressures were at work in Protestant Ulster. Britain was, in the medium term, able to hold the ring and prevent widespread inter-communal violence because it was under parliamentary control and public opinion remained important. This was in stark contrast to the widespread massacres of Armenians by the Turkish state during the First World War, on the grounds that they were enemies of the state. The British state also provided a useful scapegoat for both sides in Ireland: nationalists could blame the state for not coercing the unionists, while unionists could criticise it for threatening the Union. This allowed both nationalism and unionism to ignore the enemy within, and both were responsible for the consequences of this.[31]

The outbreak of war certainly postponed the particular explosion for the immediate future, but it did not remove the essential conditions promoting confrontation. Redmond's decision to support the war was endorsed by most sections of nationalist Ireland. It provided an opportunity for co-operation between nationalist and unionist Ireland within the British Empire, but it was an opportunity that went unrealised. It may be that if Irish regiments had been formed, with Irish Catholic officers in command, the outcome would have been different. Certainly there was considerable disappointment, if not anger, when Irish nationalist recruits were absorbed into 'British regiments'. The Irish Volunteers split over participation in the war. Redmond led the vast majority (approximately 150,000) out of the Irish Volunteers and formed the National Volunteers. About 10,000 remained within the Irish Volunteers, now dominated by the Irish Republican Brotherhood (IRB), and pursued an active anti-war policy while also preparing for insurrection. Public opinion, in so far as it can be detected, continued to support Redmond in 1914 and 1915, a factor recognised even by those planning insurrection. There is some evidence that anti-recruiting activity had support but this remained limited.[32] Redmond invoked strong nationalist symbolism to justify support for the war, a justification that was supported by his long-time enemy William O'Brien in Cork. In particular the symbolism of 1778 and 1782 was used for the purpose of securing harmony between north and south. Redmond's assertion that Irishmen could safeguard the island against a possible German threat was couched in such a way as to generate the widest possible support within Ireland.[33] The editor of a Wexford newspaper with Sinn Féin sympathies found it necessary to modify its anti-war sentiments to retain readers; as late as March 1915 he concluded that, 'If the blood shed in France and Belgium only helps to allay the distrust between North and South in this country, it will not have been shed in vain.' Fitzpatrick notes that in Clare enthusiasm for the war was weakening by 1915, at least as represented in the local press.[34] It is probably safe to conclude that Irish nationalist opinion remained broadly in favour of the war effort until 1916, though by this time opinion was becoming more sceptical about what benefits it might bring to Irish nationalism. It is noticeable that even prior to the Rising in 1916, William O'Brien, a useful barometer in these matters, is depressed in his correspondence. A further point to be considered is that insurrectionary conspiracy remained limited to a narrow circle of revolutionaries, and it is open to question whether even a majority of Volunteers, while still disagreeing with the tactics of most nationalists supporting the war, were in favour of insurrection.[35]

The evidence produced here does not do full justice to the complex mosaic of opinion within Irish nationalism between 1914 and 1916. There is a danger, when looking at it, of falling into the trap of seeing events through a lens provided by the victorious Sinn Féin elite which came to power in independent Ireland, though it is also important to resist the nostalgia for Redmond's Ireland, which can be a reaction to the 'official' history of the period. I have suggested already that by 1914 there was an expressly Irish nationalist political culture in place in Ireland, that it reflected deep-seated and popular values within that community and that it exercised a high degree of authority within the nationalist community while effectively contesting the British state and its legitimacy. Moreover, it was politically sophisticated, self-confident and determined to achieve its main political objectives, primarily Home Rule for a united Ireland. If this is the case, was the decision to enter the war confirmation that Irish nationalism was fundamentally flawed (as Mazzini claimed and Mill had hinted at)? The IRB leadership certainly believed this to be the case, but also recognised the opportunity that this provided for a return to revolutionary action. The war led D.P. Moran to break with Redmond and to pursue an anti-recruiting policy in the *Leader*. Likewise, Arthur Clery considered that Irish nationality itself was threatened by the war, echoing an earlier view of Moran's: 'There are certainly some traits to be found in Ireland which stamp the people as a distinct race even yet; but they characterise her torpor and decay rather than her development.'[36] For those willing to interpret 1914 in this negative light, it reinforced the radical nationalist view that Redmond and the IPP had betrayed Irish nationalism. Much later Daniel Corkery commented: 'If that split between parliamentarians and the separatists had not taken place, we certainly should not today be living under a native government in Dublin.'[37] This is a view which has characterised Irish political opinion since the War of Independence. The 1916 Rebellion, the 1918 election, the War of Independence, the Treaty and the Civil War become a seamless (and inevitable) consequence of the war and the division in the Volunteers, but more powerfully (and self-servingly) these actions (especially 1916) could be justified on the grounds that they contributed to securing Irish independence and protecting Irish nationality.[38]

It is not necessary to accept Moran's pessimism about the state of Irish nationality to recognise that Irish nationalism had entered uncharted waters in August 1914. Those Irish Volunteers who accepted Redmond's view that the war provided an opportunity to safeguard Home Rule did not consider themselves to be British when doing so. In defending the state, Irish nationalists believed that they were also defending their nationality. The militant minority rejected this view, believing that it compromised nationality. It is mistaken to conclude that the militant is the representative figure for Irish nationalism and dismiss the views of the mass of the people as anti-Irish or Anglicised. For example, John T. Lemass (Seán Lemass' father) was presented with his wife to Edward VII when he visited Dublin in 1903, but this did not prevent him from being a nationalist, advertising in Moran's *Leader* or supporting the political activities of his sons. The reason John Lemass could do so was that relations between the state and nation had improved and moderate nationalists could see the monarchy in a positive light.[39] If the interpretation of a situation is left to the political militant or the utopian ideologue, there is a strong possibility that the context will be misunderstood.

Garret FitzGerald revisited this issue in a series of articles written in 1991 for the seventy-fifth anniversary of the 1916 Rebellion. His analysis echoes the view of the militant wing of Irish nationalism that Ireland had capitulated to the British in 1914. He goes on to claim that the Rebellion was the last opportunity to establish the political conditions for Irish independence. For FitzGerald, independence in 1922 'was in fact secured almost at the latest date at which it could have been conveniently achieved'. Consequently, Irish national identity would have been lost without the violence of this period, a view FitzGerald seems to have gained from his father, Desmond, a former militant.[40] Yet is this the case? Was Irish nationalism really undermined by Redmond's decision to support the British war effort? As suggested in the previous chapter, the evidence we have is that Irish nationalism was quite self-confident in the decade before 1914. It is open to question whether such a nationalism would have discarded its identity as easily as implied by FitzGerald. Yet, there is a paradox in this. Some 206,000 Irishmen joined the British forces during the war. The rate of enlistment actually increased during 1915, while in 1916 and 1917, as David Fitzpatrick has shown, the rate declined appreciably. Interestingly, there was an increase in enlistment immediately after the 1916 Rebellion, though this was clearly not maintained.[41]

Significant numbers of UVF and Irish Volunteers members enlisted in 1914 and 1915, if for somewhat different reasons. It may be that joining the British army was a way to continue the Home Rule confrontation by other means and never provided a basis for co-operation. Certainly Carson and the UVF believed that their status within the United Kingdom would be secured by their involvement in the war effort, that this loyalty would be rewarded in a postwar settlement. Similar reasoning contributed to the decision by Redmond, Dillon and O'Brien to support the war, though for some such as Tom Kettle the rationale for fighting was extremely complex and cannot be reduced to one simple ingredient.[42] Fitzpatrick has emphasised the role of group loyalty in encouraging enlistment, and this is a more persuasive approach than poverty, intimidation or excitement taken in isolation. This feature should be linked to political considerations, especially in the minds of Irish nationalists. In contrast to the UVF, Irish Volunteers had a choice in 1914 and 1915. They could have remained with the IRB-dominated Irish Volunteers after the split or simply dropped out of Volunteering entirely. Some Volunteers were radicalised by the war and remained committed to an independent strategy, while others simply ignored both the militarists and the pro-war camp. But was Irish nationalism fundamentally undermined as a consequence of the majority of Irish nationalists supporting the war? There is less evidence for this. The IPP maintained its political dominance through to 1916; indeed by late 1915 Redmond was in a position to ignore O'Brien in Cork and the party judged that his influence was in terminal decline. Police reports confirmed that prior to 1916 militant nationalism was relatively weak in most parts of the country.[43]

Nor did Sinn Féin or the Irish Volunteers offer a serious challenge to Redmond prior to 1916. Support for the war was never automatic or unanimous. The British state was mistaken to expect this. Redmond's support relieved British anxiety that Irish nationalism might not give its consent to the war. But the British government never recognised that Irish support for the war was always contingent. Irish nationalism was giving its consent for Ireland (or at least the part which it represented) to join in a struggle with an ally. The influence of 1782 is not far off in this reasoning, an image returned to by Redmond and others. Those who accept a state-based view of the contemporary world might misunderstand the limited and contingent nature of Irish support for the war. The enthusiasm reflected a belief that participation was in Ireland's interest, that it would confirm and secure Home Rule and that it might provide the basis for consensus among Irish people once the conflict ended. Consequently Irish nationalist support for the war was ultimately based on the considered interest of nationality and not on the fact that Irish nationalists were subjects of the Crown. There was Catholic jingoism, which was nationalist, and there was Protestant jingoism, which was unionist. In the excitement of 1914 and 1915 it is easy to conflate them. However, the reality is that Ulster unionists supported the war because they were British while Irish nationalists did so because they were nationalists. In the short term, Irish nationalists provided strong support for the war, as the figures for enlistment demonstrate. However, because support was based on nationalist concerns, there was a danger of instability if circumstances changed. Irish nationalists owed primary loyalty to the nation not the state, and if a conflict between these occurred then the nation would take priority over the state. Between 1914 and 1916 the interests of state and nation coincided but this could never be taken for granted. It can be argued that most recruits from within nationalist Ireland (especially those who had been members of the Irish Volunteers) were not Anglicised by this involvement, but were responding to what was considered to be the national interest. This was also the opinion of a majority in nationalist Ireland up to 1916, if not 1918. Nor should this be surprising. Elsewhere in Europe, people made decisions on the war by reflecting on national interest rather than state interest if these were in conflict. In Ireland the short-term outcome coincided with the interest of the state and the nation.[44]

The First World War provided an opportunity for revolutionary and radical groups to reassert the superiority of the elite over the opinion of the mass of citizens. Lenin and Mussolini welcomed the war because of the opportunity it provided to break with continuity, but also because it provided an opportunity to reject the 'tyranny' of democracy and its enfeebling impact on the revolutionary potential of the people.[45] The driving force behind the Irish revolutionaries in 1916 had a similar origin. Pearse, Connolly and the IRB recognised that the war provided an opportunity for radical intervention in the political process, and, moreover, that if such action was not taken the mass of the Irish people would accede to the politics of compromise central to the parliamentary system. The war provided an opportunity to destroy the legitimacy of the IPP and democratic politics in Ireland. By definition, the revolutionary is never a representative figure. Few people have the will or certainty to commit themselves to violent action in anticipation that this will change politics radically. All revolutionaries share this will and certainty, but few get the opportunity to put it into effect. The revolutionary situation requires the commitment of the revolutionaries, a domestic crisis which provides an opportunity to act, and a permissive international environment. What the First World War did in Ireland was challenge the long-term dominance of constitutional politics and provide the opportunity for a revolutionary elite to ignore the will of the electorate and representative institutions.[46]

Pearse was clear about the opportunity. The war had undermined the moral authority associated with constitutional politics: 'The last sixteen months', he wrote in December 1915, 'have been the most glorious in the history of Europe. Heroism has come back to earth.' He emphasised the importance of violence in this world: 'The old heart of the earth needed to be warmed with the red wine of the battlefields.' Pearse conceded that 'War is a terrible thing' yet welcomed it as an opportunity to destroy what he considered to be the bankruptcy of the previous twenty-five years of Irish history: 'What if the war sets Poland and Ireland free? If the war does these things, will not the war have been worth while?'[47] The socialist James Connolly expressed similar sentiments, as did Lenin and Mussolini. In each case violence was justified as a means to undermine existing institutions.

The impact of the 1916 Rebellion on Irish nationalism

There were a number of factors which created the environment that led to the 1916 Rebellion. The first of these was frustration with constitutional politics by radical nationalists, associated with a belief that the war and patriotism had seduced the mass of the people. There had been a revival of the militarist tradition after the fall of Parnell. Of particular importance were the celebrations in 1898 accompanying the centenary of the 1798 Rebellion. These events gave a focus for nationalists disillusioned with more conservative parliamentary politics and glamorised the '98 Rebellion and its separatist message. Other contributory factors included the Boer War, the Volunteer movement, cultural utopianism and the organisation and maintenance after 1914 of an armed revolutionary force, one which was not repressed by a state at war. The radicalisation of nationalist opinion in the face of partition and the failure to realise Home Rule in 1914 also contributed, as did the war itself and the successful recruiting campaign in 1915. These features convinced the IRB that an insurrection should be attempted. What came into play was the historic belief that armed insurrection had the best chance of success when Britain was engaged elsewhere. However, if there is one factor which more than any other accounts for 1916 it is the threat of partition and the organisation of Ulster to defeat Home Rule. It is clear that if Home Rule had been agreed for the island, Pearse, Connolly and the IRB might have been critics of the new dispensation, but would have remained within democratic and parliamentary limits. It was the threat to Home Rule from Carson and the UVF which facilitated the growth of the Volunteers and placed the IRB in a crucial leadership position. After the split in the Volunteers in 1914, a minority of nationalists identified with the more radical version of politics. This was not equivalent to supporting the use of violence. It is also important to ask what the insurrection was aimed at. It is an incomplete explanation to say that it was the British presence in Ireland. If Britain had been defeated in Dublin in 1916, the Volunteers would still have been faced with the task of controlling the northeast. It is unlikely that unionist Ulster would have accepted republican rule. It is more likely that the northeast would have been used by Britain to launch a counterattack. Even if the British state had been defeated in 1916, British Ireland in Ulster would have been able to maintain its presence.

That those who fought in 1916 believed they were acting against the British state is, of course, true, but the residual power of the British state in nationalist Ireland disguised a far more serious and deeply rooted obstacle to a united Ireland: Protestant Ulster. In his last major political essay, Pearse demanded sovereignty over 'all men and things' in Ireland.[48] The possible sovereignty of Ulster unionism was implicitly denied, thought there is no way of knowing whether Pearse would have coerced Ulster unionism into a united Ireland. But if the leaders of the 1916 Rebellion wanted to achieve this objective, then force was the only method available to do so. The political heirs of Pearse and Connolly certainly threatened violence against unionist Ulster and on occasions sanctioned it, though this provides only indirect evidence that other leaders would have done so.[49] British disengagement from nationalist Ireland predates the War of Independence. The British state during the Home Rule crisis was not engaged in a last-ditch defence of the Union, but was securing the best terms for its dependants (especially in the south) and attempting to limit the fall-out for the empire. Augustine Birrell, who was Chief Secretary from 1907 to 1916, advanced the policy of conciliation with Irish nationalism throughout this period. His policies assumed that there would be devolution of power to a Home Rule parliament in Ireland and his actions acknowledged that power (if not yet institutions) had already moved decisively in favour of Irish nationalism. It was also difficult for the British state to appease nationalist opinion in 1914, as this would have required going to war with Ulster unionists, a relatively well-armed force by this time. In so far as these matters can be determined, this is precisely what Irish nationalism wanted the British state to do, and when it did not do so organised to do so itself. To claim that Ulster unionism and the threat of partition was not a cause of 1916, and indeed the War of Independence, is similar to saying that slavery was not the cause of the American Civil War. The 1916 Rebellion and the War of Independence were directly aimed at British rule in Ireland, but it was the existence of Ulster unionism and the threat of partition which created the conditions for Irish nationalism to take up arms against the British state. If Ulster unionism had not existed, armed conflict would have been far less likely because most of what Ireland wanted in 1912 could have been conceded by the state.

The insurrection itself was a failure, with the insurgents surrendering within the week. It is not my task to discuss whether the outcome might have been different if circumstances had been more favourable to the conspirators. The leadership often misread the situation due to its conspiratorial nature. Yet, all else being equal, it is likely that a state under severe pressure in Europe would have produced the necessary force to regain control. The question I wish to address is whether 1916 was a necessary condition for Irish independence, in the sense used by FitzGerald and Corkery. Was it the one last chance to redeem a degenerate nationalist consciousness? The causal relationship does appear to be there. Although the insurrection was defeated, radical politics successfully reappeared in 1917. Sinn Féin, newly reorganised, led the campaign against conscription, won a number of by-elections and in 1918 defeated Redmond and his party at the polls. The War of Independence followed from this, and so ultimately did the Treaty, which secured Irish independence. It is possible to accept the causal relationship without agreeing that the majority of Irish nationalists were Anglicised in 1916 and required this stimulus. It is also important to distinguish between what actually happened (the historical record) and what could have happened (alternative routes). To describe the historical sequence is not the same as giving causal priority to one or other trend. But was the route taken the only possible one? Because something happened does not mean that it was inevitable or that there was no alternative.

The 1916 Rebellion is one of the key moments in twentieth-century Irish history. Three leaders of the state fought in the insurrection, while two of the main political parties owe their origin to the sequence of events which followed. For republicans, the Rebellion provided the catalyst which finally undermined British rule in Ireland and created the foundations for an independent Irish state. On this reading the Irish state was established in violence by a revolutionary movement committed to transforming the political environment. Though the outcome was different from that anticipated by the leaders of the Rebellion or their successors, this legacy remains influential and potent. In the articles discussed earlier Garret FitzGerald defends the view 'No 1916 — No independence'. But was this actually the case? Both FitzGerald and republicans endorse the view that Irish nationalism had been seriously compromised in 1914 and that the movement for self-determination had been weakened as a consequence. The evidence provided for this argument is the continuing recruitment of Irish nationalists to the British armed forces. This was a minority view within Irish nationalism between 1914 and 1918, but was revised when the victorious Sinn Féin wrote the official history of the period. That history was rewritten by the victors should not surprise historians, but this does not make it an accurate account. There was no contradiction between joining the British forces and being a good nationalist for the majority of National Volunteers. For the most part they believed they were advancing

Ireland's interest by joining the British army. The Rebellion was not necessary to save Irish nationalism from itself, even if those who participated in it deluded themselves that this was the case.

If the Rebellion was not necessary as an awaking, perhaps it was necessary to secure Irish independence. FitzGerald makes the case that, without the Rebellion, Ireland would not have achieved independence in 1921 and consequently it would have been postponed indefinitely. This is extremely doubtful as it is based on the assumption that the demand for self-determination by nationalists was weak and that a moderate degree of devolution would have been enough to satisfy Irish nationalism. While independence would have been different without the Rebellion, there was every likelihood that an independent Irish state would have been established. This might not have happened in 1922, but in all likelihood it would have occurred. It is only possible to maintain the view put forward by FitzGerald if one accepts that Irish national identity was weak at the time, and the evidence we have suggests otherwise. It might be argued that without the Rebellion there would have been little opposition to conscription. Yet again this is questionable. If Sinn Féin had not existed there would still have been widespread opposition to conscription, because Irish nationalists of every variety denied the British state the right to conscript Irishmen. It is probable that there would have been mass opposition to conscription even if there had been no 1916 and no reorganised Sinn Féin. The Rebellion was important in that it determined *when* Ireland became independent and contributed to a more radical momentum. Furthermore, the political success of Sinn Féin in 1918 and the collapse of the IPP's electoral support generated a new dynamic within nationalist Ireland and created a crisis in the relationship between Britain and Ireland. While these events are important for understanding why independence came when it did, one should not take at face value the view of the militants that this was the last opportunity to act decisively.

As a consequence, the 1916 Rebellion retains an importance which is not the case for earlier rebellions. The Rebellion disrupted the constitutional continuity of Irish politics and contributed to the weakening of the IPP between then and 1918, when it collapsed in the face of Sinn Féin. Unlike earlier revolts, the 1916 Rebellion continued to impact on politics after its defeat. There is continuity between 1916 and independence, but not necessarily a causal link. It can be argued with as much confidence that the First World War or the organisation of the UVF is as causally related to Irish independence (in the form it emerged) as are the events of 1916. To put this in its strongest form, the Act of Union itself could be said to have 'caused' the collapse of parliamentary politics after 1916, but the relationships involved in this claim are too tortuous to provide a satisfactory causal explanation. Are there criteria that we can apply to allow us to choose between different candidates for a causal relationship? The difficulty in establishing a causal claim is that the links are what we see after the completion of the event and the disappearance of other alternatives. The outcome is never clear at the time. Notwithstanding this, 1916 is not like other earlier militarist enterprises in that it left a significant political legacy that continued to affect the behaviour and choices of groups and individuals thereafter. It is possible — and necessary — to incorporate 1916 into an understanding of the multiple processes that led to independence without necessarily ascribing to it the heroic status it has received. Also, in contrast with Russia in 1917, Ireland had representative institutions in place in 1916. Redmond and the IPP continued to represent the majority of Irish nationalists and had received an electoral mandate in 1910. By-elections continued to take place and be won by the IPP during the war and opinion could be gauged by this method. In addition, the British state was open to influence exercised by Irish MPs at Westminster, providing leverage for Irish nationalists to obtain concessions from the government. The position taken by the *Irish News* in Belfast immediately after the Rebellion reflected not only the general view among nationalists in 1916, but also one that was maintained by most nationalists subsequently: 'Had it been possible to take a vote of the people of this country on the issue, 99 per cent of them would have declared against such an attempt without hesitation, and with all the power they could muster'.[50] The Rebellion was in fact an unrepresentative putsch organised by a minority of nationalists with little public support. Sinn Féin subsequently rewrote the history of the war to suit its ideological purposes, but this does not affect the conclusion that the Rebellion was an assault on democratic government in Ireland.

Sinn Féin's political success cannot be equated to mass endorsement of the Rebellion by Irish nationalist opinion. It was a consequence of Sinn Féin adopting an electoral strategy which accepted democratic principles, one which allowed it to challenge the dominance of the IPP. There were weaknesses in Redmond's strategy and Sinn Féin became the means to expose them. Paul Bew has argued that the IPP, though successful in a number of by-elections, was already encountering some strains and opposition within its own community by 1916. A police report by the Cork County Inspector in October 1915 suggested that some sections of the nationalist community were already hostile to the war and to recruitment. J.J. Lee has speculated that there might have been more support for the insurgents than conventional wisdom allowed.[51] The traditional view has been that the Rebellion was opposed by a majority of Irish nationalists, that martial law and the executions distressed, if not alienated, nationalist opinion and that the mismanagement of Irish affairs by the British state contributed over the subsequent eighteen months to the radicalisation of nationalist opinion. It is possible to reconcile the traditional view with that of Lee by invoking a notion of collective loyalty. The initial response to the Rebellion was one of bewilderment, resentment and anger as individuals attempted to fit it into existing conceptual frameworks of meaning. In the very short term, the shock led to condemnation. However, this may have been superficial, leading over the following weeks to a reconsideration of the event and its consequences. Adjustments took place; events were reordered to take account of deep-rooted values, norms and attachments. A contemporary analogy can be found in the reaction to specific atrocities in Northern Ireland. After an atrocity all sides normally condemn the extremists, but this response has rarely been translated into a long-term cross-denominational force for ending violence. The memory of each atrocity is retained by the community upon which it is perpetrated, but is weakened appreciably in the perpetrator community. Each community remembers the atrocity perpetrated on it, while forgetting the atrocities that it perpetrated. Thus, Bloody Sunday and the Enniskillen Remembrance Day bombing are remembered and forgotten differently in each community. What happens is that collective identity overrides the shock and anger of an atrocity, retaining its significance only for those who have been attacked. What occurred after 1916 is an example of the national community responding in the short term with anger and shock, but subsequently re-evaluating that response in the light of further information becoming available and invoking certain collective memories embodied in the national consciousness. The actions of the British state immediately after 1916 were understandable for a state at war, but given the contingent nature of Irish nationalist loyalty there was no guarantee that such actions would be endorsed.

There is also some evidence that the immediate response was more ambivalent and nuanced. Tom Johnson, an English socialist, noted in his diary that most of the people he met were 'compelled to admire the courage and resources of the young men and their leaders'. Seán Lemass recalled not only the relief of his parents when he was released without being deported, but a degree of pride in his activities.[52] James Stephens, who completed a book on the Rebellion on 8 May 1916, slightly over a week after the surrender, reflected on some of its ambiguities. Rather prophetically, Stephens sensed that the mood of the Irish, at least in Dublin, was already changing: 'Ireland is not cowed. She is excited a little. She is gay a little. She was not with the revolution, but in a few months she will be.' Stephens was prepared to 'name this date as the first day of Irish freedom, and the knowledge forbids me mourn too deeply my friends who are dead'. Not only was he sympathetic to the insurrectionists, but he openly endorsed the need for a blood sacrifice, 'The blood of brave men had to sanctify such a consummation if the national imagination was to be stirred to the dreadful business which is the organising of freedom.'[53] Stephens' day-by-day account of the Rebellion is valuable in that it captures various moods in snapshot, showing the confused and ambiguous response to the event. Tracey Connolly has demonstrated in her research that a new consensus emerged quickly, once the first shock was over. This in turn led to a significant shift in public opinion in nationalist Ireland.[54] The execution of the leaders of the Rebellion, the murder of the pacifist Francis Sheehy-Skeffington and the introduction of martial law certainly contributed to the shift, yet this is an incomplete explanation. The default position among nationalists and unionists was quite different. Unionists believed that all nationalists were traitors, and the Rebellion simply confirmed this for them. Accordingly, nationalists could not be trusted. For nationalists, in contrast, the default position was far more complex, leading to growing sympathy for the rebels and eventually forgiveness.[55] The question is: why was this the case? John Dillon was reported as claiming in the House of Commons on 11 May that 'Thousands of people in Dublin who ten days ago were bitterly opposed to the Sinn Féin movement and to rebellion were now becoming infuriated against the Government on account of these executions ... that feeling was spreading throughout the country in a most dangerous degree.' His fellow MP, Arthur Lynch, linked the leaders with previous martyrs in the nationalist canon, recognising the powerful symbolism involved in their death.[56]

One way to account for the rapid change of opinion on the Rebellion is to refocus the lens through which it is perceived. The *Irish Times*, and unionist opinion in the south, viewed the Rebellion through a lens affected by their political and social demise. The British government's actions were all subordinated to the need to manage a war and defend the state. For the British state, Ireland had priority only because of the war and the threat to prosecuting it after the insurrection. For Irish nationalism the lens used was influenced by a particular history, one which distrusted British and unionist motives in any set of circumstances. This distrust came into play once the Rebellion was over and the authorities began to act in response to it. Irish nationalism had a more selective vision of the events, and the response differed as a consequence. Much of the immediate newspaper reporting on the Rebellion was extremely general and often incoherent. This is understandable, as censorship and confusion prevented careful assessment.[57] However, within another week a more considered editorial line began to emerge. By the middle of May, there was a growing concern that the executions would alienate Ireland from Britain, that Irish nationalism was embittered by its treatment and that there was growing sympathy (though not support) for the rebels. Police reports confirm that opinion changed very quickly. The Carlow County Inspector reported that 'somewhat more sympathy is being extended towards those who took part in the recent rising than was at first the case. This is chiefly due to the idea that too many unnecessary arrests have been made.' Similar reports appeared from Fermanagh, Monaghan, Kilkenny and Down.[58] Opinion on the Rebellion by the middle of May is already following more predictable lines, with nationalists becoming more sympathetic to the rebels. There are two factors interacting here: the short-term events — the Rebellion, executions and arrests — and the long-term structure of the political culture. The latter imposes a coherence and order on the former, especially if the former is novel or shocking. Increasingly, the most persuasive response on the part of Irish nationalism was the view that, though mistaken, the leaders of the Rebellion should not have been executed. When this is then placed in the broader context of the political dynamics of the second half of 1916, a new process becomes evident.

To suggest that this sympathy for the rebels was immediately translated into political support for Sinn Féin is mistaken. But the response to the Rebellion by mid-May surely indicates that Irish nationalism was not becoming Anglicised: indeed it lends support to the opposite conclusion. Irish nationalist opinion was sophisticated enough to draw a distinction between the act of violence (which was generally deplored at this time) and the motivation behind it (which was often considered noble and patriotic). National unity is retrieved in the face of British behaviour which is considered inappropriate, even for an act condemned by the nation. National unity was given priority in the conflict with the state, even though that state was at war and the Rebellion could be considered a stab in the back by Britain. This was not how it appeared to Irish nationalists, many of whom were increasingly critical of British behaviour during the war. The contingent nature of opinion is evident among those who supported the war and condemned the Rebellion. Redmond's leading supporter in Cork, John Horgan, claimed that Sinn Féin influence was growing in the city even prior to the Rebellion and believed 'We will be in serious trouble if conscription is introduced.'[59] Those nationalists who supported the war drew a distinction between voluntary enlistment, which they encouraged, and conscription by the British state, which was considered by all shades of nationalist opinion to be an intrusion into Irish nationalist authority. What can be seen here is a difference in policy among nationalists, not a disagreement about the principle of Irish autonomous authority.

One of the immediate effects of the Rebellion was to put Home Rule back on the agenda of British politics. On 12 June, the Ulster Unionist Council abandoned its reservations about Home Rule by agreeing that six counties would be excluded, while the twenty-six counties would achieve Home Rule. In early July, the IPP met to respond to this and to the British government's initiatives on the issue. In effect, Redmond and his party were being asked to abandon the aim of a united Ireland in return for Home Rule. The IPP accepted this compromise very reluctantly, but did so on the grounds that it would be temporary. What Redmond was not aware of was that Carson was convinced that the exclusion would be permanent. Concern was also expressed at the IPP meeting about the status of nationalists within a unionist-controlled north. Yet Redmond and the party leadership accepted this outcome on the grounds that it would bring harmony to Ireland and was in the best interests of the country.[60] While the potential in the July 1916 arrangements was never realised, the decision to accept partition had an increasingly negative impact on the IPP. One response to this accepted the reality of partition while complaining that giving the unionists six counties was overly generous and had sinister consequences. Arthur Clery, writing in the *Leader*, continued to claim that Ulster unionists were alien to Irish nationalism, while at the same time recognising the openly sectarian nature of the conflict. His realism about unionism did not lead him to a sympathetic view of that population or any optimism about future relations:

> Were it not for the traditional nonsense of calling East Ulstermen Irishmen, no one would look upon the Catholics of Armagh or Fermanagh as anything else. They are in a sense the victims of the lie we have all been keeping up about Protestant Ulster. If Protestant Ulster now insists on keeping them, it can only be as hostages. It should be said in fairness that similar remarks apply to the small Protestant district that lies just across the borders of Donegal.[61]

Clery asked his readers whether the Ulster Protestants 'are ... such a loss', making explicit the often latent hostility to Protestant Ireland on the part of

Irish nationalism. His own reply was in the negative, but most other nationalists did not share this view. William O'Brien appears to have been devastated by the Rebellion, blaming Redmond and the IPP for driving 'the unselfish young men of Ireland' into revolt. In contrast to Redmond, Dillon and Horgan who praised the northern nationalist leader, Joe Devlin, for his loyalty in accepting the exclusion of the six counties, O'Brien condemned partition unreservedly, whether temporary or permanent. In reply to a clerical correspondent who believed that the exclusion of the six counties handed northern nationalists 'over to the old ascendancy party in Ireland', he demonstrated how radicalised he had become in response. O'Brien feared for the future, believing that there was no opposition to partition: 'In all our history there is no more abominable disgrace than that a public offer should be made of six counties of Ireland to the Orangemen and that, up to the moment, the so-called nationalist representatives of Ireland should not have uttered a word of protest or taken their countrymen into their confidence.' O'Brien warned Lloyd George and Carson that a partitionist resolution of Home Rule 'would hand the country to the Sinn Féinners'. Partition would furthermore 'destroy the very name of Ireland and split her into two hostile religious and racial "compounds"'. If this was put in place, he predicted that a 'new and more formidable rebellion in Dublin and Belfast' would be the most likely consequence.[62]

O'Brien was an ambiguous and flawed individual in Irish politics, yet his response to the First World War, to 1916 and to the threat of partition seems to have been representative of mainstream nationalism. While despising Redmond, he remained deeply pessimistic about the future, believing that the people would side with the 'traitors' against any initiative he might pursue. Despite this, it is already possible to see the contours of a new anti-partitionist coalition emerging. William Martin Murphy, the proprietor of the *Irish Independent*, became increasingly critical of the British administration and the IPP, using his newspaper to devastating effect after the Rebellion. He also wrote to O'Brien offering support for an anti-partitionist campaign. Among AFIL members, there was increasing pressure to work closely with Sinn Féin on the issue. Some of O'Brien's correspondents claimed that his newspaper, the *Cork Free Press*, was now extending its readership because of O'Brien's stand on partition. Alfred O'Rahilly, on the way to becoming one of Ireland's leading Catholic intellectuals, wrote supporting O'Brien in the 'present crisis'. Lawrence Casey, who was a member of the organising committee of the Anti-Partition League (a dissident nationalist organisation established in 1916) claimed to detect a new and considerable hostility to Redmond in Dublin, Wexford and Waterford.[63] Various currents were emerging in late 1916 which contributed in time to the success of Sinn Féin in 1918, yet this was not inevitable.

O'Brien's support for the war deprived him of influence among radicals after the Rebellion.[64] However, the hardening of his position on partition, and his reluctance to openly support the war after 1916, marks the beginning of a transition for him and the AFIL. In the short term it is his weakness, and that of Redmond's opponents, which is most obvious. O'Brien's last direct intervention in politics came in the West Cork by-election in November 1916. There were three candidates, including Frank Healy for the AFIL, and the official IPP candidate won on a plurality. What is of interest in this election is not that Redmond's candidate won the contest, but that the combined vote of the two anti-Redmond candidates was greater than that of the victor. An editorial in the *Cork Examiner* claimed that this defeat marked the demise of O'Brien as a political force in Cork. This was in large part true of his active influence, and the *Cork Free Press* ceased publication shortly after the election.[65] The victory in West Cork provided some evidence that the IPP was not dead, despite encountering difficulties. Its ability to win a seat where O'Brien had influence indicates that the party could still muster support among the electorate. It is noticeable that both anti-Redmond candidates claimed association with Sinn Féin, though Sinn Féin denied any direct affiliation. O'Brien was now considered to be a Sinn Féin supporter in all but name by the IPP in Cork, and to have repudiated 'parliamentary methods' of politics.[66] It was the beginning of a process of disillusionment with the existing parliamentary consensus within Irish nationalism which led to the by-election victories for Sinn Féin in the course of 1917. What the by-elections demonstrated was that there existed a constituency within Irish nationalism for a more vigorous approach to the issue of self-determination, and increasingly open support for a republic. Sinn Féin success in 1917 was all the more remarkable as the by-elections were fought on the existing and restricted franchise. Sinn Féin was now successfully appealing to voters who had previously supported the IPP, but who were now prepared to jettison this loyalty. Nationalist politics, even before the extension of the franchise in 1918, had become more competitive and was under serious internal strain.[67]

The priorities of the British state and those of Irish nationalism diverged to a considerable extent after 1916, while Ulster unionism's priorities overlapped with those of the state. The period up to 1916 can be characterised by convergence between the three forces, but thereafter Irish nationalism's commitment to the war was subordinated to the need to achieve some form of self-determination for Ireland. In contrast, the state had only one priority: winning the war. Carson recognised this and benefited from it, but then his movement remained united whereas Redmond was faced with a serious political challenge throughout 1917 and 1918. Moreover, the cost of partition for the British government was relatively low and could be borne politically. This was not the case for Redmond or Irish nationalists generally. For them, partition came into conflict with long-standing beliefs about the nature of Ireland, its people and the authority of nationalism itself.[68]

Most nationalists were not prepared to concede a right to self-determination to Ulster unionism. James Stephens reminded his readers that nationalism's stock response to unionism was to dismiss it as 'rooted in ignorance and bigotry', but that the challenge remained. Even if unionism was ignorant and bigoted, he added, this did 'not explain the Ulster standpoint'. Stephens believed that Redmond and the IPP had made no attempt to understand unionism in Ulster — indeed had wilfully ignored it and outraged it by their own behaviour: 'Let the Party explain why, among their political duties, they neglected the duty of placating Ulster in their proper persons. Why, in short, they boycotted Ulster and permitted political and religious and racial antagonism to grow inside of Ireland unchecked by any word from them upon that ground.' This had been the basis of O'Brien's strategy, to engage in negotiations to prevent division among those living on the island. O'Brien recognised his own inability to achieve this end, one of the reasons he boycotted the Irish Convention in 1917–18.[69] In contrast to either of these positions, de Valera's response to Ulster unionism was stark; he 'did not believe in mincing matters, and if Ulster stood in the way of the attainment of Irish freedom, Ulster should be coerced. Their natural political enemies were Unionists.' Nor was this an isolated view; Bowman has provided a careful analysis of de Valera's and Sinn Féin's views on Ulster unionism, which not only are uniformly hostile but display no understanding of the community.[70] Although some nationalists might not have shared the view that Ulster should be coerced, virtually all believed that partition undermined Irish nationality and its historic claims. Nor did Sinn Féin accept Stephens' view of the nature of Irish nationality: 'Before we can talk of Ireland a nation we must make her one. A nation, politically speaking, is an aggregation of peoples whose interests are identical; and the interests of Ulster rather than being identical are antagonistic.'[71] De Valera shared with Griffith and O'Brien the view that the unity of Ireland was so central to the self-image of Irish nationalism that no compromise on the issue could be entertained.

Divisions within nationalism

In 1917 the possibility of compromise with unionism eroded quickly. Nationalist opinion became increasingly hostile to the British state and to Irish unionism, due to the threat of partition and conscription. In March the IPP withdrew from Westminster in protest against partition, but it was Sinn Féin that benefited politically from this confrontation. Sinn Féin now provided a political umbrella for the most militant Irish nationalists, those opposed to partition and voters alienated by the IPP.[72] Nationalist politics also became seriously divided for the first time since the Parnell split. These divisions went to the heart of democratic politics in Ireland. After the East Clare by-election in July 1917, when de Valera easily defeated the IPP candidate, the influential dramatist Edward Martyn wrote to John Horgan in Cork claiming that Sinn Féin 'is going through the country like an epidemic'.[73] By the end of 1917, O'Brien claimed that the IPP was no longer the only constitutional party in Irish politics and that Sinn Féin was now a legitimate force.[74] Frank Gallagher confirmed to O'Brien the growth of Sinn Féin in Dublin and Cork, claiming that there were some 3,000 members in Cork alone. He also told of a meeting he had had with de Valera, noting 'my opinion of him is that he is politically the man for the moment but whether he will last is another thing. He seems to lack something. One thing is certain — that something isn't honesty.' In reply O'Brien effectively endorsed Sinn Féin, in the full knowledge that this would go back to de Valera and the Sinn Féin leadership: 'the Sinn Féinners have saved the country from Partition, from conscription and from parliamentary corruption, and they were the only force in Ireland that could have done it'. At roughly the same time Frank Healy, the unsuccessful AFIL candidate at the West Cork by-election, was comparing the 1916 rebels with the Manchester Martyrs, attacking the Irish Convention and advocating abstention from the Convention itself.[75] Lloyd George established the Irish Convention in July 1917 in an attempt to secure agreement on Home Rule and its implementation. Sinn Féin and the Labour Party boycotted the proceedings and Sinn Féin militants attacked meetings supporting the convention. It was a last attempt to secure agreement between the IPP and Ulster unionists as both sent representatives to the convention. However, the differences were already too wide and the Irish Convention ended in failure in April 1918. The significance of O'Brien's support for Sinn Féin is that it confirms a drift away from traditional constitutional politics on the part of those who had supported it previously. By the end of 1918 the AFIL had effectively dissolved itself to allow Sinn Féin a free run in the general election, 'to afford an opportunity to the younger minds to work out the realisation of Ireland a nation'. The decision was welcomed by Sinn Féin.[76]

What is of considerable interest during 1917 and 1918 is the failure of Redmond and the IPP to meet the Sinn Féin challenge. One should also not underestimate the ability of the Sinn Féin leadership or its attractiveness to former IPP supporters, especially as Redmond appeared unable to deliver Home Rule. The IPP was also placed in an invidious position, simultaneously supporting the war and attempting to represent Ireland's interests with the British government, but unable to prevent partition or conscription. Increasingly, these two loyalties pulled the party apart, undermining its influence within Ireland and with the British government. John Horgan and his colleagues attempted to come to terms with these new political realities. During 1917 and 1918 Horgan wrote or co-wrote with his father-in-law, Bertram Windle, the President of University College Cork, a large number of editorials for the *Cork Examiner*. Windle had been appointed to the Irish Convention and, unlike O'Brien and Sinn Féin, both he and Horgan believed that this offered the last hope for a peaceful settlement in Ireland. Considerable emphasis was placed on the experience of Canada, Australia and South Africa, all of which it was noted had 'full responsible Government, with fiscal autonomy and complete control of their own affairs'. Moreover, while an imperial veto over colonial legislation existed, it had never been used. On Ulster, however, Horgan and Windle provided no easy answers. Indeed for the most part the discussion of this issue never moved beyond generalisations and high hopes. Among the suggestions discussed for reconciling the divisions between nationalist and unionist, the introduction of proportional representation and a federal system were the most important.[77]

Horgan had contributed an article to the *Leader* in December 1916 that included a proposal on Ulster. In his memoirs, Horgan claims that Lloyd George commended him on this proposal, regarding it to be of considerable value. In the article Horgan claimed that 'The fears of the Ulster Protestant are entirely fictitious' and had been used by the 'Ascendancy party' in Ireland for its own selfish needs. Accordingly, 'The only certain cure for the mental disease of the Orangeman is direct legislative association with his brother Irishmen.' Horgan also rejected O'Brien's suggestions that Ulster should have an absolute veto over legislation and that it should receive double representation in an Irish parliament, on the grounds that they were 'undemocratic and humiliating'. Horgan recommended that an Ulster committee be established, within an all-Ireland parliament, which would have the right to review all legislation. If a majority of this committee rejected a proposal then it could not be applied to Ulster, though it could apply to the rest of Ireland. If legislation on taxation was rejected by two-thirds of the Ulster committee, it could not become law for any part of Ireland. Horgan believed that his scheme had the merit of retaining an all-Ireland political unit, while allowing time for the elimination of distrust and ignorance, which he considered to be at the heart of the Irish problem. Horgan's proposals were discussed at the Irish Convention but, as he noted retrospectively, the political conditions necessary for acceptance were missing in 1917.[78]

Horgan's position can be contrasted with that of Sinn Féin and the Volunteers, especially de Valera. Whereas the Redmondites sought compromise with the Ulster unionists in the Irish Convention short of a partitioned Ireland, Sinn Féin ignored the challenge of unionism and merely insisted on Ireland's right to self-determination. The other difference from the IPP was that while Sinn Féin was a political party with growing electoral support, it co-existed with the Irish Volunteers which proclaimed the right to use violence. Though de Valera led both movements by the end of 1917, the relationship between the two was complex and ambiguous. Sinn Féin had been reorganised in October 1917 and the new body included both constitutional nationalists alienated by the IPP and physical force nationalists committed to the armed struggle. While the constitutionalists were probably in the majority, the militants were the most powerful force in the new party. The Volunteers remained a conspiratorial movement controlled by the IRB, despite Sinn Féin's electoral success. The militarists remained committed to armed insurrection, though at what point and under what conditions this might occur was not clear.[79] The tension between those nationalists who believed that a more active promotion of policy was in order and those who were prepared to use violence was to remain a significant feature in Irish politics for the next five years and to affect the nature of its politics. This tension is evident in Eoin MacNeill, who, though committed to active nationalism, also believed that the right to use force had limited application and no justification in 1916. Likewise, though O'Brien moved close to Sinn Féin, neither he nor his close supporters favoured the use of violence.[80]

Electoral support for Sinn Féin in 1917 and 1918 should not be equated with support for the use of violence against British security forces or the police. Sinn Féin pursued a quasi-democratic policy and its electoral success in 1918 was an endorsement of Ireland's right to self-determination, not a mandate for war. At the Clare by-election in July 1917, de Valera offered conflicting messages to the electorate. On one occasion he declared 'although we fought once and lost, it is only a lesson for the second time'. But this militancy might be contrasted with his view on another occasion that 'every vote you give now is as good as the crack of a rifle in proclaiming your desire for freedom'.[81] Within Sinn Féin there were those who emphasised constitutional politics, while there were those, such as de Valera, who seemed determined on a return to armed struggle. The Sinn Féin manifesto for the 1918 general election committed the party to abstention and to the establishment of a constituent assembly to determine Ireland's future and attend the Paris Peace Conference to make Ireland's case to the victors in the war. However, the demand for a republic was clearly enunciated and Sinn Féin claimed that it would make 'use of any and every means available to render impotent the power of England to hold Ireland in subjection by military force or otherwise'.[82]

There is little evidence that the majority of those who voted for Sinn Féin in 1918 were endorsing a war strategy. They were endorsing a more militant version of Irish nationalism and were now favouring the establishment of a republic, rather than the introduction of Home Rule. Sinn Féin's public appeal in 1918 took account of this and its message reflected the need to appeal widely. This is not to say that the Volunteers were now constitutional democrats; far from it. But Sinn Féin had to balance the pressure from its militants with a more moderate appeal to sections of the electorate who wanted change but not revolution. After all, Sinn Féin claimed to be the party representing the nation and as such had to be sensitive to the diverse range of opinion that made up its support base. Sinn Féin also had to avoid condemnation by the church, always a danger when violence or conspiracy was involved. In fact, the new party succeeded in achieving a balance between the various forces pulling at it. When the War of Independence did begin, however, it had considerably more legitimacy than had the 1916 Rebellion. The Irish Republican Army (IRA) was supported by the elected representatives of the nation, who, in turn, received continuous support from the nationalist electorate. The Dáil and its institutions (of which the IRA was only one) challenged the British state successfully between 1919 and 1921, in electoral, institutional and military terms. Yet there were limits to how much violence the nationalist population would accept. The Catholic Church continued to have misgivings about the use of violence throughout the War of Independence, and most clerical supporters of Sinn Féin drew a clear distinction between support for Sinn Féin electorally, the withdrawal of legitimacy from the British state and support for armed rebellion. Augusteijn suggests that 'the use of violence by Volunteers was not popular', but he also shows, as does Miller, that this unease was rarely translated into open opposition to Irish nationalism or its aims. Most Irish nationalists distinguished between the violence of the state and the violence of the nation: the latter, though criticised, was tolerated more than the former. It may well be that Sinn Féin was supported by a majority of Irish nationalists despite its use of violence, and that British state violence provided Sinn Féin and the IRA with justification for their actions. For most Irish nationalists, Dáil Éireann, the Dáil

Courts and Sinn Féin acquired the legitimacy denied to the British government in Ireland. This legitimacy was based on electoral success and the establishment of quasi-legal institutions. The IRA also had a qualified legitimacy in the minds of most Irish nationalists, but support for violence was limited and could be withdrawn.[83]

The evolution of Horgan's political strategy between 1916 and 1918 is of considerable interest in this context. Horgan had been one of the more influential of the younger IPP politicians. He was close to the IPP leadership and was a personal friend of Willy Redmond, but he had also been close to Griffith's Sinn Féin. He corresponded with many leading political and literary figures, including Eoin MacNeill. He became vice-president of the Cork branch of the Gaelic League and was active in the promotion of Irish industry. Horgan was also a contributor to Moran's *Leader* and to the Jesuit monthly *Studies.* Based in Cork, Horgan is important as a representative figure among younger nationalists, irrespective of political affiliation. The main division between them tended to be on the use of violence, not on the objectives of Irish nationalism. Horgan had condemned the Rebellion from a democratic and Catholic perspective; politically it had never been justified:

> No one living in Ireland in 1916 could truthfully say that we were living under intolerable oppression, or that all legitimate means of redress had been tried and failed. On the contrary a whole series of ameliorative measures dealing with every aspect of Irish life had been secured by the Irish representatives in the British Parliament, and a final measure granting full self-government had been passed into law, and only awaited the conclusion of the war to be applied. Nothing but our own action could thus prevent the sure growth of freedom in Ireland.[84]

Horgan continued to support constitutional politics on the grounds that Home Rule could be secured. For Horgan, as for many moderate nationalists, the threat of partition, the failure to introduce Home Rule and the prospect of conscription in early 1918 changed his thinking. There was a widespread and justified belief that the united front generated against conscription weakened the will of the British government to implement it. Furthermore, Sinn Féin demonstrated its capacity to co-operate with other sections of the nationalist movement, while maintaining its own more radical strategy for political independence and a republic. By November 1918 Horgan was writing in the *Cork Examiner* that, while 'every sensible nationalist would take full self-government within the Empire were it honestly offered as an immediate settlement . . . It is not so offered, and no Irish nationalist now believes that it will be.' Horgan now embraced Sinn Féin's view that Irish nationalism should be represented at the Paris Peace Conference, where it should demand self-determination for Ireland. This demand had the support 'of the overwhelming majority of the Irish people', notwithstanding their political differences. If such an objective could be achieved, Horgan concluded, 'we can after full discussion decide by referendum what form of government we desire'. This view could have been modelled on de Valera's presidential address to the Sinn Féin ard fheis in October 1917, reflecting perhaps an increasing overlap between these political activists in nationalist politics. Horgan also believed that such an approach would provide the 'real and democratic way to deal with northeast Ulster'.[85]

Horgan was not an abstentionist at this stage, though he believed that if the Peace Conference rejected Ireland's right to self-determination, then absenteeism would be justified. In a letter to his friend Stephen Gwynn MP just prior to the December 1918 general election, Horgan all but rejected the parliamentary position he had maintained up to then. He questioned the honesty of the British state in respect of the war, contrasting the nature of European diplomacy with President Woodrow Wilson's idealism. Although Horgan had supported the war, he now appeared to reject his original view that Britain had the moral right in the matter. It is on the question of a united Ireland and Ulster that Horgan demonstrated the shift in emphasis. Whereas Gwynn believed that Ulster should not be coerced, Horgan considered that a measure of coercion might be warranted. He invoked the example of the United States' determination to defeat the secessionist south in the American Civil War, though acknowledging that the Slave South might have had some justification for secession. Accordingly, the demand made by unionists for the right to remain outside a united Home Rule Ireland was not considered a legitimate one and could not be supported by nationalists. Horgan maintained that 'if there had been no Curragh mutiny and Larne gunrunning in 1914, there would have been no rebellion in 1916'. He continued to believe that the Allied cause was justified, adding that Wilson's principles would meet Irish claims at the Peace Conference:

> We are not drawing out of the war because we might be assisting England *but because we would not be assisting Ireland*, a far different reason. The answer to your argument can be put in one sentence. Give Ireland the right to 'self-determination' both as regards Ulster and conscription and then we can get on with the War.[86]

Horgan maintained that the Peace Conference, and President Wilson especially, 'cannot refuse to hear Ireland if she speaks with a clear and united voice', but warned that the Peace Conference was the last opportunity short of 'internal revolution (in England)' or 'external pressure' to achieve self-determination in his generation.[87]

This view led Horgan to propose a motion at the Cork county executive of the IPP that a united front of nationalists should be allowed to present Ireland's demands for self-determination at the Peace Conference in Paris. To this end and to 'avoid internecine strife at the forthcoming General Election', Horgan and his supporters believed that a conference attended by all nationalists could agree on how best to achieve this.[88] John Dillon's reply to Horgan outlined the obstacles to such a course of action and highlighted Sinn Féin's unwillingness to make any concessions prior to the elections. He also refused to accept a policy of abstention because unionists would dominate the House of Commons in the absence of Irish representation. Subsequently Dillon appealed to Horgan to oppose Sinn Féin in Cork, insisting that he was 'eager that the city should be contested and not handed over without a fight to the Sinn Féinners'.[89] While the IPP nominated candidates for the general election, Horgan and his close allies were unwilling to support Dillon and resigned from the party. This did not place them in the Sinn Féin camp, as was the case with O'Brien, but it did mean that a formidable obstacle to Sinn Féin was removed.[90] Sinn Féin believed that the 1918 election provided a retrospective imprimatur for 1916, and there is some force in that argument. But Sinn Féin received support in 1918 because of its militant, but non-violent, activities in the cause of Irish nationalism and this qualifies the claim that the election provided either justification for 1916 or a rationale for a return to military struggle. Many Sinn Féin candidates were clearly militarists, but Sinn Féin also had to address a constituency that was not as radical as its party members. The 1918 general election involved a change of leadership in the nation, but not a radical departure in the nature of Irish political culture. It was the failure of the IPP to adequately represent the nation in 1917 and early 1918 that provided the opportunity for Sinn Féin to challenge the IPP.[91]

Forging a new nationalist consensus

For a brief moment there was a real threat that these divisions would disrupt the unity of Irish nationalism. However, the main difference between the two parties was over abstention, though clearly the IPP's view of self-determination was more moderate than Sinn Féin's. A rupture was prevented by a number of factors, but the main one was Sinn Féin's decisive electoral victory in December 1918. It was no accident that in Ulster the Catholic bishops enforced an election pact, while not interfering in the rest of the country in the election. Sinn Féin's victory laid the basis for the establishment of Dáil Éireann in 1919 and the assertion of self-determination by the democratically mandated body. The Dáil quickly acquired considerable legitimacy in nationalist Ireland, more so than any military force could have achieved. Once the election was over, Dáil Éireann proved strong enough to lead nationalist Ireland and receive assent from the community up to the Treaty in December 1921. The failure of the Labour Party to contest the election has often been seen as a lost opportunity for the left in Ireland, but this is to misunderstand the context of the election. This was not a conventional election. Labour's reluctance to fight the 1918 election reflected the continuing appeal of nationalism in the face of external challenge, and a reluctance to damage national unity. The reconfiguration of Irish nationalism in 1918 included a greater inclusiveness than previously, but its message was basically the same: an Irish homeland/state for the nation. This was something that Labour could share. The priority in 1918 was to give effect to the demand for self-determination, and in such circumstances national unity was of greater significance for most nationalists than party competition. This proved to be the case not only for the Labour Party, but also for

Horgan and O'Brien in Cork as well.[92] This led to a consensus in Irish politics after 1918, one that transferred to Sinn Féin the legitimacy which the IPP had once enjoyed. There was considerable discontinuity in Irish public life between 1914 and 1922, but the main attributes of Irish nationalism remained intact.

Sinn Féin's vote was a national one, and as a consequence national authority passed from one party to another. About two-thirds of the electorate in 1918 were first-time voters, but they did not vote in a vacuum. The young voter, and the first-time female voter, who went to vote in December 1918 had already been socialised by a complex mosaic of ideas, institutions and organisations within nationalist Ireland. The environment in which most Irish people grew up between 1890 and 1918 was one where nationalism was the dominant view. This environment did not predispose these voters to support Sinn Féin, but it did limit the choice to nationalist parties for the vast majority of voters. When first-time voters went to the ballot box in 1918, their political opinions were informed by membership of a nationalist community. In 1918 Sinn Féin was best placed to address the concerns of this community and give political expression to them. It may be that some of those who voted for Sinn Féin in 1918 regretted that decision later, but this does not eliminate the significance of the support at this time.[93] The *Freeman's Journal* acknowledged that the election had restructured nationalist politics: 'The party [Sinn Féin] will now occupy the position held for forty years by Parnell and his colleagues and their successors.' The paper warned, however, that Sinn Féin would not be able to realise its objective of achieving an Irish republic.[94] There may have been elements of continuity in 1918, but the success of Sinn Féin tilted the balance within Irish nationalism away from gradual reform and constitutionalism to a more aggressive and at times violent assertion of sovereignty. This strategy challenged the constitutional basis of Irish politics between 1919 and 1922, and in such a context there was little room for compromise on either side. Sinn Féin's success in 1918 secured a mandate for a more active promotion of self-determination, a strategy that was both republican and separatist.

Nor should the role of the Catholic Church be ignored in this process of change. Sinn Féin and especially de Valera were deeply concerned not to alienate the bishops and worked assiduously to demonstrate loyalty to the church; they also sought to persuade the bishops that the movement was not endorsing a conspiratorial form of politics. At times this was difficult to achieve, given the widespread violence in 1920 and 1921, but it was imperative for Sinn Féin that the IRA would not be condemned by the Irish hierarchy. In an innovative argument about the role of the Catholic Church in Irish politics, Emmet Larkin concluded his path-breaking study of the new relationship between the Irish hierarchy, the Land League and the IPP in the following terms: 'What saved the Irish state from the tyranny of the "Leader", the "Party", and even the majority, was that in the last analysis the church had enough real power and influence within the consensus to resist effectively any attempt by either the "Party" or the "Leader" to overrule the consensus.' The existing consensus between the church and the IPP effectively collapsed between 1916 and 1918. De Valera was anxious to reach agreement with the church and activate a new consensus. He was successful in this, though the use of violence during the War of Independence sometimes placed it under strain. Despite these tensions, the consensus between church and nation was maintained in the confrontation with the British state. Violence also disrupted Irish nationalism's commitment to democracy and cast doubt on its continuing importance for the political culture. After fifty years of relatively peaceful political advance, the use of violence in 1916 and the War of Independence challenged the consensus in favour of parliamentary politics. However, a democratic consensus was remade during and immediately after the Treaty and Civil War, allowing the government of the Irish Free State to marginalise the 'irregular' forces and the militant wing of Sinn Féin. The church played a central role in this by supporting the duly elected government and by contributing to the re-establishment of the consensus and public order.[95] The church guaranteed the maintenance of constitutional politics as the *main* feature of nationalist politics, even during the War of Independence. During the War of Independence the church, in common with much of nationalist opinion, frequently condemned the killing of policemen by the IRA. However, clear distinctions were often drawn between the acts of the IRA and those perpetrated by the Crown forces. Cardinal Michael Logue, for example, criticised the assassinations carried out by the IRA on 'Bloody Sunday', 21 November 1920, but considered British reprisals in Croke Park on the same day to be more worthy of condemnation. This is not surprising, since virtually all nationalist communities draw a distinction between the violence carried out by their forces and those of the state or another nationalist community.[96]

The Irish War of Independence was a national liberation struggle fought in exceptional circumstances. If the 1916 Rebellion had no democratic justification, the 1918 general election and the establishment of the First Dáil provided a legal basis for secession. That Britain chose to ignore this reflected the government's continuing commitment to the imperial system and the fear that Irish independence would undermine the entire structure. In this matter the pessimists were certainly correct and the War of Independence can be seen as the first instalment of the break-up of the British Empire. Yet there were limits to what Sinn Féin and the IRA could achieve by violence or mass mobilisation. Time and again between 1918 and 1922, nationalists demonstrated their support for Sinn Féin but the new leadership could never attract support from unionists or indeed fulfil its claim to represent all those who lived on the island. The Irish Free State was not the republic fought for in 1916 or demanded in 1918 and the commitment to this institutional outcome obscured the important of the Treaty for Irish self-determination. Furthermore, the continuing demand for a united Ireland plagued the politics of independent Ireland and the relationship between north and south for the next seventy-five years. In many respects the main legacy of 1916 was the inevitability of partition, but republicans remained unwilling to concede this. In retrospect the 1918 general election is the most important event of the period 1910–22. It demonstrated that the will of the nationalist community was now settled on self-determination. But is also restored a degree of legitimacy to democratic politics, a legitimacy which the partisans of armed struggle denied but which remained central to the politics of war and peace in Ireland.

The priority until the Treaty in December 1921 was to maintain national unity and this was in large part achieved. There were strong elements of continuity during the decade 1912–22 at the level of political values and in respect of the long-term sources of nationalist identity. It was at the institutional level and in the realm of individual action and behaviour that the most significant changes took place. The most important individual changes were the political success of Sinn Féin in 1918, the successful defence of alternative republican institutions under the direction of Dáil Éireann in 1919–21 and the establishment of the Irish Free State in 1922. None of these changes challenged the underlying stability of the political culture: indeed they reinforced it. Political action and behaviour also changed quickly and in new ways. Irish nationalism became more inclusive, both electorally and socially. Political opinion became more varied by 1922, ranging from a radical republican socialism on the left to conservative clericalism on the right. Yet across the nationalist spectrum, unity was the main feature of the political culture until the Treaty. Subsequent divisions were concerned with the institutional arrangements related to nationalism, rather than about the nature of the political culture. Irish political life was disrupted between 1912 and 1922 and this provided the means to challenge certain aspects of the power structure. It also introduced a lethal aspect to the politics of Irish nationalism, through its use and glorification of violence. Violence could be attributed to the breakdown of liberal order in Europe during and after the First World War, but in Ireland the preconditions for violence were already in place before the war. It was the failure of nationalism and unionism to reach agreement which laid the basis for violence and the willingness of both communities to sanction its use. Both nations reserved the right to retain a monopoly of the use of violence both to defend the nation and to coerce the other nation into submission. One of the first tasks of the Irish Free State was to discipline the forces which continued to reject its right to this monopoly and to re-create the conditions for the integration of all sections of Irish political life into a constitutional framework.[97]

3

From Civil War to National Integration

The Nature and Consequences of Irish Independence, 1923–1945

Cumann na nGaedheal's achievement

The Irish Civil War was a bitter conflict, but the outcome reinforced Ireland's commitment to parliamentary democracy, weakening anti-democratic forces in the society. It is mistaken, therefore, to argue that 'it was evident that there were no real victors' in the Irish Civil War.[1] Without a clear and decisive victory over the republican forces, the new government would not have been in a position to govern. It is true that the legitimacy of the state was weakened because a section of the electorate did not accept it, but this opposition was quickly neutralised by vigorous policing and then political inclusion. The government's ruthlessness in the Civil War and subsequently against the IRA was absolutely necessary to secure the state and its democratic institutions. Otherwise, the IRA would have established a parallel government in permanent opposition to the duly elected government, as was its intention. That this intention failed dismally was not due to a lack of will on the part of the anti-democratic forces, but was a consequence of their inability to challenge the government's legitimacy when new institutions were established between 1923 and 1927. The acceptance of parliamentary democracy in Ireland was never a forgone conclusion, but democracy's foundations were stronger than the size of the opposition indicated. Of particular importance was the refusal of most sections of Irish society to countenance the use of force against the state after 1923. The new state insisted on, and largely received, the right to a monopoly of violence. This can be seen in the neutralisation of the so-called Army Mutiny in 1924 and the acceptance of the Garda Síochána by the vast majority of citizens as a legitimate police force.[2]

Likewise, Cumann na nGaedheal was never a counter-revolutionary government. Despite Sinn Féin's rhetoric in 1918, or the use of violence by the IRA, the War of Independence had limited and conservative objectives. The demand for independence was a serious challenge to the British state, but not in itself revolutionary. Revolution cannot simply be equated with the use of violence, but must be accompanied by radical change in the political, economic and social system. In the Irish case socio-economic continuity was maintained, though the demand for sovereignty destabilised the British state. Irish independence involved a structural change in Britain, but did not imply a radical departure for Ireland. The political scientist Robert Dahl developed a scale to measure the nature of government change that ranged from pure office seeking to revolutionary transformation. In the Irish Free State there is a change of personnel and some constitutional change to give effect to devolution, but little evidence of radical political or socio-economic transformation.[3] In isolation from other changes, independence would not be revolutionary. In 1922 the majority were prepared to accept a form of devolution short of the full independence demanded by the republican movement. Nor was the republican minority in 1923 offering a radical alternative to the Irish Free State. Partition reflected the divided nature of Irish politics and society and the opposition of Irish unionism to nationalist demands. The War of Independence can be characterised as a war of national liberation, with quite limited political and social aims, and consequently the Irish Free State was not unlike other successor states in Europe after the First World War.[4]

Because these aims were limited, more radical political options received little support. The need to maintain nationalist unity during 1919–21 disguised the uneasiness within the nationalist political community with the use of violence. But violence never replaced electoral politics. The 1918 general election was a mandate for change, not necessarily for violence. The 1923 general election confirmed the Treaty settlement democratically. This settlement was conservative but not counter-revolutionary and Cumann na nGaedheal reflected the will of the nationalist people of Ireland voting in an election. The government was able to mobilise a conservative majority in favour of the Treaty and subsequently institutionalise democratic politics in the new state. The use of the term counter-revolutionary in this context deprives it of any real meaning and ignores the representative nature of the pro-Treaty majority. The anti-Treaty minority refused to accept the decision of the electorate in 1923, thus placing itself outside the democratic process.[5] The outcome of the August 1923 election was crucial to the consolidation of parliamentary democracy after the Civil War. While de Valera and Sinn Fein refused to accept the verdict, those in favour of the Treaty settlement received overwhelming support. With a turnout of 59 per cent, slightly less than the 60.27 per cent at the 1922 general election, parties in favour of the Treaty received approximately 70 per cent of the vote while the anti-Treaty vote accounted for less than 30 per cent.[6]

The 1923 election was an electoral re-run of the Civil War, without the deaths but with the same outcome. The election itself was primarily about the national question, or more accurately about what type of state the nation should consolidate. Without its military victory in the Civil War and its electoral success in 1923, Cumann na nGaedheal could not have secured Irish democracy as quickly as it did. While many IRA veterans may have been described as 'unenthusiastic democrats' by Tom Garvin, the majority of those who participated in the War of Independence quickly accepted the parliamentary system after the Treaty. The contribution of Michael Collins, Richard Mulcahy, Kevin O'Higgins and William T. Cosgrave was crucial to the success of this process. In different ways, these individuals moved Irish society away from the violence of the period 1916–23 and rediscovered the democratic roots of Irish nationalism. Their actions guaranteed that an independent Ireland would also be a stable democratic one. The defeat of the anti-Treaty forces in the Civil War was total and decisive. This defeat was not simply a military one: it also had significant political consequences. The government won the Civil War with the support of a majority of the electorate and its legitimacy was endorsed by the results of the 1923 general election.[7]

The Irish Free State was one of only a small number of successor states to preserve democratic politics during the interwar period. Ireland was not unusual in adopting parliamentary government after the First World War. There was a wave of democratisation in Europe at this time, but most new states did not survive as democracies. Ireland was unusual because it maintained intact its democratic system. One of the main reasons for this was that democracy, which had been used to legitimise the Irish nation against the British state and unionism prior to independence, could now be used against the minority of nationalists who refused to accept the democratic outcome. Irish nationalists had argued throughout the nineteenth century that Britain should accept the right of the majority within Ireland to determine its own future. This belief in majority outcomes was maintained in the Irish Free State. The government argued that a majority of Irish nationalists accepted the Treaty and the new state and that republicans were rejecting the democratic will of the people by refusing to acknowledge this. During the course of the Civil War de Valera had argued in an interview with the *Daily Mail* that 'We are in arms against and resisting now exactly what the whole nation resisted in 1919–21', adding for emphasis that 'The only difference is that in the earlier period England was maintaining her claims directly. Now she is maintaining them indirectly through Irishmen.' As late as 1925, when the Irish Free State was clearly consolidated, he continued to insist that the electorate had not recognised its 'true' interests:

> Recently an opportunity was given to the people to declare their will. They did not declare that will *as we know it to be their will*, and, perhaps, there are people listening today who, if you had an election here tomorrow, would be a party to misrepresenting the national position. It is a shame that Irishmen who know what the majority want — this country free and independent — should go to the polls and register their votes in such a way that it will be held that these are votes for the Free State. I do not know what it is. It is the

> result, so far as I can see, of the teaching that you have been listening to for the past three years. …There is no use in looking to a small body of men to free the nation. It is for the people to right the wrong they did a couple of years ago and which apparently they have been doing since.

The Cumann na nGaedheal government could ignore de Valera's anti-democratic elitism, as it commanded majority support in the Dáil and among the electorate. With this support it could act with a determination against internal enemies and maintain its legitimacy, something the British had never been able to achieve.[8]

The Labour Party criticised de Valera for not recognising that constitutional means were the only ones which would achieve change in the Free State. The IRA, Sinn Fein and, for a time, Fianna Fáil shared a fundamental hostility to the operation of the Irish parliamentary system. This hostility was all the more intense as it was directed against former friends and allies.[9] Given this attitude, the achievements of the Cumann na nGaedheal governments were remarkable in comparative terms. In a Europe where democracies faltered and failed throughout the next two decades, Ireland was one of the few which sustained and enhanced its democratic political culture. Ireland was a predominantly Catholic and rural society, but one which successfully institutionalised a competitive parliamentary political system with widespread legitimacy. In 1927 Fianna Fáil was still a disloyal opposition, reluctant to accept the Treaty settlement and overtly hostile to Free State institutions. By 1932 it had formed a government, an outcome which in large part can be attributed to the way in which Cosgrave and his political allies ran the state and refused to compromise with the intransigent elements. Most democracies in the 1920s were Protestant or secular, whereas a Catholic democracy seemed to be a contradiction in terms on some accounts. The Vatican was not sympathetic to democratic politics, as its compromise with Italian fascism and the German Nazis indicated. In addition, agrarian societies were often more prone to political instability and proved attractive to anti-democratic politics. Although there may be economic prerequisites for democratic government, these are weaker than sometimes thought. It is the actions of individuals and their ability to bring order and discipline to the political system which facilitates the stabilisation of democracy.[10]

Democratic nation building

Irish democratic success was based on three factors. One was the influence of the British parliamentary tradition, which had deep roots in the political culture, while another was the presence of a land-owning majority. On their own, however, these factors could not have secured Irish democracy. Other states have been deeply influenced by Britain, but are not democratic, while the existence of peasant proprietorship did not prevent many states becoming authoritarian during the interwar period or later.[11] The most important contribution was an existing democratic tradition among Irish nationalists. Irish politics remained democratic even during the violence of 1919–21 and this was reasserted by the pro-Treaty majority in 1922–3. Cosgrave and his allies were able to draw on Irish nationalism's commitment to majority outcomes to legitimise their actions.[12] As a consequence historians have probably underestimated the Cosgrave governments. The period between 1923 and 1932 has often been characterised as conservative, reactionary and narrow, while the leadership provided by Cumann na nGaedheal has been seen as uninspiring or venal.[13] Yet the achievement of this period was, in many ways, more important than that of Fianna Fáil. By 1932 the Irish state had acquired widespread legitimacy, even among its opponents. More fundamentally, Cosgrave forced the majority to come to terms not only with a native government, but also with the responsibilities associated with self-government. One of the reasons for Cumann na nGaedheal's success was that it persuaded its citizens that the Irish Free State had acquired the necessary status required for self-government.[14] A government will normally be viewed positively by the electorate if it is able to acquire status for the state. The Irish Free State in the 1920s was overwhelmingly Catholic, comprehensively rural, relatively well educated in a comparative context, reasonably affluent in European terms and politically nationalist and partitionist. The achievement of Cumann na nGaedheal was to take these factors and locate them within an embryonic democratic political system which, within a decade, became pivotal to the state and the political culture of nationalist Ireland. In addition, the new government had a self-conscious belief in the need to force the Irish people to accept its responsibilities for democracy and political order. Even the republican opposition had to accept this by 1927.

The Free State government worked hard to enhance the new state's sovereignty and to advance Irish nationalism's political objectives. It used the 1922 constitution as a basis for political development. Hugh Kennedy, Law Officer to the Provisional Government in 1922 and first Attorney General of the Irish Free State, described his role during the negotiations with Britain on the constitution as primarily to resist clauses at variance with the objectives of Irish nationalism and to provide amendments more favourable to that position. Kennedy believed he had achieved a considerable amount by the time the constitution was accepted. While the second schedule to the constitution included the controversial oath of allegiance which Dáil deputies were expected to take, this oath was to the constitution of the Irish Free State and not to the King as such. It is also questionable whether, as Coakley claims, 'the sovereign British Parliament was the ultimate source of legitimate authority' in the Irish Free State, though it was explicitly the case in Northern Ireland. Article 2 made clear that sovereignty resided in the people of Ireland and the Irish negotiators successfully neutralised British attempts to weaken this principle.[15]

Though the Irish input into the constitution was not enough to prevent civil war, the history of the Irish Free State fully sustained the position of those such as Kennedy and Cosgrave who maintained that the Treaty settlement provided the basis for realising the objectives of Irish nationalism. In 1931 the Minister for External Affairs, Patrick McGilligan, insisted that the King 'functions entirely, so far as Irish affairs are concerned, at the will of the Irish Government'. He added that negotiations after 1922 had placed the Irish government in an even more favourable position with respect to the monarch. The government pursued a moderate policy on Northern Ireland on the grounds that this would aid reconciliation.[16] It also promoted the Irish language, introduced various reforms in education and provided a system of free elementary education. Despite the unrest in the army in 1924, civilian control was exercised over all aspects of Irish life then and subsequently. In addition, local government was reorganised to make it more accountable, while strict rules were imposed on the civil service to protect it from political interference. In contrast to many successor states, and indeed France and Italy, Ireland was remarkably free of corruption in public life between the 1920s and the mid 1960s.[17]

Cumann na nGaedheal's conservatism can be better appreciated in its successful campaign to restore order. The Cosgrave government quickly assembled a political coalition committed to restoring order in politics and society. It did so in part through coercion, but also through receiving a democratic mandate from the electorate. The fear of social revolution passed quickly, left-wing and trade union demands were successfully defused or defeated and the family farm regained its dominance at the heart of Irish society.[18] The Catholic Church provided crucial support for the restoration of order, highlighting on numerous occasions the threat from instability and the modern world. Some Catholic militants urged the government to act more decisively and in some cases action was taken.[19] The campaign against prostitution in Dublin throws light on the government's assumptions in moral matters. Under pressure from lay Catholic groups and with the co-operation of the gardaí, the government initiated a campaign against the 'Monto' red-light district in north inner-city Dublin. While it proved difficult to prosecute brothel owners, the campaign was quite successful in limiting prostitution itself. One report to the Minister of Justice claimed:

> The existence of such places is a blot on the reputation of a Catholic city. The parochial clergy despair of reforming them and do not visit such areas. It is only by a vigorous campaign, and the institution of homes for the reception of women found there, that the evil can be eradicated. Men visitors, bullies, [pimps] etc., should also be punished.

In its review of the campaign, the Department of Justice believed that considerable progress had been made between 1925 and 1929, but that the problem had not been eradicated. In 1931 further action was recommended and this resulted in the 1935 Criminal Law (Amendment) Act. According to Liam Ó Murchada, Commissioner of the Dublin Metropolitan Police, an Irish solution would have to be found:

> This whole question of prostitution, morality crimes, etc., should be dealt with from an Irish point of view and *not from the rather slack English standpoint.* In general the onus of proving innocence should in all such cases rest on the accused. The penalties should be drastic and mandatory.

The government was concerned not only to safeguard the state, but to use it to promote political order, social morality and traditional values, though in this and other cases it did not adopt a policy with the recommended degree of severity.[20]

Too much emphasis has been placed on the repressive elements of the Cumann na nGaedheal government and not enough on its positive contribution to the growth of the Irish Free State. This is particularly true in economic terms. I am not the only one who has criticised the policies adopted by the Cumann na nGaedheal government and compared them unfavourably with those of Fianna Fáil. The most frequent charge is that the government was too cautious and conservative or that it failed to represent the interests of significant sections of the population. This argument is open to considerable doubt, although aspects of it have strength. While economic policy in the Irish Free State during the 1920s was similar to the conservative consensus which emerged in Europe after 1919, the Irish experience cannot simply be reduced to this. The government had a strong commitment to stabilising the society after the Civil War, but it was also a nationalist government with a commitment to economic development. It believed that the best strategy for economic development was to concentrate on the most successful segment of the economy, agriculture, and to generate growth from that dynamic. On the basis of this, it was asserted that there would be a knock-on effect for other sectors of the economy. However, as agricultural prices were falling during the 1920s, this policy may not have been as sensible as the government thought. Alternatively, Irish exports and foreign earnings were higher at the end of the 1920s than at any time for the next forty years. In addition, the government engaged in state-led infrastructural development such as the Shannon scheme to promote the expansion of electricity usage. Furthermore, while some sections of Irish industry were competitive and benefited from free trade with Britain, the Fiscal Inquiry Committee reported in 1923 that most Irish industries were inefficient and uncompetitive. In response to this, the government set up the Tariff Commission in 1927 to provide an institutional environment where the case for protection could be made. The government never abandoned free trade or the commitment to agriculture, but a radical alternative, as demanded by Fianna Fáil, was inappropriate before 1932, if even then. The government throughout the 1920s largely achieved the balance between economic stability and innovation.[21]

Per capita income in the Irish Free State was affected by the post Civil War economic downturn, but probably increased again by the end of the decade. Although serious questions remain concerning the way in which income was distributed, this does not make Ireland any different from most other European states, where income distribution was often inegalitarian. An increase in income suggests that the economy performed quite well during the 1920s, though not all benefited from it.[22] The decision to establish the vocational education sector in 1930 to promote training in technical subjects was also an important departure, even if sensitivities concerning the Catholic Church prevented it from achieving its full potential.[23] Cumann na nGaedheal successfully stabilised the Irish Free State by 1927 and consolidated the institutional foundations of the state between then and 1932. The majority of the electorate quickly accepted the parliamentary system established in 1922 as the only legitimate forum for political decision making. The Cumann na nGaedheal government also introduced legislation to give effect to its nationalist and religious objectives. Its most decisive contribution to Irish democracy, however, was the recognition by Fianna Fáil in 1927 that political influence could be achieved in Ireland only by accepting parliamentary politics.

Fianna Fáil's challenge

If Cumann na nGaedheal was so successful in consolidating the Irish Free State, why then did Fianna Fáil replace it in 1932 and remain in power for a further sixteen years? When we look back over the history of independent Ireland, it is Fianna Fáil that appears to be the dominant political force. With the exception of the decade 1922–32, Fianna Fáil's presence and influence seems ubiquitous. One reason for this outcome was that Fianna Fáil quickly accepted the rules of the political game as established by Cumann na nGaedheal. There continued to be unease about the Irish Free State among Fianna Fáil deputies up to 1932. Hostility to the government, the memory of the Civil War and the party's relationship with the IRA maintained a distance between parliamentary democracy and Fianna Fáil until at least the first de Valera government was formed. Even in 1932, many Fianna Fáil deputies continued to believe it was a 'slightly' constitutional party, as Seán Lemass had famously phrased it in 1928. There was a tendency among Fianna Fáil supporters to place its republican idealism above a commitment to constitutionalism. IRA actions between 1927 and 1932 were often supported by Fianna Fáil. De Valera may have condemned the murder of the Minister for Justice, Kevin O'Higgins, by the IRA in 1927, but Fianna Fáil's relationship with the IRA remained highly ambiguous.[24] As late as October 1931 in the Dáil, de Valera continued to condemn the Treaty as a *coup d'état,* and he offered what at its most sympathetic was a confused and ambiguous interpretation of the principle of majority rule and parliamentary sovereignty:

> I have said that the doing of wrong is never right, no matter who did it. There was an apparent and obvious wrong. Now, let us be clear on that. What appeared to be an obvious wrong was being justified by the idea that it was backed by the majority vote of the people. I said that that did not justify wrong. ... Therefore the majority rule does not give to anybody the right to do anything wrong, and I stand by the statement that a majority does not give a right to do wrong.[25]

Despite becoming the dominant party during the 1930s, Fianna Fáil remained reluctant to acknowledge the achievements of Cumann na nGaedheal. It was left to Seán MacEntee to openly endorse what had been achieved during the first ten years of the Free State. In a remarkable statement, while responding to interruptions during a speech in the Dáil in December 1935, MacEntee said: 'Yes, I am quite prepared to say that Deputy Cosgrave and his Party established that principle [majority rule] and we are here to preserve it.' Following this, the Wolfe Tone Fianna Fáil cumann in Trinity College Dublin (TCD) passed an angry resolution 'noting with amazement' MacEntee's statement and calling on the Fianna Fáil national executive to repudiate it and discipline him. In his reply to the national executive, MacEntee robustly defended himself against the charges. The first of these was that by making the statement he was reversing the republican analysis of the Treaty and Civil War, which denied that the pro-Treaty forces were fighting for majority rule. In effect this charge was correct, but MacEntee insisted that he was not prepared to 'condemn the Republican attitude during the Civil War'. To do so, he continued, 'would be to condemn my own part in it, and I do not feel that there are any grounds for that'. Despite this, he returned to the substance of the original claim and reiterated his position in considerable detail. MacEntee insisted that the general argument for majority rule should stand and his reasoning is quoted at length here:

> Before the principle of majority rule can be applied effectively it is essential that there should be an assembly which the community in general are prepared to accept as representative. Therefore to my mind the political development which holds most promise for the future well-being and progress of this country has been the acceptance by the vast majority of our people of the Oireachtas as the representative assembly of the state.
>
> Everything that Fianna Fáil has been able to do since 1927 has been consequent upon this. The abolition of the Oath, of the Appeal to the Privy Council, and of the Seanad as at present constituted, in my view would never have materialised but for the fact that the Oireachtas has been so accepted. And this occurred and indeed to an extent was compelled during Mr Cosgrave's regime. It may not have been the object which the then Government had in view, nor the end which they really sought, but I cannot enter into their minds and none of us was in their councils. In any event it was the consequence of their policy — and for the consequences, in my view, if they have proven to be beneficial to the Nation, they are entitled to credit.

MacEntee continued by praising the decision of Cumann na nGaedheal to call an election immediately after the end of the Civil War, 'an irretraceable step which helped to establish here the fundamental principle of representative democracy, which is majority rule, as the governing factor in our public life'. He then highlighted the threat to representative democracy which emerged at the time of Fianna Fáil's narrow election victory in 1932:

> Our opponents accepted the verdict of the electorate notwithstanding, and surrendered power to the representatives of the majority. In doing so, they, to my mind, finally established the principle of majority rule here — and

> that without any reference or prejudice to the merits or otherwise of the respective sides in the Civil War.

In discussing the Civil War itself, MacEntee observed that both sides were driven by a 'revolutionary temper', which left little room for applying the principle of majority rule. He also maintained that some members of the national executive, some Fianna Fáil public representatives and some of the electorate took different sides in the Civil War. He hoped that the Civil War 'will always be a dead issue', that each side's viewpoint would be appreciated by the other and that all should 'do our utmost to ensure that the same spirit of national respect and toleration will encompass the nation as a whole'. MacEntee scathingly dismissed the criticism offered by the TCD cumann, invoking Wolfe Tone's plea for unity as his own guideline and insisting that nothing he said was contrary to Fianna Fáil policy. He also believed that the issues raised 'are of such fundamental significance to me' that he would prefer to retire from politics than to have to maintain the opposite.[26]

To the best of my knowledge, MacEntee's Dáil comment was the only public one made by a serving Fianna Fáil minister between 1932 and 1948 which recognised the important role played by Cumann na nGaedheal in stabilising the Irish state after 1922 and providing the foundations for the changes introduced by Fianna Fáil when it came to power. Coogan recounts a conversation between de Valera and his son Vivion shortly after the 1932 election when de Valera acknowledged that the previous government had done 'a magnificent job', but he never found it possible to do so in public.[27] Although MacEntee was the only one to say so openly, the reality for Fianna Fáil after 1932 was that it had accepted the 1922 settlement, while still committed to changing it. Fianna Fáil ceased to be an anti-system party as a consequence. It was no longer committed to radical transformation, but sought to use existing institutions to change the system democratically.

This in itself would not have secured power for Fianna Fáil. If it had remained a narrowly republican party, or tried to compete with Cumann na nGaedheal at the conservative end of the political spectrum, it would probably not have been very successful. This can be seen from the change in its electoral fortunes between 1927 and 1933. Fianna Fáil's vote in the June 1927 general election was not significantly different from the republican anti-Treaty vote in 1923. The decision to end its abstensionist policy (by which it refused to take its seats in the Dáil) prior to the September 1927 general election made Fianna Fáil more attractive to voters who might have welcomed alternative policies but remained wary of Fianna Fáil's hostility to the state. Fianna Fáil's vote jumped from 26 to 35 per cent nationally, and increased in virtually every constituency, but especially in urban areas. Republicans had previously performed badly in cities and large towns, but Fianna Fáil made significant inroads into these areas in September 1927 for the first time. In the Dublin region the party improved its position by 5 per cent, but in Cork and Waterford it nearly doubled its vote. While the gains were not as significant in Galway and Limerick, this can be attributed to the already strong support for republicans in those cities. Fianna

Fáil set out quite consciously to attract voters in the cities and big towns. Lemass devised an imaginative socio-economic programme to appeal to those voters, in what proved to be a successful strategy. His economic radicalism was designed to appeal to the working class and others who had not been given a voice in the new state. This appeal was not socialist or left wing, but rested on the view that it was necessary to generate socio-economic development for inclusive nationalist ends.[28]

Fianna Fáil had become the main party of the urban working class by 1932 while also drawing significant support from small farmers and rural labourers outside the urban areas. By 1932 Fianna Fáil had become the largest party in the political system, drawing electoral support from most social groups. In the 1933 general election Fianna Fáil received 40 per cent of the vote in the Dublin and Cork regions, while in Galway, Limerick and Waterford its vote ranged between 50 and 60 per cent.[29] Two further factors contributed to Fianna Fáil's success by 1933 and maintained it subsequently. The first was that Fianna Fáil was now a democratic party with a national appeal which could challenge Cumann na nGaedheal as a nationalist party. Fianna Fáil's nationalism was more active and inclusive than Cumann na nGaedheal's, promising welfare for the disadvantaged and a more vigorous promotion of the state as an agent of nationalism. Similar links between nationalism and welfare were being made by the New Deal in the United States and by the Social Democrats in Sweden at this time.[30]

The second factor was de Valera's success in meeting the expectations of Fianna Fáil's republican constituency, while deflecting criticism of the party's radicalism by Cumann na nGaedheal. The party's 1932 election manifesto was cautious, emphasising the need for change but recognising the necessity for a gradualist approach. The party took the strategically important position that 'we shall not in the field of international relations exceed the mandate here asked for without again consulting the people'. The commitment to abolish the oath of allegiance was absolute, but was defended disingenuously on the grounds that 'This article is not required by the Treaty. It stands in the way of national unity and of willing obedience to the law. Government by coercion is the result.' Fianna Fáil promised that it would respect the law, would not act in an arbitrary fashion and would not threaten civil rights. Its caution was an implicit recognition that Cumann na nGaedheal had stabilised the Irish Free State and consolidated its parliamentary system. This did not prevent Cumann na nGaedheal from criticising Fianna Fáil as a radical party bent on destabilising the economy or society. In response, Fianna Fáil insisted that it would use democratic means to bring about change, and accused the government of being anti-national and dependent on Protestant votes to win elections.[31]

Despite the animosity between the two parties, the 1932 election was the first stage in the regularisation of the post-Treaty party system. Both parties were national in appeal and nationalist in policy, though emphasising different policies. There may have been considerable enthusiasm during the campaign but there was remarkably little violence. Patrick Hogan, the Minister for Agriculture, feared that the IRA would disrupt the election through intimidation. The Department of Justice played down these fears, noting that Garda Commissioner Eoin O'Duffy was responsible for the peaceful running of the campaign and that the department had every confidence in him.[32] In fact the threat to democracy in 1932 came not from the IRA, but from O'Duffy. He attempted to put in place plans for a coup in the event of a Fianna Fáil victory, going so far as to circulate a proclamation in favour of a military government. In the event, the army remained opposed to such action and Patrick Hogan's brother James, a historian and a former Director of Intelligence in the National Army during the Civil War, went to O'Duffy and persuaded him to give up the action he was intent upon.[33]

Fianna Fáil became the largest party in the Dáil in 1932, though it was dependent on Labour support to form a government. It achieved this in part because it was better organised and more disciplined than Cumann na nGaedheal, but also because it offered a clear and distinct policy choice to the electorate.[34] Fianna Fáil was not merely an updated version of Sinn Féin; it was a new national party appealing to and attracting voters from virtually every section of Irish society. It quite consciously appealed to sections of the electorate that Cumann na nGaedheal ignored or alienated, offering policies that would clearly benefit them. Fianna Fáil's success in 1932 and again in 1933 transformed the Irish political system, leading to the emergence of a new two-party system around the twin poles of Fianna Fáil and Cumann na nGaedheal/Fine Gael later in the decade.[35] The basic cleavage in the Irish party system by the 1930s did not rest simply on how parties aligned on the Treaty settlement, but also included how each party used nationalism to promote socio-economic development. By 1932, Fianna Fáil and Labour were on the same side, promoting an active and interventionist strategy, while all other parties advanced conservative policies. Lee has suggested that 'Cosgrave was in large measure the author of his own electoral misfortunes. His basic strategic error was the shift to the right. He should have consolidated the centre ground. In particular he should have striven to retain Labour support.' This, however, may not have been a realistic option for Cumann na nGaedheal. This is to accept the conventional interpretation of Fianna Fáil as the continuation of Sinn Féin and to ignore the social appeal which the party was now making. Because the constitutional question was not the only issue, this meant that there was no centre and the political culture was being remade with a strong left–right basis to it.[36]

Although a minority government, Fianna Fáil acted decisively in most policy areas. At the heart of its strategy was the need to enhance national sovereignty. The decision to abolish the oath of allegiance, the refusal to pay land annuities and the sidelining of the Governor General reflected this priority. British retaliation for the decision to withhold the annuities led to a six-year economic war between the two states. The economic war provided Fianna Fáil with an added opportunity to orchestrate a campaign for national consensus against British 'aggression'. It also removed some of the internal obstacles to nationalist economic policies in respect of industry and agriculture. All of this secured Fianna Fáil's position as a nationalist government and most of its policies had an activist nationalist focus to them. Fianna Fáil assumed that national welfare would benefit from self-sufficiency in economic and political terms. Fianna Fáil equated the national interest with the promotion of nationalist policies, insisting that all policies should be judged by nationalist criteria.[37] Consequently, Fianna Fáil sought to disrupt the existing diplomatic arrangements between Ireland, the United Kingdom and the Commonwealth. MacEntee urged de Valera to pursue a revisionist strategy to isolate Britain in Europe and undermine the Commonwealth. The contrast with the outgoing government was stark. Though cautious at times, de Valera's new government was iconoclastic on foreign affairs and interventionist in domestic policy. Fianna Fáil reconfigured government policy in a most nationalist and vigorous fashion.[38]

Fianna Fáil's position was quickly consolidated and confirmed at the January 1933 general election, when it won a majority of the seats while Cumann na nGaedheal's vote declined by 5 per cent. A number of factors contributed to this success. Fianna Fáil's policies appeared to benefit a wide range of interests in the state. Fianna Fáil outbid Cumann na nGaedheal with a more aggressive version of nationalism. Furthermore, former Cumann na nGaedheal supporters were more willing to vote Fianna Fáil because it had accepted democratic politics. The conflict with Britain also contributed to the new government's popularity, as did its evident capacity to act in a decisive manner in respect of both domestic and foreign policy. Over the next six years Fianna Fáil was strategically placed to acquire its own political legitimacy and to defend its policy departures by reference to its more vigorous version of nationalism.[39]

The politics of opposition under Fianna Fáil

Cumann na nGaedheal was ill-suited to opposition and this prevented it from developing a new strategy to compete with Fianna Fáil. Its conservative leadership feared that Fianna Fáil would undermine democracy and destroy the rule of law:

> Continuation of Fianna Fáil policy is bound to lead to anarchy. The greatest menace which any Government in the world has to face to-day is the menace of Communism. Yet the Fianna Fáil Government gives an absolutely free hand to communistic elements in the State, and at the same time by their policy which increases unemployment and creates political unrest, provides an atmosphere most favourable to the growth and spread of such doctrines.[40]

Cumann na nGaedheal continued to oppose Fianna Fáil's policies on the constitution, the economy and diplomatic relations with Britain. The differences between the two parties were extremely wide at this time, yet Cumann na nGaedheal had to be careful that its opposition to Fianna Fáil could not be construed as support for Britain in its conflict with Ireland. Cosgrave insisted that it was 'not for us to make the case', when Desmond FitzGerald supported Britain's right to impose penal tariffs in retaliation for non-payment of the annuities. The party's dilemma can be appreciated from its position on the annuities: 'Don't say that the people should not pay; say that the Government should not collect. If the Government meant business at all they should have waited until our people got rid of the year's cattle.'[41] While Cumann na nGaedheal may not have been pro-British, its policy commitments placed the party close to Britain on many of these issues. This allowed Fianna Fáil to unfairly characterise it as anti-national. In other respects, it reflected the economic and social interests of cattle exporters and big business, as its objection to protection shows: 'Without any tariffs against foreign food or preferences for Irish food we will benefit by any return of prosperity to England. ... The connection between Ireland and England in this respect is as close as between Dublin and the surrounding county.' Cumann na nGaedheal was a conservative nationalist party, but was unable to provide a sustained critique of Fianna Fáil's emotive nationalism.[42] Richard Mulcahy recognised this when he provided a rational, if regretful, appreciation of Fianna Fáil's success in the 1933 election:

> Government policy political and economic has been before the Dáil and the country. There is little doubt of its political success within the State. Its ultimate political and economic progress is speculative. What had better be conceded is that Fianna Fáil worked and toiled industriously and energetically to achieve their present position. The politicians have beaten the Statesmen, and however unpalatable it may be, it was the fault of the Statesmen.

He also admitted that Cumann na nGaedheal had been badly organised and that the party leadership lacked an awareness of public opinion.[43]

Although Cumann na nGaedheal was conservative, some of its fears were justified. The informal alliance between the IRA and Fianna Fáil was maintained after the 1932 election and for a time there was a threat to civil liberties when opposition meetings were being attacked. Both Fianna Fáil supporters and the IRA endorsed the catchcry 'no free speech for traitors'.[44] Eoin O'Duffy's dismissal as Garda Commissioner in February 1933 was construed by the opposition as another move towards authoritarianism by de Valera. In the same year, the full impact of the economic war was felt by the cattle exporters, many of whom supported the opposition. This accounts for the formation of the Army Comrades' Association to defend opposition politicians from attack, but does not explain the growth of a paramilitary organisation or the adoption of the blue shirt and beret in March 1933.[45] The most dangerous phase of this confrontation passed when the threat by O'Duffy's Blueshirts to march on the Dáil on 13 August 1933 was met by severe government countermeasures. While there may not have been a serious threat to democracy in 1933 and 1934, there was a degree of instability which provided an opportunity for political extremists, such as O'Duffy. This was not a propitious moment for European democracy. Hitler had come to power, Mussolini had consolidated his position and elsewhere parliamentary systems were under serious threat.[46] O'Duffy and others on the right in Ireland were highly critical of the existing system and flirted with authoritarian and corporatist solutions to what they described as the corruption of parliamentary politics. In addition, the severity of the Depression reinforced the belief that democracy could no longer adequately deal with economic disruption.[47]

How serious was the threat to Irish democracy? There was a degree of uncertainty in 1933 and the political system was unstable. The decision to form Fine Gael in September 1933 reflected the opposition view that a new party was necessary to counter Fianna Fáil. The appointment of O'Duffy as President of Fine Gael appeared more radical at the time than proved to be the case. There is little evidence that Fine Gael's leadership had become radicalised or authoritarian, whereas in continental Europe traditional conservative elites had abandoned democracy and parliament. Nor did political conditions merit such a change. Public order was restored by Fianna Fáil and the threat from the IRA to the opposition quickly diminished. Nor was the government using dictatorial methods to achieve its ends. The opposition might dislike the government's policies, but these were enacted in parliament with majority support. Fianna Fáil might be anti-liberal, but it was not a dictatorship. Moreover, with some exceptions, most of the opposition remained committed to the parliamentary system, despite the presence of the Blueshirts. Perhaps the distance between rhetoric and reality is best expressed by the appeal made by the Young Ireland Association (one of the names used by the Blueshirts) to Dáil deputies to wear the blue shirt 'from time to time' to symbolise the links between the older politicians and the new younger organisation.[48]

What occurs in Ireland is quite different from the general experience in continental Europe. What radical potential there was in the Blueshirt movement was neutralised and domesticated by the conservatives themselves. Fascism did not fail in Ireland because it was too intellectually demanding for Irish minds, but for other quite concrete reasons. Fascism elsewhere had attracted the young and those alienated from the political system. Despite the tensions encountered in Ireland during the years 1932–5, it is a period characterised by integration rather than exclusion.[49] Moreover, the right in Ireland found it difficult to appeal to militant nationalism because of its own origins in repressing it, though O'Duffy begins to sound like a right-wing republican by the end of 1934. It was the governing party that mobilised the marginal elements in society and incorporated them into a political party. Though this had some similarities with mass fascist and communist movements, it was achieved by democratic methods, not in authoritarian fashion. The political space for fascism was thus limited, and in so far as it generated any significant support this can be accounted for by the conflict over the annuities and the collapse in the living standards of substantial bourgeois farmers. This limited militancy to a narrow section of the opposition's electorate. In so far as there was violence and rejection of the government and the rule of law, this tended to be concentrated in those areas most affected by the farming crisis. Other sections of the rural community were subsidised by the government in one fashion or another, and neutralised.[50]

But perhaps the most striking difference between Ireland and the continental European context was the extent to which the conservative elite remained committed to parliamentary methods and the rule of law.[51] This was quite conscious and one can detect the discomfort of the leadership with the increasingly radical statements of O'Duffy and his associates. O'Duffy may have been President of Fine Gael, but his power base was in the National Guard (which replaced the Army Comrades' Association in July 1934) and among the Blueshirt youth organisations. This popularity was challenged by the conservative elite within the party during August and September 1934. By this time the government was in command of the political situation and had been bolstered by the results of local elections in June 1934. These elections demonstrated that there was no real swing to the opposition, as Fine Gael had hoped. Fianna Fáil was the largest party after the elections: it won 728 seats, whereas Fine Gael won 598. With Labour Party support, Fianna Fáil was able to control most local councils. Cosgrave admitted that the elections were a setback for the new party and he blamed the outcome on Fine Gael itself, adding, in a strange echo of de Valera a little earlier, 'We have to teach the people to understand that if they vote wrong the opposition cannot pull the chestnuts out of the fire for them. Fianna Fáil is neither honest nor democratic, nor national. But we have not succeeded in getting that over to the people. We have taken no steps to make them [understand].'[52] The choice for the party, after this, was either to accept the democratic verdict or to move towards some form of extra-parliamentary confrontation. O'Duffy was prepared to challenge the constitutional order and called on farmers to refuse to pay the annuities to the state. If this had received Fine Gael backing, it would have marked the beginning of a major confrontation with the government.

Cosgrave and the party leadership contributed to the defence of democratic institutions during August and September 1934 in much the same way as de Valera had while in opposition. Cosgrave restrained those bent on confrontation by insisting that change could be effected only by legal and electoral means. The challenge which Cosgrave delivered was formidable and might have led to the destruction of Fine Gael. He warned the party executive that anti-democratic behaviour would play into the hands of the government and allow de Valera, 'the son of a Mexican', to bring in a 'Mexican state', a very powerful image in a Catholic society concerned with the persecution of the Catholic Church in Mexico. For Cosgrave, 'There is a courage that is higher than physical courage and it is moral courage. We have to make up our minds "are we going to stand for law?"' He maintained that the government was strong but the opposition was weak, and that in such circumstances confrontation would lead to a dictatorship, which would destroy the opposition. He concluded that 'The people have the right to control the ballot boxes', and that this should not change.[53] It is doubtful whether individuals such as Cosgrave, Mulcahy or T.F. O'Higgins ever contemplated an extra-parliamentary resolution to the tensions of the years 1932–5. What concerned them immediately after the 1932 election and during 1933 was the apparent complicity between the government and the IRA, as well as the attacks on political meetings. Cosgrave certainly shared these concerns, but he and a majority of the party refused to move beyond the defensive stance taken at this time. The differences between the majority and O'Duffy in September 1934, when that relationship came to crisis point, focused on whether Fine Gael would go beyond the bounds of constitutional politics. O'Duffy was prepared to do so, but Cosgrave was not. Nor, it should be added, was the government prepared to allow O'Duffy the political opportunity to do so.[54] After a discussion with senior members of the Fine Gael executive, O'Duffy agreed to a compromise and to accept party discipline. However, James Dillon subsequently complained to the party leadership that almost immediately after the meeting, O'Duffy made a speech that contravened the compromise. This prompted James Hogan, a Fine Gael Vice-President and party to the agreement, to resign on the grounds that O'Duffy was not following party policy and was moving dangerously close to paramilitary politics. Hogan later claimed that O'Duffy intended to organise politically in Northern Ireland and agitate there. Hogan considered that this would lead to violence and destabilise both the Free State and Northern Ireland, insisting that the only solution to partition was a peaceful one.[55] On 20 September O'Duffy submitted his letter of resignation to Fine Gael, while re-emphasising his belief that Fianna Fáil was in decline. This in turn prompted the party to act decisively against him. At a special meeting of the party executive on 21 and 22 September the main issues were discussed and O'Duffy's resignation accepted. The League of Youth was reorganised and placed under the control of Commandant Ned Cronin.[56]

Once Fine Gael had eschewed anti-democratic politics, its choices were fairly narrow. By 1937, when it again performed badly at a general election, it was a party in disarray. Though Fine Gael remained more conservative than Fianna Fáil, the policy differences between the two parties had narrowed appreciably. Fine Gael's political supporters might disagree with the government on tax, land or industrial policy, but did not necessarily disagree with it on foreign policy, the constitutional changes or with some aspects of development policy. By 1936 Fine Gael TDs reported that the party organisation had been seriously weakened, even in its midlands heartland. The ard fheis in the same year gives the impression of an extremely conservative party on the defensive against a confident government.[57] When Patrick Hogan died in a road accident, his brother James fought the ensuing by-election in Galway in August 1936. Hogan's political views during the election campaign and on the 1937 constitution were closer to Fianna Fáil than to his own party.[58]

Fianna Fáil became the dominant political force in Irish politics by 1936, an outcome reinforced by its electoral success in 1937 and 1938. However, electoral success is only one reflection of Fianna Fáil's impact on Irish political life. De Valera's governments republicanised the Irish Free State through democratic means and in a way that proved acceptable to more conservative groups, such as Fine Gael. Fine Gael recognised this by remaining a loyal opposition, even if the party had yet to find a political identity under the new order. Fianna Fáil focused on transforming the economy, the constitutional framework and diplomatic relations with the United Kingdom. In doing so, de Valera also created the conditions for changing the nature of Irish politics itself. Fianna Fáil's economic strategy and the related economic war with Britain were based on the need to control all aspects of the Irish economy. By refusing to pay the land annuities, de Valera could portray his government as being in conflict with the old enemy and generate further political support. Furthermore, under the leadership of Seán Lemass in the Department of Industry and Commerce, the new government embarked on an ambitious programme of economic and industrial development. This programme was based on the nationalist assumption that Ireland's economic and social well-being could not be guaranteed by involvement in the world economy. Consequently Fianna Fáil was committed to greater intervention in the Irish economy, when compared to the previous Cumann na nGaedheal government, but also to the isolation of the economy from international pressures. Ireland became more self-sufficient during the 1930s, though it also became more isolationist and inward looking. The primacy given to domestic expansion deprived Ireland of the benefits of its privileged access to British markets, which in turn led to an increasingly inefficient economic structure.[59]

Likewise, in agriculture and in social policy, Fianna Fáil's attention was focused on the requirements of the nation, not the benefits to be gained by involvement in an internationally competitive system. At the political level Fianna Fáil built an electoral coalition which included republicans, radicals and conservatives as well as trade unionists, farmers and constitutional nationalists. The support range was extraordinarily wide and was held together by Fianna Fáil's nationalist ethos and the benefits derived from nationalist policies. Furthermore, by 1937 there was broad acceptance among the main political parties of what had been achieved. Fine Gael may have faulted the government for being too radical and Labour may have criticised it for not being radical enough, but neither challenged the government's legitimacy. In addition, as long as Labour remained in an informal alliance with Fianna Fáil, there was little likelihood of an anti-Fianna Fáil coalition. While there were extremists on the left and right of the political system, these forces were increasingly irrelevant for the development of Irish political life. After four years of rapid change, Irish life had become quite stable by the beginning of 1937.[60]

A republican democratic constitution

Fianna Fáil's political success and the consequent stabilisation of Irish politics provided the opportunity for de Valera to introduce a new constitution. By early 1937, de Valera had already disabled the 1922 constitution, changing the nature of constitutional government in Ireland. De Valera wanted a constitution with a clear normative content, one which 'should inspire as well as control, elicit loyalty as well as compel it'.[61] He intended to reconcile Irish democracy with nationalism and Catholicism, while simultaneously creating a sovereign and republican state. Considerable attention has been paid since 1937 to the Catholic nature of the new constitution and perhaps not enough to its republican and democratic content. Notwithstanding this, it is going too far to suggest, as Keogh does, that the constitution was an essentially liberal document.[62] This is to misconceive what de Valera set out to achieve. Most of the innovative sections of the 1937 constitution were anti-liberal, particularly when compared to its 1922 predecessor.[63] An early draft of the preamble reflected Catholic thinking and was fundamentally at variance with the American or British liberal traditions: 'The Irish people acknowledge their defender almighty God, thanking him for the preservation of their nation and dedicating themselves to his service, accepting the Ten Commandments as fundamental law give themselves to this Constitution.' Nor did the revised version of the preamble depart significantly from the original formulation.[64] De Valera also explicitly eschewed British precedents when he elaborated new political titles in the constitution. His adoption of Taoiseach and Tánaiste (in preference to President and Vice-President) drew on the archaic Gaelic past and his search for a unique political language had more in common with the interwar continental right than with liberal traditions.[65]

Though regularly redrafted, the constitution retained its nationalist and religious philosophical foundations. These were predominantly anti-liberal and grounded in irredentist nationalism and fundamentalist religion.[66] In most parts of Europe during the 1930s, nationalism was anti-liberal but so too was the Catholic Church. By linking religion and nationalism in the constitution, the Irish presented themselves as God's chosen people, claiming that their nationalism and religion made them special.[67] The normative sections of the constitution all had an anti-liberal character. In particular, Articles 2 and 3, which asserted the nationalist claim over Northern Ireland, overturned the careful and realistic strategy developed by the Cosgrave government and had the effect of deepening hostility between unionists and nationalists in Ireland north and south. This reasserted a pattern central to the political relationship between unionists and nationalists in Ireland. The more vigorously nationalists promoted their political objectives, the more likely they were to alienate unionist opinion. The most advanced nationalism was also the one most likely to copper-fasten partition. Furthermore, Article 9. 2 declared 'Fidelity to the nation and loyalty to the State' to be 'fundamental political duties', echoing the most extreme demands of loyalty from authoritarian nationalism in Europe. This anti-liberal intent was reiterated in Articles 41–44, which regulated the family, education, property rights and religion. Embedded in these articles were the central tenets of Catholic social policy as elaborated by the papacy over the previous century. For Ireland, natural right was 'antecedent to positive law' (Article 43) and this was spelt out in detail in articles on the family, private property, education and religion. In each case, the official position of the Catholic Church was emphasised in the constitution, especially in respect of the family as the core unit of society and the prohibition on divorce. Furthermore, in Article 45, the Directive Principles of Social Policy, the constitution brought together both nationalist and Catholic conceptions of the good life.[68]

Though not a liberal constitution in any conceivable sense, it was based on democratic principles and the rule of law. The 1937 constitution represented one of the first attempts to reconcile Catholicism, nationalism and democracy.

In this, de Valera was quite successful, even if Irish democracy had a majoritarian rather than a liberal basis. It is possible to have a liberal constitution without it being democratic, but it is also possible to have a democratic constitution that is not liberal. The weakness of the Irish liberal tradition was evident in 1937; it had largely been a British import and had few domestic roots. De Valera excised what liberalism there was, replacing it with a strong Catholic-nationalist democratic foundation which resulted in the 1937 constitution being more enduring and popular than its predecessor had been. Fianna Fáil itself was often anti-liberal at this time, but so too were Fine Gael and the Labour Party, if for somewhat different reasons. In so far as liberal elements remained in the text, these were residual and subordinate to the anti-liberal foundations.[69]

The most important feature of the new constitution was that it gave normative effect to the core values of Irish nationalism. It achieved a synthesis between Catholic, nationalist and democratic values in a way that provided a stable basis for constitutional continuity for the next forty years. The constitution avoided the authoritarian attractions of European Catholicism without alienating the church in Ireland, but also offered the promise of inclusiveness to all Irish citizens. Nor did the new constitution clearly distinguish between the secular and the religious sphere, as is normally the case in liberal societies. In the Dáil, on radio, in the newspapers and in day-to-day business and social activity priest and people, the sacred and the secular, not only met in a formal sense but also meshed and interconnected. This created a moral certainty that could be arrogant and intolerant. Seán MacEntee's comment on Winston Churchill at the time of the abdication crisis in Britain reflects the worst of this. He observed that 'a very large portion of the British people have very lax views in regard to marriage and divorce', dismissing Churchill 'whose house was founded by a man who betrayed his first patron, James Duke of York, and who allowed his wife to pander to an erotic Queen'. The government also considered it necessary to engage in a question-and-answer session with the Archbishop of Dublin, Dr Edward Byrne, on the appropriate (Catholic) behaviour to be followed in respect of the President (a Protestant).[70]

Despite this, the constitution's aim was to balance nationalism with Catholicism within a democratic state. It would never be possible, while retaining democracy and continuing to endorse a republican world view, to meet all the demands made by the Catholic Church, especially a papacy as authoritarian as that led by Pius XI and Pius XII. But it was possible to neutralise Irish Catholic criticism by emphasising the nationalist elements of the constitution and the extent to which it was necessary to compromise on some Catholic demands for the sake of national unity and Northern Ireland. As originally drafted, Article 44.1 acknowledged the Catholic Church as the 'church of Christ' and as the 'true religion', 'established by our Divine Lord'. While this was subsequently amended to a form more acceptable to other churches, the changes were prompted by nationalist rather than liberal considerations. Gerry Boland and other Fianna Fáil members opposed the original version on the grounds that it was sectarian and excluded the Protestant tradition from

Irish nationalism. Boland threatened to leave Ireland if the constitution was enacted in this form. The protests had their effect, though Boland remained critical of the final version. The final draft was more nuanced than earlier versions, but de Valera would not have endorsed a document that did not meet his political requirements. Electoral considerations should also not be ignored. If the constitution alienated too many groups in Irish society, it might have been rejected. In the event a referendum in July 1937 endorsed the new constitution by a narrow majority.[71] De Valera recognised the tensions between religion, nationalism and democracy, but insisted that the new constitution had 'the character of the public law of a great Christian democracy'. One of the major difficulties for de Valera and for Catholic politicians in continental Europe was that while they shared with the Pope a suspicion of liberalism, they all departed from him on the issue of democracy. The papacy was not to be reconciled to democracy until after 1945.[72]

The constitution established the parameters within which government policy could be defended or challenged. For nearly forty years after 1938, the Supreme Court acted to strengthen the Catholic, nationalist and patriarchal nature of the constitution.[73] The constitution reinforced the distinction between male and female spheres of activity. For de Valera, reflecting both Catholic social thought and nationalist preconceptions, a woman's place was in the home with her children, while that of the male was in work and the public domain. This fitted in well with contemporary nationalist notions of masculinity, not only in Ireland but also throughout Europe. At the heart of this conception was the heroic, aggressive male who sacrificed himself for the nation. To complement this, women were asked to sacrifice themselves to the male, the home and children to provide for the continuity and security of the nation.[74] Although the Catholic Church often disapproved of the cult of masculinity, especially in its fascist form, it could endorse the separation of the sexes and the curtailment of work opportunities for women. The focus for legislative attention was married women, but some restrictions affected all women. The Conditions of Employment Act 1936, introduced by Lemass, imposed a number of restrictions on women in work. The section of the act providing for the exclusion of women from various employments had been promoted by Fianna Fáil TDs and by a number of trade unions. There was already a marriage bar in the civil service, and in a number of other areas, including banking, women normally retired on marriage. A marriage bar for women primary schoolteachers was introduced in 1933, remaining in place until 1958. There was little opposition to these changes, even among the professions. Strong informal pressure was brought to bear on women who continued in employment after marriage in sectors without a formal marriage bar.[75]

The constitution formalised this position, leading the journalist Gertrude Gaffney to compare Fianna Fáil's social policy with that of Nazi Germany. A number of women's organisations compared de Valera's constitutional proposals unfavourably with the 1922 constitution, arguing that women would be placed in a less favourable position, effectively restricting their role to that of wife and mother. The *Irish Press*, acting as de Valera's mouthpiece, denounced this criticism of Articles 40, 41 and 45, but refused to engage in debate on the matter. In one case, criticism was dismissed as a 'gratuitous libel'. In a meeting with women's groups, de Valera claimed that the constitution would not restrict the political rights of women, but this had never been the criticism. The critics emphasised that what was intended was the restriction of women in the public sphere, especially in employment. Women's organisations highlighted a number of areas where serious discrimination existed. De Valera on occasions did meet delegations to discuss individual concerns, but neither he nor his ministers were sympathetic. In January 1937 de Valera suggested to one delegation 'that any inadequacy in the representation of women in the legislature and in public bodies was attributable to the state of public opinion. It would be difficult to do anything to give women a larger place in public life while public opinion remains as it is.' This was a circular argument, for if opportunities were not created for women it was unlikely that public opinion could be changed. Nor was de Valera prepared to listen to the advice given to him by his friend Dorothy Macardle, who recommended that an anti-discrimination clause be included in the constitution. While de Valera ignored Macardle's plea, more congenial was the advice received from J.J. Walsh, former Cumann na nGaedheal minister and successful protectionist businessman, who claimed that the groups looking for changes were 'unrepresentative' of women. John Charles McQuaid gave similar advice, including citations from papal encyclicals.[76]

De Valera also encountered some difficulties with the constitution within Fianna Fáil. In September Kathleen Clarke, Fianna Fáil senator and widow of 1916 leader Thomas Clarke, demanded that the national executive accept that party members 'have the right of free expression of opinion on any matter of national importance, which is not a Party or Organisational question'. The national executive agreed that 'the free expression of opinions on non-party matters' was not against the party rules. In abstract terms this discussion was vague, but another executive member, Seán O'Donovan, who gave notice that he would introduce a motion at the next meeting, made the substance of the argument clear. This motion read: 'That this Executive considers that support for the Constitution at the recent plebiscite was an obligation on all members of the Fianna Fáil organisation and party.' At the next meeting the motion was seconded by Oscar Traynor, the Minister for Posts and Telegraphs. An amendment was also tabled but not seconded. O'Donovan was requested to withdraw the motion but, when he refused to do so, the national executive agreed to move to next business without discussing the motion.[77] Some of these tensions surfaced again at the Fianna Fáil ard fheis in October, when de Valera told the party that criticism of the constitution was mistaken, malicious or partisan.[78]

Once the constitution was enacted, many Fianna Fáil members had unrealistic expectations of what could be achieved. De Valera believed that the constitution provided the means to end partition peacefully, but his speeches on this theme were so unrealistic as to question his contact with political reality: 'The time is now ripe — and it was not ripe until that Constitution was adopted by our people — for a united national movement towards securing the unity of our country.'[79] This optimism gave way to a more cautious attitude in private when members demanded action on the north. A motion to the national executive in February 1937 to establish an all-Ireland convention to promote reunification was defeated. After the ard fheis in October, Eamonn Donnelly, a former TD for Laois–Offaly (1933–37), moved a motion:

> That, as the present phase of National politics definitely ends on 29th December, the Fianna Fáil organisation, as at present constituted be remodelled and made applicable to all Ireland under its present title, or, if necessary, under another name with a view to recommending:
>
> Contesting all parliamentary seats in Northern Ireland at coming general election;
>
> Holding a General Election in southern Ireland on same date;
>
> The formation of an all-Ireland National Party under the leadership of Mr de Valera with head quarters in Dublin.

However, de Valera rejected any radical action or initiative which would destabilise the already delicate relations between the United Kingdom and Ireland in the period immediately prior to the introduction of the constitution.[80] The executive did establish an Anti-Partition League with a more limited set of objectives, but without any real sense of direction or purpose. Indeed, de Valera proved to be extremely conservative on the north when it came to action. In July 1938 he intervened directly at a party meeting to have a proposal that two nationalists from Northern Ireland be appointed to the new Senate rejected.[81]

If Fianna Fáil believed the 1937 constitution would provide a basis for ending partition, then the party, and de Valera, seriously miscalculated. At a time when Ireland was moving further out of the orbit of the Commonwealth, the British watched with unease these developments, as did the unionist government in Northern Ireland. On the one hand Irish ministers insisted that a united Ireland was necessary to overcome the historic animosity between Britain and Ireland, yet at the same time Irish policy reiterated that any change would be on terms dictated by Ireland.[82] De Valera's notion of sovereignty was incompatible with permanent membership of a body such as the Commonwealth. To all intents and purposes Irish policy in respect of Northern Ireland ignored the region itself, while insisting that the United Kingdom government withdraw its support for the unionist government there. This, it was believed, would create the conditions for the integration of Northern Ireland into the Irish state. The introduction of the constitution had the opposite effect in reality. Unionists in Northern Ireland were not attracted to the new constitution or to the Fianna Fáil government or its policies. The constitution was considered by most unionists to reflect the narrow interests of the Catholic Church and nationalist Ireland. The constitution appealed to northern nationalists, but this in itself was reason for unionists to reject it, such was the polarisation within the region.[83]

Anglo-Irish negotiations, 1938

In 1938 the British and Irish governments negotiated the end of the economic war on terms generally favourable to Ireland. At the beginning of the negotiations the British Prime Minister, Neville Chamberlain, highlighted the changing nature of the relationship between the two states when he insisted that 'discussion would take place on a footing of complete equality and without any conditions'. The threat of war was a major consideration for de Valera, because if the Irish ports remained under British control Ireland would become a target in any conflict.[84] De Valera warned that in the event of war, he would be placed in the same position as John Redmond in 1914, who 'found himself faced with difficulties which proved beyond his control'. For de Valera, partition was at the heart of the negotiations, and he insisted that it was Britain's responsibility: 'If the problem of partition was not solved it was inevitable that agitation and grave unrest must continue on an increasing scale and that incidents might occur which would be misunderstood by the Government and people of the United Kingdom.' He went on to claim that it had been the threat of partition which had brought him into politics in the first place, and it was the issue which 'caused a deeper and more intense feeling throughout Ireland than any other questions'. Chamberlain replied that it was a mistake to believe that the United Kingdom government wished to keep Ireland divided, but added that agreement had to be reached between the two Irish governments. However, de Valera wanted Britain to exert pressure on the unionists, emphasising, in particular, the need to withdraw any subsidies. When the Dominions Secretary, Malcolm MacDonald, pointed out that the situation would not be changed even if the British government did withhold subsidies, de Valera ignored this and declared that 'in the absence of some arrangement regarding partition it was out of the question to hope to get greatly improved relations' between the two states.[85]

On all matters except partition some progress was made during the first set of meetings in January 1938, and this was built on, despite some difficulties, over the following weeks. Irish diplomacy in respect of the main questions was competent, realistic and in some cases tough-minded. However the issue of partition continued to loom large for the delegation and the government. It was as if the rhetoric surrounding the introduction of the Constitution overwhelmed the realities of reaching diplomatic agreement. The Minister for Finance, Seán MacEntee, quickly concluded that the prospects for agreement had been weakened by de Valera's obsession with partition. In a pessimistic letter to his wife, he claimed: 'We shall not get the ports, and... if we do reach agreement about trade and finance... it will be much less satisfactory than it would have been if we had been prepared to deal with obvious facts and not to go window-dressing now about partition.' In February, MacEntee wrote to de Valera charging that he was obstructing agreement because of partition. The terms, MacEntee continued, were the best available and most Irish people would accept them. Moreover, the stabilisation of the economy and the need for national defence overrode all other considerations. MacEntee was also scathing about the prospects of the British forcing the unionists into a united Ireland:

> I feel that the partition problem cannot be solved except with the consent of the majority of the Northern non-Catholic population. It certainly cannot be solved by their coercion. Hitherto *we as the Government here have done nothing of ourselves to secure a solution, but on the contrary have done and are doing certain things which have made a solution more difficult.* The demand which we make continuously that the British should compel the Craigavonites to come in with us, has only had the effect of stiffening them against us.[86]

MacEntee accused de Valera of bad faith in the negotiations. He believed that Fianna Fáil would suffer and that it would be bad for the country if an agreement was not reached. MacEntee went so far as to claim that de Valera remained the sole obstacle to realising the government's diplomatic aims: 'The three objectives which six weeks ago we thought practicable appear to be within our grasp. The question is whether we shall secure them now, or abandon them because we cannot get immediately what we all, with maybe the exception of yourself, feel is at the moment unobtainable.'

MacEntee insisted that public opinion was not opposed to an agreement short of ending partition. He noted, however, that there were those within Fianna Fáil opposed to an agreement and who wished to continue the economic war, including cabinet members Gerry Boland and Oscar Traynor. They were openly rejecting government policy in respect of the negotiations, and MacEntee demanded to know how they could remain in the cabinet while criticising the government's actions. MacEntee could not understand why Boland in particular had not resigned, given the extent of his disagreements. Nor was MacEntee slow to follow the logic of his position, offering his own resignation to de Valera. He added that if the negotiations broke down because of de Valera's intransigence over partition he would leave politics and not stand for election again. Although not always evident in public in 1938, tensions had emerged within the party on how best to negotiate with Britain. MacEntee represented one opinion within Fianna Fáil, but it was not the only one. De Valera had been worried that disagreement over the negotiations would lead to details being leaked to the press. In January 1938 he asked party members to be 'extremely discreet' about matters discussed by the parliamentary party during the discussions. Later in the year he complained that strict secrecy was not being maintained following party meetings. This proved difficult to achieve, and in October de Valera refused to continue a discussion on a policy matter on the grounds that secrecy had been breached after an earlier meeting.[87]

Was de Valera's use of the partition question during these negotiations merely ritualistic or was it a clever attempt to deflect critical republican opinion within and outside the party? MacEntee's concerns indicate that some sections of the party were indeed critical of any accommodation with Britain and that de Valera was alert to this threat. However, the tone of MacEntee's criticism lends support to the view that more was at stake and that de Valera had reservations about the outcome. There was always a strong ideological element to de Valera's thinking on Northern Ireland and on the relationship with Britain. If, as he himself said, partition was the issue which brought him into politics, it is likely that this remained a key element in this thinking, especially if he believed that the 1937 constitution provided the means to realise his objective. His disappointment must have been great when he realised that the British government had no intention of forcing the northern government to come to terms with its neighbour. Indeed a case can be made that de Valera's own actions had widened the gap between the two parts of Ireland. MacEntee's distress over the exchange is clear, as there is no evidence that his February 1938 letter was written for anything more than private circulation:

> We have had differences of opinion as to the wisdom or unwisdom of a line of policy and I have always been prepared in the last resort to defer to your judgement. But I cannot concede that full deference now, because in regard to partition we have never had a considered policy. It has always been an affair of hasty improvisations, a matter of fits and starts.

Moreover, when MacEntee was interviewed in later life he denied that there had been serious divisions about partition at the time, perhaps a case of not being willing to remember an uncomfortable episode in his relationship with de Valera.[88]

De Valera eventually came to terms with the cabinet majority. Lemass, MacEntee and the Minister for Agriculture, James Ryan, had been deeply engaged in the discussions and were in favour of the agreements reached. De Valera had to override his own misgivings in the matter and accept the outcome or face the prospect of a revolt among some of his ablest supporters. Irish negotiating tactics were extremely successful in obtaining the government's objectives on most matters except partition. The outcome provides an early example and confirmation of the view that a small state may be in quite a strong position to negotiate favourable outcomes even with a much larger and stronger power, as long as both are democratic. As a small state, Ireland could concentrate its diplomatic resources exclusively on obtaining the best outcome for itself, whereas a large state with many interests is rarely in a position to do so. Ireland also benefited from Chamberlain's policy of appeasement, which worked to de Valera's advantage on this occasion. A further consideration is that Chamberlain was concerned with the possibility of war in Europe, if for different reasons to de Valera, and this generated an environment conducive to agreement.[89]

The endorsement of the new constitution by the electorate in 1937 and the Anglo-Irish Agreement in 1938 allowed Fianna Fáil to claim that it had achieved most of its objectives. At the 1937 election the party asserted that 'Bit by bit the British connection has been broken and the new Constitution heralds the final advance on the road to freedom.' This had been achieved because the government's policies were 'based on the proudest traditions of our race'. Erskine Childers had predicted in 1934 that if Fianna Fáil realised its social and economic objectives, then the 'Results will be sufficient to compel whole nation to give vote of confidence to government. Griffith's and Lalor's aims will have been achieved.'[90] Notwithstanding this optimism, the electorate proved resistant to these blandishments. In the referendum on the constitution, 56.6 per cent voted in favour, while 43.4 per cent voted against. (In addition, 10 per cent of the votes cast were either spoilt or blank; these votes were not included in the calculation.) Sinnott concluded that the outcome was 'hardly an overwhelming endorsement'. At the general election Fianna Fáil's vote fell in comparison with 1933, but it still won 50 per cent of the seats. Labour increased its vote quite significantly, but the trend for Fine Gael was down.[91] If 1937 reflected uncertainty in respect of Fianna Fáil and de Valera's constitution, this had disappeared by 1938, when Fianna Fáil was safely returned again. Despite this, there were fears that the constitution would not receive the respect due to it. Childers complained to the national executive that the use of Éire as an English term was 'an obvious attempt to nullify the effect of the designation of our country in the Constitution by identifying the Irish name with the 26 counties exclusively'. The issue was also raised at the parliamentary party, when de Valera was asked by Cormac Breathnach TD to elaborate on the appropriate use of the terms Éire and Ireland in the constitution. De Valera admitted that the current usage was not entirely satisfactory, 'but under the circumstances the limited area included under the name Éire would when partition is abolished render it possible for the name to apply to the whole country'.[92]

The stabilisation of Irish nationalism

By the end of 1938 consensus was widespread. Fianna Fáil had achieved a considerable amount in six years and this was endorsed by the electorate and (reluctantly) by the opposition. This is likely to happen in a nationalist community when most constitutional, institutional and policy conflicts have been resolved. That they had been resolved on terms favourable to one particular political party does not weaken the claim, as Fianna Fáil had proved to be the most successful political force in implementing its objectives. While Fianna Fáil's electoral support waxed and waned, support for the constitution consolidated quickly, becoming almost unanimous by the early 1940s. De Valera had predicted that in time the constitution would receive the support of 90 per cent of the Irish people, and in this he was correct as it applied to nationalist Ireland. Another reflection of this process was the increasing stability evident in Irish society after 1938. Domestically, Ireland had become an independent developmental state along the lines sketched out by Fianna Fáil during the 1920s, while the constitution reflected a clear break with the Treaty settlement. Only in respect of partition could it be charged that Fianna Fáil had not met its objectives, though here de Valera insisted, mistakenly, that the other changes brought this closer. The difficulties associated with the restoration of Gaelic as a widely spoken language could be disguised by its privileged position in the constitution in a predominantly English-speaking state. The 1938 general election reaffirmed Fianna Fáil's underlying strength in the party system, while providing a positive verdict on the recent constitutional and diplomatic changes.[93] After 1938, and in the face of uncertainty in the external world, consolidation and stabilisation were the main features of Irish political culture and its political system. Indeed the Irish response to uncertainty for the next thirty years was to maintain its internal stability and to meet the challenge of change by largely ignoring it.[94]

Despite the stabilisation of Fianna Fáil rule, some republican objectives were not realised. It had been assumed by republicans that an independent economic policy would remove the incentive to emigrate, yet emigration once again increased after 1936. Despite the changes in the Irish economy between 1932 and 1938, by 1937 it was evident that emigration was again reaching record levels. De Valera and Lemass insisted that the solution to emigration was within the capacity of Irish policy makers, yet Fine Gael was able to claim that there was more emigration under Fianna Fáil than during the previous administration.[95] Irish ministers often denied that living standards and opportunities were superior in Northern Ireland, but the Department of Finance provided evidence that a gap did exist between the two parts of the island.[96] Economic conditions were probably not significantly different between north and south in 1939, when levels of taxation and others factors are taken into consideration. Economic advantage and disadvantage were not at the heart of the debate over partition, but were used as propaganda tools by both sides. It is unlikely that Fianna Fáil would have accepted free trade with the United Kingdom, even if the advantages had been obvious. Nor would northern unionists have been attracted by a united Ireland if it had been more prosperous. In a public statement in October 1938, for example, de Valera offered northern businessmen the prospect of access to southern markets, whereas in private negotiations with Britain earlier in the same year he and Lemass had strenuously opposed any such concessions. Northern Ireland was so heavily dependent on global and British Empire markets that the limited southern market could not absorb its industrial production, even if de Valera had been serious.[97] De Valera might have believed that 'So far as the Northern businessman is concerned the case for the termination of partition is quite unanswerable', but this was never a persuasive case for industrialists in the north. It also highlighted one of the long-standing inconsistencies in Irish nationalist thinking. Fianna Fáil rejected free trade with the United Kingdom on the grounds that it did not benefit Ireland. But when attempts were made to persuade unionists of the merits of a united Ireland, de Valera and Lemass continuously put forward arguments in favour of free trade between north and south which they had already rejected when applied to the global economy.

Economic policy became more insular after 1932, as did the society generally. Self-sufficiency provided the main incentive for production, rather than the market. Consequently producers were less inclined to export, even when production increased. Between 1922 and 1932 about half of output had been consumed in Ireland; by 1939 this had increased to nearly two thirds. One industrialist, whose company had previously exported 70 per cent of its output, claimed that by 1939 exports had dropped to 25 per cent, despite increased production.[98] The Irish economy was heavily protected by the state after 1932, providing a domestic market for new industries but also for Irish companies that had previously exported. There was little competition for domestic producers, who were generally inefficient and unlikely to export. Lemass in Industry and Commerce found it difficult to police native Irish industry in respect of quality, efficiency or competitiveness.[99] The Commission on Banking, which reported in 1938, warned that further protection would not benefit economic growth or help to increase employment. The report was critical of the industrial policy pursued by Fianna Fáil on the grounds that it diverted resources from agriculture. Yet despite this critical analysis, and the end of the economic war, de Valera remained suspicious of any economic policy that reintegrated Ireland into the world economy. He was especially sceptical of the benefits to be derived from cattle exports, which revived after the 1938 trade agreements. In contrast, MacEntee in Finance argued that Irish economic growth was linked to increasing exports, especially those from the agricultural sector. The consequences of the economic war, according to MacEntee in 1937, were that Ireland imported more and exported less, while the state spent more on subsidies of one kind or another. Increased pressure on the exchequer and on the balance of payments was the main consequence of this.[100]

The Department of Finance and MacEntee provided the main internal critique of economic nationalism during the 1930s, yet the position advanced was not an unreservedly conservative one. Alone among the civil service departments, Finance recognised the harm which economic nationalism caused to the Irish economy and the real cost of the various interventionist policies. Although politically constrained by Fianna Fáil's nationalist presuppositions, Finance attempted to limit the damage caused by unrestricted self-sufficiency and economic nationalism. The case for economic nationalism had always been a weak one economically in Ireland, as it, unlike other European agricultural exporters, continued to have access to the United Kingdom market which itself was protected. Despite this, neither MacEntee nor his department was strong enough politically to promote a dynamic export policy or to overcome the reluctance of the government, the party and industrialists to be more innovative. After 1938 Ireland had the worst of both worlds. It resumed exports to the United Kingdom, but in a passive fashion, while maintaining the most negative features of protection. Lemass sought to develop a more dynamic economic policy in 1938, but this did not involve a break with economic nationalism. Nor had his methods changed. MacEntee, in contrast, made an important contribution to economic stability by insisting on maintaining the link with sterling, by criticising the more autarkic aspects of policy and by highlighting how government policy was not contributing to Ireland's economic welfare.[101]

Agriculture continued to be the mainstay for Irish exports, but this sector was never given adequate political support by Fianna Fáil. Furthermore, the agrarian economy remained extremely stable in terms of output and production throughout this period.[102] The Agricultural Credit Corporation (ACC) estimated that at least £100 million (in 1940 terms) would be required to bring Irish agriculture up to the standards prevailing in Denmark, its main competitor on the British market. One leading official in the ACC was extremely pessimistic about the farming sector: 'There are many of the poorer farmers in this country and nothing will help them. You could not think of putting capital into some of those farms to make them fit to live on.' While this was an economically rational conclusion, there were other influential views on the role of farming in Ireland. Bishop Michael Browne, who chaired the Commission on Vocational Organisation, argued that agricultural policy should attend primarily to 'the social welfare of the community as a whole'. For him, 'There is the question, not of the economic, but of the social and moral valuation, and that is a matter for the ordinary citizen as well as the economist.'[103] In a predominately agrarian society, there will inevitably be a tension between economic considerations and those associated with the welfare of the community. The need to export and to compete will normally provide a discipline which will give priority to efficiency and competitiveness over other considerations. During the 1920s the balance in favour of competitiveness was maintained, but after 1932 the balance altered appreciably against efficiency and in favour of security and non-economic considerations. This trend was reinforced by the favourable outcome of the 1938 agreements, which provided enhanced protection for farmers. In addition, by the end of the 1930s Ireland was characterised by high levels of dependency and extensive subsidisation of economic activity.[104] This created expectations that the state would provide an alternative to the market. Increasingly the state was second-guessing the market, seeking by institutional means, by pressure and by subsidies to achieve its objectives. There is evidence to suggest that, among small farms in the west of Ireland, family considerations took precedence over those of the market and that this sector was not deeply integrated into the market economy.[105]

The decision to accept the 1938 agreements with the United Kingdom demonstrated the limits of Fianna Fáil's economic nationalism. After this, self-sufficiency remained an objective, but the political means to achieve it were no longer available. And yet, the agreements did not facilitate a return to free trade, as this was not acceptable to Fianna Fáil's nationalist sensibilities or to the new industrial bourgeoisie which owed its wealth to economic nationalism. Lemass also lost the political initiative in 1938. His section of the party welcomed the self-sufficiency associated with industrial development and he had used the economic war to promote a policy that might not otherwise have been so successful. Despite the short-term success of industrialisation between 1932 and 1938, the opportunity provided by the economic war was closed off in 1938. Lemass' failure to realise his developmental strategy at the end of the Second World War is further testament to the stability of society and politics as well as his own political isolation. Institutional initiatives such as the Central

Bank reinforced the stable aspects of the Irish economy and did not involve a significant departure from the existing consensus. In socio-economic terms, the decade after 1938 can be characterised as one of consolidation and stabilisation *without* innovation. Policy formulation by 1940 was more conservative than theretofore and was generally designed to be preservative. At the beginning of the Second World War, the Labour Party considered that MacEntee was close to Fine Gael on economic and social policy, while Fine Gael accepted the general policy parameters established by Fianna Fáil once the United Kingdom market was open to Irish producers again.[106]

This is not to say there were no outstanding divisions within Fianna Fáil or in the party system generally. However, by 1939, when Fine Gael accepted neutrality, no significant issue divided the main parties, except on how best to manage the system. The division within Fianna Fáil over Children's Allowances was not a division between left and right but between a Christian democratic conception of the state's responsibilities and a more traditionally conservative and restrictive one.[107] MacEntee's concern in this controversy was for the 'small and middle class [tax] payer who has little marginal expenditure available'. He argued that it was 'neither politic nor justifiable' to increase taxation on this sector of the population. He emphasised that status as well as income was involved, with middle-class marginal income being invested in housing, education and the provision of services for the family. Increased taxation would divert these resources to other classes and would result in a decline in living standards and status, an outcome that would affect employment as well. In April 1939, MacEntee recommended that expenditure should be cut, while maintaining taxation at existing levels. When he lost this debate in the cabinet, he again offered de Valera his resignation. He complained bitterly that the cabinet decision had made his position as Minister for Finance untenable, as taxes and expenditure would rise. He added the following argument: 'But as Minister for Finance I stand in a fiduciary capacity to every citizen irrespective of party or personal consideration, and my obligations in that regard override all others.' While de Valera did not accept MacEntee's offer to resign, he was moved from Finance in a cabinet reshuffle in September and was not to return to that department until 1951.[108] Yet MacEntee's defeat in April 1939 was not a victory for Lemass or for expansionary politics. It demonstrated more the capacity of spending departments to win cabinet battles than any innovative strategy for growth. More seriously, the economy had been damaged by Fianna Fáil's economic nationalism. The economic war had been driven by nationalist ideology, not by rational economic assessment. Fianna Fáil discarded the advantages associated with free trade, but gained little in return. Indeed, it is arguable that Ireland did not recover from this self-inflicted wound for fifty years.[109]

Neutrality and isolationism

When the Second World War began in September 1939, Ireland declared its neutrality, as did other small democratic states in Europe. A little before this,

MacEntee had used the threat of war to urge a reduction in public expenditure. He complained that military expenditure was wasteful on the grounds that there was no military threat to Ireland from the United Kingdom and that if Ireland was attacked by any other state Britain would protect it. MacEntee was quite cynical in his assessment. He concluded that even if the worst occurred and the United Kingdom attacked Ireland, defence could only be temporary and consequently the Irish armed forces should not be expanded.[110] While no one else in the cabinet expressed this view, Ireland's strategic policy in respect of neutrality operated within similar assumptions. There was little preparation in advance of war, and even when, after June 1940, the international situation deteriorated the basic policy involved little more than mass mobilisation of a people's militia. While the enthusiasm of the volunteer militia is not in doubt, especially during 1940 and 1941, it was never a credible military force. In contrast to Sweden or Switzerland, where extensive preparations were made to defend the country, Ireland was ill-equipped to deal with an invasion. If blindness and ignorance are discounted, then the cynical explanation is the most likely one. Irish leaders believed, though only MacEntee said so, that Britain or its allies would not invade Ireland, and that if Germany threatened it the allies would come to its aid.[111]

If Ireland was ill-prepared militarily for war and neutrality, in some ways it was no better prepared in political terms. Opinion was divided on the war, as the response of two republican veterans indicates. For J.J. Walsh, the former Cumann na nGaedheal minister, as for others, the war provided another opportunity to conclude the unfinished business of partition. In a letter to the *Sunday Independent* in April 1939, he argued that Ireland should support the Germans on the grounds of Irish nationalist self-interest. He reasoned that 'The vanquished of the [First] World War, so brutally treated and cheated, are having their revenge, and as far as the people of this country are concerned, we wish them well.' Walsh claimed that he was now bitter at the Treaty and its consequences, though at the time he had supported it. He hoped that the forthcoming war would weaken Britain, but complained that the government's policy seemed to be to protect Ireland 'against England's enemies'. He asserted that if this was the case it meant that 'we are prepared to shed our blood, if needs be, to maintain the partition of our country, and at the same time to save England's skin'. More ominously, he concluded his letter by asserting that 'there [is] no shortage of determined men in Ireland to-day who mean to finish the job this time if the chance comes their way'. There was a substantial body of opinion in Ireland in 1939 which welcomed the policy of neutrality followed by the government, and believed that a defeat for Britain would bring about Irish unity. Walsh's words were given military meaning when the IRA declared war on Britain and then engaged in a bombing campaign to back up its demands. The IRA at this time was close to Nazi Germany, both ideologically and tactically. While Hitler was unable to benefit from this alliance, the militarists in the republican movement clearly believed it could achieve a breakthrough in its struggle to remove the British from Northern Ireland.[112]

MacEntee represented another school of thought. He had believed in 1932 that it was possible to isolate Britain within Europe, but by 1940 his view of the situation was more sanguine and realistic. He speculated in 1937 on the possibility of creating an all-Ireland defence system in response to external threat, believing that north and south could co-operate in a common defence structure as a prelude to unification. This was, in large part, wishful thinking and there is no evidence that the British or Irish governments gave any consideration to such an ambitious plan, though Britain hoped to negotiate a defence agreement after returning the ports.[113] MacEntee's attitude to the war was complex and in 1940 such plans could have had greater potential. He was not one of the pro-German faction in Fianna Fáil, but neither was he pro-British. However, it is more than likely that he wanted Britain to win the war, as an exchange in 1940 suggests. One of MacEntee's correspondents criticised the government for its pro-British stance on various grounds, including the influence of Jews in Britain and Freemasons in France and the economic imperialism practised by these two countries and the United States. MacEntee asked his correspondent not to forget that Pius XI had published an encyclical condemning the behaviour of the Nazis towards the Catholic Church in Germany. He added that 'It is difficult in these days for an Irishman, a Belfastman and a Catholic to reconcile all the incompatibilities in international politics.' Nevertheless, he believed that even if economic dominance had been exercised by the Allies in the past it had positive consequences for Ireland, 'For there is no country in the whole world that could give or was prepared to give as high a price for our staple products as Great Britain was.' MacEntee argued that his attitude was 'neither pro-German nor pro-British, but pro-Irish', and while this was certainly the case he leaned decidedly in the direction of Britain for the following reasons:

> But if she does go down we shall be under no illusion as to the re-actions which that event will have upon our economy and upon the ultimate history of our race in this island. No continental power enjoying hegemony in Europe will buy from us upon the same scale and at the same high prices as Great Britain did.[114]

There was a wide range of opinion within Ireland concerning the legitimacy of the war, but the decision to declare neutrality was understandable in the context of Ireland's relationship with Britain and the need to assert further its sovereignty.[115]

The decision to opt for neutrality in 1939 was based on the assumption that the war would be similar to the First World War and that neutrality would protect most states, as it had the Netherlands and Denmark on that occasion. In 1939, therefore, the Irish government was defending the national interest and reinforcing its sovereignty by declaring its neutrality. Although not clear at the time, there were a number of unintended consequences of neutrality, which were to have long-term consequences for Ireland, north and south. Under de Valera, neutrality was not simply an exercise in diplomacy; it was also a method of generating consensus within Ireland and mobilising nationalist opinion against Britain and partition. There were also complicated questions involved in the threat of war. De Valera rejected Britain's authority to conscript Irish citizens in Britain or to extend conscription to Northern Ireland, on the grounds that nationality could not be determined by a British act of parliament.[116] The British government proposed that conscription would be introduced for most categories of men normally resident in Britain. It would have applied to the many Irish men who had emigrated to Britain over the previous five years and to any Irish man who had been resident in Britain for longer than this. Chamberlain intended to extend conscription to Northern Ireland also. In April 1939 the Irish High Commissioner in London, John Dulanty, challenged British sovereignty in Northern Ireland:

> At least a third of the population there are cut off from Ireland against their will. Any attempt to conscript them would be resented as an outrage. ... The introduction of conscription in the Six Counties by the British Government for the British Army can be regarded as an act of war against our nation and will provoke the bitterest hostility to England wherever there are Irishmen throughout the world.[117]

A little earlier, the Fianna Fáil national executive discussed a motion which called for the evacuation of Northern Ireland, presumably in the event of war, though one wonders how the south could have handled the influx of Irish nationalists from Northern Ireland and those from Britain who wanted to return. It defies reality to expect that northern Protestants would have actually moved south in the event of an evacuation promoted by the Irish government, and shows how unrealistic Irish thinking was in respect of Northern Ireland.[118]

The requirements of diplomacy may have restrained some of the more aggressive versions of Irish nationalism, but that did not prevent the government from pursuing its narrow view of conscription throughout 1939. Dulanty reported to Dublin that the British Prime Minister, Neville Chamberlain, had responded sharply to the Irish message, asking why it should be so concerned. Chamberlain complained that he was dismayed by the way Ireland 'seemed to dog his steps', noting that de Valera's speeches on the north had alienated the unionists. Chamberlain revealed to Dulanty that he had drafted a letter to the Northern Ireland Prime Minister, Lord Craigavon, after de Valera had approached him on the conscription issue, but decided not to send it because de Valera's speeches had inflamed the situation. The problem here was that the British Prime Minister considered conscription to be a domestic issue, whereas the Irish government rejected this. Dulanty, perhaps intentionally, emphasised how different Ireland was from other members of the Commonwealth:

> My rejoinder was that there could clearly be no kind of comparison between Canada, South Africa, Australia, or New Zealand, and ourselves. Apart from our fundamentally different attitude towards the Commonwealth conception none of these had part of their territory occupied in the way our six Northern

> counties were occupied. In that part of our country — I emphasised the words 'our country' — nearly half a million of our people had maintained unbrokenly the position that they were in a state of bondage to a Government they detested, had not the rights of free men, and were coerced into separation away from their fellow-countrymen in the rest of Ireland.

Dulanty threatened 'strife and bitter struggle' if conscription was introduced. What is of interest in this exchange is not the rights and wrongs of conscription, but the narrowness of the Irish view in respect of the international situation. It seemed to have no conception of the negotiations between Germany and the United Kingdom or the impact that Irish hostility to conscription might have on Hitler's strategic designs. At the most delicate moments in the months before the war the Irish position, at the least, was selfish, at worse wilful intrusion into the internal affairs of another state. In addition, the unionist attitude was entirely ignored by the Irish government. When Chamberlain drew Dulanty's attention to the consequences of this, his reply was again to threaten the British:

> I said the difficulties for the British arising out of exclusion [from conscription] of the Six Counties were as nothing compared to the difficulties for us, and later for the British, by their inclusion. Mr de Valera felt that no situation fraught with such extreme dangers had arisen since he took office over seven years ago.

Dulanty informed Dublin that in his opinion the British government had not thought through the consequences of its proposal, and that he was not optimistic that Northern Ireland would be excluded.[119]

In the event, the pressure worked. In May 1939 Chamberlain confirmed that the cabinet had agreed that conscription would not be extended to Northern Ireland. The unionist government accepted that the decision should be in the hands of the British government, though they were prepared to provide all means to support the government. Although Chamberlain was anxious to dispel the view that the government had given in to 'a last moment pressure from Mr De Valera', this is precisely what happened:

> They were not to be understood as admitting that as yet Mr De Valera had any jurisdiction in the Six Counties. The British Government had reached this decision because it had been made clear to them the very serious difficulties in which the proposal would involve both Mr De Valera and themselves. It was their earnest wish to develop the most harmonious relations with the Irish Government and further it would be a pity to allow differences which really had no connection with the question of British defence to add to the grave problems at that moment confronting the British Government.

Dulanty's reports highlight Ireland's incomprehension in dealing with the British on this question. Dulanty believed that Chamberlain was relieved that the issue had been resolved, adding that 'It seemed neither necessary nor desirable at that moment to ask the obvious question as to why they had ever entertained such a proposal.'[120] This can be attributed to the key role, perhaps the only role, which partition played in Irish diplomacy. The Irish government was hostage to its own constitution, to Irish nationalists in Northern Ireland and to the threatened militancy of the IRA and its supporters. While de Valera was prepared to crush the IRA for domestic reasons in the south, there was a continuing ambiguity about its actions in the north or Britain. That Ireland's chief diplomat could, in the months prior to the outbreak of war, spend an inordinate amount of time pressurising a government to desist from an action which would be considered normal in any other jurisdiction is of considerable importance.

The decision to declare neutrality in 1939 was the logical extension of Fianna Fáil's nationalist ideology. It reflected the continuing assertion of Irish sovereignty and a determination to remain free of the major powers. As a result, ideological concerns often had a higher priority for de Valera than diplomatic considerations. Neutrality was the expression of nationalism in diplomatic form. One of the main diplomatic architects of the policy, Joseph Walshe, Secretary of the Department of External Affairs, argued that neutrality was a matter of principle, not a diplomatic position:

> Neutrality was not entered upon for the purpose of being used as a bargaining factor. It represented, and does represent, the fundamental attitude of the entire people. It is just as much a part of the national position as the desire to remain Irish and we can no more abandon it than we can renounce everything that constitutes our national distinctiveness.[121]

This was written shortly after the collapse of France, at a time when Walshe and de Valera believed that Britain would lose the war. Walshe was sympathetic to the Vichy regime in France, and believed that Ireland should not abandon neutrality even if a German invasion was threatened. The American Minister in Dublin, David Gray, later claimed that Walshe spent his holidays in the summer of 1940 with the German Minister, Eduard Hempel.[122]

Neutrality has generally been presented as the best policy for Ireland in all circumstances, though in my opinion the counterarguments have often been too quickly dismissed. At issue is not whether neutrality was the right policy, but whether it was the best policy at all times and under all circumstances between 1939 and 1945. This also raises the question whether the policy could have been altered on occasions without fatally compromising the policy itself, for example by providing transhipment facilities for convoys arriving from North America. Circumstances change, and what was appropriate in 1939 might not have been in 1940 or 1944. If neutrality was not simply ideological, then the case must be made on each occasion why it was in the national interest to continue such a policy at the appropriate moment. Thus it is possible to agree that neutrality was in the national interest in 1939 or 1940, but not when the United States entered the war in December 1941 or when the American and British governments asked that Axis diplomats be expelled from Ireland early in 1944. A more flexible approach to neutrality might focus on the possible conditions when Ireland might change its policy.

On the wider issue of neutrality, there is circularity in the way the issue has been perceived. If neutrality was a matter of principle, as implied by de Valera and Walshe, then the issue of national interest does not arise as in all circumstances and under all conditions neutrality will be in the national interest. It excludes any possibility that a situation would arise when neutrality would not be an appropriate policy stance, or where the implementation of policy would be amended or altered. It was also an essentially passive policy in the Irish case, dependent on the decisions (and the good will) of other powers. Yet even when a strong case for national interest can be made, some serious questions remained unanswered. Ireland was ill-prepared for war and remained so throughout the conflict. There were real divisions within Ireland on the issue, though these can be exaggerated. It is assumed that the national interest can be defined objectively, yet in the Irish case Fianna Fáil successfully identified the national interest with its own interests and persuaded or intimidated other political parties to accept this. This can be equated with the national interest only if the interest of the government or the largest party is considered equivalent to the national interest. It is mistaken to assume that the interest promoted by a government is identical with the national interest. Fine Gael certainly believed Fianna Fáil coerced it into accepting its view on all major matters during the war, though without reciprocal concessions.[123] Moreover, government control of the media through its draconian censorship deprived most Irish citizens of even basic information to form opinions on what constituted the national interest. Sean O'Faolain complained in the *Bell* that when Mussolini was forced to resign as head of government in 1943, it was the third item on the Irish radio news, following a report on a pilgrimage to Croagh Patrick and a Muintir na Tíre conference in Cork. Nor was everyone able to receive the news, even in this truncated form. The novelist Elizabeth Bowen, who reported to the Minister of Information in London on Irish attitudes during the war, found that political debate was severely restricted by censorship in 1942, while the independent TD James Dillon complained that his speeches on neutrality were often not reported in the newspapers. Furthermore, in rural areas, where the majority lived, news was sparse due to the lack of batteries to power radios in the absence of electricity, and the shortage of print for newspapers. Censorship, centralisation and surveillance allowed Fianna Fáil to intimidate, manipulate and control the Irish population throughout the war. This reinforced the authoritarian instinct in Fianna Fáil, reflected not only in the censor's office but also in other government agencies. Whether there was a conscious effort to weaken Irish democracy during the war it is difficult to judge, but the actions of the Fianna Fáil government weakened the capacity of the Irish people to arrive at well-informed conclusions about Ireland and the world.[124]

Fianna Fáil's success in defining national interest does not entail that its policies actually achieved this end. If partition was the real obstacle to Irish participation in the war (or in NATO subsequently), as alleged by successive governments, then opportunities to change the political environment in this respect can be considered in the national interest. One such opportunity was the British offer in 1940 to promote Irish unity in return for Irish involvement in the war. Irish historians have generally dismissed this offer as nonsense and regarded de Valera's decision to continue neutrality as justified. By 1940 circumstances had changed dramatically. The United Kingdom was now isolated in Europe and faced a German invasion. The Irish ports which had been returned in 1938 took on a new importance for the British government, and there was considerable speculation that a British invasion might take place to reacquire them. The response of the British government was not, in fact, to invade but to seek accommodation with the Irish government to secure the ports and other facilities. The fiasco after Britain infringed Norwegian neutrality earlier in the year must have been fresh in the minds of British planners, though the situation was more serious after June. While Chamberlain conceded that an invasion was justifiable to secure the ports, the cabinet agreed to offer a declaration in favour of a united Ireland in return for Ireland's entry to the war. Malcolm MacDonald engaged in intensive negotiations in June 1940 to persuade de Valera that the British were serious, though to no avail.[125]

De Valera's attitude to neutrality was essentially inflexible. Richard Mulcahy concluded, after a discussion with de Valera in July 1940, that there were no circumstances when Fianna Fáil would support joining the war, even if Irish unity could be achieved. In fact, de Valera's policy was essentially one of isolation, of which neutrality was the public face. In the discussions with MacDonald, de Valera insisted that Britain support a united Ireland and that the island remain neutral and he guaranteed that the island would not be used for aggression against Britain. If this had been agreed, it would have involved Britain giving up any naval advantage it had in the North Atlantic, exposing further its supply lines from the United States. This reflected de Valera's indifference to the outcome of a conflict which, he believed, did not directly affect Irish nationalism. The Irish state's only concern was to remain outside the conflict, while obtaining any benefit it could without significant cost to itself.[126] On 26 June MacDonald returned to Dublin with a six-point proposal, including a declaration in principle for a united Ireland, a joint north–south defence council and a commitment by Ireland to join the war. Lee dismisses the offer as a 'bizarre proposal', arguing that de Valera 'rightly rejected the offer'. Keogh warns against reading the offer in a positive sense, though O'Leary urges a more positive approach, suggesting that it could have formed the basis for a historic agreement between the two parts of Ireland.[127]

It is possible to make a positive assessment of this offer, while recognising that there were serious obstacles to an agreement. The crisis after the fall of France forced the British government to act in a more innovative fashion, of which the offer to Ireland was but one point of departure. Churchill's abortive plan for an Anglo-French union can also be seen as part of this process. As such, the politics of the early 1940s may have been more open to genuine change than some historians suggest. However, this is not to underestimate the obstacles to realising any such departure. One obvious problem was the resistance of Ulster unionists, who were excluded from the discussions. Yet unionism was in a weak position to oppose an agreement which might have helped the defence of the realm and the empire. Lord Craigavon was a weak and ineffective leader of the government and Northern Ireland was ill-prepared for war. There was some hostility to Northern Ireland within the British government and there is also evidence that some senior unionist politicians would have considered a new arrangement with the south as a response to the crisis.[128] In practice, de Valera was in a stronger position to negotiate with Britain in 1940 than Craigavon was. In the first place, de Valera had something the British wanted quite badly and they were prepared to negotiate with him to obtain it. Secondly, de Valera was the democratically elected leader of a sovereign state, whereas Craigavon was the weak and ineffective leader of a devolved regional government with a poor civil rights record. It is also likely that, notwithstanding his own belief in the matter, de Valera could have persuaded the nationalist minority in the north as well as the majority in the south that an arrangement with Britain was worth it in the national interest. It should be remembered that a significant number of northern and southern Catholics voluntarily joined the British armed forces during the war. While de Valera was justifiably concerned that such an arrangement would seriously divide opinion in nationalist Ireland, it is possible to overestimate the extent of opposition. With the exception of Frank Aiken and Oscar Traynor, most of the Fianna Fáil leadership were in favour of a British victory, if only on the grounds identified by MacEntee in 1940.

After a series of meetings with de Valera and senior Fianna Fáil ministers, Richard Mulcahy summarised the state of opinion in July 1940. He concluded that it was unlikely that de Valera and Cosgrave together could retain enough support to bring Ireland into the war:

> Dev would have to swerve his party away from their present road. He could only get half, Cosgrave two thirds. We would be left with a divided front. One third of the country opposed to us. This would be a matter of terrible difficulty. The one third of the country would be that part with the greatest possible capacity for nuisance and damage.

Indeed, as reported by Mulcahy, the opinion among the party leaders was that nationalists in Northern Ireland would pose the most serious obstacle to any decision to join the war: 'There are two things about Partition: (1) The Northern nationalists are pro-German (2) the section in the South who are pro-German would probably not be so but for partition.' Any change in policy and any offer from Britain would have to appreciate this, according to Mulcahy: 'they should have something definitely reassuring to say about Partition, and the favourable reaction of military security should be thoroughly understood'. This was written at the same time that de Valera rejected the British proposals. It lends support to the views of those who believe that de Valera took the correct policy decision in 1940. It is evident that Mulcahy was not aware of the extent of the British concessions. Likewise, MacDonald was of the opinion that

Lemass and other members of the cabinet were not fully aware of the proposals. At a meeting attended by MacDonald, de Valera, Lemass and Aiken, Lemass explored the possibility that Ireland could maintain its neutrality but permit British use of the ports and other facilities.[129] Of greater importance was the fact that on 28 June the British government amended its original proposals to meet Irish objections, strengthening the commitment to a united Ireland but deleting those sections committing Ireland to immediately join the war. The British now asked for facilities to be granted in respect of the ports and airfields, but this does not appear to have included Ireland declaring war on Germany. This revision seems to have been prompted by Lemass' remarks during the earlier meeting and was probably a direct attempt to influence the Irish decision. Whether acceptance of these proposals would have prevented attacks on Ireland by German forces is problematic and in all likelihood Ireland would have been drawn into the war on the Allied side eventually. It certainly would have compromised neutrality, if not undermined it. Notwithstanding this, the important point is that the United Kingdom was prepared to amend its original proposals in a significant fashion to meet Irish reservations. At the very least it presented the prospect of further negotiations, but these do not appear to have taken place. I can find no evidence that the 28 June proposals were discussed by the full cabinet, though the original ones were. It may be that de Valera, Aiken and Walshe did not reveal their full contents to other senior Fianna Fáil ministers and that when de Valera rejected the British proposals in July, these members were under the mistaken belief that it was the original proposals that were being rejected. De Valera's note to the British government is couched in such a way as to strengthen this view.[130]

On the basis of the limited information available to Mulcahy, Fine Gael continued to support neutrality, yet if the full extent of the offer had been revealed the political context could have been changed irrevocably. De Valera claimed, during a meeting with Sir Emerson Herdman early in July, that the offer to end partition had come too late for him to respond positively, as Ireland was too weak militarily to repel attacks. This, of course, was a situation of Fianna Fáil's own making, but de Valera also argued that to abandon neutrality would be divisive: 'The Fianna Fáil Government could not carry it, even with the support of Fine Gael. That the people were pro-German and that this would drive whatever instinct they had now the other way completely on to the German side.'[131] This reads as post-hoc rationalisation and may have been intended for Fine Gael and British eyes in any event. It is conceivable that de Valera could have created a nationalist movement in favour of the war (or the more limited involvement contained in the 28 June proposals) if he had wished to do so. This is not to say it would have been easy, but de Valera's skills were formidable and intervention at such a fluid time could have changed the direction of Irish politics. In the event, his conservative mind-set, his dislike of Britain and perhaps also his belief that the British would lose the war made him refuse the opportunity to explore further possible amendments in these negotiations. By doing so, he further reinforced partition, increased the divisions within Ireland and especially within Northern Ireland and exposed the Catholic community in Northern Ireland to harassment by security forces and sectarian attacks by the Orange Order. Control of the media would have allowed pro-Allied supporters in Ireland to promote the most positive cause in favour of the new departure. The defence of neutrality is only persuasive if one accepts that all elements remained constant. The British changed this in June 1940, but de Valera was unable to respond to this new environment. What is also overlooked in this process is public opinion. Irish involvement in the war would have changed public opinion in Britain and in Northern Ireland, providing a more favourable environment for changing the relationship between the two parts of the island. If de Valera was serious that the political changes he had introduced provided the opportunity to bring about unification without violence, then he missed this opportunity in 1940. It is strange that de Valera did not adopt the position in 1940 that England's difficulty was Ireland's opportunity to acquire further concessions from the United Kingdom.

That Britain was serious about reaching an agreement in 1940 receives some support from a conversation between Dulanty and an unnamed British cabinet minister in 1942. It is probable from the internal evidence that the minister was Ernest Bevin, perhaps the most influential member of the War Cabinet after Churchill. The minister emphatically rejected Dulanty's argument that the British government and Churchill in particular would not have delivered Irish unity in exchange for support in 1940. The British minister claimed that the original idea for an agreement had come from him, but had been accepted by Churchill because he believed that it was an opportunity to achieve unity and friendship within Ireland and between the two islands. The minister insisted that 'an absolute guarantee for a United Ireland' was the intention of the negotiations, and said that he was disappointed that nothing came of them. He paraphrased Churchill to the effect that he would pressurise the Northern Ireland government in any way possible short of using force against them.[132] Though this interview took place two years after the original negotiations, they seem to have remained fresh in the minds of both parties to this conversation. It does not provide irrefutable evidence of British intentions, but coming from Bevin, if this is who it was, it provides powerful additional confirmation that the British government was serious in its approach to the Irish government at the time.

On a number of occasions de Valera reiterated his government's aim to maintain good relations with the United Kingdom, yet its actions at times do not lend support to this view. Although de Valera remained extraordinarily sensitive about any threat to Ireland's sovereignty, his interference in the affairs of other states was often crude and self-destructive to Irish interests. His opposition to Franklin D. Roosevelt during the 1940 presidential elections did not endear him to the American administration, nor did Frank Aiken's heavy-handed and insulting meeting with Roosevelt in 1941 help the Irish position with the United States. One consequence of this was the deterioration of diplomatic relations between Ireland and the United States, reflected in the mutual hostility between the American Minister to Ireland, David Gray, and the Irish government. Furthermore, when the question of conscription emerged again in May 1941, de Valera used the opportunity to reassert the Irish irredentist claim over Northern Ireland and over all those living in the area, including Catholics and Protestants.[133]

A case could be made for special treatment for northern Catholics, but the Irish government never developed it. At issue was not that certain categories of people should be exempted from conscription, but that the British government had no legal right, according to de Valera, to legislate in Northern Ireland. This may have been self-evident in Fianna Fáil, but international law did not sustain the Irish position. In international law, Northern Ireland was part of a sovereign state, although its status was contested by the south. Given the continuing disagreements between the two states, it is likely that concessions would have been made to the conscription law. However, the Irish government, during a war, was challenging the right of a sovereign state to legislate for its own state, a claim which would have been rejected in most circumstances by other states. De Valera's position was actively endorsed by nationalist MPs in Northern Ireland and by the Catholic Church. Dulanty energetically lobbied the British government, engaging in acrimonious exchanges with Churchill. The proposal was dropped when the cabinet accepted that the threat of violence from the Catholic minority would make conscription unworkable. The narrow-minded nationalism of de Valera and the Department of External Affairs not only obstructed the British war effort but increased the obstacles to any possible reconciliation between the two parts of Ireland. In a context where the majority in Northern Ireland believed it could afford to ignore the minority, and indeed to repress it if need be, the failure of the Irish government to create bridges between itself and the British government amounts to a dereliction of duty on its part.[134]

The inflexibility of Irish neutrality is the most obvious feature of the war years in Ireland and this can be attributed to the role played by de Valera. In these circumstances appeals to national interest are ambiguous, if no alternative policy could be considered. Whatever about June 1940, there were other opportunities when joining the war would have served the national interest, as well as being safer for Ireland. James Dillon recognised this when he publicly called for an end to neutrality once the United States entered the war. Likewise, by 1944 Ireland could have entered the war with relatively little cost and considerable advantage to itself.[135] Yet this never seems to have been entertained by Irish diplomats or politicians, not because Irish diplomacy was more moral than that of other states but because Ireland had a sense of superiority in relation to the combatants, one which was enhanced by its isolationism during the war. In one of her reports to London Elizabeth Bowen highlighted both the religious sensibility of the people and its associated superiority and isolationism.[136] Neutrality fitted in well with de Valera's nationalist vision, expressed most romantically in his famous radio broadcast on St Patrick's Day, 1943, but it was also widely endorsed within Catholic-nationalist Ireland. It was a view which was also to be found among many of those Irish citizens who joined the Allied war effort, whether in British factories or in the armed forces. These volunteers drew a distinction between their individual decision to join up and the national community's decision not to do so.[137] However, the longer term impact of neutrality increased isolationism in Ireland, an outcome which had a marked effect on Irish political culture until the 1960s, if not beyond. This can be seen in the building of a moral community on the foundations established by Irish independence, the 1937 constitution and the policy of neutrality.

4

Building a Moral Community

Church, State and Society, 1937–1961

The Catholic and nationalist nature of Irish society was enhanced by the success of the 1937 constitution, providing powerful reinforcement for the moral certainties identified with Irish nationalism. Fianna Fáil, the Catholic Church and cultural elites (especially revivalists) intended that the constitution should be a vehicle for realising the main aims of the moral community as defined by them. This was an elite-driven enterprise, but it also had mass support and enthusiasm, though not in every area. The strongest support was for religion, nationalism and the agrarian vision of society, whereas that for the language revival was more diffuse. Nevertheless, in comparison with other European attempts to create moral communities during the interwar period, the Irish case was established on a popular democratic basis, while retaining considerable support for over a quarter of a century. Other moral communities received popular support, but most were anti-democratic and coercive despite that. The strength of Ireland's moral community was that it was both popular and democratic.[1]

In the Irish constitution, individual rights are subordinate to those of the community as institutionalised by the state. De Valera acknowledged the communitarian nature of the Irish state when he replied to John A. Costello's criticism that subjecting rights to 'public order and morality' was a means of restricting those very rights. This, according to de Valera, was to confuse liberty with licence:

> I say that you should not give to the propagation of what is wrong and unnatural the same liberty as would be accorded to the propagation of what is right. Every state has to protect itself against the abuse of liberty that otherwise would be rightful liberty. We want to protect liberty, but in the interests of the community as a whole we want to see that rightful liberty is not abused.[2]

The use of censorship, the introduction of legislation reflecting the requirements of the dominant denomination and the spread through official promotion of a narrowly configured cultural ethos were all aspects of this process. The aim was to create a harmonious moral community based on the communitarian values considered vital to a small-scale face-to-face society. While seeking harmony, such societies frequently generate conformity, a process reinforced in the Irish case by its growing isolationism after the Second World War. Disagreement and dissent are threats to such moral communities, though in Ireland such challenges were carefully regulated by church and state as well as through the welcome expediency of emigration. This is not to claim that such a society is necessarily oppressive; its moral integrity could not have been sustained unless it maintained a popular basis, which it was capable of doing for a lengthy period.[3]

While one senior Department of Justice official admitted that he was 'prejudiced against a written Constitution at all', this was not a representative view by the early 1940s, when the constitution had received widespread support.[4] The experience of war seems to have increased the confidence of some that Ireland's moral community could be used as an example to others, not least the victorious Allies. The sense of superiority implicit in this was well established when Seán Brady, TD for Dublin County, proposed to the Fianna Fáil national executive in July 1945 that the party should establish a committee to contact Canadian and American military personnel then visiting Dublin. The committee was to be asked to consider how best to provide these visitors with 'national propaganda, tourist information, and protection from street beggars'.[5] It is not clear from the subsequent minutes whether any action was taken on this, nor does the committee appear to have been established. The need to maintain a harmonious and agreed version of the past prompted Dan Breen, TD for Tipperary, to complain at a party meeting in 1941 about *A Short History of the Irish People*, written by Mary Hayden and George A. Moonan. He criticised the book as 'misleading and untrue', because of its treatment of the Invincibles and some aspects of the War of Independence. Tom Derrig, the Minister for Education, revealed during the discussion that, after consultation with the authors, agreement had been reached to remove a section on the Civil War from the published version. However, he rejected Breen's call to have the book withdrawn from schools and colleges on the basis that he, as minister, had no control over private schools. He also defended the book itself on the grounds that it 'was written from a Catholic point of view and in that sense was in demand. Other histories have, of course, been written, but as they are the work of Protestants, they were not likely to be sought after.'[6] Despite this close scrutiny by the Fianna Fáil party, the book continued to be used widely in Irish secondary schools until the 1960s.

Some images were more successfully internalised by the political culture than others. At the heart of Fianna Fáil's programme was its commitment to de-Anglicising Irish culture, through the revival of the Irish language. Yet there were many difficulties associated with this aim. Censorship could not entirely cut off Ireland from liberal and external influences, though some 249 periodicals were prohibited between 1946 and 1953. If the ultimate aim of policy was to create an Irish-speaking barrier against English and liberal influence, its success was patchy to say the least. A primary reason for this was that the majority of Irish citizens continued to use English as their only mode of communication. Even within Fianna Fáil the response to calls for more use of Irish was lukewarm. At a meeting of the parliamentary party in late 1943 it was proposed that at least one speech a day should be made in Irish in the Dáil. This did not have the intended effect, and a stronger proposal was introduced the following year, demanding that Fianna Fáil should promote the language more vigorously. One contributor to the debate criticised TDs from Kerry for their alleged failure in this matter. However, the Cork West deputy Ted O'Sullivan rejected the charge, countering that 'he [the proposer] was wrong in throwing the onus of learning Irish on the members of the party. They were too old to learn Irish and had to earn their living. Also Ministers and Parliamentary Secretaries together with being too old had too much business to attend to.'[7] During the Inter-Party government of 1948–51, the Minister for Education, Richard Mulcahy, criticised the authorities in University College Dublin (UCD) for not setting examination papers in Irish, following complaints from some secondary schools who taught through that medium. The minister castigated UCD for adopting what he described as 'a cowardly and incompetent approach' to the use of Irish, attributing it to UCD's fear that it would not compete with TCD for students if it did so.[8] Problems with the revival can also be seen in the failure to sell books produced in Irish. When An Gúm, the government-funded Irish-language publisher, was established in 1941 one of its aims was to increase the availability of Irish literature. Take-up was poor; by 1948 at least 140 titles were considered 'dead-stock'. In some cases not a single copy had been sold. It was estimated that the publishers had over 100,000 copies of books it was unlikely to sell.[9]

What is perhaps surprising is that despite the use of considerable resources, the policy to revive Irish failed so disastrously. By the 1950s there were a considerable number of schools teaching through Irish, while various incentives were provided for individuals to learn and use the language, yet there was an underlying resistance to this, as noted above. The total number of those speaking Irish had been in decline prior to 1926. Between 1926 and 1936 a significant increase took place, but this was followed by further decline. Within the Gaeltacht itself, the total population of both Irish and non-Irish speakers declined during the decade after 1936. By 1946 non-Irish speakers outnumbered Irish speakers for the first time in the Gaeltacht, though the situation then stabilised somewhat until the early 1960s. By the 1950s over 70 per cent of those able to speak Irish were living outside the Gaeltacht. It is also clear that the traditional life of the Gaeltacht was seriously disrupted by emigration and economic change, forcing native speakers to leave Ireland and not just the Gaeltacht.[10]

Outside the Gaeltacht, knowledge of Irish privileged some sections of society and excluded others. It created a vested interest among the better educated and middle classes, especially in education and the civil service, providing them with access to employment. The Irish-speaking middle class became a powerful and influential sectional interest in Ireland, contributing to the political coalition favouring protection for all matters Irish. The Irish language was an economic as well as a cultural resource, providing access to scarce urban employment in a predominantly agrarian society. The main losers in this were those with poor educational standards in urban and rural Ireland and the Protestant community in general. According to one report prepared for Mulcahy after he became Minister for Education, Protestants had a high failure rate in Irish examinations, one of the consequences of which was that few Protestants were able to enter the civil service or join the school inspectorate in the Department of Education. Nor was the department sympathetic to Protestant church leaders who complained about the teaching of Irish in their schools. Officials invoked a strong ethnic memory in respect of the divisions between Catholics and Protestants when responding to Protestant concerns. In a note prepared for Mulcahy in 1948, one senior official in the Department of Education expressed considerable distaste for the Protestant schools:

> Inspectors are unanimous that the level of intelligence in Protestant rural schools is low — due they say, to intermarriage. I saw a few of them myself when I first started inspection and I can bear things out. I cannot imagine a more distasteful assignment than to have to teach in some of the Protestant schools I saw.

It is difficult to see how Irish Protestants could have remained members of the moral community in these circumstances, though they were recognised as citizens.[11]

A more ominous threat to the self-image of Ireland's moral certainty emerged when the Armistice Day commemoration was revived in November 1945. During the 1920s Armistice Day had been widely commemorated, though republicans frequently disrupted these ceremonies with violent attacks on the participants. The Free State government had generally protected the participants against such attacks. Restrictions had been imposed on the British Legion's right to march following Fianna Fáil's election in 1932, while the commemoration had been prohibited during the war. A large number of Irish citizens, perhaps as many as 100, 000, had joined the Allied forces during the war, but for Fianna Fáil and for a section of public opinion this placed them outside the moral community.[12] In 1945, the government decided not to prohibit the wearing of uniforms due to the presence of United States and Commonwealth personnel visiting Dublin, but the Garda Commissioner remained opposed to the event itself. Just prior to the commemoration, the march to Islandbridge was banned on public order grounds. The rationale provided to Gerry Boland, the Minister for Justice, was that:

> This year the British Legion in Dublin wished to resume the pre-war practice of holding a parade of ex-servicemen and sympathisers on Remembrance Day. In the past these parades were regarded by a large section of the community as provocative demonstrations antagonistic to national sentiment.

> The police authorities were opposed to the holding of the parade, as they would have had to take extensive precautions, entailing the deployment of large bodies of police from other duties, to ensure against breaches of the peace.

In the Dáil, Boland simply repeated this defence of the prohibition. James Dillon, the only member of the Dáil to openly support the Allied war effort, accused the government of removing the protection of the constitution from the British Legion by denying it the right to free assembly contained in Article 40. He rejected the minister's charge that 'these men contemplated a breach of the peace'. Dillon affirmed the idealism of those who had fought in both world wars and pointedly asked Boland whether he would ban a march led by de Valera if evidence was available that subversives might disrupt it. He added that minorities deserved special protection when they were threatened. Dillon feared that 'This country may after all become the last citadel of Fascism if we start banning processions without any just cause, but merely because of a rumour that there may or may not be a riot.' Boland denied that he had taken the decision, but supported the Garda Commissioner's right to do so. He referred especially to the riot that had taken place on VE day (8 May) when students from TCD had burnt the national flag and the fear that similar disturbances would take place. He refused to meet Dillon's arguments, beyond returning to the breach of peace response. The decision to ban the 1945 march reflected continuing hostility to Britain over partition, concerns about neutrality and a fear that large numbers of Irish citizens might participate in what was an end-of-war celebration by any standard. Fianna Fáil was clearly uncomfortable with the evidence that a large number of Irish men and women had joined the Allied war effort. The government, and nationalist opinion generally, considered participation in the war to be anti-national. Consequently, the 1945 ban reflected the need to exclude Irish citizens from the rather self-satisfied postwar society which continued to pride itself on the moral superiority of its neutrality.[13]

Ireland's isolationism was also reflected in the widespread anti-Semitism apparent during this period. Speaking in the Dáil in July 1943, Oliver J. Flanagan demanded to know why the government's emergency powers were not used against Jews, rather than against the IRA. He complained that Jews 'crucified our Saviour' and 'are crucifying us every day in the week'. He suggested that the Irish government should follow Germany's example: 'There is one thing that Germany did and that was to root the Jews out of their country. Until we root the Jews out of this country it does not matter a hair's breadth what order you make.' Flanagan's outburst has often been represented as an isolated and unrepresentative voice in wartime Ireland, yet the attitude was more pervasive than this. Flanagan returned to his criticism of Jews on a number of occasions after the war, and there is no evidence that his views were unpopular or unrepresentative.[14] During her visits to Ireland during the war, Elizabeth Bowen found anti-Semitism to be widespread. A memorandum produced by the Department of Justice in September 1945, after the war was over and the full horror of the holocaust known, declared that the government's policy was to 'restrict the immigration of Jews' into Ireland. The grounds for this policy were similar to those of Flanagan, that Jews were wealthy and influential; furthermore, 'As Jews do not become assimilated with the native population, like other immigrants, there is a danger that any big increase in their number might create a social problem.' Widespread Christian anti-Semitism allowed the Department of Justice to reject applications from Jewish refugees to live in Ireland. Catholic refugees from Europe were not faced with the same obstacles as Jews during the postwar period. While it is difficult to measure the extent of anti-Semitism, a survey carried out in the early 1970s reported quite pervasive anti-Semitism in the Dublin area.[15]

Nor were these attitudes restricted to the Department of Justice. Lemass in Industry and Commerce questioned the ethnic background of those proposing to build a new factory in Ireland in October 1945. An official was sent to interview the project's promoter on these matters and he was able to confirm that 'the aliens would not be Jews and that the capital backing would not come from Jewish sources'. In June 1943 one Fianna Fáil member wrote to MacEntee objecting to the candidature for the general election of Robert Briscoe, sitting Fianna Fáil TD in Dublin City South and a Jew, on the grounds that the 'people are thoroughly opposed to Jews'. Following a complaint in October 1944 by Mark Killilea and Patrick Beegan of the Fianna Fáil parliamentary party concerning aliens purchasing land, the Minister for Lands assured his colleagues that relatively few foreigners purchased land in Ireland, and of these only one was a Jew.[16] Perhaps the most serious expression of anti-Semitism can be found in the decision of Mr Justice George Gavan Duffy in the case *Schlegel v. Corcoran & Gross* (1942). When Mr Gross purchased a dental practice from Mr Corcoran, the owner of the property, Mrs Schlegel, refused to transfer the lease to Gross on the grounds that he was a Jew. The High Court had to determine whether this was reasonable. Gavan Duffy considered that this was indeed a reasonable view, given the extent of anti-Semitism in Ireland. He dismissed the contention that Schlegel's objection was 'a caprice or mere prejudice' on the grounds that

> Anti-Semitism ... is notoriously shared by a number of other citizens; and, if prejudice be the right word, the antagonism between Christian and Jew has its roots in nearly 2,000 years of history and is too prevalent as a habit of mind to be dismissed off-hand, in a country where religion matters, as the eccentric extravagance of a bigot.

Gavan Duffy found in favour of Schlegel, doing so in a fashion that reduced Gross to an inferior position before the law. Schlegel was described as 'Irish and a Catholic', while Gross was merely 'a Jew'. Gross was not an 'alien', but in fact was an Irish citizen, a feature which made the finding more serious. It would appear that Gavan Duffy was not prepared to provide the protection of the constitution for an Irish citizen who happened to be Jewish by religion; being Irish and Catholic bestowed superior legal rights on an individual because of his or her religion. Gavan Duffy apparently could not imagine circumstances where someone could be both Irish and Jewish, a view maintained by other nationalisms in Europe at this time. Gavan Duffy was the most nationalist and Catholic of the Irish judiciary, but while he had some influence, this did not translate into a comprehensive Catholic nationalist legal tradition. Nevertheless, his conclusion in this case reflected a sinister aspect of nationalist thinking within the legal environment.[17]

In 1945, Erskine Childers privately complained to Seán MacEntee that anti-Protestant sentiment had noticeably increased; that a recent court case involving a bigamous marriage (the Hunt case, which is discussed briefly below) reflected this; and that he had evidence of discrimination against Protestants in public appointments. He returned to these concerns again in 1948, when he claimed that Robert Barton had hinted that a Protestant could not become a minister in a Fianna Fáil government. As one of the few leading non-Catholics in Fianna Fáil, Childers would be worried about the implications of a more openly denominational culture in Ireland. He was also reflecting a growing concern within the Protestant population about its position in a society which was more vigorously Catholic, which did not share its identity with Britain and whose policies in respect of the Irish language excluded Protestants from some posts.[18] At about the same time as he expressed these private views, Childers issued a public statement denying that Protestants in Ireland 'did not prosper' or 'were not happy', a charge made by J.E. Warnock, the Northern Ireland Minister for Home Affairs. This, Childers retorted,

> was an entirely baseless allegation...The Protestants of the 26 counties lived in an atmosphere of complete tolerance, their share in industrial and commercial activity far exceeding the proportion of their numbers, and in connection with all government and local appointments where examinations were held, there was no religious test whatever.

The public statement clearly contradicts his private views. That he was prepared to conceal his doubts attests to the strength of nationalism and the pressure on Protestants to conform to nationalism's public image.[19]

In a democratic society, without a strong liberal tradition, there will be a tendency for the majority to enforce its world-view in legislative and social terms. Those in the minority, especially if they are relatively small in numbers, do not have the electoral weight to counter this, nor do they have allies within the dominant majority in the absence of liberalism. After 1937, the bias towards Catholicism became more imprinted in the social life of Ireland. Two issues concerning marriage remained unresolved; the first was the exact status of nullity in the Irish courts and the other concerned the legal enforcement of pre-nuptial agreements between Catholic and Protestant spouses. De Valera was committed to prohibiting remarriage after divorce under any circumstances and agreed in 1940 to introduce legislation if the constitution, as enacted, could not do so. However, nullity by the Catholic Church posed a different problem. The Attorney General was not willing to prosecute in the event of remarriage after a church nullity, but could not prevent cases coming before the courts or intervene to deal with property or related matters.[20] Notwithstanding this, two cases of bigamy were heard in Irish courts, one in 1945 and the other in 1946. The best known is the Hunt case, mentioned by Childers and one that received considerable publicity at the time. Hunt had been married in a registry office and when that marriage broke down he entered into another relationship. He was encouraged by the local Catholic clergy to marry in a Catholic church, as the Church did not recognise the validity of the original marriage. In the opinion of the Church Hunt had never been married. However, the Irish constitution prohibited remarriage under any circumstances and in the eyes of the state Hunt had committed bigamy. This proved embarrassing for the government and seemed to confirm a complaint by the *Standard* in 1937 that the constitution would deny individuals a right which the church recognised. An article in the *Irish Ecclesiastical Record* by William Conway, later Archbishop of Armagh and Primate of All Ireland, condemned the courts for finding the individuals guilty of bigamy. According to Conway, the church not the state should 'determine the circumstances in which a marriage shall be valid and binding'. Conway admitted that a change to bring the law into conformity with the Catholic position might produce injustices for non-Catholics, but maintained that Catholics could not be considered married if the ceremony was not in conformity with church teaching, even if both parties had given full consent. The issue of marriage, nullity and bigamy highlights difficulties in the relationship between church and state in Ireland. The view adopted by the state was that there could be no remarriage under the constitutional prohibition. This was not the Church's view, but the constitution did not reflect the subtle difference which the church made between marriages performed in a Catholic church and those performed by the state. The state had to regulate all marriages and this came into conflict with the Catholic view of the issue. Although church and state differed on the matter, the state was not prepared to actively pursue the issue. However, as the Hunt case demonstrated, independent action by individual citizens could force it to act despite its misgivings.[21]

The Tilson case raised other serious issues concerning the regulation of marriage, the impact of the constitution on arrangements made by individuals prior to marriage, and the limits which the constitution placed on the application of English legal precedent.[22] Under the *Ne Temere* decree, the Catholic Church insisted that the non-Catholic party to a marriage performed in a Catholic church should provide an undertaking that all children would be raised as Catholics. This ruling had been in place for a considerable time, but did not have legal power. These were private arrangements between two individuals intending to marry, whereas the legal position inherited from English precedent was that the father had the sole right to determine the education of the children. The *Ne Temere* decree had caused controversy earlier in the century, but remained a private undertaking until the Tilson case. Though private in form, it was the Catholic Church which imposed the conditions. If a Catholic wished to marry a non-Catholic in a Catholic church, then the conditions had to be met. It might be argued that there is an element of coercion surrounding what is a delicate matter at the best of times. A couple intending to marry may believe that no difficulties will impede their lives and that such a promise can be easily met. However, life is never that simple. Moreover, the Catholic Church in Ireland was not just an important institutional force; it also had a strong emotional hold over its members. The choice for non-Catholics was either to agree to the conditions or not to marry a Catholic; for Catholics it was to marry in a non-Catholic ceremony or persuade the other party to accept the conditions or not marry a non-Catholic.

In the Tilson case the Catholic party was sixteen years of age and pregnant when the non-Catholic party, Ernest Tilson, signed the promise to bring up the children as Catholics. The coercive nature in this case was greater than in others due to the pregnancy, yet Tilson did agree to sign and four children were subsequently born to the couple. In 1950, Tilson removed three of the children from the family home and placed them in a non-Catholic institution, with the intention of raising them in the Church of Ireland. In the High Court, Mr Justice Gavan Duffy found in favour of the wife, referring explicitly to Articles 41, 42 and 44 of the constitution to sustain his conclusion. Gavan Duffy rejected English precedent which gave primacy to the father on the grounds that this deprived the wife of all rights in relation to the children's education. In effect, Gavan Duffy overturned the legal precedent and concluded that husband and wife had equal rights in the matter, thus enforcing the pre-marriage agreement. The outcome of this was that no one party to a marriage could arbitrarily violate the rights of the other.

The case then went to the Supreme Court, which again found in favour of the Catholic party. In an earlier judgment the Supreme Court had made the important observation that existing precedent could not have priority over the 1937 constitution.[23] The Tilson judgment built on this, though it was more narrowly framed than Gavan Duffy's decision. The Supreme Court concluded that the existing precedent of paternal supremacy was inconsistent with the rights of parents contained in Article 42.1 of the constitution. The court extended the right of the wife in a marriage to that of equality with the husband, invoking what could be seen as a mutual veto. As a consequence, the validity of pre-marriage agreements was upheld. The decision was important legally because it recognised the equality of both parties to a marriage. In this it reflected the republican and democratic nature of the constitution, but it was also controversial because it provided the force of law to an arrangement that had hitherto been a private one. It also changed the balance of power within marriage, providing Catholics with legal justification to enforce their position in court. Moreover, it reinforced and extended the position of the Catholic Church as arbiters in inter-denominational relationships, giving it a power of veto over such marriages.[24]

Whether the Supreme Court majority intended these and other consequences, it is impossible to judge. But it is important to emphasise that the decision was based on Article 42 of the constitution, which dealt with the rights of parents, and not Article 44, which was concerned with the special position of the Catholic Church. While certainly welcomed by the church, the decision itself was based on considerations other than those contained in Article 44. In the High Court, Gavan Duffy had based his decision on both the rights of parents and the Catholic nature of the constitution, but the Supreme Court majority provided a more limited conclusion based on equality between parents.[25] In his careful assessment of the decision, Hogan notes that writers on church and state have often misrepresented the judgment. Notwithstanding this, the narrow legal decision has to be placed in a wider context. The decision had an immediate impact on the non-Catholic minority in the Republic, placing it further on the defensive in its social relations with Catholics. By providing a legal sanction for pre-marriage agreements, it guaranteed that any non-Catholic who married a Catholic had to abandon any possibility of his or her children being brought up in or appreciating his or her religion. One consequence was a growing religious apartheid, where members of the different denominations inhabited parallel but different social spheres.[26] As Ireland was a highly stable society, the social consequence of the Tilson decision was to polarise further the Catholic–non-Catholic nature of Ireland and to erode the non-Catholic presence in the state. The most striking confirmation of this can be found in the population statistics. Whereas the Catholic population fell by 3.62 per cent between 1936 and 1961, all other denominations or none fell by 25 per cent.[27]

If Irish society became more insensitive to religious minorities during the 1940s and 1950s, it frequently neglected more vulnerable sections of the population. One intervention by the Department of Local Government and Public Health led to a diplomatic incident. The Sacred Heart convent at Bessboro in the Cork suburbs was one of a number of homes established to provide a refuge for women who were pregnant but unmarried. In common with other homes, it was operated by a religious order, but funded by the state. Towards the end of the war a new nursery was built at a cost of £10,000, but this did not improve conditions for babies born there. According to James Deeny, the department's Chief Medical Adviser, infant mortality had been extremely high in Cork for some years. The number of deaths in Bessboro was extraordinarily high; in one year alone there had been 180 births, but over 100 of these newborn babies had died. Deeny then made an unannounced visit to the home and examined the nursery in detail. At first he could not detect anything wrong, but after personally examining the babies he found that all were suffering from a 'purulent infection' (discharging pus) of the skin and all had diarrhoea. While recognising that he had no legal authority to act in the case, Deeny believed that the infections had been consistently covered up and that there had, at the very least, been serious neglect. He closed down the unit and removed both the matron and the medical officer from their posts.[28]

At this point the Bishop of Cork, Daniel Cohalan, intervened by registering a formal protest through the Papal Nuncio, Paschal Robinson, with the government. He complained of 'illegitimate interference' by the Department of Local Government and Public Health in the 'religious government' of the convent. Although no medical investigation, aside from Deeny's, had taken place, the bishop assured Robinson that the 'matter is now in hand'. Cohalan complained that he had not been consulted about Deeny's visit, while insisting that 'one could not conclude from that one experience that neglect was the cause of the high mortality'. The Department of Local Government and Public Health took the view that the matron (Reverend Mother Martina) should be removed from her post. However, Bishop Cohalan replied that 'the removal or continuation of a religious superior in this office was not a matter for the civil authorities'. He also objected that the inspection took place on a holy day of obligation when the nuns were in church. Deeny claimed that the department did not wish to interfere with the religious or ecclesiastical sphere of the convent, but still required that the matron be removed from her responsibilities in respect of the children's home. The bishop insisted that no distinction could be made between the two posts held by the individual, as 'Reverend Mother Martina and Reverend Mother Superior are the same thing'. Accordingly, 'there could be no case in Canon Law for the removal of such a person from office'.

Deeny successfully defended the right of the authorities to act in this case, maintaining that the nun should be removed. This did not occur until a high-level exchange between the Department of External Affairs, the Taoiseach and the Papal Nuncio had taken place. The Department of External Affairs was subsequently informed that Bishop Cohalan had agreed to transfer the matron after a further review. The Papal Nuncio reported that the bishop was now 'deeply shocked', agreeing that he was 'satisfied from the beginning that S. Martina was gravely at fault and he had no difficulty in accepting the Government's view that she should be moved'. Robinson advised the government that in future the authorities should inform the local bishop of any such action and secure his consent before acting against a religious order.[29] Deeny's actions were those of an individual who had the imagination and foresight to act when his medical investigations discovered a glaring discrepancy in the data available to him. His action in confronting church authorities who did not wish to be answerable to the state was unique at this time. For those women unfortunate enough to become pregnant and not get married, their fate was to be denied existence in respectable society. In 1939 some 1,781illegitimate births were registered in the state, accounting for 3.18 per cent of all births; by 1945 this had grown to over 4 per cent, the highest recorded figure between 1864 and 1977. Although not high by international standards, the trend during the war was upward, especially as the possibility of travelling to Britain to have a baby was excluded by wartime restrictions. There is also evidence that infanticide and backstreet abortions increased. It was also reported in 1954 that the infant mortality rate for 'illegitimate' children in Ireland was considerably higher than that for 'legitimate' children in Ireland or that for 'illegitimate' children in Britain.[30]

The Irish Catholic moral community's concern to control sexuality was not limited to Ireland. It was alleged in the British media that a significant number of Irish women arrived pregnant, though this was denied by Irish sources. The Catholic Church was concerned that babies born to Irish women in Britain were 'lost to the faith', as they were normally given up to non-Catholic adoption agencies. In 1953 an emissary of the Bishop of Cork, Cornelius Lucey, approached the Department of External Affairs seeking co-operation to repatriate such children on the grounds that 'It is entirely in the interest of the children's religion that they should be brought back here.' While there were assurances that 'their temporal needs would also be attended to', the main priority in Irish Catholic circles was the faith of these babies. The government was unwilling to act in matters that occurred outside the state. But in a cruel irony, it also denied these babies Irish citizenship on the grounds that, as citizenship was determined by the father not the mother, and there was no way of knowing who the father was, they did not qualify. Thus a pregnant woman forced out of Ireland because of the moral climate had Irish citizenship denied to her baby.[31] Part of the problem was that Ireland did not have an adoption law until 1952, in large part because the Catholic Church was not satisfied by any of the proposals put forward. It was only when American publicity uncovered the trafficking of Irish babies to the United States that the government acted. It only did so in close co-operation with the Catholic Church, and Archbishop McQuaid and his representatives were involved in every stage of the bill. Milotte concluded that the Irish state abdicated its responsibilities for the welfare of these children and their mothers during this process, though Whyte suggested that the objections to legal adoption were 'intelligible and not unreasonable'. Given the new evidence which has emerged about the Adoption Bill, this is a view which can only be sustained if one accepts that the position adopted by McQuaid and the hierarchy was the only one available. The eventual Adoption Act reflected Catholic thinking on the matter in virtually every clause.[32]

This moral community had two components, nationalism and religion, yet it was not obvious how these would impact on the political system. In his pioneering study of church–state relations in Ireland, John Whyte claimed that two distinct philosophies of government were in competition by the mid 1940s, vocationalism and bureaucratic centralism. The former emphasised the need to diffuse power among interest groups, to decentralise and to weaken the power of the existing state structures. Its most significant success was the publication of the report of the Commission on Vocational Organisation in 1944. Archbishop McQuaid, for example, not only favoured the Pétain government in France, but believed that its decentralisation of power from the state to the regions should be introduced in Ireland.[33] In contrast, the bureaucratic alternative involved greater centralisation by government and the civil service, resting on a strong belief in ministerial responsibility. According to Whyte, the 'intellectual shortcomings' of the bureaucrats may actually have been worse than those of the vocationalists. Whyte concluded that the civil service was behind Fianna Fáil's rejection of the report of the Commission on the Vocational Organisation in 1945, citing the evidence of the Secretary of the Department of Finance, J.J. McElligott, to the commission to sustain this view.[34] The juxtaposition of vocationalism and bureaucracy is misconceived, while Whyte's view on the influence of the civil service and the nature of bureaucracy is flawed. It is true, as Whyte suggested, that there was a conflict in

Ireland by 1945 between competing conceptions of government, but bureaucracy was not the main opponent of vocationalism. What Fianna Fáil ministers and a number of civil servants were defending after 1945 was representative government and democracy, not centralisation or bureaucracy as such.[35]

Seán Lemass, frequently the focus of criticism by vocationalists, recognised that totalitarian societies were often successful because of the absence of representative institutions, but democracies had to meet the challenge: 'If democracy is to work, however, particularly in time of war, it can do so only by getting through voluntary co-operation with the central authority the same effective combination of all efforts to the same objective that in the totalitarian states is secured by regulation and control.'[36] Although the Commission on Vocational Organisation presented its findings as a deepening and extension of democracy, in reality the consequences of implementing its recommendations would have dismantled parliamentary democracy. While some criticism of the report dealt with institutional questions, the main reason for rejection was political. Industry and Commerce believed that the state was the most appropriate vehicle for defending consumer interests, while Agriculture asked, if the report was implemented, 'what would remain to be done by the Government and by Government departments?' This could lead to the abolition of the Dáil and parliamentary democracy, it was claimed. Finance used the opportunity to put a nail in the coffin of a nuisance (and a vocal critic of the department), but made the case in terms of defending liberal democracy. The implementation of the report would 'completely undermine in the long run political democracy as practised in this state where the unit is the individual voter and the underlying philosophy is that the aggregate of these units will regard the nation as a whole as their concern, even though, in giving expression to their views they may range themselves with different political parties'. Finance agreed with the other departments that the existing system was most appropriate for Ireland's political needs, one where weaker groups could offset strong ones through the actions of political parties and the state, a view echoing the classical contribution to political theory by James Madison in *The Federalist Papers*.[37] It was unlikely that the commission could have been anything other than hostile to modern government, to liberal democracy or to the existing state system. It drew on Catholic social thought, on a rather narrow conception of nationalism and on a traditional rural identity to give expression to a view of the world which was just then being defeated in Europe. Although not fascist, vocationalism drew on ideas which fascism shared with the Catholic Church and with the authoritarian Catholic right. Corporatists, authoritarian nationalists and fascists had frequently co-operated during the interwar and Second World War period. For over a decade after 1945, advocates of the report surfaced in various guises, the most significant being the Maria Duce movement but evident also in Fine Gael, National Labour, Clann na Talmhan and Clann na Poblachta. Although weakened by Hitler's defeat and the democratisation of Catholicism in Western Europe, vocationalism's appeal to rural ideals and its antimodernist sentiment continued to be influential in Irish political life into the 1960s, though it attenuated over that period.[38]

Fianna Fáil insisted that the Dáil, parliamentary politics and perhaps democracy itself would be undermined by the introduction of vocationalism into Irish public life.[39] Bishop Michael Browne of Galway, who chaired the commission, invoked Catholic social teaching and Pope Pius XI in defence of vocationalism, as did other clerics. One of the leading advocates of vocationalism was Dr Cornelius Lucey, later Bishop of Cork, who explicitly placed the moral law in a superior position to formal democracy. This view remained central to Catholic conceptions of politics then and thereafter. Lucey endorsed the Portuguese state on the grounds that it was 'translating our Catholic social principles into practice along authoritarian lines'. For Lucey, the Portuguese dictator, António de Oliviera Salazar, remained an exemplary leader, authoritarian but not totalitarian: 'What is original about Salazar is that he was not content with writing Christian principles into a Constitution, but took steps he thought necessary to make them effective in the everyday life of the people as well.' Lucey's remarks on Salazar were probably a veiled criticism of de Valera, who might be accused by some Catholic critics of introducing a Christian constitution but not making determined efforts to give effect to its principles in everyday life.[40] Fianna Fáil's decision to oppose vocationalism after 1944 was based on a strong commitment to democratic republican principles, whereas a vocationalist political coalition including Fine Gael, Clann na Talmhan, the National Labour Party and Clann na Poblachta would have endangered the democratic foundations of the state. In what was possibly the most acute assessment of vocationalism at the time, James Hogan, though sympathetic to the Catholic concept of subsidiarity, admitted that a vocational system was 'in fact incompatible with political democracy'. In 1938 Hogan had condemned many aspects of liberal democracy, while recommending corporatism based on Catholic principles as an ideal form of government. By 1945 he was enthusiastically endorsing liberal democracy and dismissing vocationalism as a marginal element in politics. Indeed, Hogan's comments on vocationalism in 1945 are not very different from those made by Fianna Fáil ministers or civil servants at the time. Hogan had been radicalised by the deep divisions in interwar Europe, but had come to recognise by the end of the war that parliamentary democracy was more valuable than he had considered it in 1938.[41] If we return to the infant deaths in Bessboro, centralisation in this case prevented the continuation of serious neglect on the part of the matron and staff at the home. The Bishop of Cork clearly had a vocational system in mind when he insisted that the government should not interfere. If a vocational system had been in place in 1945, Deeny's limited powers would have been non-existent. The alternative to liberal democracy would have involved granting considerable resources to non-elected bodies, with no means to ensure compliance with basic criteria for operation.

More seriously, the campaign to eradicate TB initiated by Fianna Fáil and expanded by Noël Browne would not have been successful if implementation had remained in the hands of the local government authorities. Centralisation in this case provided the means and the finance to achieve a virtual eradication of the disease. In the area of health care there were vested interests whose primary concern was the control of institutions (the church) or the maintenance of their income (much of the medical profession). Their primary interest was not in the health of the community, though both the Catholic Church and the Irish Medical Association (IMA) used this to obstruct change. Both were markedly self-serving during the Mother and Child controversy, reflecting narrow interests, not those of the general public or the national interest. The Catholic Church applied a theological assessment to health policy, not unlike the ideological demands made in Stalin's Russia. Such a stance could undermine a policy which was for the benefit of the majority for non-medical reasons. The defeat of the Mother and Child proposals can in part be attributed to the weakness of the Inter-Party government, Noël Browne's inflexible nature and the opposition of the IMA. But it was fundamentally a victory for the vocationalist forces within Ireland, who opposed it on the grounds that it would further centralise medical provision. The nature of the hierarchy's opposition to the Mother and Child scheme can be seen in Archbishop McQuaid's critique of the proposals:

> The right to provide for the health of children belongs to parents, not to the State. The State has the right to intervene only in a subsidiary capacity, to supplement, not to supplant. It may help indigent or neglected parents; it may not deprive 90 per cent of their rights for 10 per cent necessitous or neglected parents.[42]

It is probable that the Irish state's reluctance to introduce legislation on adoption was a consequence of its inability to satisfy the church's demands. Furthermore, where decentralisation did exist, such as in education, hospitals and children's homes, there is now evidence of widespread physical and sexual abuse in some of these sectors. But there was also an absence of accountability on the part of those in authority, thus providing the environment for violence and abuse. Most of these self-regulating institutions wanted the state to provide finance, but to maintain its distance from the institutions themselves. The demand for decentralisation during the 1940s and 1950s reflected the concern of powerful institutions to maintain their control over resources and people. The most successful of these was the Catholic Church, but it was not the only one.

Fianna Fáil's defence of democracy and political institutions may have been self-serving, but it was also due to a genuine commitment to parliamentary democracy as the best method available for representation. Part of the difficulty with Whyte's analysis is that there is little understanding of the notion of power and especially how that power is distributed in a fairly stable democratic environment. Within the equilibrium established, the various interests continued to exercise power and extend their influence. Even in a homogeneous society, there will be points of difference between interests, though operating within a consensual framework. For example, Irish industrialists sought to employ their monopoly position within the Irish economy to achieve further protection from the government, effectively removing all external competition.

The state, in this case represented by Industry and Commerce, for the most part resisted these attempts.[43] Similarly, Gaelic revivalist interests increased pressure for further resources (financial and institutional) to accelerate the movement to an Irish-speaking Ireland. This consensus is also reflected in anti-partitionism. Indeed, by the end of the 1940s it is almost impossible to discover any liberal or pluralistic sentiment on the question of Northern Ireland. De Valera's position, as reflected in the constitution, becomes the only view within the political culture. This was demonstrated in the Dáil when the decision was made to declare a republic, in the hostility to the Ireland Act 1949, and by the unanimous support given to the all-party anti-partition campaign. Some individuals questioned the necessity to declare a republic in 1949 on the grounds that leaving the Commonwealth would not aid reconciliation with Northern Ireland, but such views were isolated.[44]

It would be remarkable, in these circumstances, if the Catholic Church did not also seek to extend its position and reinforce its control over those areas of public and private life it considered to come within its remit. At the margins of political activity there was a concerted campaign by lay Catholic activists to amend Article 44 of the constitution, which recognised the 'special position' of the Catholic Church but also recognised other churches. For some Catholics, such a compromise was unacceptable, and the campaign's objective was to amend the constitution to recognise the Catholic Church as the 'one true church'.[45] This was not a major issue, however, and its potential force was weakened by the failure of the hierarchy to actively promote it. Notwithstanding this, there were other areas of possible difficulty between church and state. The maintenance of a denominational educational system was one area where church and state regularly interacted. An internal report prepared for Tom Derrig, the Minister for Education, in 1947 put the case quite bluntly:

> The educational process is essentially religious and must be treated as such in accordance with the wishes of parents and the teaching of the church to which they belong. It is taken for granted, therefore, that the place of religion in the whole life of the school will be re-organised, and that the education of the child will be one simple process embracing the religious and moral as well as his [*sic*] intellectual, physical and social training.[46]

It may have been important for the Department of Education to insist on this, as very powerful forces were carefully watching its actions. Dr Cornelius Lucey rejected the view that the Irish educational system was 'in the strict sense Catholic at all', insisting that in a legal sense it was an 'undenominational state system'. He further charged that 'the only rights conceded to the Church are the rights to make suggestions, lodge protests and select text-books where alternative text-books are given'. What was required, he believed, was 'a system giving us both the legal form and the reality of Catholic education'.[47]

Martin Brennan, Professor of Education at Maynooth College, criticised the vocational education system in February 1941. His basic challenge was that this was a secular system, which was unacceptable in a Catholic society, while complaining that the presence of boys and girls in the same classroom 'is a form of naturalism that is not tolerated even in Nazi Germany'. While Frank McNamara, the General Secretary of the Vocational Education Officers' Organisation, responded vigorously to this attack, his reply was defensive and sought to assure the clerical critics that their fears were not justified.[48] At the time this discussion took place, the future of the vocational education sector was in some doubt. De Valera, who was then acting Minister for Education, openly questioned the value of the sector in the Dáil in 1940. His public preference was for the system to be absorbed by the primary schools, but in private he offered the entire sector to a religious order to remove it from state control.[49] Shortly after this, the Department of Education issued a memorandum for the direction of vocational educational committees and teaching staff, known as V.40. It openly sought to meet clerical criticism of the system by insisting that 'Continuing education must be in keeping with Irish tradition and should reflect in the schools the loyalty to our Divine Lord which is expressed in the Prologue and Articles of the Constitution.' V.40 provided a strong endorsement for the inclusion of religion in the vocational curriculum. The local clergy attached to the schools received the same status as the teaching staff. This was not simply an acknowledgment that a priest should instruct members of his religion; the memorandum also stated: 'It is necessary not only that religious instruction be given at certain times, but also that the teaching of every other subject be permeated with Christian charity, and that the whole organisation of the school, whether in work or recreation, be regulated by the same spirit.' J.P. Hackett, who was head of the technical and instruction branch of the Department of Education and who chaired the internal committee to deal with the issue, wrote V.40. It is probable that this was directly prompted by de Valera to avoid further clerical criticism, as Hackett wrote it after extensive discussions with Derrig. James MacDwyer, a colleague of Hackett at the time, confirmed that the reason for producing V.40 was to deflect criticism by the church. If the department hoped to avoid further criticism, it was not successful, and the Commission on Vocational Organisation rebuked the sector in no uncertain terms in 1944.[50]

As part of the same response, the Department of Education produced an information film on vocational education, which emphasised the Catholic, rural and wholesome aspects of the sector. MacDwyer scripted this film under the direction of Hackett, the main intention of which was to show that the sector did not differ in any religious or moral sense from the primary sector. The parish priest plays a crucial role in the film, being placed at the centre of the school's activities, and the spiritual dimension is given a superior place in the scheme of things. Of interest in the light of Brennan's criticism is that male and female students do not mix in the film, except during the religious instruction class, when they are in separate rows of seats.[51] These actions do appear to have deflected de Valera's proposals, though criticism did not disappear. However, the cost was quite considerable. Any hope that vocational education could become an element in the expansion of technical instruction was neutralised by the continuing suspicion of the church authorities, the defensiveness of the Department of Education and the failure of the government to consider the sector a policy priority. In addition, the sector itself became more demoralised and was short of resources, especially at a time when in Europe technical education was being favoured. Postwar education policy has been described by Ó Buachalla as offering 'a static vision of Irish society', and nowhere is this more evident than in the failure to recognise the potential worth of vocational education. During the Marshall Plan, American officials criticised the absence of technical skills in Ireland, but the Department of Education often resisted recommendations from them.[52]

A little later, Hackett admitted that the attempt to reconcile the secular with the sacred had not been realised. This was because of the anomalous situation in the education system:

> They have their roots in the conflicting educational aims of the past, in the attempts at compromise, and in particular in the struggles of Catholics to maintain their own system of education in the face of determined efforts to establish two other systems. The objection to Vocational Education Committees is that they tend to perpetuate the second of these systems — that they are in fact essentially Undenominational Education Committees. Memorandum V.40 was an effort to effect a reconciliation by the denominationalisation of continuing education. I am now satisfied that no reconciliation is possible and that there is no real future for continuation under Vocational Committees as at present constituted, notwithstanding the success of their day courses and the value of the work which has been done to date.[53]

Nor did the change in government in 1948 affect this policy environment; Mulcahy simply embraced the preconceptions of the Department of Education on these issues. While drifting through the 1950s the expansion of the sector was inhibited by the refusal of the church to accept any institutional competition with the secondary school system and by limited state resources.[54]

The experience of vocational education may affect Whyte's discussion of church and state. At a formal level nothing actually happened, but below the institutional surface there was a subtle but important shift. The Department of Education was under pressure (certainly from the clergy, but also from de Valera) to eradicate any aspect of vocational education which might be construed as secular, non-denominational or in competition with schools controlled by the Catholic Church. The way power is being exercised here is more subtle and circuitous than that proposed by traditional pluralist models or advanced by Marxists. The relationship between church and state in Ireland has some similarities with that between business and government in the United States. In policy making, the default position (the policy that would automatically be adopted, all else being equal) will be that of the business community, even if these interests have not been directly consulted. Public officials and public opinion will often, though not always, accept the privileged position held by business and act accordingly.[55]

The analogy between business in a market society and a church in a democracy can be taken too far. However, there are similarities. In the Irish case, policy makers were extraordinarily sensitive to the needs of the church. In some cases, anxiety expressed on the part of the hierarchy led to action by the authorities; in others no prompting was required because the public culture shared many of the concerns expressed by the church. Whyte identified some sixteen measures where he had evidence that the hierarchy or individual bishops 'were consulted or made representations'.[56] With the opening of government archives, a more comprehensive calculation of consultation and representation can be made. This, however, remains inadequate, because by using this method it is difficult to measure influence when it is not expressed through consultation or representation. In the case of V.40 and the production of the film on vocational education, these cannot be causally connected to consultation or representation. It is possible to infer, though, that the behaviour of public officials in this matter was a consequence of their awareness of the unease of clerical opinion in respect of the sector.[57] Nor is this an isolated case, because indirect and direct influence is exercised by the Catholic Church on various issues throughout the history of the Irish state. Whyte did recognise that his list probably understated the actual influence exercised, providing additional cases where consultation was in all likelihood probable.[58] This can be taken a step further. While the influence exercised by the church in Ireland may be similar to that of business in the United States, their status is not comparable. During this period (1940s and 1950s) the Catholic Church in Ireland encountered little public opposition. Indeed, what is noticeable is the virtual absence of public criticism of the church and the public expression of views hostile to the church, even at the time of the Mother and Child controversy in 1951–2.[59]

It may be that the media were hesitant to publish hostile views on church issues, but if so this confirms the indirect influence exercised. The position of the Irish church was unusual in that it received overwhelming loyalty from the majority of its adherents. Most public officials were infused with the core religious, moral and ethical values associated with Catholicism, and though this did not necessarily make them zealots, it certainly legitimised what can be described as the default position, which was instinctively that of the church. This was particularly true in matters related to education and health, but extended beyond this. The consent to Catholic influence was spontaneous since Irish nationalist political culture, both elite and mass, had for over a century internalised Catholicism as one of the key values in its world-view. This provided the church with a privileged position within the state, but this privilege was unlike that which the Catholic Church received in Italy, Spain and Portugal, where it was based on coercion. The privilege accorded to the Irish church by the state was not based on coercion, but on the willing acceptance of that position by the majority of Irish nationalists. This is what, in different circumstances, Antonio Gramsci described as 'hegemonic' power, though his usage attempted to explain why the majority of the oppressed accepted their subordinate position willingly. In the Irish case, this acceptance was not due to 'false consciousness', but was a product of the majority's loyalty to the church.

The Catholic Church's position in Ireland was hegemonic precisely because coercion was not required and because the church's power and influence was not resisted.[60]

This type of power and influence is not easy to measure, as in many cases no direct influence is exercised. What occurs is that certain policies simply rule themselves out, before they are even considered. Thus, the prospect of increasing the limited state sector in education never arose as a realistic policy, even when other related issues were being seriously reviewed.[61] What reinforced this was the loyalty of Irish Catholics to the church and its teaching. During the Mother and Child controversy, individual politicians defended Noël Browne (including Oliver J. Flanagan), but not a single one, including Browne himself, denied the church's right to pass judgment on the legislation. The Taoiseach, John A. Costello, condemned Browne for discussing publicly matters which should have been kept private: 'All these matters should have been, and ought to have been, dealt with calmly, in quiet and in council, without the public becoming aware of the matter. The public never ought to have become aware of the matter.'[62] Nor was this an isolated outburst during a government crisis. Costello frequently confused his personal piety with his role as Taoiseach, blurring the institutional and political line between church and state.[63] Most other contributors to the Dáil debate on Browne's resignation as Minister for Health reinforce the view that the political elite was loyal to the church and, in public at least, to its teaching.

The attitude of the elite rested on the strong devotional culture in the community at large. Attendance at mass, probably the highest in the world, was one reflection of popular participation in the church's rituals. In rural Ireland the integration of church and community was total, whereas in urban Ireland it was somewhat less so but everywhere the pressure to attend mass was socially intense.[64] A Catholic weekly such as the *Standard* could sell upwards of 50,000 copies per issue, and at times of controversy perhaps many more. The Catholic press extended from the intellectually sophisticated, such as *Studies*, to didactic devotional tracts and children's magazines.[65] It is not the purpose here to assess the overall quality of these publications, but it should be emphasised that the contributions to some of them were of a high standard, with many of the features written by academics and intellectuals. That most worked within a Catholic intellectual framework does not (and should not) take away from the intellectual quality of their contribution. In terms of social organisation also, the influence of the church was immense. Muintir na Tíre had been established in 1931 as a rural social organisation by Father John Hayes, an admirer of Mussolini, and by 1949 about 200 parishes were sending representatives to its rural weeks.[66] Muintir na Tíre was one of the organisations involved in establishing the National Farmers' Association during the mid 1950s.

Nor was this influence restricted to rural Ireland. The President of University College Cork, Alfred O'Rahilly, organised adult education programmes for trade union officials. The stated purpose was to provide trade unionists with the skills required for their duties, and to do so in a Catholic environment. Likewise, the Jesuits established the Catholic Workers' College in Dublin to fulfil a similar function. In 1954, the Workers' Union of Ireland, once led by James Larkin who for a time had been a member of the Communist International, had its headquarters dedicated to the Blessed Virgin Mary. Similarly, the rules of the Marine Port and General Workers' Union included a section emphasising the importance of papal encyclicals on social issues for the union. Brendan Corish, later to be leader of the Labour Party, asserted in 1953: 'I am an Irishman second; I am a Catholic first … If the Hierarchy gives me any direction with regard to Catholic social teaching or Catholic moral teaching, I accept without question in all respects the teaching of the Hierarchy and the Church to which I belong.'[67]

Anti-communism was popular and widespread, reinforced by the persecution of Catholicism in Eastern Europe after 1945. A demonstration in support of the imprisoned Hungarian Primate, Cardinal Josef Mindszenty, on 1 May 1949 could draw up to 150,000 people, while £20,000 was collected at church-gate collections for the Italian Christian Democrats prior to the 1948 elections.[68]

There is no question that Catholicism was popular or that the people's faith was genuine, but it could also give rise to intolerance. The writer Hubert Butler suffered ostracism in his native Kilkenny when it was claimed that he had 'insulted' the Papal Nuncio, Gerald Patrick O'Hara, at a public meeting in October 1952. Likewise a little later in the decade very little tolerance was extended to the Protestant population of Fethard-on-Sea in County Wexford, when a Protestant woman and her children left her Catholic husband because of disagreements over their religious upbringing. The subsequent boycott of the Protestant population was actively promoted by the local clergy and enthusiastically supported by some sections of the Catholic community. De Valera never actively condemned the boycott, reserving his harshest criticism for the woman at the centre of the controversy and urging her to return to her husband.[69] An American priest visiting Ireland in the early 1960s noted the pervasive influence of the Catholic clergy on public life.[70] As a result, there was little conflict between church and state before the 1970s, but when differences did emerge between lay and clerical interests it sometimes proved difficult to mediate between them. The church was not used to its authority being challenged by lay people, while the laity were frequently unable to deal with that authority, as can be seen in the Mother and Child controversy. There was a major confrontation in Ballina, County Mayo, in 1956 when the lay principal of the primary school retired and the Bishop of Killala, Patrick O'Boyle, decided to introduce a religious order, replace the lay staff and appoint a clerical principal. The Irish National Teachers' Organisation (INTO) opposed the change, pointing out that a Catholic lay teacher had traditionally been appointed to this post. The controversy lasted until 1962, during which time the bishop refused to accept a compromise brokered by Archbishop McQuaid. This in turn led to a strike by the INTO in 1962, which prompted the Minister for Education, Patrick Hillery, to intervene and devise an acceptable solution. Though the outcome was a compromise, Bishop O'Boyle was eventually forced to make concessions to the teachers, and similar actions were not publicly entertained by other bishops.[71]

The nature of the Catholic Church's power in Ireland has been the focus of considerable discussion since the 1950s, especially following the Mother and Child controversy. In response to the revelations published by Noël Browne, the *Irish Times* complained that 'the Roman Catholic church would seem to be the effective Government of this country'. This was also a viewpoint elaborated in considerable detail by an American liberal critic of Catholicism, Paul Blanshard, who spent nine months in Ireland researching his book *The Irish and Catholic Power*. The published work was written in such a way as to offend Irish sensibilities, especially as Blanshard compared the Republic unfavourably with Northern Ireland.[72] Seán MacBride was probably reflecting Catholic opinion fairly accurately when he denounced the book as anti-Catholic, adding that he did not think Blanshard was 'a reliable authority'.[73] Blanshard asserted that 'The Irish Republic is a clerical state', but qualified this somewhat by accepting that it was unlike other clerical states such as Portugal and Spain. Most importantly, he recognised that the situation was not simple: 'Its political democracy is genuine, and it grants complete official freedom to opposition political parties and opposition religious groups. In Ireland the Catholic church has no official share in government, which is officially democratic.' His charge was that there was an unofficial church–state alliance, for which he provides considerable evidence. After detailing this evidence, Blanshard drew a number of conclusions. Formal political democracy is not an adequate defence against clerical dictatorship, he claimed, especially when the hierarchy 'controls the organs of public opinion'. Even a partial union of church and state, as in Ireland, creates the conditions for clerical dictatorship. Blanshard also cited the impact of denominational education, 'an unrealistic sexual code', censorship and the impact of the Tilson Supreme Court case on non-Catholics as evidence for the strength of this informal alliance between church and state. Indeed, for Blanshard, a tolerant democratic society can become the victim of a 'tightly organized and well-disciplined sectarian and nationalist pressure group', and such pressure can have a disproportionate effect on the rest of society.[74]

Blanshard's case received some support from an unlikely source a little later. In a Catholic Truth Society pamphlet, Catholic jurist, Donal Barrington suggested that the Irish constitution was generally compatible with Catholic teaching, and where it was not this could be attributed to nationalist concerns about Northern Ireland, not a consequence of liberalism. He openly rejected the medieval view that the Pope had the authority to depose a secular ruler on the grounds that the church had a more acceptable method of expressing its political power in the modern world: 'In a democratic state the citizens can peacefully remove a government which is following a policy which the church considers immoral, so that it is quite possible for the church to make itself felt in the temporal sphere without ever resorting to anything in the nature of force or legal coercion.'[75] As a consequence, an explicitly confessional state was unnecessary in Ireland, because of the relationship between religion and nationalism. The constitution reflected this, leading Barrington to assert that the existing constitutional and institutional arrangements best served the interests of the church.[76] Put more critically, this is very similar to what Blanshard had been saying in his book. The French diplomat Jean Blanchard, in his sympathetic account of the relationship between church and state, asserts that in Ireland 'there are no religious questions *per se*, public life being religious, since the nation is devoutly Christian'. Jeremiah Newman, later to be Bishop of Limerick, added that despite the continuing influence of nationalism and some liberal aspects, the Irish state 'must take account of the official teaching of the Catholic church, irrespective of its proximate origin'. In policy terms, it is clear that this is precisely what happened, as can be seen from the evidence provided in Blanshard's study and from subsequent academic studies such as Whyte's. Despite their differences, there is remarkable agreement between these various writers, though they draw very different inferences from this. What is clear is that conventional notions of church and state or of the secular and the sacred are inappropriate in the Irish context. The conventional view that the sacred and the secular inhabit separate spheres does not reflect the reality of Irish public and private life before the 1970s.[77]

Is the relationship between church and state in Ireland unique, because the society does not distinguish between the sacred and the secular as is normal for liberal societies? It is possible that Blanshard, though accurate in his description, failed to appreciate the closeness of the ties between religion and society. The evidence does not sustain the view that Ireland was a confessional state, but neither was it a normal liberal democratic state. The Mother and Child crisis in 1951 is often presented as a key piece of evidence to sustain the charge that Ireland was a confessional and clerically dominated state. It was a serious dispute because it led to Browne's resignation as a minister and, indirectly, to the collapse of the government and the withdrawal of the legislation. When Fianna Fáil formed the next government, it engaged in extended negotiations with the hierarchy to secure agreement on revised legislation.[78] While Fianna Fáil did not capitulate to the bishops, as the Inter-Party government had done, it quickly met most of their objections. De Valera wrote to Lemass recommending the following approach to the legislation:

> I would suggest that each particular proposal of ours to which objection was made be taken up with the Archbishop [McQuaid], and that he be asked to make a draft with the qualifications which would satisfy him. This draft could then be examined from our point of view, and amended if necessary, until an agreed text was arrived at. That was more or less what happened in regard to the corresponding articles of the Constitution.[79]

In his classic study, Whyte offers a different reading of the crisis: 'The hierarchy's decision in the mother and child episode, then, was one which it cost most ministers nothing to accept. It provides us with no evidence of how the government would have reacted if the hierarchy had produced some ruling with which they strongly disagreed.' More recently, Keogh has dismissed traditional explanations of the crisis, arguing that the hierarchy was in a weak position and would have been defeated in open conflict. He further suggests that the controversy has been 'erroneously' described as a crisis between church and state, whereas it can more accurately be described as an 'internal government crisis'.[80]

Even if the Mother and Child controversy is taken in isolation, the evidence does not sustain the views of Whyte or Keogh. If it is placed within the wider context of the moral community during the 1940s and 1950s, then a pattern is apparent where the Catholic Church extends its already powerful position within Irish society and with the state. Moreover, for a quarter of a century after this controversy, none of the political parties were prepared to confront the hierarchy on education, health or moral issues. As late as 1965 Lemass immediately withdrew tentative suggestions in respect of marriage and divorce once it became clear that Archbishop McQuaid was opposed.[81] On moral, educational and health matters, political parties accepted the church's position unconditionally. In most cases conflict did not emerge because of a wide-ranging consensus about these matters, one shared by the church and secular elites. The absence of conflict does not mean that tensions between church and state did not exist: only that the parties did not confront one another. The Mother and Child controversy confirms this because no one, including Browne, was prepared to challenge the church's authority in matters of faith or morals. Keogh is surely correct to emphasise the role of the medical lobby, yet to conclude from this that the hierarchy was used by the doctors or was in a weak position strategically stretches the evidence too far. The IMA's opposition created difficulties for the legislation, but Browne could have maintained the support of his colleagues in the face of that challenge. The crucial point for the cabinet was the hierarchy's opposition. Once this became clear, Browne was effectively isolated and the legislation withdrawn. James Deeny has argued that Browne was the wrong person to become minister in such a sensitive department and his behaviour undermined the carefully cultivated relationship between the church and the department.[82]

Deeny's evidence and the behaviour of the cabinet during the Mother and Child confrontation illustrate further the pervasive influence of the Catholic Church on the public mind during the 1950s. For virtually every politician, confrontation with the hierarchy was not even considered. Throughout this period, it is the government not the church which appears weak. The nature of the Inter-Party government weakened it in any event, but the response of successive Fianna Fáil governments provides further evidence that the political parties were at a disadvantage when confronted with issues considered of primary importance by the church. The reason it cost the Inter-Party ministers nothing to accept the hierarchy's view in the Mother and Child controversy was that they could not conceive of a situation where they would oppose the church on such matters. The question to be asked is why successive governments framed legislation in such a way that the hierarchy did not have to formally intervene to influence it.[83] This can be explained in part by the position of the Catholic Church in the hearts and minds of the vast majority of Irish people. The influence of the church rested on its moral power in a religious society, though it clearly had institutional power as well. What is remarkable about the

Mother and Child controversy is that it never led to anti-clericalism or to hostility to the church. The church was not weak at this time, but only unused to having its relations with the state discussed in public.

Conventional views on church and state do not adequately address the nature of the relationship in Ireland. Ireland was not a theocratic state by any definition, nor was it priest-ridden if by that is meant that the priest exercised an unwelcome influence over the population. Nor was the institutional relationship between church and state similar to that prevailing in Italy, Spain or Portugal at this time. Nevertheless the church was not simply another interest group similar to a trade union or professional organisation. The Catholic Church had a special position in Ireland and this rested on the identity and loyalty of both the elite and mass of Irish Catholic society. The extent of this identification and loyalty can be measured in a number of ways. Church attendance is one, the low number of marriages in registry offices another, while Blanchard has estimated that less than 1 per cent of people refused extreme unction when dying. We also have a survey of opinion carried out by an American Jesuit, Bruce Biever, during the early 1960s, which provides important evidence to sustain this view. Though the research was confined to Dublin, there were 969 respondents and the author also carried out follow-up interviews. The majority of those interviewed had been politically socialised during the high point of Irish nationalism between 1890 and 1940. The survey was carried out before the changes which occurred during the 1960s could have had any impact. It is safe to conclude that the opinion in the survey broadly reflected the catholic nationalist consensus.[84]

The picture that emerges from the survey is one where the Catholic Church is accorded a status unchallenged by any other group or interest in the society. Its teachings are widely endorsed, as is its right to act and influence a wide range of areas in the state and society. On the question of sexuality the respondents confirm the impression made on Humphries a decade earlier, that the majority endorsed a fairly restrictive notion on the subject. Some 82 per cent rejected the possibility that church teaching on sexuality was out of date, while 83 per cent rejected the proposition that the church took a negative stance on sexual attitudes. Furthermore, some 88 per cent of those questioned rejected the view that a celibate clergy could not give advice on marriage and sexual matters. In both the survey and in individual interviews, sex is often considered dangerous and at times evil. However, those interviewed were more divided on where the fear of sex arose from; 30 per cent believed that it was church teaching, whereas 50 per cent rejected this view. Among those questioned, economic, family and social explanations were favoured to account for the phenomenon. Other factors highlighted were the influence of the mother on a son's decision to marry and the importance of the public house as an alternative to marriage for many men.[85] Table 4.1 reports some of the respondents' views on issues associated with sexuality.[86]

Table 4.1: Church teaching on sex (%)

Proposition	*Agree*	*Neutral*	*Disagree*
Sex is like dynamite; it must be watched carefully.	66.0	11.0	23.0
Sex has one purpose: to beget children.	57.6	15.5	26.9
Sex pleasure is basically good.	19.2	7.5	73.3
Priest can give no help in marriage problems.	23.1	—	76.9
The number of children a good index of devout Catholic marriage.	5.0	14.7	80.3
Church view of total abstinence no answer to the problem of birth control.	11.5	4.5	84.0

Source: Biever, *Religion, Culture and Values*, Table 26, p. 482.

While 57.6 per cent believed that sex was permissible only to have children, some 26.9 per cent rejected this view and doubt was more frequently expressed by younger respondents and by women. At the same time, as can be seen from Table 4.1, a large majority rejected the view that big families are a good index of devoutness. This led Biever to state: 'What the Irish will not concede is that there is any direct causal relationship between this fact and their Roman Catholicism.' Notwithstanding this, opinion as presented here correlates quite strongly with the views of the Irish Catholic Church on these issues, though clearly the respondents' claim that they have not been coerced into holding the views. Not only is contraception condemned by the sample, but Biever reported that 'the Irish by and large consider abstinence the only legitimate manner of curtailing procreation'. However, he also revealed that in interviews many considered that abstinence 'frustrated' God's will, a contradiction he proved unable to reconcile. What is impressive is that behaviour does appear to follow opinion, as can be verified by the low levels of illegitimacy, a low rate of marriage and by the large number of children born to those who do marry.[87]

The self-image presented by the respondents is of a Catholic population self-confident in itself and in its attachment to its religion. Indeed, in some respects, lay opinion was more 'orthodox' than the Pope. Biever found that 88 per cent were convinced that they knew what papal infallibility meant; 39 per cent agreed with the proposition that it entailed that the Pope could not make mistakes (which is not what the doctrine is), 59 per cent had some doubts that this was the case, but only 19 per cent rejected the claim outright. In turn, there is overwhelming support for church teaching on sin and hell, but a rejection of the view that the church overemphasises these features in its teaching.[88] The Ireland revealed in this sample was fairly intolerant. Some 76 per cent agreed with the proposition that non-Catholics do not have truth and should not be allowed to remain in their ignorance, while 55 per cent agreed that the prospect of salvation for non-Catholics was not as good as for Catholics. An interesting distinction was made between the possibility that 'non-Catholics *can be* better persons than Catholics' and the assertion that 'Catholics *in fact* have higher morality than non-Catholics'. Whereas 58 per cent agreed that it was *possible* for non-Catholics to be better persons than Catholics (29 per cent disagreed), 71 per cent endorsed the view that *in actual fact* Catholics had a higher morality. An overwhelming 75 per cent would not marry a non-Catholic, while 92 per cent did not agree that one church was as good as another. On other matters, opinion was more divided. Some 44 per cent rejected the view that the enemies of the church were narrow-minded and selfish. Furthermore, while 44 per cent thought it possible that a non-Catholic could be a true Christian, 48 per cent did not think this was the case.[89]

The data also threw up a number of other interesting findings. When asked whether the 'Church has the right to dictate behaviour in all areas, not just in those of religion and morals', 51 per cent agreed that this was the case, though 43 per cent disagreed. Some 61 per cent of the respondents said that they would do whatever the church told them, 'whether it makes sense or not', though, in qualification of this, only 19 per cent said they would accept communism if told to do so by the church.[90] Not a single respondent agreed with the proposition that they 'put too much stock in church teaching'. From this evidence it is clear that Irish Catholics willingly accepted church authority on faith and morals, fairly generously determined, with few if any reservations. When church authority in these matters overlaps with political and social issues, the situation becomes more complex. The refusal of a large majority to endorse communism, even if the church asked them to do so, introduces further complexity. It indicates that the church is not the only influence at work and that opinion remained capable of critical analysis. The Irish may have been intolerant but they were not thoughtless or ignorant about their beliefs. Their ideas about the world, both secular and sacred, were derived from Catholicism and reinforced by being in a predominantly Catholic environment. This was an illiberal community, but one which most Irish Catholics accepted willingly. Although the survey did not deal directly with political issues, on a number of occasions it did so indirectly, especially when addressing issues of church and state. Table 4.2 sets out what a representative sample of Dublin Catholics thought about the relationship between church and state at the beginning of the 1960s.

The respondents placed the Catholic Church in a special position, unanimously distinguishing its divine nature from man-made institutions. As a consequence, most of those interviewed believed that a clash between the state and the church could not occur, but if one did the church would be given preference. Supplementing this, 52 per cent agreed that Catholicism was the greatest aid to patriotism, 75 per cent believed that those who followed the church's teaching made the best citizens, and 66 per cent agreed that attendance at church 'is a good index of the nation's morality'. Although not expressed strongly here, there is some evidence that tension between Catholicism and nationalism was possible. Respondents were anxious to reject any possible conflict, but also to deny that their religion and nationality were related.[91] The church's role in education was overwhelmingly endorsed, with 84 per cent continuing to favour a church school even if a state school was available. Respondents also rejected the suggestion that the role of the church in the education system was either authoritarian or negative.[92] When asked about church influence in politics, opinion becomes more divided. Only 15 per cent endorsed the view that a Catholic should vote along religious grounds, when better non-Catholic candidates were available. When asked if the 'church must keep politics on a high moral level', 51.9 per cent agreed though 32 per cent disagreed. In addition, individuals interviewed by Biever were sometimes critical of the church on specific issues, though none of them would voice such opposition publicly.[93]

Table 4.2: Irish attitudes to church and state questions (%)

Proposition	*Agree*	*Neutral*	*Disagree*
Church cannot be compared to any other social institution.	100	—	—
State to be preferred to church on hypothesis of conflict.	3.5	10	86.5
Rome control significant.	3.0	5.0	92
Church too much involved in politics.	7.5	10.5	82
Church usurping role of state.	5.0	15	80
Irish church a national church: nation and church inseparable.	27	10	63
Church and state *totally* independent of each other.	4.0	23	73
Church harms itself by political involvement.	28	13	59
Church should be *more involved* in state matters than it is.	29	13.4	57.6

Source: Adapted from Biever, *Religion, Culture and Values,* Table 7, p. 311.

When Biever completed his fieldwork in Dublin, the moral community it described remained intact and dominant. It would be a further decade before organised dissent began to make an impression, by which time circumstances had changed significantly. In 1961, the fixed points of that community — religion, nationalism and its democratic political system — were little changed from what they had been in 1922. What had changed was that the social acceptance of these features had been given powerful recognition institutionally by the constitution. Despite Blanshard's fears, Ireland remained an open and democratic society, though most politicians were unwilling to challenge the authority of the church. The society was clearly permeated by theocratic assumptions, but religion, perhaps even more than nationalism, seemed to give meaning to everyday life. In politics, in education and in medicine as well as in normal social interaction, religion provided an institutional and emotional environment for behaviour. What is surprising is that there was no serious attempt to mobilise this opinion to make Ireland a more Catholic state. A number of factors contributed to this, but the most important was the continuing separation of church and state. The state was never theocratic, notwithstanding the extent of theocracy within the general population. Fianna Fáil in particular sought to exclude theocratic tendencies from the state, not always successfully. Its hostility to the report of the Commission on Vocational Organisation had its basis in this need to maintain distinct spheres. Ironically perhaps, it was Fianna Fáil who eventually and most successfully defended the British state tradition in Ireland.

In the main this was a genuinely harmonious society, one in which religion dominated the public and private life of the citizen. For most, it remained a comfortable property-owning society, but was disturbed at the end of the 1950s by mass emigration and economic crisis.[94] Biever's snapshot provides a fairly accurate picture of a traditional society just before it begins to change. He also identified where change might come from. Although still a very small group, Biever reported that the better educated were more likely to be critical of the church than any other section. This was particularly true of younger university-educated males. Women and those with less than eight years' education, on the other hand, had few, if any, reservations in respect of the church. This cleavage between male and female and in respect of education is not unusual and can be found in other Catholic societies at this time. In the Irish case, however, the proportion of those with twelve or more years of education remained small, though it was rising. The percentage of Dáil deputies with secondary education passed 50 per cent in 1961 for the first time, while those with university or professional qualifications also increased.[95] This is not to claim that education is the only variable involved in explaining change or indeed the rise of anti-clericalism in Ireland. It is to suggest that the expansion of educational opportunities in the 1960s offered an expanded environment to those who wished to challenge and criticise aspects of the traditional political culture in Ireland, of which the church was often seen to be the most important aspect.

Conclusion

The year 1961 was a Patrician year and was widely celebrated by Irish Catholics. This emphasised the continuing importance of religion in the institutional and daily life of the Irish people. But 1961 was also a year of new beginnings in terms of Europe, nationalism and economic policy. Despite this, Ireland's moral community had changed little since 1937. This was particularly the case in respect of religion and the Catholic Church in Ireland. Despite the changing nature of Irish life in the 1960s, the moral community remained largely intact for some considerable time thereafter. The majority of Irish citizens did not question Catholicism or nationalism during the 1960s, though a new critical elite did challenge some of the certainties. In his critical survey of Irish Catholicism, Blanshard underestimated the strength of Irish democracy and the uniqueness of the relationship between Catholicism and democracy in Ireland. Though the church's influence was strong, it was never a dictatorship. Ireland was never a clerical state, nor was it priest-ridden and it most certainly was never theocratic. No church was established and the formal boundaries between church and state, if blurred at times, remained in place.

It is at the popular level that theocracy is most evident. By the 1950s Ireland was in some respects a theocratic society, but the state resisted these tendencies. The 1937 constitution, various court decisions, especially the Tilson case, and the evidence from the Mother and Child controversy provide significant evidence that religion was encroaching on the state. Ireland was becoming a more illiberal society and this could be uncomfortable for those who did not share the values of the moral community. Yet there were limits to this. The strength of Irish Catholicism was its voluntary nature. The church had little coercive power and depended on the loyalty of its members to secure its authority. While its institutional position was strong, the church's success rested on its role within the moral community. However, it should also be acknowledged that the defeat of the Mother and Child scheme weakened the Irish state during the 1950s in this and other policy areas. Indeed, the state never recovered from this defeat, as can be seen by its reluctance to confront the hierarchy subsequently on education policy, divorce or abortion. Despite this, the unique characteristic of the moral community was its consensual nature. Most Irish people accepted the place of the Catholic Church in this community, acknowledging the superiority of the spiritual over the material. In doing so, the moral community echoed de Valera's vision of the good life and reaffirmed its commitment to the core values of Irish life as set out by him.

5

Emigration and the Failure of Rural Ireland, 1945–1961

The importance of rural Ireland

For most of the twentieth century Ireland was a property-owning democracy. Rural values provided an important barrier against the materialism, secularism and permissiveness associated with Britain and the United States. The writer and critic Daniel Corkery highlighted three factors he considered central to Irish identity: 'The three great forces which, working for long in the Irish national being, have made it so different from the English national being, are (1) The religious consciousness of the People; (2) Irish Nationalism; and (3) The Land.' In the 1937 constitution and in his 1943 St Patrick's Day broadcast, de Valera emphasised the importance of rural values for Ireland and its distinctive identity.[1] In European terms, Ireland remained a predominantly rural society after 1945. By that time, however, rural Ireland was no longer secure, though it continued to be the mainstay of the economy and the main source of exports. The harshness of rural life was poignantly portrayed in Patrick Kavanagh's 'The Great Hunger', a poem that touched on the desperation accompanying rural life, but also one that highlighted the attraction of the land and the security associated with living on a family farm. The difficulty for Ireland by 1945 was that the negative features of rural life were enhanced, while the positive ones no longer provided adequate compensation.[2]

Irish agriculture, in common with much of rural Europe, faced serious challenges after 1945. Industry rather than agriculture now provided the main sources of growth and employment, while the traditional family farm often proved to be uncompetitive in an increasingly mechanised age. Rural Europe was often successful in using its political strength to maintain its privileged position, but for the most part the national interest was no longer associated with agriculture.[3] In Ireland, agricultural production had increased during the Second World War, due to British demand, but the expansion was not subsequently maintained. While Ireland was one of only five Western European states that exported more food than it imported, its export surplus remained quite small when compared to Denmark or the Netherlands.[4] Yet Irish agriculture had a major advantage over Denmark or the Netherlands at the end of the war. It maintained its privileged access to and increased its share of the British market. As a consequence, Ireland became more dependent on agriculture for exports, while these exports were concentrated on a single market and a narrow range of products. Irish agriculture was weaker in 1945 than it had been in 1929, due almost entirely to Fianna Fáil's hostility to the cattle economy. This had been the most efficient and commercial sector of the rural economy, yet Fianna Fáil deliberately undermined it for ideological reasons during the 1930s. However, Fianna Fáil's commitment to agricultural self-sufficiency failed and cattle exports resumed after the 1938 Anglo-Irish Agreement. Yet the blow to the cattle economy had been severe, depriving the sector of political support and weakening its capacity to adapt to the postwar environment.[5]

Notwithstanding these problems, in 1950 the agricultural sector still accounted for 75 per cent of all exports. Writing in 1944, de Valera's economic adviser, Timothy Smiddy, argued that agriculture continued to bring significant benefits to Ireland: 'Generally the countries which are largely agricultural but whose industries cater only for the domestic market and which were able to import raw materials at depressed prices but which had normally no industrial exports, such as Ireland, were not adversely affected from the point of view of unemployment.' The logic of this position was that Ireland should remain primarily an agricultural economy, limiting its industrial expansion and restricting its commitment to international trade, almost the opposite of what every other state in Europe did after 1945. He warned: 'As countries become highly developed economically, which they can only do by participating in international trade, they become part of a highly integrated system, and must pay the penalty of any maladjustment in the machinery of that system.'[6] This was a view shared by de Valera, who remained sceptical about the benefits to be derived from the cattle export economy or from international trade. De Valera failed to make the connection between the lack of economic growth, unemployment and emigration, continuing to cling to the illusion that only a small-farming tillage economy could provide income and employment growth and also be the means to reduce emigration.[7]

Differences between Ireland and other European states had been opening up during the interwar period, but at first the gap was not significant. Between 1913 and 1950 Irish growth rates were about the same as those for the United Kingdom but somewhat less than the Western European average. Ireland, however, fell well behind the growth rates for Sweden (which was about three times the Irish average), Norway, Finland (both about twice the Irish average) and Denmark (about 40 per cent above the Irish average). Where Ireland stands out from Europe is in the small size of its industrial sector and in the predominance of agriculture. A high dependence on agriculture in itself was not a disincentive to economic growth. In 1914 most of the states with high per capita incomes were agrarian.[8] However, as economies of scale and technical innovation grew during the century, it became more difficult to sustain labour-intensive agriculture. Increasingly, high productivity in agriculture was closely related to levels of investment and the commercial nature of the sector. In the Netherlands and Denmark the success of agriculture was based on high-quality low-cost production for export, usually to expanding industrial and urban markets. While this process was halted by the Depression, it revived after 1945.[9] Industrialisation became the method by which economies previously dependent on agriculture addressed the problem of how to deal with unemployment and displacement as a consequence of the structural changes in agriculture. The danger for agrarian states was that emigration would reach very high levels unless the surplus rural population could be provided with employment in alternative areas. Norway and Sweden had emigration levels almost as high as Ireland at the beginning of the century, while Finland and Austria were not far behind. The growth of an industrial base accompanied by tertiary employment in an urban/industrial environment reduced emigration levels in most of these states after the First World War, and reduced them significantly further after 1945. By 1950, the Irish emigration rate was about twice what it had been in 1901–10, and much higher than the European average. Ireland moved from a position of being within reach of the norm/mean in Europe to one where it was the exception. Although the tendency for this to occur was there earlier, the most pronounced impact of it took place between 1945 and 1960.[10] It is no part of this argument to suggest that the transition for these states was easy. Indeed the 1950s in Denmark were quite difficult, with unemployment running at about twice the Swedish or Norwegian levels. In Germany, also, unemployment was high during the first half of the decade. Yet each of these states emerged from the transition period stronger economically, more prosperous and more dynamic than Ireland. Nor was post-1945 performance necessarily linked to historical experience.[11]

The failure of agriculture

Ireland seemed ill-equipped to make this transition between 1945 and 1960. The features that characterised most agrarian societies seem even more pronounced in Ireland during the interwar years and were exaggerated after 1945. One contributory reason was political. The strength of farmers' disquiet had been expressed in the electoral success of Clann na Talmhan at the general elections in 1943 and 1944 (when it won fourteen and eleven seats respectively). Although Fianna Fáil was a national party, it received significant support from rural Ireland and remained committed to further land division and rural settlement. At times the party was dependent on this support to form a government and the leadership was particularly sensitive to criticisms from its rural deputies. Rural TDs were highly critical of government policy on a number of issues and Fianna Fáil deputies Mark Killilea and Patrick Beegan, representing Galway East, put down a motion for the parliamentary party on 16 October 1944 in respect of government land policy. This was a policy of considerable concern to Beegan and Killilea, as they were in contention with Clann na Talmhan for votes in their constituency. Galway East was an interesting constituency, where Clann na Talmhan received 29 per cent of the vote in 1943 and 39 per cent in 1944. Clann na Talmhan was the only party other than Fianna Fáil to field candidates in that constituency in 1944, and the incumbent deputies were clearly under pressure on the land issue, which was a focal point of Clann na Talmhan agitation. Fine Gael had been virtually wiped out by Clann na Talmhan, receiving approximately 8 per cent of the vote in 1943 and being unable to field a candidate the following year.[12] The Minister for Lands, Seán Moylan, responded to his colleagues' criticism by arguing that there should be no small or uneconomic holdings: 'We should make people farmers or leave them as labourers.' He then outlined the position of the party on the issue of land as he conceived it: 'The Fianna Fáil party was not merely a political party, it was a national party as well. They had to set their faces against wrong things. In land division uneconomic holders come first.'[13] Policy makers were not clear on how to deal with agriculture. The majority report of the 1938 Banking Commission maintained that agriculture should provide the primary means for economic development, a view that continued to be widely held into the 1950s. The committee on postwar agricultural policy, set up in 1944 and chaired by Smiddy, emphasised the stability of the agricultural sector and the narrow variation in its output (whatever the incentive or disincentive). Smiddy noted that agricultural efficiency would have to be increased, but he reported that the committee was at a loss 'to suggest even the outlines of a policy'. The objective of policy should be 'the social welfare of the community as a whole', while the 'real problem is to devise methods by which farmers may be induced to adopt measures to increase their efficiency'. Neither Smiddy nor other specialists on agriculture considered that there might be a contradiction between welfare and efficiency. Although the agricultural sector employed about half the labour force, it contributed just over a quarter of the national income. In contrast, industry accounted for about 15 per cent of the labour force but contributed over a third to national income. Furthermore, while the agricultural community contributed about 30 per cent to the state's revenue, Smiddy estimated that it received 59 per cent of all public expenditure.[14]

Smiddy hoped that Irish agriculture would become more competitive and efficient during the postwar period. If necessary the government should adopt 'drastic measures' to achieve these ends:

> The methods of the past have failed to increase efficiency even a little. Hence, the necessity for attempting more radical methods. Those which the committee suggests are moderate and the minimum required to increase our output. If this is not achieved there is a real danger of a serious fall in our standard of living and an unbearable increase in the burden of taxation to which we have committed ourselves by our increasing social services especially as otherwise our national income will be substantially lowered. There is no economic or social problem of more importance for the welfare of the community and the maintenance of our standard of living than increased agricultural efficiency.

Agriculture was constrained by the policy imperative of balancing industry and agriculture; consequently neither was dominant, although agriculture did have a residual priority. The danger for Irish agriculture after the war was that it would not be competitive on the British market and other suppliers would displace Irish exports. This would begin a cycle of decline in rural Ireland: 'The effect will in the long run tend to lower our standard of living as compared with that of the UK. If our standard of living is materially lower, workers, both agricultural and non agricultural, will tend to emigrate to the UK, thereby further increasing the flight from the land.' Smiddy's assessment was realistic though not very optimistic. He recommended that tariffs should be used sparingly in the future and reviewed by a tariff commission, as had been the case prior to 1932:

> Increased agricultural efficiency will lower costs of production and increase the farmers' purchasing power which forms approximately 50 per cent of the total population. ... By this and no other means the standard of living can be raised and the size of the 'national-cake' increased. Leaving the cake the same size and giving some sections of the community a larger slice than others will not increase wealth or employment. Such a policy may have the opposite effect.[15]

Despite this succinct analysis and apt warning, the politics of postwar recovery in Ireland did not include a reorganisation of tariff policy or a desire to utilise the competitive advantage in Irish agriculture. While all small dependent agricultural economies experienced problems in the decade after 1945, Ireland is almost unique in its inability to pursue an active export strategy. The comparison with Denmark and the Netherlands is especially relevant here. These states encountered difficulties, but in contrast to Ireland both successfully unblocked the obstacles to growth within their economies by maximising exports and adopting new and innovative industrial and trade policies.[16]

Most European states after 1945 recognised the need to industrialise, but Ireland did not. Irish policy makers were not prepared to jettison the commitment to agriculture for economic, political and cultural reasons. Even Lemass, probably the most innovative Irish politician of his generation, failed to appreciate what was required to change the direction of Irish policy. His full employment proposals produced in 1944–5 failed due to the opposition of his colleagues and the inertia within the Irish economy itself, something Lemass failed to appreciate. The political consequences of these proposals were clear to some of his colleagues. MacEntee argued in April 1945 that planning on a national scale — which is what Lemass required to achieve his objective — faced 'insurmountable obstacles'. It was the Minister for Agriculture, James Ryan, who drew the most obvious political conclusion. Ryan reminded Lemass that even a commitment to tillage would not necessarily provide enough additional jobs to achieve full employment in the economy. If mechanisation of agriculture continued, the need for labour could actually decline. Such a view was heresy within Fianna Fáil, but Ryan took the argument further: 'In the case of the rich pasturelands something more than encouragement to till would be necessary and it is probable that a measure of compulsion would have to be applied to ensure that a fair number of workers would be kept in employment and that the experience of tillage introduced in recent years would not be lost.'

The basic contradiction in agricultural policy was that increased production would not necessarily lead to enhanced employment in rural areas. Increased production and mechanisation could lead to enhanced income for those remaining on the land but a reduction in those gaining their livelihood from farming. Most Irish politicians, especially those in Fianna Fáil, patently ignored trends in other economies, in the belief that Irish conditions were special. Lemass had recognised that Irish farming had not been optimal in terms of efficiency or production, but his 'solution' was to remove 'bad farmers' and allow other 'good' farmers to utilise the resources. This was not attractive politically. Ryan countered that 'this would be a most delicate and difficult matter', while admitting that there were 'many farmers in the country who for one reason or another make a poor contribution to the general output'. There might be a case for the state to take action if it could be proven that a farmer was senile or in other ways incapacitated. Yet these cases were exceptional, and Ryan held out the possibility that in the longer term improvements could be achieved:

> There are a number of holdings, however, in every parish falling below a reasonable productive capacity due to some failing on the part of the present owner but who probably has a young family growing up, one member of which would in time pull the place together and become in due course a first class farmer. In the meantime the family somehow or other are reared and set out in life as useful citizens. Indeed the lessons which the poverty of the home teaches them very often make them good workers wherever they go. It would be unthinkable to disturb the family in such cases no matter how much below the desired standard the farm might presently be.

Ryan also highlighted the serious political and social implications of an active state intervention policy. He believed, and not without good cause, that if Irish farmers were disrupted as a result of these proposals, 'there would be danger of serious agitation and public disturbances'. The general elections in 1943 and 1944 drew attention to high levels of dissatisfaction in rural Ireland, often among those who had previously voted for Fianna Fáil. Moreover, although Ryan did not mention it, the 1937 constitution would have made it virtually impossible to engage in compulsory purchase of 'inefficient' farms. The Department of Agriculture believed that reducing costs to farmers would contribute to increased output, but that this would need to be linked with the modernisation of farm equipment and facilities. There were also cultural reasons why young people were leaving the land, 'a tendency which is encouraged as much by the drab and hard conditions of farm life as by the prospect of higher wages' in urban areas.

If the quality of life was improved in rural Ireland there was every likelihood that people would stay on the farm. But it was also necessary 'to give the farmer security in price and market'. This was the point of contention between Lemass and Ryan. Lemass argued that farm output was stable and that Irish farmers limited output when a certain income was achieved; consequently the price mechanism in agriculture operated in a subtle and complex fashion. Ryan and his officials believed that this was not the case, citing evidence that output had increased since the early 1930s. Furthermore, Ryan calculated from figures produced by Smiddy that there had been an increase in the volume of net output between 1929/30 and 1942/3 of about 10 per cent, though, as noted above, Smiddy claimed that Irish agricultural output was essentially stable. Two assumptions remained essential to the Department of Agriculture, as reflected in its postwar policy deliberations. The first involved retaining privileged access for Irish agriculture to the British market, as officials believed there was no alternative for Irish output. Secondly, it was assumed that stability of price and guaranteed markets were the optimal method for achieving the best results in agriculture.[17]

Fianna Fáil was slow to respond to dissatisfaction in rural Ireland. Clann na Talmhan's political success demonstrated a political threat to both the major parties in rural Ireland. After the defeat of Fianna Fáil in two 'rural republican counties' (Kerry South and Wexford) in late 1945, Aodh de Blacam, a member of Fianna Fáil's national executive, produced a memorandum critical of the party's rural policy. De Blacam recognised the strength of Clann na Talmhan and the threat it posed. He believed that the electoral system would deny Fianna Fáil an overall majority at the next election and deprive the party of the means to 'carry out any part of its National policy'. In sharp contrast to Lemass' industrial strategy, de Blacam believed that Fianna Fáil's rural policy was the key to success or failure: 'The drift against us in rural counties is the more disturbing, because we won power mainly on the support of the small-holding counties: always the backbone of the patriotic cause. If we renege the policy of 1932, on which we were returned, and which we are assumed to be maintaining, we will deserve defeat.' De Blacam dismissed industrial and urban policy as irrelevant to Ireland: 'it is essential to happiness and prosperity to have at least double the present rural population'. This was within the capacity of the government to achieve, he maintained, but current policy conflicted with the constitutional aim of repopulating rural areas. He asserted that 'Ireland will die if it is deserted.' Accordingly, de Blacam considered that Ireland was equivalent to rural Ireland. He strongly recommended that all emigration be prohibited, claiming that there was enough employment available as domestic help in the countryside. These concerns were decidedly conservative, embracing as they did a nostalgic traditionalism which bore little relationship to the reality of Irish life. De Blacam advocated an increase in the rural population at a time when most of Europe was recognising that agriculture alone could not sustain an increased population. Cities were dependent on the countryside, according to de Blacam, requiring a solid rural hinterland to survive and unable to be self-sustaining. Interestingly his commitment to traditional norms led him to recommend that a number of women should be appointed to cabinet positions on the good conservative grounds that 'women will uphold the moral integrity and idealism of Government'. This view was justified by an analogy with the farmer's wife who was necessary to run the household, a job the male could not do on his own. De Blacam also promoted the decentralising proposals contained in the 1944 report of the Commission on Vocational Organisation. His Ireland was one where the small farm flourished as an independent self-sufficient unit, where the family acted as the core of social life and where all production decisions were directed to maintaining the maximum number of people on the land.[18]

De Blacam's vision was similar to that expressed by de Valera in his 1943 St Patrick's Day broadcast and he tapped an important and extremely rich seam of Catholic nationalist thought in his memo. His hostility to the city, to the banking system, to industrialization and to emigration as well as his promotion of further land division had been central aspects of Fianna Fáil's rural and national appeal. Change in rural Ireland was undermining not only this message, but also the social foundations for its realisation. The most corrosive consequence of this was emigration and the apparent failure of a Fianna Fáil government to stem it. Closely linked to this were the anti-modernist sentiments of the Commission on Vocational Organisation, commended not only by de Blacam but also by significant sectors of the political establishment outside Fianna Fáil; as we saw in Chapter 4, most of the political parties advocated some aspect of vocationalism after the war. MacEntee, who was Minister for Local Government and Public Health at the time, castigated de Blacam's views in a reply written a little later. He defended the system of local government in Ireland and the safeguards built into it, claiming that de Blacam's recommendation that the county manager system be abolished would restore a system originally introduced by the British. MacEntee's most scathing remarks were in response to the claim that rural Ireland was not receiving the housing it required to preserve its population or to permit marriage. De Blacam wanted 50 per cent of all new housing to be built in rural areas. MacEntee showed that there was no discrimination between urban and rural Ireland in respect of expenditure or need. Local authorities had built about 12,000 more houses in rural than in urban areas under all Housing Acts up to March 1946, while over twice as many houses had been privately built with state aid in rural Ireland as had been built in urban areas. Whereas by 1946 urban areas had received about a half a million pounds in grants under the 1932 Housing Act, the figure for rural areas came to £3 million. MacEntee denied that the government had ignored rural areas and he also rejected the view that its policies were preventing individuals getting married. He concluded that de Blacam's criticism of local government amounted to open hostility to the government, a view confirmed when de Blacam resigned from Fianna Fáil to join Clann na Poblachta just prior to the 1948 election.[19]

Some of these problems were addressed by the Department of Lands in early 1945. It recognised that the original objective of the Land Acts had been 'largely fulfilled'. Most large estates had been divided into what were described as 'economic holdings'. A change in policy might be required and a reconsideration of the position was now necessary, it added. This re-evaluation of policy 'led to the conclusion that an unlimited and irresponsible ownership of land can no longer be admitted'. The department continued to believe that the best policy for agriculture involved breaking up certain sizes of farms, especially those which would revert to cattle and grass once the opportunity presented itself. A number of properties had been identified with an average of 250 acres (in south Tipperary alone there were 866 such holdings in 1936), the majority of which could be profitable sub-divided. Departmental policy continued to concentrate on providing enough land for a family (approximately a thirty-acre holding in most cases), but it was also recognised that more could now be expected from the farmer in the way of productivity, given the size of the subsidy received by those given land: 'There is a contractual obligation imposed on the trustee to add to the national resources and to contribute to the common pool of national wealth in his use of the property entrusted to him. An allottee who merely maintains himself with negative results to the community remains a liability.' Despite the changes which had taken place in rural Ireland under Fianna Fáil, it was generally recognised that in comparison with continental Europe or with urban Ireland the standard of living was lower in the countryside and the spread of consumption goods slower.[20]

The poor state of Irish agriculture was not just attributable to the effects of wartime privation, but was a product of Fianna Fáil agricultural policy and the search for security on the part of producers against competition. The 1938 Anglo-Irish Trade Agreements governed the export of Irish cattle to the United Kingdom market. During 1947 the two governments engaged in protracted discussion on various matters affecting the relationship. It was, however, left to the Inter-Party government to conclude these discussions, and in July 1948 James Dillon was in a position to announce that agreement on trade issues had been reached between the two governments.[21] However, the announcement of the Marshall Plan and the beginning of the European Recovery Programme (ERP) raised concerns in Dublin that Britain's policy towards Irish agriculture would be changed, especially if the Americans objected to Ireland's privileged access to United Kingdom markets. Britain was anxious to address United States concerns in respect of exports to dollar areas and Irish officials feared that this attitude would affect Irish trade to Britain. So serious was this threat that R.C. Geary, Director of the Central Statistics Office, claimed that 'it could be argued that the whole future of agricultural policy, and even the future of the race from a population point of view, were involved in the issues raised on agricultural matters in London'. Another official feared that Britain might be 'endeavouring to induce a shift in the pattern of Irish agricultural production and export policy'. Irish officials were concerned that access to British markets might be affected and that the Americans should not learn of the British proposals as this would increase the pressure on Ireland.[22] The government valued the 1938 and 1948 trade agreements with the United Kingdom because they 'provide the basis for long term arrangements for the disposal of Irish agricultural exports'. Irish export strategy was based on the view that: 'The ideal Trade Agreement, therefore, in respect of Irish agricultural produce is one which guarantees the Irish producer a price equivalent to that obtainable by the British producer, and permits him to exploit the British market without limitation of quantitative character.' The objective was to avoid multilateral commitments in agriculture and to maintain privileged access to the British market. The Irish government was concerned that American initiatives on multilateral trading would affect Ireland's access to British markets. American pressure on the Organisation for European Economic Co-operation (OEEC) to liberalise also worried Irish policy makers. While Ireland was not an active participant in the OEEC, it was party to agreements within the organisation.[23]

The election of a Conservative government in Britain in 1951 also threatened the stability of Irish trade. The incoming government preferred to use free market criteria rather than bulk purchases by the state, which had been the case with the Labour administration. Pressure on Ireland increased, though the Chancellor of the Exchequer, R.A. Butler, and the Minister for Food, Gwilym Lloyd-George, disagreed on the percentage of Irish agricultural exports which should go to dollar areas. Irish exports of frozen meat, for example, increased from $2 million in 1950/51 to $6 million in 1951/2.[24] Butler believed that this was a positive development because of the dollar-earning capacity involved, whereas Lloyd-George complained that agricultural exports to the United States were a loss to the British consumer. Even though the United States was paying twice the UK price for meat, Lloyd-George wanted the Irish to agree to limit non-UK exports to 10 per cent of existing exports. If productivity was increased this would allow for an increase of volume to the US as well as to the UK. He feared that in the absence of an increase in output, the UK consumer would suffer. The tactic pursued by Britain during 1952 was to use its coal exports to Ireland to gain concessions on meat exports. Lloyd-George echoed a view widely held outside of Ireland at this time, especially by the Americans: 'The Irish economy is indeed largely complementary to that of the UK. Our aim should surely be to exploit this to the full rather than to encourage the Irish to loosen the economic ties that bind them to us.' During trade agreement negotiations in 1953, the British largely achieved this aim.[25]

Lemass was suspicious of British motives, believing that the negotiations limited Ireland's export opportunities with other states and discouraged the development of the meat trade. He argued that the interests of Britain and Ireland were different on trade issues, especially because the UK wanted supplies of cattle at the lowest price: 'The British government, being the purchaser of our best cattle and meat and also the body which determines ultimately the price of our stores, is in a strong position to influence the trend of the trade.' According to Lemass, Ireland's interest required it to develop alternative markets, especially for meat rather than live cattle.[26] Despite this intervention, little was achieved and Britain remained the main market for cattle and meat. During the negotiations for a European supranational agricultural community between 1951 and 1955 (the Green Pool) the Irish position throughout assumed that the only option for agriculture was continued access to the British market. The Department of Agriculture opposed any harmonisation of European agriculture on the grounds that it would be 'essentially inimical to the interests of the country'. Accordingly, Irish national interest was best served by remaining outside any integrationist arrangement while persuading the British to do likewise. The department feared 'that participation by Ireland in a European Agricultural market might involve, inter alia, a complete revision of the basis of our trading relations with Britain'. There is no evidence, notwithstanding Lemass' view in 1952, that the Irish government or the Department of Agriculture considered alternative trade strategies which would change the direction or the type of Irish exports. The Minister for Agriculture dismissed any advantage which might result from multilateral arrangements in farming: 'The Irish government are unable nevertheless to accept the thesis that the agricultural unification of Western Europe is economically or socially feasible and that furthermore the government feel that no Supranational Authority could give to farming communities the assurance and confidence which they could hope to obtain from National governments.'[27] Nor did this situation change in 1954 when Lemass led a delegation to London to negotiate on trade. By this time there was no suggestion about diversifying the export trade. The objective was to maintain Ireland's position within the British market on terms favourable to Irish producers. Total exports of cattle, sheep and pork had increased appreciably during the previous year, and Irish policy was now to retain its position in the face of some British pressure to erode Ireland's preferences. In the event, these negotiations concluded rather satisfactorily for Ireland, with Britain agreeing to maintain existing concessions made to Irish farm exports.[28]

One of the weaknesses in agricultural policy was highlighted shortly after this. During 1953 and 1954 there had been a considerable increase in the export of carcass meat due to the high price obtainable for it, but virtually the entire increase was wiped out in 1955 when price changes quickly led to a revival of the live cattle trade. The fluctuating nature of exports made Ireland even more dependent on British markets, a point noted by one British civil servant early in 1956: 'The Irish have no other market for their cattle. I only suggest we should bear this in mind when we negotiate, especially as to the amount of coal we supply. Everybody else has had their coal reduced, and I see no reason why the Irish should be a complete exception.'[29] The basic stability of Irish agriculture and its continuing dependence on one market restricted the state's options between 1945 and 1960. Access to the British market was fairly secure, and the price received was generous enough for Irish policy to maintain that focus. Indeed, for much of this period, across five separate governments, what is noticeable is the lack of imagination in trade policy. At no time before 1961 were alternative economic strategies considered, especially if they challenged the relationship with Britain.

The contrast with other small European states is instructive. The more innovative of these, Belgium, the Netherlands and Luxembourg, recognised the new imperatives in a context where uncertainty was the determining factor. NATO, the European Coal and Steel Community and the EEC were all responses to uncertainty by politically sovereign states. Indeed the gamble was that uncertainty could be better regulated in a multilateral world. Although not as decisive, the Danish response in the 1950s also presumed uncertainty, and its policies reflected this. Even Franco's Spain seized the opportunity provided by the Green Pool negotiations on agriculture to promote an active European strategy, in contrast to the passive Irish one.[30] In the Irish case, uncertainty was feared and avoided where possible, an outcome which the relationship with Britain facilitated. Furthermore, the Irish state continued to subsidise the farming community extensively. Domestic prices for a range of agricultural products were maintained above those of imports or the world price level, while direct subsides were paid for flour, butter and sugar beet among others. These support mechanisms created links of dependency between the state and the farmer and made it politically more difficult to change them if a government wished to do so. Tony Fahey has convincingly demonstrated that housing policy was formulated to address agrarian requirements, especially the need to maintain the family farm. He also suggests that Irish policy in respect of agriculture led to considerable redistribution of resources, though it is probable that middle-class farmers gained most from the process. The overall objective of Irish state policy was to limit the impact of the market economy on the family farm. In this, it was remarkably successful, protecting this economic unit by policy, subsidy and diplomacy for a considerable period.[31] A contributory factor was that after 1948, with a new government in place, Fianna Fáil was faced for the first time since 1932 with a realistic government alternative. In rural Ireland both potential governments were in competition for farmers' votes, and it was in their interest to claim, as the Inter-Party government did, that it could guarantee farmers' prosperity more adequately than the alternative. Another factor also affected the Irish capacity to act. In a number of European states, including Denmark and the Netherlands, the pressure on the agricultural sector was minimised by the introduction of a comprehensive welfare system and the availability of employment outside of agriculture, whereas in Ireland the weakness of the economy and the limited nature of its welfare system cut off these safety valves.[32]

The challenge of emigration

During the fifteen years after 1945, rural life in Ireland was seriously disrupted. The agrarian economy could not maintain its existing population at a standard of living considered appropriate. Adequate alternative employment was not available off-farm, especially in towns or cities. However, not only was employment available in Britain, but it was supplemented there by the introduction of a generous and comprehensive welfare system. Emigration had been high during the war, but it accelerated immediately after 1945. Irish policy makers had not expected this, and throughout the 1950s the number of emigrants continued to rise as economic conditions deteriorated. Moreover, the new emigrants were predominantly women, a cause of concern to lay and clerical opinion. De Blacam argued that no one should be allowed to emigrate unless they 'can prove the impossibility of getting work at home'. He maintained that there was no shortage of work in the Irish countryside, but if this was the case many men and women were unwilling to take it up. Emigration also questioned Fianna Fáil's socio-economic policy and weakened its anti-partitionist strategy.[33] This is not to claim that conditions were easy for Irish workers in Britain. There was always the prospect of hostility to the newcomer, especially if he or she spoke or behaved differently. Religious differences within Britain in the postwar period may not have been as significant as during previous periods of Irish emigration, but they did persist, especially in cities such as Liverpool and Glasgow. For many, the choice was not as easy as the statistics might lead one to think. Indeed, the pressure from within Ireland must have been especially strong to generate the exodus that occurred between 1945 and 1960.[34]

Most of those who travelled to Britain were from rural Ireland and the majority were unskilled. Nearly 90 per cent of women leaving Ireland in 1946 were destined for employment as nurses or domestic servants, whereas males travelled for unskilled or semi-skilled work.[35] The government discussed various proposals to restrict or control emigration, but no realistic policy was ever formulated. It was noted on one occasion that demand for nurses in Britain was high and that conditions there were superior to those in Ireland. The Catholic hierarchy was deeply concerned and, after a cabinet meeting in June 1946, Archbishop McQuaid was informed that the government had taken a decision to prohibit girls under the age of eighteen from travelling to Britain unless they had explicit parental permission; however, it was recognised that little could be achieved unless a complete ban was introduced. As long as wartime restrictions remained in place, some control could be exercised, but most controls were removed by 1947 and the movement across the sea intensified.[36] If 'Emigration is a great national problem', as one writer claimed, Irish governments found it difficult to respond to the phenomenon. In an independent Ireland emigration should not take place, and if it did then a scapegoat had to be found. Two contributory factors were often isolated: irresponsible parents and foreign agents offering inducements to work abroad. In April 1947 'a very marked increase in the emigration of women' was noted. This was attributed to the removal of travel restrictions on women by Britain in July 1946 and an increasing number of advertisements in newspapers offering work to women in Britain. During the first six months of 1946 just over 6,000 women emigrated, slightly less than the number of men; however, during the second half of 1946, once the British controls were removed, the number of women emigrating jumped to over 12,000. For most of the next fifteen years the majority of emigrants were women.[37]

Various methods for attracting Irish women to Britain were identified. Newspapers were a primary source, but British employment agencies also recruited in Ireland. Irish people already living in Britain secured work for relatives, who then travelled to these occupations. While higher wages may have been the main incentive, other considerations included 'more personal freedom, shorter working hours and better living quarters'. Social status attached to these occupations may also have been higher in Britain than in Ireland. 'Although there is no shortage of employment for domestic servants in Ireland money wages and working and living conditions are generally speaking less attractive than in Britain', one departmental official minuted.[38] While the government was less concerned with male workers emigrating, the Federation of Irish Manufacturers (FIM) complained that large numbers of skilled workers were being attracted to Britain. The FIM demanded that existing travel restrictions be 'rigorously enforced' on male workers and 'reimposed' on female workers. Commenting on the situation in early 1948, the President of the FIM, P.L. McEvoy, complained that the previous year had been a difficult one for Irish industry, a situation compounded by the shortage of skilled workers.[39] Industry and Commerce believed that the main problem for Irish labour was the differential in wage rates that existed between Britain and Ireland. These rates were attracting Irish workers even from relatively well-paid work. One report highlighted the situation in the west of Ireland:

> The Girls are Going: Of the twenty-three knitting machines in the Gaeltacht Industries factory at Bauntrach, Ballinahowen, seventeen are now idle for want of girls to work them. Recently three more girls left the factory to go to England. The average wage earned by girls in the factory amounts to about £2 per week, but some people have actually earned £4 per week and even higher.

A number of employers in Cork and in the west of Ireland complained about the shortage of female textile workers after the travel restrictions were removed. This indicated that some (at least) of the women were leaving employment in Ireland to seek higher salaries rather than fleeing unemployment.[40]

Policy makers in 1947 were also concerned with the moral and social danger to women who emigrated. The government conceded privately that 'there is no evidence that their economic interests are at all endangered', as young domestic workers could easily change jobs or demand better conditions in a market where labour was in short supply. It was believed that men were less open to moral danger because of the nature of their work and their tendency to live and work together and to congregate in Irish areas where the church had ready access. This was not the case for the female domestic workers who would not have the protection of a Catholic Irish environment. This could expose them to a 'moral atmosphere' which 'young and inexperienced girls are only too often unfitted to withstand'. The real problem according to the government was that nothing could be done officially once the young women had left home and emigrated. The problem was getting worse rather than better. One calculation claimed that the rate of female emigration in the immediate postwar years was twice the rate for the period 1926–36 and the percentage of those under twenty-one years of age was increasing. In 1949, 39 per cent of women who emigrated were under twenty-one. Continuing emigration posed a demographic, social, moral and economic challenge to the Irish state, but one which was not easily addressed. One proposal sought to restrict emigration by women to those over twenty-two years of age, when it was determined that 50 per cent of female emigrants were under this age. It was hoped that women would marry in the interim and those who waited until they were twenty-two would be more mature and capable of handling the threats in Britain. Other ideas included a quota system and an official notice given out by the gardaí to prospective emigrants warning them of the 'difficulties and dangers' an individual might encounter in Britain. None of these proposals proved acceptable due to the serious objections raised in respect of them.[41]

The pressure to be seen to respond to emigration increased in 1947 as a consequence of the success of Clann na Poblachta, but also in response to the Catholic hierarchy. In October 1947, the hierarchy issued a statement expressing concern at the level of emigration, complaining that conditions facing emigrants in Britain 'are full of danger to their religious and moral well being'. In a letter sent to de Valera these fears are emphasised:

> The Bishops view with great alarm the continuous drain on the womanhood and future motherhood of the country as the result of the present wave of emigration, and they consider it contrary to the spiritual and temporal welfare of the nation that foreign agents should be allowed to enter the country to attract girls abroad with promises of lucrative employment, the fulfilment of which no one in this country could control.

De Valera responded quickly to the bishops. The Minister for Social Welfare, James Ryan, reported to the cabinet that there was little the government could do to control the flow of people out of the country. Ryan also dismissed allegations that 'foreign agents' were at work in Ireland, luring young people to Britain. Ryan regretted that the joint Anglo-Irish controls over travel in place between 1942 and 1947 had been removed, as these had been advantageous to Ireland. De Valera was unhappy with Ryan's report on the grounds that this 'would not be sufficient' to meet the hierarchy's concerns. He demanded that the gardaí investigate further the possibility that 'foreign agents' were involved, but no criminal activity could be detected. The evidence available to the government in 1947 suggests that coercion was not involved in the decision to emigrate and that potential emigrants were not being seduced by 'foreign agents' or misleading advertisements.[42]

With the removal of all British controls on movement between the two countries in 1947, the Irish government lost its only method of affecting emigration. But Fianna Fáil was not prepared to address the core issues involved in emigration. This is highlighted in de Valera's reply to the hierarchy: 'Their Lordships may be assured that the Government both in the legislative proposals and in administration have consistently in mind, not only the State's function as guardian of the common good, but also the respect which is due to the fundamental personal and family rights.' The government, he continued, was deeply concerned about emigration and was especially anxious about women. De Valera asserted that many emigrants were leaving 'without having experienced real difficulties in finding suitable employment at home'. He was not, however, in favour of prohibition, as this would interfere with basic human rights and could only be justified in an emergency. De Valera also claimed that agents did not cause emigration, asserting that the way forward was increased agricultural and industrial production to provide employment. This had been the stock Fianna Fáil response to criticism in the past, yet, even during times of expansion, employment creation had rarely been adequate to meet the demand for jobs.[43] The census evidence for the period 1926–61 showed that the Irish population was in decline, notwithstanding a slight increase in the 1945–51 figures. (The increase in population between 1945 and 1951 was slight, less than 5,000, and the downward pattern was quickly resumed.) The disparity with Northern Ireland is illuminating, as the population there had increased in every period between 1911 and 1951, though emigration had also been high in that region. The persistent nature of emigration and population decline drew attention to the existence of social patterns which direct rule from London (before independence), rule from Dublin under a free trade system (under Cumann na nGaedheal) or significant state intervention (under Fianna Fáil) left untouched. Fianna Fáil promised that a nationalist government could address this phenomenon by organising the nation to achieve its objectives, but this proved to be optimistic. Most of the policy prescriptions involved greater state control to prevent individuals leaving the country, but little else. The reason for this was the belief expressed by de Valera, among others, that people were leaving for frivolous reasons. De Valera's letter to the hierarchy was political in that he was seeking to avoid public confrontation, but beyond that his defence highlighted the impossible position the government was in.[44] The reason that 'foreign agents' were invoked by the hierarchy and critics of emigration was that it was necessary to claim that young people did not know their own minds and were persuaded to emigrate as a result of inducements. If this was indeed the case, it implied that pull factors were at play, drawing young people to Britain for high wages, bright lights or better marriage prospects. If this was not so, then perhaps it was the push factor which was central to the decision made. In this case lack of employment opportunities, absence of marriage prospects and the dullness of rural life, as well as the lack of social opportunity, 'drove' people out. For a nationalist neither of these factors could be easily admitted. To do so would be to accept the weakness of Irish economic and social policy and, in the light of a forthcoming election, was even more difficult for Fianna Fáil to admit in early 1948. In any event, the reality of emigration was more complex than either explanation. The decision to emigrate was a personal one, with individuals from very similar backgrounds making different decisions. It is probable that push and pull factors operated, but that a particular event occasioned the individual to leave Ireland.[45]

Shortly before the 1948 election, the Department of External Affairs produced an incisive analysis of the emigration problem. It drew attention to the main reasons for emigration and sought to provide a reasoned evaluation of trends and consequences. It started from the assumption that emigration was a real problem, while noting that deploring emigration would not end it: 'The trouble is that so many people are content simply to exploit the sentimental feeling about emigration which we all share, without making any effort to analyse the problem or make constructive suggestions for its solution.' It was essentially a rural problem; the urban population had increased since the state was established while most of the population loss occurred in the countryside. However, the Irish economy had never provided adequate employment to absorb those coming on to the labour market in any given year. Two processes were at work: internal migration, mainly to Dublin, and emigration, primarily to Britain. The 'ideal solution' would be for the agricultural sector to absorb the surplus population by increasing employment prospects to provide for this. The evidence for the period following independence demonstrated that this was not the case. Indeed the pattern of emigration was similar to that which characterised Ireland between 1850 and 1921. Moreover, rural migration/emigration was dominated by women, who in any event could not find employment in rural areas or could not marry.[46] These trends were reinforced by the tendency for rural populations to decline throughout Europe, no matter what system of production was in place. Denmark, despite having an efficient export-based agricultural sector, was also experiencing a flight from the land. In other words, enhanced agricultural production would not, in itself, solve the problems associated with rural depopulation. The rural economy might be wealthier, but the cost could well be fewer people living on the land. Thus, one of the identifiable characteristics of the postwar world was that all societies experienced a degree of rural–urban migration. However, where Ireland was different was that its total population was in decline, and its rural population had declined even when its urban population had increased. In most other European states the overall population increased during the first half of the twentieth century, normally as a consequence of growth in urban areas. In the case of England and Wales the rural population was roughly the same in 1951 as in 1851, but the urban population had increased dramatically to dwarf those living in the countryside. Of considerable comparative interest in the Irish context, Norway, Denmark and Switzerland had experienced significant increases in urban population but each had also seen their rural population increase over the century.[47]

One of the favourite policies advocated by nationalists to deal with emigration was further land division. Fianna Fáil, Clann na Talmhan and Clann na Poblachta all advocated this approach, but it also had wider appeal. Further land division providing holdings of twenty-five acres would lead to the creation of about 18,000 new farms, it was claimed, and those holdings could accommodate approximately 90,000 people (assuming a family of two adults and three children), a development which it was hoped would lead to an increase in the rural marriage rate. Some 18,000 men would acquire a degree of status and property to permit marriage. This, in turn, would lead to an increase in the number of children being born. But it would not mitigate emigration as only one son would inherit the farm and this would simply contribute to future pressure on those without property or skill to look elsewhere for employment. The conclusion drawn was rather stark: 'Whatever happens, therefore, you are going to have a certain degree of migration from the land. The question is whether that migration need become emigration from the country itself; and the answer to that depends entirely on the rate at which new employment openings can be created in the country in occupations other than agriculture.'

This indeed was the crucial question, for in the most comparable states in Europe emigration was limited by the provision of non-agricultural employment. Nor does one have to use comparative statistics on this; within Ireland most of the employment creation occurred in the industrial sector: 'The essential truth which we must grasp is that courageous and well considered programmes of investment in our own country offer, in present circumstances, the best and most hopeful means of checking the stream of emigrants.'[48] To all intents and purposes this had to take place in the industrial and commercial sectors, agriculture having exhausted its potential to create new employment. This would in turn require an acceptance that urban policy should receive primacy over rural policy. Non-agricultural employment increased between 1932 and 1939, continuing this upward growth after 1945. Industrial production and employment in particular recovered more quickly than agriculture after the war. There is evidence to suggest that a proportion of those who went to Britain during the war returned subsequently when industrial production resumed. Those who returned to Ireland after the war were only a proportion of the total, but their return supports the view that if industrial employment had been available many more might have done so.[49]

It is arguable that even if wages were higher in Ireland emigration would have continued, but would this necessarily have been the case? Irish wages may have been higher than those in Britain in the 1930s under conditions of protection and strong trade unions, but employment was also more limited. Outside the well-paid jobs, work was often scarce, infrequent and not always well paid. A stable employment market was in place by the end of that decade and this pattern reasserted itself after the war.[50] Consideration might, of course, be given to prohibiting emigration, in exceptional circumstances. However, in a democratic state this could be justifiable only in an emergency such as wartime, and then only for a short period. To the claim that emigration was a national evil and therefore the individual did not have the right to emigrate (which is what de Blacam was saying in 1946), the Fianna Fáil position in late 1947 is well reflected in the Department of External Affairs' memorandum's conclusion on the issue of a prohibition on emigration:

> The point is one on which opinions may differ but, to the mind of the Government, it admits of only one answer. We consider that no Government has such a right. Any such prohibition would involve an unjustifiable and dangerous infringement of the freedom of the individual. It would mean the Government substituting its own judgement for that of the individuals concerned and their parents. It would be an unwarranted invasion of human responsibility. It would lower national morale. Far from effectively countering the psychological causes of emigration, it would turn the country into a prison house in the eyes of those who wanted to emigrate, making the far off hill greener than ever.[51]

An editorial in the *Irish Press* at the end of 1948 was highly critical of the new Inter-Party government for its failure to stem emigration. Citing the economist

Professor John Busteed, who had been close to Fianna Fáil in the past, it claimed that, while Irish emigrants might find bright lights attractive, the real cause of emigration was poverty, especially among rural workers. The editorial commended the Dutch, Swedish, Danish and Belgian approach to farming and contrasted it favourable with that of Britain. The United Kingdom was not, it added, a good example for Ireland, and neither was the concentration on cattle. Policy should focus on emphasising output per acre, as this would assure 'maximum utilisation of land, minimum dependence on imports of dollar costing grains, and the fullest employment of Irish workers on the farm'.[52] This had been Fianna Fáil policy since 1926, and it was now being adopted to criticise the policies of James Dillon, Minister for Agriculture in the new government. Yet Fianna Fáil in opposition was as far away from drawing the radical conclusion about the link between Irish agriculture and emigration as it ever was.

The Commission on Emigration

Nor did the Inter-Party government have a clear view of what might be done to address the problem. There were considerable policy differences among the coalition members. Fine Gael remained committed to agriculture and particularly the cattle and export sectors. While this was a positive approach, it did not generate employment in rural Ireland. The new government did take a decision to establish a Commission of Enquiry on Emigration and other Population Problems on 24 February 1948. The Minister for Social Welfare, William Norton, appointed the commission on 5 April with James P. Beddy as Chairman. The members included James Meenan, Peadar O'Donnell, Dr Cornelius Lucey and Alexis Fitzgerald. Two Jesuits were included, as was Aodh de Blacam, but he died prior to the publication of the commission's report in 1954. The terms of reference were general and it is open to conjecture whether this was another attempt to neutralise debate on sensitive issues.[53] The commission's membership was wide-ranging, but this did not prevent Clann na Talmhan from complaining that there was no farmer's representative, advising farmers to boycott the enquiry.[54]

Seán MacBride, the leader of Clann na Poblachta and Minister for External Affairs, circulated a memorandum written by de Blacam to his cabinet colleagues in May 1948, and, while it does not seem to have been discussed, it drew attention to the rural policy of Clann na Poblachta. De Blacam reiterated the claim that Ireland could have a population of twenty million, making it a 'big nation', but instead it was dying. The fault lay with Fianna Fáil: 'not only did it fail to stop the decay of population, but its leading spokesmen even condoned the flight in the very years when the rural population had become so depleted that all branches of agriculture were faltering'. This, he concluded, was an 'unnatural' situation. The main cause, however, was not economic but 'spiritual':

> a loss of the natural instinct to survive, among the people, and a lack of purpose to revive that instinct, in the late rulers. Give us a truly patriotic

> Government, passionately resolved to save the race from extinction, and let such a Government lead the revival of national aspiration, and the economic measures necessary will be easily recognised and effected.

For de Blacam, will-power would provide the necessary conditions for solving this problem, while economic policy would remain secondary. 'The nation must be exhorted to undertake the full reconquest of Ireland – meaning by that, the full repopulation of the countryside, development of natural resources to the utmost, and restoration of all phases of the national culture.'

While de Blacam was strong on exhortation, he was less forthcoming on specific policies. He did call for a 'mental renaissance' and drew analogies with the mobilisation against conscription in 1918. Interestingly, de Blacam compared Ireland unfavourably with Northern Ireland in respect of farming, noting that more people lived on the land in the north than in the south. He also asserted that domestic production was not adequately providing for the home market and that this should be the focus of policy. Yet nearly all his recommendations were extremely general or bordered on the sentimental. Local participation should be encouraged; an Irish language revival would contribute to a sense of nationhood; decentralisation, land division and an emphasis on the 'ideals of property' would contribute to success. De Blacam laid particular emphasis on educational matters:

> We would suggest that the Minister should consider the adoption of the American custom of saluting the National Flag in school every day, at the time of morning prayers. A short formula could be written in the National language, which would make the action impress upon the young mind the idea that Ireland is our home, that it should be the ambition of all save the exceptional cases (like those who go abroad as clergy), to find happiness and a useful career, in this ancestral land.

De Blacam's analysis was a conservative one, involving a policy of stabilising the society at a particular moment in time forever. When the optimum conditions were achieved, the society could be set in stone. He recommended that virtually all employment should be reserved for local people; in Dublin and Cork 90 per cent of all employment should be reserved for city people so that country people would not be tempted to migrate, not unlike the system introduced in the Soviet Union. What seems to be advocated is a heavily controlled system within which a high degree of coercion would be used to give effect to the policy objectives. Though not all members of the cabinet shared de Blacam's specific prescriptions, his general emphasis was one which most politicians in the government could agree with. More generally, de Blacam's assertion that nationhood was weak was not only misconceived, but it ignored the economic reality that even nationalists had to find work and earn a livelihood.[55]

Despite continuing emigration between 1948 and 1951 there is little evidence that the Inter-Party government considered the issue to be of such importance as to require specific action. The government hoped that the commission would provide it with proposals to take action or, if not, that it could use the existence of the commission as an excuse not to act. W.A. Honohan, who was a member of the commission and Secretary of the Department of Social Welfare, in a confidential note to the Taoiseach in August 1951 reported that there had been eighty full sessions of the commission, that the collection of evidence had been completed in 1950 but that he did not anticipate that the report would be signed before Christmas 1951. The report, he added, would not revolutionise thinking on the issues referred to it: 'Its value, *in my opinion*, will be largely in the keen analysis and interpretation which it will provide, rather than in its practical recommendations. It may also be of some value to secure a common viewpoint (from a rather diverse group of citizens) on a subject which has, up to now, been rather controversial.'[56] Despite Honohan's cautious observations, expectations were high among the public. The journalist Gertrude Gaffney identified a number of problems in rural Ireland of long standing, while the author Shane Leslie believed that Ireland was probably the happiest country in the world, with only emigration taking away from its idyllic circumstances.[57] Con Lehane, a Clann na Poblachta TD, asked the Minister for Social Welfare to prohibit advertisements for Irish women to go to Britain to study nursing on the grounds that the promises made were dishonest. The Limerick-born Archbishop Duhig of Brisbane appealed to young Irish people not to emigrate to England, warning that 'there is always a danger there of infection from paganism and materialism'. When the new census was published in 1951 the *Irish Catholic* compared the slight increase in the population of the Irish Republic with the significant increase of 90,000 'in our six separated counties'. As on previous occasions this newspaper drew attention not only to population decline, but also to the moral threat which Irish emigrants in England encountered, especially women.[58]

In August 1951 R.C. Geary of the Central Statistics Office claimed that in 1950 some 73,000 people emigrated while 36,000 returned to Ireland, 'for more or less permanent employment'. He also noted that women were more likely to emigrate and that Ireland now had the lowest proportion of women in the population in Europe if not the world. By 1950 the rate of emigration was about four times the 1947 figure.[59] Fianna Fáil returned to office after the indecisive election in June 1951. In the Dáil shortly after this, de Valera admitted that the figures on emigration 'are really very disquieting and have been progressively increasing over the years'. Despite this he seemed incapable of addressing the difficulty: 'If serious action is not taken the result will be the complete impoverishment of our country through the departure of our people. I was in England recently and heard there appalling stories about the conditions under which some of the workers who go from this country are living.' He warned those intending to travel for work: 'It is a very sad thing indeed to think that our people who leave this country and go to other countries live in conditions in which nobody would dream for a moment of permitting them to live here.'[60] The threat posed by mass emigration does not appear to have dawned on Fianna Fáil. There is a notable fatalism in Dáil debates and in the media throughout this period, usually accompanied by a high moral tone about the dangers accompanying emigration.

The *Kerryman* newspaper reported in 1953 that of those who had attended one local school between 1917 and 1946, only 26 per cent remained in the parish; 20 per cent had migrated within Ireland while 54 per cent had emigrated. The impact on women was even more extreme. By the end of 1952 less than 11 per cent of the women who had attended the school remained in the area. Cornelius Lucey, a member of the Commission on Emigration and recently appointed Bishop of Cork, argued: 'Not partition, then, not the balance of payments, not every other Party crisis of today or yesterday is Ireland's major national problem. That problem is rural depression and decay — the disappearance of so many uneconomic holdings, so called, the drying up of the very well springs of national population.'[61] For him, as for many others, the flight from the land was equivalent to 'race suicide' and to the implosion of Irish-Ireland. It was thought that Ireland could be saved only by preserving the existing social conditions in rural Ireland. Alternatives, such as those discussed in the External Affairs memorandum in December 1947 or by Seán Lemass at various times, were discounted because they ran counter to the belief that Ireland's future lay with agriculture. The failure to appreciate that industrial expansion and a market economy provided the best means of survival can be attributed to the narrowness of the political culture and the nature of the constitution itself. The severity of the situation by the early 1950s was brought home to de Valera when one of his constituents wrote to him concerning the impact of emigration on her family. All five of the correspondent's children, aged between eighteen and twenty-three, were working in England, but she wanted them to work in Ireland. In particular two of her sons wanted to attend evening classes in University College Dublin. This letter confirms other evidence that emigrants were 'economic emigrants', forced out of Ireland through lack of opportunity. It was noted that most ministers received similar letters and it was thought necessary to co-ordinate employment information for them, especially those who were not directly responsible for employment or economic issues.[62]

De Valera's response was to call on Irish emigrants to return to Ireland. In August 1951 in a strongly worded speech in Galway he condemned the conditions of Irish emigrants in urban centres in Britain. He argued:

> There is no doubt that many of those who emigrated could find employment at home at as good, or better, wages — and with living conditions far better — than they find in Britain. Moreover, not only do they fail to improve their own circumstances by going abroad, but they leave enterprises for the development of our national resources without sufficient labour to enable progress to be made as rapidly as we would all desire.

While de Valera stopped short of declaring that those who emigrated were traitors, he certainly implied that the emigrants were to blame for their own plight. Not only was the attraction of Britain false, he asserted, but by going there emigrants took away from economic success in Ireland. There was certainly a case to be answered in some urban areas in Britain. A report from the Irish Ambassador in London, F.H. Boland, pointed to overcrowding, costly accommodation and dirty conditions for many of those working in Birmingham. In this city particularly there was a general shortage of accommodation, while conditions in many of the small firms in which the Irish worked were described as shocking by Boland. He believed that 'The degrading condition under which Irish workers in Britain live and work has a grievously lowering effect on their prestige and morale and has grave consequences from the health, moral and religious points of view.' Boland had also been in contact with Michael Foot, Labour MP and later party leader, who had agreed to publicise the conditions there. However, Boland believed that it was necessary to publicise the conditions in Ireland and warn those who might be considering emigrating. A report prepared by the Young Christian Workers' Association compared the security of a Catholic family life in Ireland with the temptations of 'mixed marriages, immorality or non practice of the faith' in Britain. Considerable emphasis was placed on the impact of emigration on women, highlighting the number of Irish women who arrived pregnant or who entered into relationships while in Britain and became pregnant subsequently. There was also some evidence that some Irish husbands had in effect abandoned their wives in Ireland and were establishing new relationships with women in Britain. In addition, a significant proportion of those charged with drunkenness each week were Irish. There was also a fear that a sizeable proportion of Irish emigrants were now lapsed Catholics or practised their religion infrequently.[63]

De Valera's speech received considerable publicity in Britain and Ireland. Peadar O'Donnell, another member of the Commission on Emigration, criticised it on the grounds that employment was not easily available in Ireland, citing this as the primary reason for emigration. The British press was generally hostile and public representatives in Birmingham and elsewhere claimed that conditions for Irish workers were no worse than those for anyone else. The Mayor of Coventry condemned the speech as 'ridiculous, irresponsible and unjustified so far as it relates to Coventry'. The *Irish Independent* noted that many of the letters it received were critical of de Valera. Those in the *Irish Press* were less so, but it is difficult to judge whether this was due to censorship in what was a de Valera-controlled publication. One correspondent from Birmingham wrote: 'Mr de Valera, please leave us be, here in peace. Get on with the building of a better Eire, with decent houses, full employment, and better conditions. Then — and only then — will you get us to return. Meanwhile, I am sorry — but it's here we stop.' Oliver J. Flanagan raised concerns that there had been communist involvement in providing the information on Birmingham, while a priest claimed that Irish workers did not go to mass because they were forced to work on Sunday.[64]

The government did not have a response to the criticism or to the problem. It was one thing to encourage emigrants to return or to discourage those intending to leave, but it was another to persuade either group that Ireland could provide adequate economic security or remuneration. Lemass responded to a Dáil question on the issue with the traditional answer: 'The whole objective of the economic and social policy of the government and of the implementation of that policy through the various departments of state concerned is to create such economic and social conditions in this country as will lead to the stopping of emigration.' There can be little doubt that Lemass sincerely believed this to be the case, yet there is no evidence that he or his department or indeed the government knew how to achieve it. This is not to say that Lemass did not appreciate the relationship between economic growth, investment and emigration. He drew the conclusion:

> The fundamental cause of the persistence of abnormal employment and emigration in Ireland is the continuing low level of capital investment by private enterprise. This is due to practical factors which limit the expansion of industry, including the static population position. With a rising population, a continuous expansion of investment would be automatic. On the other hand unless an expansion of investment is induced, emigration will continue to prevent a normal population growth.

Lemass considered that only state action would realise these objectives, but there was no obvious or automatic guarantee that this would occur.[65] However, there was an increasing tendency for conditions in Britain to attract Irish emigrants. An inter-departmental committee reported in 1952 that full employment, social welfare and high wages in Britain provided the basis for comparison with conditions in Ireland. The difficulty here is that during the early 1950s the gap between the two states increased and Irish living conditions deteriorated in comparison with those in Britain.[66] There was a sense that Fianna Fáil blamed Britain for being too successful, but the political reality for the government was that developments in Britain were out of its control. Nor did Irish emigrants want to be controlled in any way by the Irish or the British governments, rarely availing themselves of the 'generous facilities offered by the British Liaison Office', once they were no longer required to do so. The British government also largely ignored Irish pressure, especially de Valera's protest of August 1951. Boland reported at the beginning of 1953 that the conditions originally complained about were 'no longer a serious factor'. By this stage the Conservative government had initiated a significant housing programme, which quickly met demand for housing and alleviated the housing shortage.[67]

Boland acknowledged, after the controversy over de Valera's speech had died down, that housing conditions had been poor for most sections of the British population, not just the Irish. He also drew attention to potential tensions between the welfare of Irish workers and the Catholic Church's desire to maintain them in one place. He cited an example from the parish of Southwark, where a local Catholic businessman purchased three houses, which now had 150 Irish tenants in them. When the Irish Ambassador questioned the desirability of so many people having to live in such conditions, the local priest commended the businessman on the grounds that keeping the Catholic Irish together made it easier for them to maintain the faith. This drew the general observation from Boland that

> The local Catholic clergy always take a great interest in the living conditions of our workers here and some of them are very active about it. But their interest in the matter may not be always quite in line with ours. They are mainly concerned with spiritual welfare and are anxious to keep Irish people together in individual houses as opposed to taking digs in English households where, although they may be materially better off, the atmosphere would often be destructive of spiritual values.[68]

Reports from London emphasised the continuing moral threat to young women in England, with loss of faith and sexual behaviour being the main concerns. The German novelist Heinrich Böll recounts a conversation he overheard between a young woman and a priest on the boat to Ireland. The woman informed the priest that she had lost her faith since she went to work in Britain, but would not tell her parents about this when she returned home on holiday. One report highlighted the threat posed to Irish women by the 'white slave traffic', while it was also claimed that a significant proportion of women in jail were Irish Catholics. There was also some evidence produced of significant movement between the two countries by young pregnant women. This caused considerable concern, as the babies born to unmarried Irish mothers in Britain were often 'handed over by the mothers to non-Catholic and undenominational Societies'.[69]

In response to the general issue of emigration to Britain, the government was approached on a number of occasions by Irish and Catholic community groups in Britain to finance the construction and operation of hostels and welfare centres for young emigrants. Such requests received very little support. Seán MacEntee, once again Minister for Finance, acting in his usual brutal fashion when it came to spending, urged the government to reject any demand to appoint a welfare officer in London: 'It is not the function of the state to assume responsibility for the economic, spiritual or moral welfare of Irish citizens resident abroad.' Nor was MacEntee alone in his views on this issue: other departments shared his reluctance to sanction involvement by the state in Britain.[70] Likewise, de Valera moved rather cautiously for one who had been so decisive in condemning conditions in his 1951 speech. He said he needed time to think over the proposals, though in the interim he proposed setting up a government committee, which he would chair, to 'examine the whole matter in detail before any definite steps are taken'. Most revealing of all perhaps was de Valera's amendment to the original memorandum. He claimed that the reference in this document to the government's willingness to welcome back emigrants was 'unnecessary', while a reference to the 'Irish in Britain with the help and co-operation of their English friends' had the words 'their English' removed.[71]

Ambassador Boland remained deeply sceptical about the ability of the Irish in Britain to look after themselves. He claimed that little could be done for emigrants because they would not do anything for themselves, believing that 'there is a barrier of habit and apathy to be overcome before any progress can be made'. He claimed that Irish emigrants spent most of their surplus money in English-owned dancehalls and bars, whereas this money could have been put to better purposes by developing specifically Irish amenities.[72] A welfare officer was eventually appointed to the London embassy late in 1954, probably due to the change in government in June 1954 and the publication of the Commission on Emigration's report. This may also account for the decision to amend the 1913 Children (Employment) Act, to restrict the emigration of children and young people for employment and aimed specifically at employment agencies. In the short term, however, little was achieved. Following discussions between the Minister for External Affairs, Liam Cosgrave, and Archbishop McQuaid, the cabinet discussed emigration again in May 1955. McQuaid urged the government to restrict emigration by young people and to control recruitment agencies. Cosgrave conceded that the government had no power to restrict emigration, despite earlier attempts to do so. While the government continued to examine the possibility of controlling employment agencies, the Irish Ambassador in London warned that care should be taken that action by the government should not be construed as providing facilities for emigration. Moreover, even if tough action was taken, there was a further danger that the agencies would move to Northern Ireland and recruit from there. From the evidence in these files it appears that Irish sovereignty in respect of emigration was limited unless coercion was used, and, furthermore; that action within the state could be circumscribed with relative ease.[73]

In 1955 the Catholic hierarchies in Ireland and England agreed that Irish priests would organise missions to British cities. Bishop Lucey returned to the issue of emigration on a number of occasions, condemning in one talk the fathers of families who emigrated, leaving their families in Ireland. In July 1955 the Irish hierarchy issued a strongly worded pastoral letter, asserting that it was the duty of Catholics to defend the faith when outside Ireland. Catholics should be 'active soldiers, showing that they appreciate the truth of their faith and its power to influence their lives. They should be proud to stand fast by it and to defend it against attack.' The pastoral had been prompted by fears among the bishops that life in Britain was undermining the moral certainty attached to the religion in Ireland. The greatest danger was no longer anti-Catholic bigotry or hostility, but indifference: 'The peril to the ordinary adult arises from a widespread indifference to religious faith and worship, a disregard of Christian moral standards in theory and practice, an atmosphere in places of work and amusement indifferent to religion and often opposed to Christian morals.'[74] The church had a particular concern. Within the Irish state it was secure, venerated and respected, continuing to be the most influential institution in Irish life. Nor is there much evidence to suggest that a change was under way during the 1950s on moral or social issues. The problem for the church was that many of its most devout members were leaving Ireland in large numbers and it did not have the capacity in Britain to maintain the institutional or psychological environment for religious socialisation or participation.

Moreover, within Ireland the social environment which had cultivated Catholic values, especially in rural society, was on the verge of collapse, with all its attendant uncertainties.

The report on emigration

The long-awaited report of the Commission on Emigration was published in June 1954, shortly after the second Inter-Party government took office. The delay was partly due to de Valera's reluctance to publish it while in office, given that the draft report had been available since the end of 1951. It contained a considerable amount of very detailed information, and provided a wide-ranging discussion and analysis of both population and emigration. However the main report concluded that the issues involved were so complex that no attempt would be made to present a summary of conclusions, as this would 'weaken their significance by divorcing them from the text'. This probably took away from the impact of the report, as its detailed nature often obscured the actual recommendations in it. It remained an extremely cautious document when compared with the 1938 report of the Banking Commission or the 1944 report of the Commission on Vocational Organisation, containing many reservations, addenda and two minority reports. The main emphasis in the report was on the need to expand agricultural production to secure employment in rural areas and thereby stem emigration.[75] It bore the hallmark of a commission where the members sought to reach agreement within a narrowly defined area. It recognised the failure of Irish agriculture to provide an increase in employment in rural Ireland, but reiterated the traditional panacea of moving to intensive farming. The commission believed that national policy should be judged on the extent to which population increased and remained in Ireland. If so, the evidence collected seemed to bewilder the commission, noting that after thirty years of independence such an objective was no closer to realisation. In fact, the report (paragraph 471) provided the main explanation for this outcome. Irish citizens chose to enhance their standard of living by accepting that the price paid for this was large-scale emigration for those who did not own property or could not obtain employment in the state. This came close to claiming that strong social mechanisms existed which pushed 'surplus' population out of rural Ireland. Yet the commission drew back from such a radical conclusion, highlighting instead the need to increase efficiency and output by a more intensive use of farmland (paragraphs 472–4). Notwithstanding this, no attempt was made by the commission, or by those who responded to its report, to explain how the rural population could be persuaded to break the cycle of emigration which now characterised the state. Indeed by the time the report was published, Britain had become the destination for increasing numbers of young Irish men and women. Britain's attraction was enhanced by the lack of opportunity and low status which most would endure if they remained in Ireland, a point explicitly recognised in the report (paragraphs 433, 438–40). In social terms, the trade-off between emigration and living standards for those who remained on the land proved acceptable and, despite some serious discussion of the problem, helps to explain why the report had such little influence in electoral or policy terms.[76]

Though the strain introduced by accelerating emigration was showing by the mid 1950s, not everyone believed that this amounted to a crisis. At a conference held in the Gresham Hotel in Dublin in May 1954, it was claimed that there was no need for pessimism on population, while R.C. Geary, who had been a member of the commission, argued that the Irish were not facing extinction, as some had charged. In his view, it was necessary for the Irish to change their attitude to emigration. Geary and others were responding to *The Vanishing Irish,* a book published the previous year. This book had been controversial, providing an extremely critical analysis of Irish behavioural patterns, especially in respect of marriage. The contributors had considerable sympathy for Ireland, but believed that emigration and marriage patterns were a major challenge to the society.[77] Yet the response to *The Vanishing Irish* illustrates further the view that those who continued to live in the country were reluctant to face up to the social basis and cost of the phenomenon. The key argument in the book was that Irish men would not marry, in part because the sexes were so effectively segregated but also because of the role of the mother in influencing choice and the nature of inheritance. While this may not have gone to the heart of the matter, it did highlight a very real social problem. In a society where women could not be seen to have children outside marriage, an increase in population could occur only if more people married and had children. Critics of this view identified a weak point in the argument, that births had increased in every decade since independence but emigration had prevented a rise in the population. Yet, the contributors to *The Vanishing Irish* were closer to recognising the problem than many other commentators at the time. By this time there existed strong social factors which acted against the propensity to marry and in favour of remaining single or emigrating. The simple explanation is that Irish society was uncomfortable with the discussion of intimacy between the sexes in this book and was unwilling to meet the challenge which some at least of the contributors posed to their attitude to emigration and its source.[78]

Nor did the Dáil debate on the report of the Commission on Emigration in February 1955 add much to the question. Out of office, Fianna Fáil adopted a high moral stand, but its policy commitments were meagre and limited. The government did not do much better, insisting that the situation was not as serious as claimed.[79] While some heat was generated, not one of the contributions provided a realistic response to what was now a serious problem. Between 1946 and 1951 net emigration was around 120,000; this had grown to 187,000 between 1951 and 1956, and was to grow again to 212,000 between 1956 and 1961. In all, around a half a million Irish people emigrated in just fifteen years, the vast majority of them to Britain. While other regions of Europe also experienced emigration, notably the Italian south, in virtually every case except Ireland the national population was increasing during the postwar decades. By 1961 the population was down to 2,818,341, compared with

2,971,992 in 1926. In some parts of Ireland not a single new house was built during the 1950s. During one of his visits, Böll recounts coming upon a house with the lights on and the morning milk outside the front door. A neighbour informed him that the individual had emigrated that day and had simply walked away from the house. While this may not have been typical of most people's departure from home, it does have a ring of authenticity about it.[80]

The report received considerable publicity, but politically the response was muted in the extreme. None of the major political parties took up the findings, though this can also be attributed to their vagueness and the real difficulty associated with them. It took over a year for the first responses to come from government departments concerned with the matter. Industry and Commerce dismissed the recommendation to decentralise industry and the civil service on the grounds that the civil service should remain in Dublin because it provided the best environment for administration. The Department of Health rejected the claim that most unmarried mothers left the country, though evidence from other sources questioned this view. The most scathing comment came from the Department of Agriculture, which concluded that the report contained nothing new: 'It merely repeats the consistent injunction of the Department of Agriculture without at any stage adverting to the fact that the Department through its advisory service and other media at its disposal consistently enjoins the farmer to make the best use of its resources.' Agriculture was particularly critical of Bishop Lucey's minority report. The department dismissed Lucey's competence, declaring him to 'have insufficient knowledge of the agricultural situation or the overall economic situation of this country'. Agriculture considered that Lucey was proposing two incompatible objectives. He wanted simultaneously to remove power and responsibility from the state in matters affecting the economy, while demanding that the state provide the means to develop a credit co-operative system. This led to the conclusion that the bishop had 'an inclination to regard the state as something which could act as a sort of benevolent money issuing institution, divorced from responsibility for ensuring that the monies issued were properly and wisely applied'. The department drew attention to 'signs of improvement' in the economy, concluding that the report had been too pessimistic about the agricultural economy and that its criticisms were unwarranted.

The Department of Agriculture's main intention was to defend the status quo in rural Ireland. This was apparent in a number of ways. One was its insistence that Irish conditions were unique and therefore could not be compared with those of other farming nations such as the Netherlands or Denmark. The implication of this approach was that supposed Irish shortcomings which arose in comparisons with these countries were more apparent than real because Irish conditions were unique. Although rather circular in formulation, this argument did have the merit of defusing criticism based on such comparisons. But the criticism had merit in its own right: it was easy for critics to highlight the positive attractions of another country without appreciating what features of that state and society provided the means to achieve the objectives admired. The departmental critique highlighted the views of Geary and M.D. McCarthy, mathematician and Deputy Director of the CSO, in their addendum No. 2 when they argued that 'The Irishman's reaction to his environment ... has usually been not only intelligible but intelligent', to insist that the existing structure of agricultural production and output provided the best possible opportunity for farming. In other words, and in contrast to the thrust of the report as well as sentiment within Fianna Fáil, the cattle economy was the one which provided Ireland with a competitive advantage in export markets. This led the department to reject Lucey's view that the norm for farms should be between fifteen and twenty acres, insisting that progress in agriculture required larger farms: 'It cannot be disputed, however, that relatively, there is a greater scope for improving farming standards on large farms than upon small holdings and that most of the larger holdings in this country would be far more valuable to the nation if they were more intensively worked.' It also rejected most of the criticism of the cattle economy on the grounds that Irish exports were drawn predominantly from this sector. In most cases the department dismissed alternatives to the cattle trade, especially the belief that resources should be concentrated on dairy products.

The Department of Agriculture's response was sober and realistic if fairly conservative. The influence of the minister, James Dillon, can be seen in it, but it also reflected the department's belief that agricultural policy had again, as it had in the 1920s, rightly focused almost entirely on the stronger farming sector, especially those who exported. There is little discussion of the family farm as a socio-economic unit, which had been Lucey's concern, nor is there a discussion of agriculture's contribution to population decline. Although not stated explicitly, there is an assumption that rural Ireland could not provide the means to sustain a growing population. This was not a view shared by the Bishop of Cork, whose minority report was almost exclusively concerned with the family on the land as an ideal unit. Nor did Lucey display any great knowledge of economics or the role of the market. It is probable that the bishop had little concern with economics as such; for him the main function of agriculture policy was to maintain as many people on the land as possible. The Minister for Lands, Joseph Blowick, shared many of these concerns. As leader of Clann na Talmhan, he considered the defence of the family farm, its income and social environment to be his primary concern, especially in the west of Ireland. Given this, it might have been expected that he would prove to be a natural ally of Bishop Lucey, yet this did not turn out to be the case. In doctrinaire fashion, Lucey accused the Land Commission of extinguishing 'far more homesteads than it has created' (paragraph 347). Blowick countered this by noting that without the actions of the Land Commission between 1931 and 1949, 'the decline would have been at least three times as great and catastrophic'. He added that more resources would have helped and concluded that if a 'few hundred' new holdings and one thousand enlargements had been provided every year the decline in holdings would have been halved. What is not clear from this assertion is whether there was a causal relationship between land distribution and population increase.[81]

Blowick considered lack of finance to be the main obstacle to securing more farms. He estimated that there were over 100,000 farms in the state which did not provide a 'secure livelihood' for a family, while 19,000 of these in the western counties were in poor condition. He complained the state was now acquiring less land than previously, and recommended a return to the more active and traditional policy. Moreover, the Land Commission had progressively increased the size of what it considered to be an 'economic holding' outside the western counties, from twenty-one acres in 1935 to thirty-three by 1949. In doing so the department also rejected Lucey's belief that the ideal size should be between fifteen and twenty acres, believing that this size was no longer a realistic one for a farm. It also rejected as utopian the view propounded by Lucey that 50,000 new farm holdings could be created, leading to an increase in the population of 150,000 (paragraph 347). Even if feasible, the cost (estimated at £125 million) was considered prohibitive. Such action would also undermine the existing stability of rural Ireland, as it would require the compulsory purchase of some 30,000 farms in excess of 100 acres. One by-product of this would have been the virtual extinction of the livestock industry and its export potential, though this might not have been unwelcome to some sections of Fianna Fáil.[82] The report and memoranda were subsequently discussed at a cabinet meeting in July 1956 and a decision was taken to establish a cabinet committee to examine the question and make recommendations for action. There is no evidence that any action was taken during the life of the Inter-Party government prior to the 1957 election.[83]

The failure of the Commission on Emigration to influence policy or to generate political debate draws attention to the weakening influence of rural Ireland and the increasing salience of urban Ireland and industrialisation in the process of economic growth. Emigration was the most public feature of the economic crisis that characterised Ireland during the late 1950s. Ireland was the major exception to the European-wide economic expansion during that decade. Emigration was in large part a symptom of the crisis, but more explicitly a reflection of the collapse of rural Ireland as a self-sustained socio-economic unit. Bishop Lucey's minority report was not in essence an economic analysis, but a defence of a way of life with assertions of how it could be maintained. Lucey started from the premise that the small family farm was the ideal unit for a stable moral community, and all his recommendations followed from that premise. He did not give any indication of how this might be achieved, given his opposition to state control. Though not the last gasp of Catholic corporatism or vocationalism in the Irish context, his minority report was the last influential statement of that position before Irish society began to change more profoundly in the 1960s. Other members of the hierarchy were more realistic than Lucey, though often critical of government policy. The Bishop of Clonfert, William Philbin, suggested in 1957 that the diminution of Ireland's population would destroy its unique contribution to the world, especially the provision of missionaries and its spiritual influence. He linked economic decline with political sovereignty and patriotism, arguing that independence might be threatened by decline. Yet while Philbin recognised the need to increase the state's overall prosperity, his concern was not significantly different from Lucey's. He believed that prosperity was necessary; otherwise

Ireland could not achieve unification: 'If only a remnant of the Irish people is left at home, living in a run down economy, it will matter little how we are governed, we shall be a negligible factor in human affairs.' The hierarchy more generally was concerned with emigration, but most bishops were attracted by the ideals of rural life at a time when it was collapsing under its own inability to maintain people on the land.[84]

A new realism?

In April 1959 Lucey attacked the reported statement of a Fianna Fáil minister that emigration would probably be a permanent feature of Irish life. The bishop asserted that the state had a duty to provide for the people by preventing unemployment and emigration. Accordingly, 'The natural purpose of any State, according to Catholic teaching, is to ensure peace and prosperity for all its citizens. Prosperity for some, even for the majority, and the dawn of the emigrant ship for the rest, does not satisfy discretive justice. All in this country must be provided for, even if it means the lowering of the living standards.' Lucey asserted that no 'civilised country washed its hands so completely of its emigrants as the Irish Republic', complaining that there was a paradox in Irish policy making associated with ever-increasing public debt while unemployment rose and emigration accelerated.[85] Yet Lucey did not have a monopoly of influence in these matters. Alternative sources of opinion were increasingly available within and outside the civil service. For example, Garret FitzGerald's economic commentaries were appearing regularly in the *Irish Times*, but also in departmental files, and his analysis owed little to the moralising of Bishop Lucey or the idealisation of rural Ireland.[86] In addition, influential reports and publications from the OEEC and other international agencies were now influencing departmental officials in key positions, the most influential of whom was T.K. Whitaker, the Secretary of the Department of Finance. In contrast to the views promoted by Bishop Lucey, Lemass — who succeeded de Valera as Taoiseach in June 1959 — was attempting to design a more modern and dynamic economic strategy. He addressed some of the issues associated with emigration in a speech to the Dublin Chamber of Commerce a little over a year after he became Taoiseach. He recognised that emigration remained a major problem for Ireland. It offered further evidence, he said, 'of the insufficiency of our efforts to date to develop a completely attractive way of life for all the elements of the national community'. He recognised that the only way to achieve this was by providing employment and living standards comparable to those available to emigrants. While highlighting the need for economic development, Lemass also referred to the Commission on Emigration, drawing attention to the non-economic, social and psychological factors contributing to emigration. He believed that these features led many emigrants to leave employment in Ireland or not to take up employment within the state when available. National policy should focus on discovering and identifying all the features leading to emigration. At the same time, he was realistic enough to counter Lucey's admonitions, openly rejecting the view 'that emigration can be ended by urging people to accept willingly lower living standards in Ireland than they can hope to attain elsewhere, or by appeals to patriotism alone'.[87]

Lemass' argument here and elsewhere suggests that a new way of thinking about the problems associated with emigration had emerged with his succession as Taoiseach. It is not that emigration disappeared automatically — indeed it was to pose a problem throughout the following decade and beyond — but Lemass was capable of dispensing with traditional rhetoric and policy to provide a more realistic response to a deep-rooted problem, and in contrast to his predecessor he seemed willing to recognise that many of the obstacles to change existed in Ireland itself and were not imposed from the outside. Yet even Lemass was not in a position in 1959 to resolve the contradictions associated with slow growth, the demand for higher living standards and the attractions of emigration. The economy was still depressed and the agrarian sector unable to provide the means for growth. A radical change in economic policy was required, and it was to this that Lemass and his new government turned, though not always with the success hoped for.

6

Conservative Nationalism and the Fear of Change, 1945–1961

Stability and isolation

Political failure is the main feature of postwar Ireland and de Valera was the politician most responsible for this. What is noticeable is that Ireland's economic performance is much weaker after 1932, and especially between 1945 and 1961, than it was between 1922 and 1932. Why should this be the case? In part it can be attributed to the growing isolationism of the political elite, the population in general and the Catholic Church after the Second World War. This was compounded by the continuation of economic policies (both industrial and agricultural) which, even if they had been appropriate between 1932 and 1939, were inadequate to the postwar challenge. A further contributory factor was the intensely stable nature of the society after 1945, a stability reinforced by the successful neutrality policy and the influence of the 1937 constitution. In a rapidly changing world, the defence of this stability, politically, economically and socially, weakened the possibility of innovative action within Ireland and deflected any real prospect of external influence. Both isolationism and stability were products of Fianna Fáil's political success and the consequent consensus which grew out of this. This achievement was so successful that none of the main parties or the population at large concluded that change was necessary.

By the 1940s much had been achieved and Irish nationalism moved into a more conservative and defensive phase of development. The aim of Fianna Fáil was now to preserve what had been achieved and defend the newly stabilised status quo. In so far as changes occur, their function is to further secure these achievements and to hold off or neutralise destabilising influences within or outside the state. By the end of the Second World War the Irish constitution was defending a traditional way of life against the changes taking place elsewhere in Europe. But the constitution was also a means for commanding internal loyalty and countering dissent.[1] Despite the shift from an active to a more passive phase of nationalism, nationalism still provided the context for politics in Ireland at the end of the Second World War. In contrast to many other political systems in Europe, political cleavages that centred on language, religion or class were weak or non-existent in Ireland. The form that political competition takes in systems organised along nationalist lines is somewhat different to those associated with linguistic, religious or class cleavages.[2] Within a nationalist political system there is a high premium on consensus and a tendency to move towards equilibrium. Unless nationalism is rejected or challenged, as it was in Ireland up to 1921 and continued to be in Northern Ireland thereafter, common ground is achievable by all the parties which participate in democratic politics. A nationalist party system within a liberal democratic society will tend towards consensus, all else being equal. This condition had been largely met in the Irish Free State after 1927 and was maintained after Fianna Fáil came to power in 1932. The division within the consensus after this was between those who wished to use the state for developmental purposes, in respect of both domestic policy and the state's sovereign status, and those who had a more limited and passive perspective on such purposes. This latter view was dominant until about 1932, while the activist view, represented by Fianna Fáil, became the dominant one after this. Not only was the Fianna Fáil view dominant, but during the Second World War it was extended to include virtually all segments of political opinion in defence of the state in wartime, cementing further the Fianna Fáil-generated consensus.[3]

A political equilibrium based on consensus within a nationalist political system can produce powerful obstacles to change. One of the paradoxes of Irish life from 1945 until the early 1960s was that the main forces within the society were committed to its stability while the social system itself was unravelling. The centrepiece of this stability was the 1937 constitution, which remained unchanged for thirty years. Moreover, the constitution served as a reminder and institutionalisation of certain values held by the society. Among these, the importance of religion, the irredentist claim to Northern Ireland and the commitment to revive the Irish language stand out. In general, the Irish constitution was a conservative system-maintaining device between 1941 and 1972, restricting change and promoting the further stabilisation of the society. It is not until the mid 1960s that serious discussion about possible change begins again; and even then the discussion is very cautious indeed. The one major innovation in Ireland between 1945 and 1959 did not require an amendment to the constitution. The declaration of the Republic in 1949 was in line with the sentiments in the document. In contrast, the attempt to abolish the proportional representation electoral system in 1959 was rejected by the electorate. This Constitutional stability was also reinforced by the full sovereignty achieved by the state and by the specific balance of forces in the society and politics after 1945.[4]

This internal stability in terms of institutions and political culture disguised a growing indifference to the outside world. As late as 1953, the Minister for External Affairs, Frank Aiken, claimed that Irish foreign policy was based on the view that Irish freedom had to be achieved before Ireland would fight for the freedom of others.[5] De Valera's decision to go to the German legation to offer condolences on Hitler's death in May 1945 reflected this indifference to the outside world, and especially to democratic opinion. This alienated Ireland from Europe, though de Valera expressed surprise at the hostile European and American reaction, claiming that he was personally opposed to the Nazi regime. The British Representative in Dublin, Sir John Maffey, responded that de Valera was behind the times and that the Allies were disappointed with him. Maffey concluded that the Irish government was alarmed that its foreign policy was proving ineffective.[6] Around the same time, Archbishop McQuaid was reported questioning Ireland's isolationism, though his actions on other issues do not lend support to this. Perhaps more representative of McQuaid's position was his criticism of the Italian Minister, Baron Gonfalonieri, for making friends with non-Catholics after taking up his post in Dublin. McQuaid refused to return a call from the Minister and subsequently complained that his behaviour was inappropriate for an Italian Catholic with two saints in the family line.[7]

The postwar Fianna Fáil government remained hostile to the Commonwealth and any continuing connection to Britain. De Valera certainly believed that Ireland owed no obligation to the United Kingdom and that, to all intents and purposes, 'This is an independent Republic acknowledging no sovereignty except that of the people, a fact which their attitude during the recent war should have amply demonstrated.' This attitude had wider implications. When Irish membership of the United Nations (UN) was rejected in 1946, de Valera dismissed the issue as unimportant in conversation with Lord President Herbert Morrison. In 1953 he was reported as saying that he was no longer interested in the UN and that if Ireland had been admitted he would probably have walked out of the organisation by now.[8] In one of life's little ironies, when de Valera made his famous reply to Churchill's attack on Ireland's neutrality during the war in May 1945, the Irish authorities had to apply to the British for permission to relay the broadcast to the United States.[9]

It has been said that de Valera 'had learned many political lessons from the world of high diplomacy between 1939 and 1945'. If this was indeed the case, policy makers in Ireland did not apply the lessons. The policy environment established by Fianna Fáil after 1932 was reinforced by the Second World War and Irish neutrality and was maintained throughout the 1950s. Ireland's distance from world and European affairs grew as a consequence. Isolationism or insularity did not concern the majority of Irish citizens. Most Irish nationalists agreed with de Valera's reply to Churchill in 1945, and this was not simply reactive nationalism on their part. It reflected Fianna Fáil's success in establishing a political consensus shared by most of those who lived in the state. Fianna Fáil's achievement was considerable in political terms, being reflected in its dominance of the party system by 1938. Fianna Fáil's deepening of Irish sovereignty vindicated Michael Collins' prediction that the Irish Free State could realise the aims of the independence movement. Fianna Fáil's success in this respect also confirmed that the Civil War had been unnecessary. With the exception of IRA extremists, most sections of Irish public opinion now accepted the view that the Irish state was best placed to achieve nationalist objectives. This convergence and consensus was marred for nationalists by the continuation of partition and by the failure to revive the Irish language, but there was general agreement that it was within the power of an Irish state to achieve these goals.[10]

The consensual, isolationist and stable nature of nationalist Ireland in 1945 created a rather smug and superior environment. Ireland was promoted as a Catholic, nationalist, democratic and agricultural alternative to the Anglo-American and Soviet worlds in and after 1945. According to the Department of Education, 'The revival of the Irish language and the fostering of the distinctive Irish turn of mind and way of life must continue to be the main aim of the educational system whatever changes may be made therein.'[11] Yet, this very self-confidence, its nationalism and its commitment to economic protection, had serious consequences, as it prevented Irish policy makers and public opinion generally from appreciating the hard choices which had to be made in the postwar world. Furthermore, isolation and accelerating emigration also removed a further incentive to acting in a more innovative fashion. In this context, postwar Ireland shared with authoritarian Spain and Portugal a distrust of the new liberal order dominated by the United States. Until 1945 Ireland could be more accurately compared with states such as Denmark and the Netherlands, but in the postwar period Ireland's continuing commitment to economic nationalism, Catholic social values and the superiority of rural over urban values placed it increasingly alongside the less developed and authoritarian states in southern Europe. Ireland still had much in common with northern European democracies after 1945, including strong democratic institutions and culture, a tradition of neutrality, close trading connections with the United Kingdom and sensitivity to sovereignty and large neighbours. Yet notwithstanding these similarities, between 1945 and 1960 Ireland's developmental path and its politics increasingly diverged from these democratic states.[12]

De Valera remained the key influence in postwar Ireland. None of his colleagues in Fianna Fáil challenged his stature, nor could any opposition leader provide an alternative. He may not have fully realised his inner vision of the perfect society as expressed in his 1943 St Patrick's Day broadcast, but in many ways Irish society was closer to this vision than to any other. The stress placed on rural social organisation as an ideal, on moral certainties reinforced by the presence of God in daily life and on a belief in the agelessness of the nation as well as its inherent goodness were affirmed throughout nationalist Ireland — as was his conviction that the 'Ireland we dreamed of would be the home of a people who valued material wealth only as the basis of right living, of a people who were satisfied with frugal comfort and devoted their leisure to the things of the spirit'. This recognised the key nationalist belief that there is more to life than mere accumulation of wealth. De Valera also insisted that Irish society had a major contribution to make to the future of Europe, a contribution that would not diminish Irish nationalism: 'We should remember also that the more we preserve and develop our individuality and our characteristics as a distinct nation, the more secure will be our freedom and the more valuable our contribution to humanity when this war is over.'[13]

However, this confidence that Ireland had a special role to play in the post-war world was misplaced. Ireland faced hostility from the Soviet Union and its allies, but more importantly the United States continued to oppose Irish neutrality and later criticised the country's refusal to become involved in the American-led anti-communist crusade. Furthermore, Irish isolationism was compounded by its continuing commitment to economic nationalism at a time when most European states were dismantling these types of policies. The experience of fascism, depression and war persuaded the United States administration and the European elite that nationalism in its traditional form could not provide the basis for political mobilisation or economic policy making. Nationalism did not disappear, but political elites were reluctant to use overt nationalist symbols in political competition. National interest was not absent, but the form it took marked a sea change from the preceding decades. During the decade after 1945 European states experimented with a wide range of non-nationalist policies. The EEC was the most ambitious of these, while interdependency among Scandinavian states provided an alternative to such integrationist schemes, as did the development of such arrangements as NATO, the OEEC and the General Agreement on Tariffs and Trade (GATT). Whereas most liberal states actively participated in one or other of these institutions, Ireland remained well outside them, because they all assumed a liberal political and economic foundation that did not appeal to Fianna Fáil's conception of the nationalist state.[14]

De Valera's response to this challenge was one of uncertainty. In an address delivered to the Historical Society at Trinity College Dublin in November 1944, he reflected on his experience at the League of Nations in the 1930s and on the prospects for small states in this new world order. He attempted to balance the key elements of his nationalist views with a recognition that the world might be changing, concluding that he could see no solution to war in the present international circumstances. Though he believed that 'the only solution which would guarantee peace is a universal World State', he also recognised that such an organisation was unrealisable. De Valera added, quite significantly, that a central authority (not defined) could serve the interests of small nations if it had enough military power to enforce decisions and override the influence exercised by large states.[15] Despite these hints, Irish diplomatic practice did not prove to be innovative after 1945. The maintenance of a narrowly nationalist doctrine had a negative impact on Irish diplomacy for at least fifteen years after the end of the war. In particular, de Valera remained obsessed with partition, as the report of a British diplomat who met the Taoiseach in 1947 makes clear:

> Unless we [the United Kingdom] made it plain that we were in favour of reunion, he [de Valera] was afraid that the extremists in Eire would again resort to the tactics of the past. They would penetrate the Ulster counties, would commit acts of sabotage and perhaps assassination, and the situation would go from bad to worse. He felt sure that this would happen, because these men were ardently convinced that their cause was right, and that they

were entitled to use armed force to promote it. Indeed he said, if he were a young man, he did not know what he himself might feel obliged to do.[16]

De Valera's pessimism extended beyond partition. According to a report prepared by Sir John Maffey:

> Mr de Valera said he could see no sign of hope in the world's affairs. To him it seemed that nothing could prevent a war between the United States and Russia. There was nothing to stop Russia marching west and occupying France and Europe generally. So far as atomic bombs were concerned, Russia would not mind them falling on Europe.

It is probable that de Valera was out of sympathy with the new world order and this had an impact on policy. His influence in Fianna Fáil was such that little could be achieved without his support, or at least the absence of his opposition.[17]

Despite the tensions that the policy of neutrality generated, relations with the United Kingdom after the war were better than might have been anticipated. There was no campaign against Ireland by Britain; indeed trade and diplomatic relations were quickly regularised.[18] Yet, partition remained de Valera's and the Irish government's obsession, often obscuring the possibility of alternative strategies both in respect of Northern Ireland and more generally.[19] There had been some anticipation in nationalist circles that a Labour government would promote Ireland's position on Northern Ireland. This was an illusion soon shattered. Sir John Maffey believed that partition was 'wrapped up in passion and hysteria' and that 'There is every reason to fear that we may be exposed to this again owing to the growing agitation on the partition issue, and its effect on the minds of the new generation of Irishmen indoctrinated with hatred and false history.' While this is a diplomatic report, there is enough evidence to suggest that Maffey's analysis was accurate and that de Valera was 'a slave to his own past'.[20] It became increasingly difficult for the Irish government to influence British policy on Northern Ireland. The unionist majority rejected the Irish claim to sovereignty and Northern Ireland's contribution to the war effort secured its position with British opinion for the next two decades. Not only was the British government unwilling to support Irish unity, but the 1947 Nationality Act provided that those who lived in Northern Ireland were British citizens. The Irish government angrily rejected this, insisting that it was not prepared to 'recognise the moral validity of partition or accept it as imposing upon Irish citizens of the partitioned area the duty of allegiance to any nation or state other than Ireland.' Furthermore, all those who lived in Northern Ireland 'owe fidelity to the Irish nation and loyalty to the Irish state as fundamental political duties', a claim just as vigorously rejected by the British majority there.[21] De Valera's fixation with partition as an institutional arrangement provided no basis for putting pressure on the United Kingdom government to reform Northern Ireland. His insistence that all those who lived in Northern Ireland were Irish citizens alienated both the unionists and the British government, while providing no help for the nationalist minority there. More generally, de Valera became more remote from world events and more exasperated by his failure to address the subtle and complex environment developing during the postwar world.[22]

Nor did policy change when the Inter-Party government was formed in 1948. What was more serious was that Irish diplomats did not appreciate the consequence of their actions. When Ireland declared a republic and left the Commonwealth, the United Kingdom responded by introducing the Ireland Act 1949 to regularise relations between the two states. This act was quite generous to the new republic, declaring in section 2 (1) that though the Republic of Ireland was not part of the dominions it was also 'not a foreign country for the purposes of any law in force in any part of the United Kingdom'. The British government could have made life difficult for the Republic after 1949, but chose not to do so for a variety of complicated reasons. Despite this, the Irish government was outraged at the act; it ignored this generous policy and concentrated on section 1 (2), which affirmed that Northern Ireland would remain part of the United Kingdom unless the parliament of Northern Ireland decided otherwise. In diplomatic terms this was not an unreasonable position; indeed in some respects it was quite a liberal response to irredentist nationalism. Yet, in response, a mass anti-partitionist movement was created in the vain hope of reversing the position. The naïvety of Irish nationalism at this time is well represented by the President of the Irish Republic, Seán T. O'Kelly, who complained to a correspondent that events after 1945 had led him to 'imagine that perhaps I'd see the unity of Ireland as an accomplished fact before my final call came, but now I'm doubtful'. He added that this hope and the friendly relations between the two states 'have been blown sky high' as a consequence of the commitments made to Northern Ireland. O'Kelly blamed the Taoiseach, John A. Costello, for his inept handling of the situation, but he could not recognise that the real difficulty was with the unrealistic expectations generated by the government that establishing a republic would achieve a breakthrough on the north.[23]

Irredentism was at the heart of Irish policy after 1945. Successive Irish governments could not accept any arrangement which acknowledged the existence of partition. It was the excuse provided for not joining NATO and it dogged every interaction between the United Kingdom and the Republic. The Minister for External Affairs in the Inter-Party government, Seán MacBride, simply maintained de Valera's view of the situation, though he expressed it in more unrealistic and hysterical fashion. MacBride complained in May 1950 that the British government was not doing enough 'to bring the North to his [MacBride's] way of thinking'. He believed that the British government could in some unfathomable way force the unionist majority to move towards the Irish Republic. The British attitude, according to MacBride, was 'definitely provocative and unhelpful', but this provoked a counter-response from the British:

> The facts were that Eire had elected to leave the Commonwealth and had repudiated her allegiance to the King, such as it was. She was perfectly entitled to do so, as any Dominion was. But the immediate and inevitable

> consequences of her action, coupled with violent speeches in the South and appeals to 'arms to take the North', was naturally to provoke anxiety in the North for the formal restatement of their position which was embodied in the Ireland Act. The Republic has no one to thank but themselves for this, and it was useless to suggest that they had any grievance against us over it.[24]

In May 1952 Lord Pakenham, Minister of Civil Aviation in the previous Labour government and long-time supporter of the Irish cause in Britain, approached the Dominions Office after a conversation with de Valera and Frank Aiken. According to Pakenham, both men agreed that they would not coerce the north, but in return they wanted the British government to declare itself in favour of Irish unity. The response of the Secretary of State, The Marquess of Salisbury, to the approach was that he could 'see no reason why we should try and use our influence to meet the wishes of the Irish government in this connection, unless the Irish government returns to the Commonwealth and fully satisfies us in regard to defence commitments or somehow or other reassures us as to the future of this connection'. When a little later the IRA initiated a border campaign, the British government criticised the Irish government for its weak response. This was attributed to the presence of the Labour Party in the government. The Irish Ambassador hinted to the British that the Irish would have difficulty with public opinion in the Republic, 'which while condemning, was not wholly unsympathetic' to the IRA campaign.[25]

A failure of nerve on Northern Ireland

If relations with Britain remained uneasy, policy in respect of Northern Ireland was disastrous. Both the Fianna Fáil and the Inter-Party governments engaged in rhetorical posturing on this issue. De Valera's influence was thoroughly unhelpful and at times obstructive. Within Fianna Fáil, some members recognised the futility of anti-partitionist dogma. As the new IRA campaign gathered strength (and some support) in early 1955, the party's anti-partition committee was reconsidering policy. Lemass chaired the committee, which included, among others, Seán MacEntee, Seán Moylan, Frank Aiken, Gerry Boland and Charles Haughey. Colonel Matthew Feehan, another of its members, offering 'practical suggestions for adoption by the party in regard to partition', effectively called on Fianna Fáil to abandon its traditional policy. He urged the party to admit that Irish nationalism had failed to persuade unionists of the validity of its case. Feehan recognised that 'when unity comes it will not be based on a perfect solution', adding that the process would be long and drawn out and would probably frustrate northern nationalist as well as Fianna Fáil supporters. One obstacle to change was the ambiguous attitude to violence on the part of some Fianna Fáil members. Feehan believed that such ambiguity was unproductive to positive thinking on Northern Ireland. He recommended that policy should no longer focus on simply getting the British out of Northern Ireland, but on creating the conditions for uniting 'all

Irishmen'. The use of force, he claimed, had undermined previous attempts to create the conditions to achieve unity:

> The supporters of force argue that we only won freedom for the 26 counties by using force against the British. This argument is false as it is now a question, not primarily of winning something from Britain, but of winning, willing re-union from our misguided fellow countrymen. To harness the enthusiasm of idealistic youth in a campaign to win over by conviction the local majority now against us, is a task the solution of which Fianna Fáil should undertake.[26]

The difficulties facing any shift in policy can be appreciated by a memorandum prepared for a national executive meeting by the Tomás Ó Cléirigh Cumann in Dublin. This advocated the coercion of northern unionists, on the grounds that persuasion had failed to achieve unity. A campaign of civil disobedience in selected areas of Northern Ireland was proposed, the cost of which would be borne by the Irish government. Force should never be ruled out, it was maintained: 'Partition will not be ended without coercing Unionists. The aim of the campaign is to force either negotiation or a plebiscite on the portion of the area selected for the campaign. In the event of this campaign leading to the use of military force aid to be given by the Irish army.'[27] Feehan's moderate and reasonable appreciation of unionist fears and nationalist failure ran counter not only to the memorandum of the Tomás Ó Cléirigh Cumann but to the prevailing ideological view within Fianna Fáil.

Lemass responded to this by preparing his own memorandum, following discussions within the anti-partition committee. At the heart of Lemass' thinking was an attempt to reconcile his own continuing hostility to partition with the recognition that traditional anti-partitionism provided no way forward. He emphasised the need to strengthen 'all links with the six county majority', not just the nationalist minority. In addition, 'any course of action which would have the effect of embittering relations between the people of both areas, or making fruitful economic and cultural contacts more difficult', should be discouraged. Clear assurances in respect of civil and religious rights had to be given, while attention should be paid to any aspect of domestic policy in the Republic which might affect this. In a practical mode, Lemass recommended economic, infrastructural and tourist co-operation as means to promote better understanding. It is already possible to see here the beginning of the new departure initiated by Lemass when he became Taoiseach.[28] Lemass sent his memorandum to de Valera, noting that the committee had agreed it. De Valera was clearly uneasy about the implications of the recommendations and, while not openly rejecting the memorandum, was concerned that its contents would create confusion among party members and northern nationalists. De Valera decided to refer the document to the central committee of the party prior to the national executive discussing it. This appears to have buried the initiative, as it was not discussed subsequently at the national executive.[29] De Valera considered that partition would come to an end because it was nonsense, yet he admitted to the British Ambassador in 1953 that his information concerning Northern Ireland was inadequate.[30]

The decision by the IRA to initiate a new military campaign against Northern Ireland postponed any conciliatory action towards the north, while confirming Feehan's fears. There was widespread sympathy, and not a little support, for the IRA campaign within Fianna Fáil. After the IRA attack on Brookeborough police barracks in County Fermanagh on 1 January 1957, one party resolution admired

> The courage and selflessness of Seán South and Fergal O'Hanlon [two IRA men killed in the attack] in fighting for Ireland and giving their lives in her cause. Further, regarding England as the sole enemy of our country, we deplore that aspect of the foreign policy of Irish Governments which compels our people to live in amity with this enemy and collaborate with her.

Following a number of similar resolutions, Lemass issued a circular to Fianna Fáil branches expressing the concern of the national executive 'that expressions of sympathy with the relatives of those who lost their lives in recent raids in the Six Counties would be so expressed as to make it clear that no approval of the policy of the organisation of which they were members was implied, and no encouragement given to others to associate themselves with this organisation'.[31] There was little hope that Fianna Fáil would pursue a new course of action while IRA activists were dying and its members were jailed by the Northern Ireland government. With an election pending, the deaths of South and O'Hanlon exposed Fianna Fáil's republican constituency to an electoral threat from Sinn Féin, the IRA's political wing. In fact, Sinn Féin won four seats at the 1957 general election, three from Fianna Fáil.[32] Notwithstanding this, Fianna Fáil comfortably won the 1957 election, while the Sinn Féin TDs never took their seats in the Dáil. Yet the emotional pressure on Fianna Fáil remained, once again preventing positive action. After Fianna Fáil returned to government, de Valera introduced internment to eliminate any possible threat to the Irish state by the IRA. At the Fianna Fáil ard fheis in November 1957, de Valera argued that the connection between the IRA in 1957 and that of his generation was spurious, while condemning what he described as the 'falsification of history' at school. In the following year in the Dáil, de Valera insisted that if force was to be used in Northern Ireland, 'that attempt could be made only by the Irish nation and by those who are authorised to act on behalf of the Irish nation. If force were to be used, it would have to be used with the authority of this House. I do not think it would be the right method in any case.'[33]

This was clearly the limit of de Valera's thinking on Northern Ireland. There was a desire to defend the state and, when opportune, to extend the sovereignty of the Republic to Northern Ireland. De Valera was less likely than Lemass to believe that changes had to be made in the Republic to accommodate unionist fears; the process he envisaged was one where the Republic would absorb Northern Ireland without any major institutional difficulty. At a meeting in July 1958 in London, the Minister for External Affairs, Frank

Aiken, discussed the issue of partition with Lord Home, Secretary of State for Commonwealth Relations. Aiken demanded that the British government support the integration of the two parts of Ireland into a single sovereign state under the authority of a Dublin parliament. He dismissed out of hand Home's reservations about the likelihood of the unionists agreeing to any such change. Unionism never seemed to intrude on Aiken's considerations. The central belief among Irish policy makers continued to be that a bilateral arrangement between the United Kingdom and Ireland would resolve the problem and that all parties in Northern Ireland would simply accept the negotiated outcome. Aiken remained in the realm of political fantasy by impressing on the British minister that a solution to partition was now an imperative since de Valera was nearing the end of his political career. Consequently, he believed that a decision was urgently required: 'because of the Taoiseach's stature in the country, any solution which he might endorse would in all probability be acceptable to the majority of the Irish people'. This continued to ignore the essence of the problem, which was the presence of one million unionists in Northern Ireland. This lack of realism can be seen in 1957 when de Valera asked government departments to prepare studies on 'practical problems arising on reintegration of national territory'. Various departments responded, though their emphasis ranged from the banal to the utopian. The Department of Industry and Commerce reported that some progress had been made but no further study was actually required or justified, Defence concluded that military issues did require further study, and Finance, though in favour of a study, believed that there was no urgency. In contrast, most other departments were opposed to any study.[34]

The contrast in tone and argumentation between de Valera's relations with the United Kingdom and that pursued by Lemass when he became Taoiseach can be seen when Lemass visited London in July 1959 and met the Prime Minister, Harold Macmillan, and Lord Home. Lemass made no demands on the British, but highlighted the prospects for co-operation between the two governments on the island. He also identified specific changes that he believed could contribute to a more open relationship between north and south. According to the Irish minutes of the meeting:

> The Taoiseach remarked that not alone must the people of the Six Counties be persuaded of the desirability of co-operation with their fellow countrymen in the twenty six counties, but the latter must also be educated in the same direction and this desideratum was not absent from the Taoiseach's mind in his recent announcements. The armed incidents which had taken place across the border had given a set back to the tendency towards a more reasonable attitude on the part of the more broadminded of the Unionists in the Six Counties.

What can be seen here is a subtle but important shift in emphasis, one which recognised that unionism was an obstacle which had to be treated seriously. This did not preclude Lemass asking the United Kingdom government to make public statements in respect of Northern Ireland, but the emphasis had shifted perceptibly.[35]

The politics of inertia after 1945

The political scientist James Hogan remarked in 1945 that 'The gratitude of a democratic electorate is notoriously short lived.'[36] Despite Fianna Fáil's long-term political success, the party was to suffer difficulties for the next twenty years. On only one occasion between 1945 and 1969, in 1957, was Fianna Fáil able to form a government with a clear majority. The 1943 general election setback was reversed in 1944, but in 1948 an unwieldy Inter-Party coalition removed de Valera from office for the first time in sixteen years. In one sense, the outcome of the 1948 election was an accident waiting to happen. Fianna Fáil had survived various political challenges, but had become arrogant and considered itself indispensable. However, there were few differences between the parties by 1948; all shared the basic assumptions of the Fianna Fáil consensus. Most importantly, Fianna Fáil had consistently ruled out coalition, in effect forcing all the opposition parties to unite to form a government. Lemass might well insist in October 1947 that 'Our comparative well being was due to the fact that we had a secure and united government', but the electorate did not endorse this view in 1948.[37]

At the 1944 election, Fianna Fáil strategists noted that there was a loose anti-Fianna Fáil mood among the other parties, reflected in lower than normal transfers from these parties to Fianna Fáil.[38] This continued into the postwar elections and Fianna Fáil's hold on government was not to be secure again until the 1960s. Yet none of this was inevitable. Fianna Fáil easily won the June 1946 by-election in Cork Borough, though Fine Gael's vote increased dramatically over its 1944 nadir. Michael O'Riordan, later to be General Secretary of the Communist Party of Ireland, succeeded in attracting nearly 11 per cent of the vote running as a socialist, while the former IRA leader Tom Barry received 8.7 per cent. What is of interest here is that the election took place in an urban environment with a strong and well-organised trade union movement, yet there is little evidence of a swing against the government.[39]

Furthermore, though Fine Gael did well in this by-election, its political prospects remained poor. It was Fine Gael rather than Fianna Fáil which appeared to be encountering short- and long-term electoral difficulties. The mood within the party itself was extremely pessimistic. A party meeting in November 1945 concentrated minds on the threat to Fine Gael, yet its leadership had little comfort to offer. At issue was whether the party would field candidates at a number of by-elections. The party leader, Richard Mulcahy, believed it might be possible to field a candidate in the Clare by-election, but he had to admit that he could not provide candidates for other constituencies. The danger for Fine Gael was that it 'could come last in all of them and this would further erode the party'. Patrick McGilligan admitted that Fine Gael was in the 'Doldrums', attributing this to the prosperity of the farming community and the extent to which emigration had short-circuited worker discontent with the wartime wage restrictions: 'It was wrong to infuse any new policy into existing circumstances and that it was better to wait for the drop in prices. We had a declining population, more illness and more crime than ever before and it was essential to go slowly.' Mulcahy concluded the meeting on an upbeat note, asserting that 'the crisis was not one which would weaken the party but, in fact, may bring strength to the party'. There is a real sense that Mulcahy and his colleagues were whistling past the graveyard, and the by-election results did not display any strong revival for the party.[40] It was to take more than this discussion to effect a change in Fine Gael's fortunes. The difficulty for Fine Gael was that it remained a national party with a wide but weakening appeal. What it did not have by the end of the war was a distinctive policy with which to challenge Fianna Fáil. Its decision to support neutrality and effectively to give up its commitment to Ireland's continuing membership of the Commonwealth undermined any remaining difference of substance between the two national parties. These changes provided the political space for an anti-Fianna Fáil government in 1948 and for Fine Gael's support for the Republic. In the short term it was Fine Gael, rather than Fianna Fáil, which suffered from this.[41]

Fianna Fáil and Fine Gael had reached an accommodation over the previous twenty years, leading to a new consensus within nationalism. The acceptance of the constitution and neutrality by Fine Gael was the corollary of Fianna Fáil accepting the Irish Free State, the Treaty and parliamentary democracy. This is not to say that the two parties were identical prior to the 1948 election, but on matters of substance little actually divided them. Indeed in a sense the main division between the two parties rested on how best to run the economy and in whose interests to do so. This might appear a big difference, but compared to possible divisions on the constitution, neutrality and democracy it was not. Fine Gael had accepted the broad parameters of Fianna Fáil's economic policy, but sought to apply it in a more conservative fashion. Fine Gael tended to endorse a conservative policy, whereas Fianna Fáil was more interventionist. The other parties in the system were overwhelmingly sectional in their appeal, although all claimed to represent the national interest. Clann na Talmhan claimed that the small farmer interest, which it represented, reflected the nation and should be recognised as such. The Labour Party and National Labour placed the working class in this position, insisting that its interests coincided with those of the nation. Clann na Poblachta was not strictly speaking an interest group, but a coalition of diverse interests which sought to replace Fianna Fáil as *the* national party. In some respects it was Fianna Fáil mark II, demanding the realisation of the earlier Fianna Fáil promises on partition, sovereignty and welfare. However, there is no evidence that Clann na Poblachta provided an advance on what Fianna Fáil had traditionally sought. Its electoral appeal was predominantly to the lower middle class in urban areas and to disillusioned republicans elsewhere. Many of its policies were designed to appeal to these sections, especially those in the public sector.[42] The challenge to Fianna Fáil after 1945 came not from the left, as sometimes claimed, but from within the nationalist consensus. Each of the parties which made up the Inter-Party government in 1948 emphasised specific aspects of the nationalist consensus, with Clann na Talmhan and Fine Gael at the conservative end of the spectrum and the Labour Party and Clann na Poblachta at the reformist end. While the Labour Party and National Labour can be placed on the left, their ideological make-up owed more to nationalism and Catholicism than socialism. William Norton, the leader of the Labour Party, was a member of the secretive Knights of St Columbanus, while the party programme was less radical or left wing than that of many Christian democratic parties in Europe at the same time. Clann na Poblachta was socially conservative in many areas, though it was committed to an activist strategy similar to that of Fianna Fáil. Fianna Fáil could, with equal justification, be considered a left-wing party on the basis of the criteria applied to Clann na Poblachta or the Labour Party.[43]

Despite the fragmented nature of the opposition and the weakness of Fine Gael, political pressure did increase at three by-elections in October 1947. Although Fianna Fáil lost two of these to Clann na Poblachta (Dublin County and Tipperary), it won the Waterford contest quite comfortably with Labour transfers; here the Clann na Poblachta candidate was eliminated after the first count. The by-elections were not a disaster for Fianna Fáil, but de Valera's response was to panic, claiming that ending partition was the only method available to him to meet the challenge. Underlying de Valera's concern was the recognition that Britain was introducing an ambitious welfare state and that Irish citizens often measured their well-being against standards prevailing in Britain. In addition, the extension of these welfare provisions to Northern Ireland meant that a welfare gap opened up between the two parts of Ireland. The Minister for Local Government, Seán MacEntee, denied that British living standards had risen appreciably since 1938, asserting in fact that they were lower. De Valera rejected the claim that conditions were better in the north than in the south, arguing that any extra welfare there had been provided by higher taxation. Taxation, he pointed out, was higher in the north than in the south. However, as Hugh Shearman was quick to retort in the *Belfast Telegraph*, this was a sign of prosperity, high exports and high consumption. Low taxation, he implied, was a product of low income and poverty in the south.[44] A Finance memorandum prepared for de Valera in August 1947 alerted the government to the attraction which Britain provided for the Irish. High wages, employment opportunities and welfare services offered an incentive for Irish workers to go to Britain. Britain's new welfare state increased the pressure on Irish policy makers to follow suit, a fact recognised by Lemass at the time. A note prepared for John A. Costello, the new Taoiseach, in 1948 suggested that some of the unionist claims were justified. It was acknowledged that the south would not fare well in a comparison and that this would lead to demands for the introduction of similar services in the south.[45]

Fianna Fáil lost in 1948 because of weaknesses within the party, dissatisfaction among the electorate and the capacity and willingness of all other parties to agree to form a government. It was unprecedented and surprising that such a disparate group of parties could do so. Yet it attests to both the subtle shift within the party system and the extent to which all parties overlapped within the Fianna Fáil consensus. In part, Fianna Fáil excluded itself from government by its refusal to compromise on its no-coalition policy, thus precluding it from seeking potential partners for an alternative government.[46] The split within the Labour Party and the formation of the National Labour Party (NLP) might have provided the basis for a social-nationalist coalition.[47] The divisions within the labour movement (both economic and political) reflected alternative versions of Irish nationalism. The Congress of Irish Unions (CIU) and the NLP were more overtly Catholic and nationalist, whereas the Irish Trades Union Congress (ITUC) and the Labour Party continued to maintain links with Northern Ireland while embracing a fairly weak internationalism associated with European social democracy. Although Fianna Fáil may not have fomented the split in the labour movement, it certainly hoped to gain from it.[48] Lemass used his position as Minister for Industry and Commerce to favour the CIU over the ITUC, thought the latter had a larger membership. Lemass and Fianna Fáil considered the ITUC to be anti-national, because of the support given to it by unions with headquarters outside the state, whereas the CIU enthusiastically endorsed the Fianna Fáil national consensus.[49]

In these circumstances, a coalition between Fianna Fáil and the NLP was possible. However, there were a number of obstacles to this course of action. Particularly important was Fianna Fáil's refusal to form a coalition with any party; moreover, with sixty-eight and five seats respectively, a Fianna Fáil – NLP coalition government would still be short of a majority and would have a precarious existence.[50] In addition, William O'Brien retired as General Secretary of the Irish Transport and General Workers' Union (ITGWU) in 1946. His successor, Thomas Kennedy, did not wield as much influence over the NLP as O'Brien had, though clearly the split was maintained. There was certainly considerable criticism from within the CIU when the NLP joined the Inter-Party government, but the trade unions were unable to exert direct pressure on the political party despite the fact that all of its TDs were members of the ITGWU. Alfred O'Rahilly, the President of University College Cork, was particularly influential with the NLP, and he engaged in a spirited and at times ill-tempered correspondence with MacEntee in the press prior to the 1948 election. O'Rahilly was not opposed to a coalition and his views carried considerable weight with the NLP. A distinction continued to be made between the economic and political wings of the labour movement, and the NLP was never simply a pawn of the ITGWU or Fianna Fáil. Moreover, although the split was divisive, the Labour Party and the NLP did not disagree on most areas of policy.[51]

The way votes transferred between parties at the 1943 and 1944 general elections is of importance in considering the decisions made in 1948. In 1943, 27.0 per cent of Labour transfers went to Fianna Fáil, 16.6 per cent to Fine Gael and 10.9 per cent to Clann na Talmhan. The split in the Labour Party took place in January 1944, and at the general election later that year 27.4 per cent of Labour Party transfers went to Fianna Fáil, 27.7 per cent to Fine Gael and 7.9 per cent to Clann na Talmhan. Transfers from the NLP to Fianna Fáil were 29.6 per cent, to Fine Gael 15.5 per cent and to Clann na Talmhan

9.6 per cent. Although these figures disguise constituency variations, there is a pattern in transfers from Labour to Fine Gael which is clearly not as strong for the NLP.[52] However, it is important not to overstress the differences between the Labour Party and the NLP. Both parties had a similar appeal, to farm labourers in particular, to trade union members in small and medium-size towns (especially where the ITGWU was strong) and to some sections of the Dublin working class. Another reason why the NLP did not support a Fianna Fáil government was that there was real dissatisfaction among traditional Labour supporters in rural Ireland. This was concentrated on the impact of inflation, the direction of wage policy and the perception that the poorer sections of the population were not benefiting from the economic recovery. Fianna Fáil had attempted to address some of these concerns during 1946 and 1947, but the perception remained. The cabinet agreed to a 40 per cent wage increase in November 1946, but this was not enough to still the dissatisfaction.[53]

The Minister for Agriculture, James Ryan, warned his colleagues early the following year that the average wage for agricultural labourers had declined in real terms during the war and that the gap between industrial and agricultural wages continued to widen. While the differential between agriculture and industry was indeed wide, perhaps even more important for agricultural labourers was the evidence that farm income had increased by over a third in real terms when compared to pre-war years.[54] Fianna Fáil was certainly sensitive to these pressures. In October 1947, just before the crucial by-elections, the government increased food subsidies by £5 million. While this was part of a bargain to persuade the trade unions to accept a wage agreement, the government also increased farm prices and revised the retail price index. However, de Valera's attempt to offset criticism was not enough to stem the rise of Clann na Poblachta or the general dissatisfaction. Fianna Fáil also revised the constituencies prior to the election in an attempt to maximise its seats. This attempted manipulation failed to secure it a majority, but it does appear to have deprived the opposition parties of some seats in vital constituencies.[55]

The 1948 general election conforms to the argument presented here that the balance within Ireland was towards stability. By this time it was Fianna Fáil that was under the greatest pressure. Some members blamed it for not fulfilling its programme and others for not pursuing a more dynamic policy. Fianna Fáil's achievement between 1945 and 1948 was in fact quite considerable. Postwar recovery was well under way, industry and agriculture were returning to pre-war levels and trade with Britain had expanded quickly. In local government, health and rural policy further modernisation was being implemented and the state was taking its first tentative steps into a wider diplomatic arena. However, the isolation of the war years continued to affect assumptions and attitudes within the state, and it is probable that the Irish public knew less about the outside world than theretofore. This was the price Fianna Fáil paid for its censorship and isolationism. While the world might be threatening, the impression given within the state was that all was well. This induced both complacency and expectations. The public expected great things of the postwar world; in this they shared the British enthusiasm. Yet the society itself remained complacent. Expectancy was reflected in wage demands, but this was not accompanied by a recognition that the economy remained weak. It also seems that the Fianna Fáil party organisation was weak and divided. Aodh de Blacam's defection to Clann na Poblachta reflected some of the strains in the party. Other Fianna Fáil members also defected and this was reflected in the 1947 by-election defeats, as well as the decline in its first preference vote in 1948. Erskine Childers was extremely pessimistic about Fianna Fáil's prospects in these circumstances. He even speculated that Fianna Fáil should have promoted a new party at the end of the war, which would have included Fianna Fáil, Fine Gael and National Labour. This may have simply been panic on his part, but there was real dissatisfaction in both rural and urban organisations. In Longford, for example, Childers encountered considerable criticism and demands for 'new blood' in the party and the government.[56] The national teachers strike in 1946 also contributed to this dissatisfaction. In April some 100 Fianna Fáil members met in University College Dublin and issued a statement urging the government to accept Archbishop McQuaid's offer to mediate and to meet teachers' representatives. However, the Minister for Education, Tom Derrig, indicated that he was unwilling to do so.[57]

In its election literature in 1948 Fianna Fáil emphasised the need to secure the nation state and its success in economic and social matters. The Dublin North East constituency organisation highlighted the social and economic progress achieved since 1932, heading its literature with the slogan: Vote Fianna Fáil and Safeguard the Nation. This was a very optimistic approach, representing what the party described as 'a progressive policy and an energetic government'. MacEntee attacked both the Labour Party and Clann na Poblachta, warning against communism, left-wing republicanism and social dissolution. Addressing his election literature 'To the People of Ireland', he invited the electorate to 'walk with us towards a new Ireland'. The emphasis here, as elsewhere, was on social advance. He highlighted the increase in national income and the share of it obtained by workers and farmers. MacEntee also played a vigorous role in the campaign, making a sustained effort to justify his claim that Clann na Poblachta was communist and anti-constitutional.[58] At the time of Seán MacBride's by-election victory in October 1947, MacEntee had questioned his association with the IRA and his loyalty to the 1937 constitution. MacBride was accused of being pro-fascist during the war and not being in favour of Irish neutrality. MacBride's election agent threatened Fianna Fáil with legal action under the 1923 Election Act if MacEntee and Gerry Boland did not withdraw 'false statements'.[59] MacEntee argued that there was a crisis in Europe and that this was why the election was required. Fianna Fáil required an overall majority to respond effectively. De Valera, Aiken and Lemass insisted throughout the campaign that Fianna Fáil was the only party which could deal with the crisis and that any other alternative would weaken the state and could not reflect the national interest. Fianna Fáil may also have been affected by allegations of corruption against ministers, allegations that MacEntee went to considerable lengths to reject.[60] The issue in the election according to Fianna Fáil was: Government or Chaos? 'Our tiny state's only chance of survival in the future, as during the six years of the late war, depends entirely upon the stability of its government. Any combination of parties cannot provide that all important stability and effectiveness in administration.'

Fianna Fáil sought to capitalise on its assertion that it was the only party capable of representing the nation and defending the state. It emphasised the constitution, the extension of sovereignty and the socio-economic progress achieved by it. Even when social and economic achievements were highlighted, they were placed in a context which emphasised national pride, for example a national airline and international airports at Dublin and Shannon, projects criticised by Fine Gael. Of particular importance for Fianna Fáil was the rhetoric of solidarity, which highlighted the need to support neutrality, end partition and national unity to face the European crisis. Fianna Fáil's self-assessment was that it had led the state in difficult times; referring to the Second World War, it claimed: 'the nation was brought safely through the ordeal and at its end, enjoyed prestige abroad never so high before in our history'. According to this view, Fianna Fáil governments 'have triumphed over the most extraordinary difficulties' and also fulfilled their promises. Three factors were identified as contributing to this: a strong government and an overall majority in the Dáil, positive leadership and definite policies, and the support of a majority of the electorate.[61] The implication again was that any possible combination of opponents could not achieve this: that Fianna Fáil was in fact indispensable.

Once the election was over, Erskine Childers sought to explain what had gone wrong. Writing to MacEntee, he claimed that vested interests had played a part in the defeat, in particular the hostility of publicans and greyhound owners. Added to this was a general postwar dissatisfaction with any government and the belief that Fianna Fáil had 'ceased to be the poor man's government'. He also blamed the limited impact of the 1947 supplementary budget, which had not had enough positive features. Childers identified a number of other difficulties: 'Even our own supporters believe we have got above ourselves', an unforgivable moral crime in Ireland, then and now. This was also closely associated with a demand for a cut in public spending and a reduction in the numbers working in the civil service and local government, a regular aspect of the politics of resentment, which Clann na Talmhan and Clann na Poblachta reflected in their election literature. Profiteering and luxury spending alienated the poor and the less well off, without necessarily attracting the rich. He wondered 'Will we lose voters if we tax luxury spending by the rich?' The real problem may have been a tactical one, according to this analysis. Fianna Fáil overestimated Clann na Poblachta and underestimated Fine Gael. The key to the next election would be how young voters acted: 'There are 250,000 voters of age 21–25 who do not believe there is any substantial difference between us and Fine Gael. They choose Fianna Fáil because of Dev and other personalities. There is in fact no policy difference save on the Irish language.' On other areas of policy, consensus is in evidence, even on foreign policy: 'Our young supporters brought up in a Fianna Fáil tradition doubt their psychological approach rather than criticise their policy.' The danger for Fianna Fáil was that this vote could prove volatile and other parties could attract it. There was also a danger that weaknesses in the party organisation would undermine efforts to recruit new members, while the failure to meet welfare demands could lead to a left-wing challenge. Childers made damning remarks on party members and their drinking habits. He also highlighted education as a serious problem and one that concerned women to a greater extent than men. Educational levels in the state were considered poor, and Childers believed that one of the reasons women voted for Fine Gael was because they considered the educational system to be bad. Furthermore, the government was blamed for the poor quality of school buildings, when in fact this was the responsibility of school managers (normally priests), not the state. He detected considerable scepticism among supporters that the revival of Irish would be achieved.

In a further letter to Tommy Mullins, the party General Secretary, Childers identified additional reasons for the defeat. One of these was the length of time Fianna Fáil had been in office and the complacency this had engendered in the party. This allowed the opposition parties to put Fianna Fáil on the defensive well in advance of the election. Furthermore, the link between TDs and the comhairle ceanntair (constituency organisation) had weakened, while party meetings were badly attended, irregular and non-existent in some cases. He noted that TDs had frequently failed to bring the government's successes to the attention of constituents by holding regular meetings. Childers identified Cork, Carlow and Kilkenny as areas where Fianna Fáil's alliance with the working class had been weakened. But perhaps the most significant reason for defeat was that Fianna Fáil candidates were tired and boring, whereas some of the candidates put forward by the other parties were young and vital. Childers noted the success of two members of the O'Higgins family in Dublin for Fine Gael: 'it would appear that younger relations of existing TDs who are able to speak well and who have some political sense, are a very valuable asset to any party'.[62]

In June 1948 Fianna Fáil held its nineteenth ard fheis, the first in opposition since 1931. The election was to be seen 'not as a defeat but as a temporary reverse'. Fianna Fáil was confident that in due course the weakness of the coalition government would be exposed and it would fall prey to sectional pressures and internal contradictions. In 1948 Fianna Fáil had 1,330 registered cumainn (branches), including one in Scotland.[63] Although publicly confident of victory in another election, this optimism was not reflected in the new Dáil. In opposition Fianna Fáil found it difficult to counter the government or to develop a realistic strategy. High-profile ministers, such as Seán MacBride, James Dillon and Noël Browne, were able to deflect Fianna Fáil criticism of the new government for the most part. The 1948 election demonstrated that Fianna Fáil was not indispensable to forming a government. The measure of Fianna Fáil's difficulties after 1948 was that its success in creating a political consensus provided the basis for establishing an alternative government. Fianna Fáil was a victim of its own success as well as the choice of the electorate in 1948.[64]

The rise of Clann na Poblachta fits well into a discussion of continuity and stability. This may appear strange, as it could be said to have contributed to the instability that characterised the party system after 1944. There is some strength to this claim, since Clann na Poblachta attracted votes which would otherwise gone to other parties. Yet its political programme was essentially a nationalist one with aspects of Catholic social policy contained within it. Its 1948 election programme included a more active campaign against partition, the repeal of the External Relations Act and the establishment of a 32-county republic. In domestic policy it was committed to full employment, national control of the monetary system (breaking the link with sterling), the development of national resources, a reduction in food prices by increasing subsidies and the introduction of a comprehensive social insurance system.[65] In contrast, Fine Gael fought a cautious and relatively unsuccessful campaign in 1948. John A. Costello identified three policy objectives for the party, all of which were conservative: reduce spending, control inflation and inhibit government intervention.[66] This did not prevent Fine Gael and Clann na Poblachta entering into negotiations to form a government, which to the surprise of many actually led to agreement. This is one of the most remarkable achievements in coalition building in postwar Ireland. Fine Gael had accepted the Fianna Fáil consensus, and by doing so contributed to the generation of a wide-ranging anti-Fianna Fáil government. The ten-point programme, agreed just prior to the formation of the Inter-Party government in 1948, included a number of Clann na Poblachta's objectives, though it contained no commitments on partition or the Commonwealth. There were specific commitments to the eradication of TB, the establishment of a Council of Education and the removal of recently imposed taxes on cigarettes, tobacco, beer and cinema seats. The incoming government also promised to provide new housing for the middle and working classes at affordable prices, and to modify the means test for certain welfare benefits. Other commitments were so general as to be at the level of wishful thinking, including increased agricultural and industrial production, a reduction in the cost of living and a tax on 'unreasonable profit making'.[67]

Seán MacBride, the leader of Clann na Poblachta and the Minister for External Affairs in the new government, was conservative on most policies. His main motivations intellectually were a dislike of the British, a strong commitment to ending partition and a belief in economic nationalism. Though not a fiscal conservative, as was MacEntee, MacBride did not show any talent for economic policy; this, however, did not prevent him intervening in policy formation in this area. He shared with his new party colleague Aodh de Blacam an unrealistic view on what could be achieved by an act of will. He never considered in any dept the implications of breaking the fiscal link with the United Kingdom, assuming that an increase in independence would enhance Ireland's economic prospects. This, however, was an act of faith rather than a considered policy. While there was a case for breaking the link with sterling, it was not one made in any convincing way by MacBride. This can be more fully appreciated in the debate between MacBride, Costello and the Minister for Finance, Patrick McGilligan, at the time of the sterling crisis and devaluation in 1949. In this discussion, MacBride appears as the radical because he was challenging the status quo, yet the counterarguments provided by

McGilligan and Costello, though based on conservative premises, reflected a more coherent and realistic understanding of economic reality. MacBride never considered the consequences of inflation or breaking the sterling link for the Irish economy. His presumption was that any break with the United Kingdom must help Ireland.[68] MacBride's economic thinking was heavily influenced by the minority report of the 1938 Banking Commission written by Peadar O'Loghlen. O'Loghlen believed that full employment could be achieved by breaking the link with sterling, reinforced by a policy of rural development and infrastructural investment to achieve this. The assumptions contained in O'Loghlen's report and the policies of Clann na Poblachta are closer to those elaborated by the Franco and Salazar regimes in the late 1940s and early 1950s than to those of the smaller social democracies in northern Europe.[69]

Nor did MacBride's period in office demonstrate his command over his department or indeed his ability in other spheres where he had an interest. MacBride's arrogance is the most obvious feature of his leadership of the party, but clearly Clann na Poblachta was more than the sum of one man.[70] The short-term success of Clann na Poblachta can be attributed to the illusion which it created that there was space for a radical republican alternative to Fianna Fáil. Yet in large part it was a party seeking to imitate the expansionary period of Fianna Fáil between 1927 and 1938. Its commitment to welfare can be exaggerated, though Noël Browne at the Department of Health provides evidence of some earnestness in this area. However, even here James Deeny, who was the Chief Medical Adviser at the department, cautions against accepting Browne's own account of these years at face value. He argues in his memoirs that Browne's influence should not be exaggerated and that the Department of Health was already dealing with the TB problem. Deeny suggests that Browne was simply the political beneficiary of a policy already in place. However, having a new and dynamic minister can help to advance a policy, as the evidence suggests was the case with the campaign against TB.[71]

It would be unrealistic to suggest that Clann na Poblachta did not receive votes from those disaffected with Fianna Fáil (and with the other parties as well). In 1948, turnout was up on 1944 (74.2 per cent as against 67.7 per cent), but lower than in any other election since 1927 (the 1943 turnout was the same as in 1948). Clann na Poblachta's share of the vote was impressive if not remarkable. The party brought together two forces which were probably incompatible. One, which included MacBride, Noel Hartnett and a majority of the leadership, were republicans disillusioned with both Fianna Fáil and the IRA. The other group included those, such as Browne, who believed that Clann na Poblachta was a new radical democratic departure in Irish politics, one which could transcend the enmities of the Civil War. Browne claimed that he was not elected as a republican but as a social reformer, and that he and others in the party were dismayed by MacBride's association with the IRA and its violence. Indeed, his own mildly anti-republican sentiments, expressed during the election campaign, led to a demand for his expulsion from the party. Richard Sinnott has described the party as one with its origins 'in republican or extreme nationalist circles drawing especially on the resentment at the treatment of republican prisoners and their sense that Fianna Fáil had reneged on its nationalist commitments', an opinion confirmed by the party's subsequent development.[72]

One of the interesting features of politics between 1945 and 1948 was the way in which political change was articulated in a highly traditional fashion and within the context established by Fianna Fáil. Clann na Poblachta was clearly the main vehicle for this change and this accounts for its short-term growth and success. Clann na Poblachta provided a comfortable alternative for those voters who were not attracted by the rural politics of Clann na Talmhan, the working-class politics of the Labour Party and the NLP or the conservatism of Fine Gael. In retrospect, the radicalism of the party was in the eye of the beholder, rather than in the party programme itself. The mixture of social Catholicism ('for a Christian state in reality, not merely in name', according to MacBride), anti-partitionist republicanism and the commitment to extending welfare appeared to have much to offer the electorate. But this was little different from what Fianna Fáil continued to offer. Perhaps in the end what mattered in 1948 was that there was indeed a momentum within the party system to replace Fianna Fáil, one that succeeded. It is possible to exaggerate the scope for change in 1948 and to underestimate Fianna Fáil's underlying strength. Not only did Fianna Fáil remain the largest party, but it was necessary for all political parties to co-operate to exclude it from government. In fact, what brought the Inter-Party government together was a shared dislike for Fianna Fáil and a willingness not to disagree on policy. The effectiveness of this change is reflected in all the parties in different ways: the split in Labour is one, while the formation of Clann na Poblachta is recognition that IRA militarism had been deprived of any legitimacy. Likewise, Fine Gael was in a no-win situation; either it accepted the republican nature of Irish public life and discarded its commitment to the Commonwealth or it faced further electoral decline.[73]

At the same time the potential for change should not be underestimated. It is mistaken to see this potential simply in left–right terms, as most authors do. The phenomenon of political competition is more complex than this demarcation suggests, even more so in a political system defined by nationalist values. A less extreme approach may be to recognise that there was some support for change, but that this was not met in the short term by the traditional parties. Electoral volatility expressed some of this discontent, but both Fianna Fáil and Fine Gael were able to recover from the electoral challenge and re-establish themselves at the centre of the political process during the 1950s. The electoral evidence from 1943 and 1948 (but not 1944) suggests that the potential for electoral change was almost exclusively in Dublin. The surge of support for Labour in 1943 and for Clann na Poblachta in 1948 was in Dublin. Clann na Talmhan should not be included here, as it can more properly be identified as a small farmer anti-system party, largely conservative in aims and objectives.[74] Although it is difficult to compare the performance of the Labour Party in Dublin in 1943 with that of Clann na Poblachta in 1948, there is some evidence of overlap in constituency terms. Labour won four seats (one each in the North East, North West, South and County constituencies), whereas Clann na

Poblachta won six seats (one each in North East, North West, South Central, South East, South West and Dún Laoghaire–Rathdown).[75] This is suggestive rather than direct evidence, and clearly we do not know whether those who voted Labour in 1943 voted Clann na Poblachta in 1948. The position is further complicated by the constituency changes put in place by MacEntee in 1947. What might be tentatively suggested is that Labour in 1943 and Clann na Poblachta in 1948 tapped into sources of discontent and a desire for change which generated a potential for mobilisation. In the case of Labour, the split undermined this, as did Fianna Fáil's counter-campaign in 1944. In respect of Clann na Poblachta, the performance of the party disappointed those believing in change, as can be seen in the collapse of its vote in 1951 after the Mother and Child controversy.

It is, of course, true that these challenges to Fianna Fáil were fragile, but the failure of Labour and Clann na Poblachta was not inevitable.[76] The significance of Dublin was that its population was increasing and the demands being made on the state and the parties were already changing the nature of political competition. Yet, Dublin was not yet dominant and its interest had to be balanced against that of rural Ireland and urban Ireland outside of Dublin as well as the more diffuse republican constituency. Not only was Clann na Poblachta less successful outside Dublin, but, with the exception of Limerick East, the party did quite poorly in urban constituencies in Munster. The average national vote for the party in 1948 was 13.3 per cent; in Munster its vote was 11.7 per cent while in Dublin it was 19.3 per cent. In Cork city the party received 9.7 per cent and in Waterford 7.7 per cent. If the appeal of Clann na Poblachta was an urban one, it appears to have been concentrated in Dublin, while the disappearance of its vote in Dublin in 1951 demonstrates the volatility of that vote.

Whatever potential for change existed was not realised in political terms. There are various reasons for this. The most important is that the Inter-Party government was not a reforming government, except in a limited way. On economic, social and diplomatic matters it reinforced the status quo or extended it by implementing policies implicit in the previous government. Furthermore, the government itself was riven with disagreement, whatever about the success or activism of individual ministers. In more specific terms the implosion of Clann na Poblachta undermined its importance as a force for change, in terms of either its own expansion or its ability to pressurise Fianna Fáil in that direction.[77] Another contributory factor was the persistence of Fianna Fáil as a (sometimes) reforming party, a feature which allowed it to appeal widely and successfully to urban Dublin as well as other constituencies. The revival of Fine Gael at the 1951 election may paradoxically have also cut off the possibility of change. Whatever promise it may have offered as part of a reform government dissipated in the 1950s. Of added interest is the growing stability of the political system after 1948. The volatility experienced between 1943 and 1948 began to decline during the 1950s and was significantly reduced during the 1960s and 1970s.[78] Various caveats and reservations should thus be entered in this discussion. The most dramatic aspect of the 1948 election was the ability of the other parties to exclude Fianna Fáil from forming a government. This was an expression of how successful Fianna Fáil had been in defining the parameters of politics. In other respects 1948 maintained the general continuity established in Irish society, policy making and culture. Although there was a limited potential for reform in 1948, this was concentrated in Dublin and was only partly realised. The Inter-Party government failed to realise its potential as a counterweight to Fianna Fáil and its behaviour in government confirmed Fianna Fáil's view that coalition weakened policy making and Ireland's interests generally.[79]

The politics of immobility in the 1950s

During the 1940s Fine Gael slowly recognised that its only hope of re-entering government was in a coalition. During the war it demanded the formation of a national government, only to be met with the rejoinder that Ireland already had a national government in Fianna Fáil. Likewise during the 1944 election campaign de Valera insisted that only Fianna Fáil could provide a one-party government and that any possible alternative coalition could not produce a common policy.[80] After the fall of the Inter-Party government and immediately before he formed his own minority government in June 1951, de Valera informed a correspondent that he was opposed in principle to coalition. Moreover, according to de Valera, 'the members of Fianna Fáil have been elected in opposition to the Coalition idea'.[81] Later in the same year de Valera rejected MacBride's proposal to establish an Economic Council with all-party support and representation to plan investment and capital development:

> I believe the national interests are best served by having a Government with a definite policy, which they put before the people and which they are elected to carry out, and an Opposition which criticise and point out any objections to that policy. That is the way in which the country's government will best be carried out. I believe that if you try to have the sort of thing to which the deputy [Mac Bride] always seems to be harking back, an all-party body, it will not work, that it is nothing but compromise, nothing can be done unless there is common agreement.

In addition to this, de Valera defended both cabinet and ministerial responsibility and, implicitly, cabinet confidentiality.[82]

The anti-coalition consensus within Fianna Fáil made political sense, especially when the Inter-Party government proved to be unstable for the very reasons claimed by Fianna Fáil. Yet the outcome of the 1948 election and to some extent that of 1951 and 1954 suggested that the electorate remained to be persuaded to provide Fianna Fáil with an overall majority. Some younger members of the party recognised that a new strategy was required and were anxious to promote new initiatives. For example, at a national executive meeting in November 1949, Michael Yeats and Eoin Ryan proposed a motion urging the party to 'formulate a policy in accordance with present day conditions'. Two areas were highlighted in the discussion, defence issues and the Irish language, but the motion was referred to a party committee to deal with specific suggestions. There is no evidence from the national executive minutes that the discussion was taken further prior to the 1951 general election.[83] The growing convergence between Fianna Fáil and the Inter-Party government was demonstrated at the 1951 general election. While there was a swing to Fianna Fáil, Fine Gael also achieved significant success at the election. Clann na Poblachta was the main loser, especially in Dublin, while the Labour Party (recently reunited) remained fairly stable. The seventeen-point programme presented by de Valera as the basis for government formation in 1951 rarely departed in any detailed way from that of the 1948 Inter-Party programme or indeed the various commitments of the outgoing government. Specific commitments were made on afforestation, on agricultural and industrial policy and on the introduction of a social welfare bill. None of these would have been out of place in the Inter-Party programme. Moreover, the incoming government promised to preserve 'all schemes and initiatives which have demonstrated their utility, and their extension and improvement where necessary'. Even on partition, de Valera recognised that a consensus had been achieved, claiming that 'ninety per cent of our people want a united Ireland'.[84]

When the second Inter-Party government was formed after the 1954 general election, its 'Principles of Policy' were not remarkably different from those of Fianna Fáil three years earlier. Macro-economic policy was broadly in line with that of the outgoing government, with perhaps a little more emphasis on agriculture than Fianna Fáil would have. The first item in its programme was 'To restore the unity of Ireland and to safeguard Irish cultural traditions'. The incoming government also promised to reduce the cost of living by controlling prices and reducing those for essential foodstuffs.[85] In a speech during the election campaign John A. Costello provided a detailed view of Fine Gael's approach to financial policy. He believed that 'careful changes' should be made to Ireland's financial and economic institutions to allow for the positive use of savings, foreign capital and sterling balances. Costello recommended co-operation between the state and the banking system as the best way to achieve its objectives in the financial area. MacEntee provided a detailed criticism of this and other contributions by Costello, but again the differences were slight. In some respects MacEntee's views were more conservative than those of Costello, though some, at least, of Costello's suggestions could have been adopted by Lemass.[86]

This posed a serious dilemma for Fianna Fáil. If the differences between the political parties had narrowed and if the electorate recognised this, what could Fianna Fáil offer to gain the support to establish a new government? The party never had an easy answer to this. The Inter-Party government had undermined the claim that Fianna Fáil was the only possible government. Notwithstanding the failure of the first Inter-Party government to hold together, another was formed in 1954. Fianna Fáil's decision to call an election in May 1954 was influenced by its failure to win two by-elections earlier that year and the evidence that Fine Gael's vote was increasing. For example, at the 1951 general election Fianna Fáil received 53 per cent of the vote in Cork City, but at a by-election in March 1954 this plummeted to 39 per cent; in contrast, Fine Gael increased its first preference vote from 29.6 per cent to 44.3 per cent. At the May general election, Fine Gael maintained its by-election success in this constituency, receiving 41.1 per cent of the first preferences, whereas Fianna Fáil received 42.5 per cent. This confirmed the fear of the General Secretary of Fianna Fáil, Tommy Mullins, that if Fine Gael maintained its by-election support, Fianna Fáil would be lucky to win three out of five seats and in the event succeeded in securing only two. Likewise in Louth, Fine Gael won the by-election and went on to win two out of the three seats at the 1954 general election. According to Mullins, 'Our own supporters have been shocked into more vigorous and planned activity and many who voted against us or did not vote will vote for us now', yet the outcome of the general election disappointed this prediction. Mullins identified a number of difficulties after the Cork by-election. Fianna Fáil had been unfortunate that its deputy director of elections had been ill during the campaign, but more seriously the party in Cork had been complacent about victory. He believed that many Fianna Fáil voters did not turn out, due in part to poor canvassing by the party, as well as the absence of big names and ministers appearing in the constituency.

Not only did Fine Gael hold the initiative throughout the by-election campaign, but it proved to be more determined and professional than the Fianna Fáil organisation. Mullins also believed that Fianna Fáil did not get across its social and economic policies, and did not address specific Cork issues to the extent necessary to attract voters. In contrast, Fine Gael made specific commitments to post office and customs and excise workers. Mullins calculated that these promises could have attracted up to 2,000 voters to Fine Gael.[87] At the time of the 1951 election, de Valera had claimed that Fianna Fáil represented 'all sections of society' but that it had 'special regard … [for] the small farmers on the one hand, and the workers on the other'. The difficulty in 1954 for Fianna Fáil was that it overestimated how many workers in urban areas might continue to support the party without inducements, which in this case Fine Gael was prepared to offer. Additionally, the economy had only just begun to recover from the deflationary policies that had been in place since 1952, and Fianna Fáil suffered from this.[88] Fine Gael's vote had been in decline since the mid 1930s in Cork city, but the 1954 by-election and general election provided the basis for its recovery. Its 1954 general election vote was the first time since 1932 that the party had received more than 40 per cent of the vote in the city in a general election.

The Limerick East by-election held on 26 June 1952 demonstrated similar problems for Fianna Fáil. The party candidate received 41.7 per cent of the vote while Fine Gael received 34.3 per cent. However, the pattern of transfers worked decidedly against Fianna Fáil, with Clann na Poblachta and the Labour Party transfers providing Fine Gael with the seat. Immediately after the defeat, Donogh O'Malley wrote to Dan Breen reporting that Fianna Fáil's vote had been concentrated in rural areas, 'but unfortunately the City left us down'. This lack of appeal to urban voters can in part be attributed to the success of Clann na Poblachta, which achieved its highest vote at this general election in

Limerick, in contrast to the party's difficulties elsewhere at the 1951 and 1954 general elections. Clann na Poblachta's appeal in Limerick was largely an urban one, and it and the Labour Party successfully attracted trade union and working-class support, despite Fianna Fáil's very explicit appeal to this sector.[89] At the general election, Fianna Fáil once again maximised its position in Limerick East by winning two of the four seats. Clann na Poblachta won 15 per cent of the vote here, in comparison with 3.8 per cent nationally.

In response to concerns within Fianna Fáil, Lemass proposed in 1952 to reorganise the constituency party in Dublin. The intention was to generate more cumainn by having an upper limit of 3,500 voters per cumann and a lower one of 2,500. Lemass believed that there was a need to strengthen Fianna Fáil's organisation in Dublin.[90] He was anxious not only to reorganise the party, but also to provide a new means for expansion. At the 1954 ard fheis a resolution was carried which asked the national executive to revise the party programme in the light of the Democratic Principles of the First Dáil. In a letter sent to a number of party members, Lemass insisted that:

> The need for a re-examination and re-statement of Fianna Fáil's programme is recognised generally, and it is politically important to let it be known that it is being undertaken. Any idea that we are standing for the view that everything that the Fianna Fáil government did was perfect and remains perfect in all circumstances, and that everything it did not do is not worth doing would be very damaging.[91]

By this time Fianna Fáil was out of office and Lemass had undertaken the task of reorganising the party in preparation for the next election. He also developed links with a number of the younger members of the party in Dublin and elsewhere; these included Charles Haughey, Kevin Boland, George Colley and Brian Lenihan, all of whom became prominent in the party. Lemass also hoped to attract support from those who would or could not actually become party members. He proposed setting up a Comhairle Ceanntair Atha Cliath under the direct control of the national executive. It would be composed of ordinary and associate members; the latter could be 'any person, whether resident in Ireland or not, and whether a member of the Fianna Fáil organisation or not'. Lemass explained that the new organisation would in effect be a 'Central Branch', 'although we do not wish it to be so described'. At first each of the Dublin constituencies would provide the members of the branch, 'but will, we hope, enrol a number of fee paying associate members'. The justification for providing associate membership was 'to extend the contacts of the organisation amongst influential people in all classes'. While the branch would not play a role in elections, it was hoped it would have a broad appeal to those 'who can make a contribution to the development of Fianna Fáil's future programme. It is also hoped by this means to keep in closer contact with Fianna Fáil many people who are unable, for personal or business reasons, to take a more active part in its ordinary work.' Charles Haughey was appointed the first secretary of the new organisation, which seems to look forward to Taca in the 1960s.[92]

The national executive was also anxious to act decisively in individual constituencies to prepare for elections. In November 1952 it recommended that Alderman Cormac Breathnach be asked to resign his Dáil seat 'in favour of an active man who could attend to the needs of the Cabra area'.[93] Breathnach had been a TD since 1932, representing Dublin North West since 1937. In a by-election on 12 November 1952, Thomas Byrne, an independent candidate and son of Alfie Byrne, had won the seat previously held by Alfie Byrne jun., with 61 per cent of the vote, while Fianna Fáil had received 31 per cent. At the 1954 general election, the Fianna Fáil vote in this constituency, with a new candidate, remained about 10 per cent lower than in 1951. In contrast, Fine Gael improved its vote by 10 per cent and John A. Costello topped the poll. In other Dublin constituencies, Fianna Fáil gained in 1954 by the admission of Noël Browne as a member, though this also created divisions among those in the party uneasy with the volatile ex-minister. One Fianna Fáil member attacked Browne at an ard fheis, accusing him of being a communist. After receiving a solicitor's letter from Browne, Francis Clarke had to publicly withdraw the charge. In 1957 another member, Kathleen Lynch, complained that the party continued to be suspect in the eyes of many Irish people because of Browne's membership: 'I would like to add that were Dr Browne a non-Catholic I would excuse his attitude but I cannot tolerate a renegade.'[94] In retrospect it is likely that it would have been difficult for any political party to contain Browne, though it says much about the nature of Irish politics that Browne himself felt Fianna Fáil was the only party he could join. That the party was able to find a place for Browne, despite some internal hostility, indicates an openness not evident in other parties. According to Browne himself, William Norton, the leader of the Labour Party, refused to consider the possibility of his joining the party, asserting that he was not prepared to sit around a table with him.[95]

More serious than this was the evidence of continuing discontent in Dublin North East. At the comhairle ceanntair, George Colley was among those claiming that 'there was a conservative element attached to the Comhairle, who looked with suspicion on any young persons joining the organisation'. According to this, the newer members had been ignored by the long-standing officers and were made to feel 'they were not wanted'. This was denied by the sitting TDs, Oscar Traynor and Harry Colley, though George Colley quickly responded that his version of the situation was correct, insisting that 'a closed shop outlook existed' in the constituency.[96] In May 1955, just prior to the municipal elections, Colley resigned as secretary of his cumann and as director of elections. He alleged that a relative of one of the Fianna Fáil candidates had attempted to secure his election by bribery. Colley further claimed that the facts of the case were well known and had been brought to the attention of senior members of Fianna Fáil, 'who I regret to say, have not taken any action whatsoever in regard to anyone connected with the affair'. Because of this, Colley was not prepared to be associated with the election:

> Remaining in the organisation when it is putting forward this particular candidate as a suitable person for whom to vote, and as a worthy standard-

> bearer of Fianna Fáil would, in my opinion, constitute at least a tacit acceptance of the lowest standards in public life and a deliberate deception of the electorate, because there is no guarantee that a similar situation will not arise again in relation to this candidate.

The losses in Dublin North East after Colley's resignation accounted for two-thirds of Fianna Fáil's losses in the local elections in Dublin. In addressing the issue subsequently, Charles Haughey doubted 'if our organisation in this Constituency has ever entered a campaign so badly organised or lost so badly'. He outlined the seriousness of the problem by claiming:

> I do not think that we can look back on the past year with any degree of satisfaction. I think that were it not for the fact that we had an excellent and disciplined organisation for so long, the events of the year might well have disrupted it completely. I should like to make this appeal to our members in all the Cumann. Stand fast by the organisation. A number of our members were inclined to despair when they saw certain happenings. I think it is true that we did suffer from an infiltration of some individuals whose interests were more personal than patriotic, but I would like our members never to forget that ours is a great national movement.[97]

Although Fianna Fáil performed well in other constituencies, this incident provided evidence of considerable strain within Dublin, an area where Lemass was anxious to maximise Fianna Fáil's vote.

Uncertainties continued to affect the ability of Fianna Fáil to meet the challenge of opposition. In early 1955 a report from East Wall maintained that the support of the 'strong pro Fianna Fáil person' continued to be available. However, it was also noted that some former Fianna Fáil voters were now critical of the party's position on prices and food subsidies. The Inter-Party government had persuaded voters that they could deliver on promises in respect of these issues. These voters were clearly more volatile than the 'strong pro Fianna Fáil person', less predictable in voting habits and prepared in 1955, at least, to give the Inter-Party government an opportunity to demonstrate what it could do. Charles Haughey had some better news to report by the middle of 1956. The long-standing independent TD in Dublin North East, Alfie Byrne sen., had died and Haughey contested the by-election against Byrne's son Patrick. Byrne was elected with 56.5 per cent of the vote, but Haughey retained Fianna Fáil's share of the vote from the 1954 general election. After analysing the electoral data, Haughey concluded that support for Fianna Fáil was stronger in 'new areas of private housing' than elsewhere in the constituency.[98]

However, as late as January 1957, with a general election in the offing, there were doubts about Dublin and a demand that membership be built up: 'It is realised that it was mainly in the City that the weakness of the organisation in 1954 contributed to the loss of seats by Fianna Fáil.'[99] Early in 1956 Kevin Boland, reporting on the municipal election campaign the previous year, drew attention to what he believed to be the state of flux among the electorate:

> At the present time it would be well for the country if that policy [full employment] of Fianna Fáil was better understood by those people who comprise what we call the 'floating voter', because it is in honest effort by our own people using Irish capital that the answer to all our economic problems lies, and an intelligent vote by these people putting Fianna Fáil back in office would bring this about.[100]

If there was some quiet optimism among the more active younger members of the party, there was also some uncertainty about the future. Party members frequently voiced traditional concerns. The prospect of increased imports affecting employment was highlighted by one cumann, while another complained about the possible threat to neutrality posed by foreign capital in Ireland. The Fianna Fáil cumann in Ballyfermot brought considerable pressure to bear on Lemass in respect of the future of the Córas Iompair Éireann engineering works at Inchicore. The fear in this case was that technical change involving the importation of components would affect employment in the company. The unions were opposed to any changes and, following correspondence, Lemass put down a question in the Dáil asking the Tánaiste, William Norton, how the employment of 338 workers in the engineering works could be protected in the circumstances. Nor were all these pressures from urban Ireland; Lemass received many requests from Fianna Fáil members in rural Ireland to obtain posts or other favours. In most cases, these were handled in an appropriate manner, with no evidence of favouritism. In one case, a party member wrote requesting assistance in obtaining a post as rate collector. Lemass wrote to Dan Breen, 'It would I think be useful if you could help him in the matter.'[101]

Lemass also recognised that rural issues had to be addressed or Fianna Fáil would lose support in these constituencies. Overemphasis on full employment, he believed, could have a detrimental effect on opinion in rural areas. In a letter to Brian Lenihan he expressed the view that 'Fine Gael is trying to give the impression that we are interested only in urban employment ... this has to be countered.'[102] Another type of influence is evident from correspondence between W.H. Lamb (of Lamb Brothers, the jam makers) and Seán MacEntee just prior to the 1957 election. Lamb claimed that he contributed to the election campaigns of all the main parties, but believed that none of them had the jam industry's interest at heart. Margins in the industry were narrow, he claimed, and a 'free for all' (i.e. competition) was something he opposed. Lamb believed that Fianna Fáil would follow the same policy on this issue as the outgoing government, the consequence of which would be unattractive to the industry: 'with an increased number of jam factories and a diminishing population we are all in a somewhat discouraged frame of mind'. Lamb wondered aloud whether 'Fianna Fáil dare come out with a policy in its election programme of fostering industry by giving encouragement to manufacturers to spend money on improving their premises, machines and amenities'. MacEntee showed this letter to Lemass, who replied that it was impossible to address Lamb's concerns, as it was not practicable to prevent price cutting among the competitors in the grocery sector.[103]

There is little evidence that by the 1957 general election Fianna Fáil had moved away from the certainties of the 1930s. In terms of general policy formulation there were few interventions after the motion promoted by Ryan and Yeats in 1949. There was a discussion of economic policy in 1953, but de Valera deflected any serious consideration of the matter. Later in the same year a motion was proposed at the parliamentary party asserting that the deflationary policy then being promoted by the government was 'no longer justified', while demanding that a more 'progressive policy' be pursued. This was not discussed until January 1954, when, after de Valera made 'a comprehensive statement on the party's general financial and economic policy', it was withdrawn.[104] At the national executive Eoin Ryan's proposal that 'adequate credit at reasonable rates' be made available to the agricultural community was agreed in amended form after a discussion. Its influence on subsequent party policy, however, is not clear.[105] Considerable attention has been paid to Lemass' public statements on economic policy during this period, especially the one made at Clery's Ballroom in Dublin, in October 1955. Lemass made few commitments in this speech, which was of a very general nature. His belief that 100,000 jobs could be generated by massive investment made headlines, but most of the criticisms of the proposal were well founded and Lemass himself moved cautiously in this policy area subsequently.[106] In September 1955, the national executive accepted a proposal from Noël Browne and Eoin Ryan that Fianna Fáil adopt the principle of 'the desirability of equal opportunities in education for all sections of the community'. A committee was set up to examine this issue, including in its membership Haughey, Lenihan and Ryan among others. A report was produced, but Browne claimed that de Valera actively obstructed any attempt to implement it, and concluded that there would be no change in Fianna Fáil while de Valera remained as leader.[107]

The final years of de Valera's leadership were associated with recession and stagnancy and his lack of direction certainly frustrated others in the party, including Lemass. Lemass was working on a new economic strategy after 1957, but de Valera provided little active support for innovative departures. Even before de Valera resigned as Taoiseach in 1959, some changes were already being promoted, but without de Valera's departure it is unlikely that anything comparable to the range of initiatives introduced by Lemass between 1959 and 1966 could have been entertained.[108] Despite this, de Valera's departure did not constitute a clear break with the past. The political, economic and social stagnancy of the 1950s was attenuated during the 1960s, but many of the factors that induced it remained important. De Valera left politics too late, depriving his immediate successor of the time to realise his own ambitions. By 1959, it was fifteen years too late. By then the world had moved on, not just economically but politically and socially as well. When Lemass became Taoiseach in 1959 he had the opportunity to promote change and did so to a considerable degree. Yet the obstacles facing Ireland by that time were immense, perhaps greater than even Lemass appreciated. Between 1945 and 1960 Ireland had ceased to be a relatively wealthy society in Europe and had become a poor one. Over that time also, and more seriously, the political culture had become extremely resistant to change, especially if change involved confronting any of the major interests in Irish society, whether this be the church, the farmers, the Gaelic League or nationalism. The conservative grip on Irish politics was not broken in 1959, nor had it been when Lemass himself resigned in 1966. Indeed patterns of political behaviour established during the 1950s continued to affect the development of Irish society well beyond the 1960s.

7

Back to the Future

Crisis, Change and the Modification of Irish Nationalism in the 1960s

By the time Ireland applied to join the EEC in 1961, the specific dynamic that had driven Irish nationalism from the Act of Union to the consolidation of a republican regime had become exhausted. This insular protectionist nationalism was challenged by the process of constructing a more modern Ireland spearheaded by Seán Lemass and T.K. Whitaker. However, to survive as a meaningful template for Irish political culture, Irish nationalism had to change. This capacity both to change and to persist explains why nationalism remains a potent force both in Ireland and internationally in the twenty-first century. Between 1800 and 1922 Irish nationalism became predominantly secessionist, and this objective was largely realised when the Irish Free State was established. Once the state was established, nationalism had to change to meet new challenges. Nationalism became conservative in respect of the state. The need to uphold national sovereignty, improve citizens' welfare by state action, enhance the cultural and social capital of the nation, and protect the state's institutions from internal and external challenge reinforced this conservative version of nationalism. The defence of the nationalist status quo becomes the main aim of conservative nationalism. After 1922, nationalism could be conservative because state and nation were now closely identified, in contrast to the period 1800 to 1922. While this conservative securing of order was the main trend after 1922, there was tension with an expansionist nationalism that insisted on Irish unity as the continuing objective of nationalism. The relationship between conservative and expansionist nationalism remained highly ambiguous, especially as the 1937 constitution, which in most respects was a conservative document, was expressly irredentist in Articles 2 and 3.[1]

This tension between a system-maintaining conservative nationalism and the destabilising potential of expansionist nationalism was never resolved under

Eamon de Valera's leadership, though, as discussed in chapters 3–6, stability and order were the predominant features of the period up to 1961. Both varieties of nationalism were in crisis by 1961. The British and Irish governments had dealt decisively with the IRA border campaign, which was effectively extinguished by 1960. But de Valera's conservative nationalism was also under considerable pressure, despite its undoubted success in maintaining the nationalist state. Certainly, de Valera's version of nationalism did not have an adequate answer to the economic and social crisis that affected the Republic of Ireland during the 1950s. By 1959, when de Valera retired from active politics, Ireland was internationally recognised as a sovereign independent state; this was reflected in Ireland's admission to the United Nations in 1955. Yet, despite its sovereign status, Ireland appeared to have lost the ability to direct its own future. The national economy, based on nationalist foundations, was in tatters, while nearly half a million of its citizens had emigrated since 1945. T.K. Whitaker's warning in *Economic Development* captures the sense of despondency at this time:

> After 35 years of native government people are asking whether we can achieve an acceptable degree of economic progress. The common talk amongst parents in the towns, as in rural Ireland, is of their children having to emigrate as soon as their education is completed in order to be sure of a reasonable livelihood. To the children themselves and to many already in employment the jobs available at home look unattractive by comparison with those attainable in such variety and so readily elsewhere.

Many thought that the entire fabric of Irish society was unravelling and that the Irish state was unable to deal adequately with the problem.[2]

While there was no single reason for this situation, much of the blame can be attributed to Fianna Fáil policy after 1932. Economic nationalism, the economic war, the reluctance to innovate after 1945 and the dependence on traditional policy weakened both agriculture and industry. Fianna Fáil squandered the positive economic inheritance from Cumann na nGaedheal after 1932 by imposing a doctrinaire nationalism on economic policy. Although not evident until after 1945, Ireland was living on its accumulated capital between 1932 and 1948, following which decline set in. The change in Ireland's status is striking, as it quickly becomes one of the poorer areas of Europe. As late as 1948, however, Ireland had been relatively well off, placed about sixth in the European wealth league. In 1950 Irish per capita income was approximately 86 per cent of the average of those states that would be members of the European Community in 1992; by 1960 this was down to 62 per cent, and the gap between Ireland and the majority of European states was widening. Comparison with Spain and Portugal was now probably more appropriate for Ireland, whereas previously the comparison would have been with Denmark or the Netherlands. Ireland maintained its relative position within Western Europe between 1913 and about 1950, though some slippage is evident before this. The real shift in Ireland's fortunes occurs between 1950 and 1960 and is not reversed until the 1990s.[3]

Nationalist communities expect their state to protect their welfare as well as their sovereignty and independence. While Irish nationalism had failed to protect its citizens' welfare during the 1950s, nationalism itself had not been openly challenged. Irish nationalism continued to receive unprecedented levels of loyalty from those who remained in the state. Yet such loyalty could not be guaranteed, nor was it unconditional. The challenge for Lemass, when he succeeded de Valera in 1959, was to harness this patriotism and channel it in a new direction. Lemass recognised that the status quo in Ireland was unsustainable, though it remained attractive to those who remained in the state. He was no less a nationalist than de Valera, but he was more flexible and pragmatic than his predecessor. A broader conception of patriotism allowed Lemass to think in a more original way and to jettison some of the key features of de Valera's legacy, especially on economic policy. De Valera's nationalism had fixed points, made in stone and inflexible. Lemass had a dynamic notion of nationalism as a structure that could be changed and remodified. He recognised that a reliance on de Valera's fixed points condemned Ireland to a dismal future, threatening not only the viability of nationalism but Fianna Fáil's dominance in the nationalist party system. The big question for Lemass when he became Taoiseach was how much of de Valera's legacy he would maintain and to what extent Irish nationalism could be modified and modernised.[4]

Lemass' primary aim during the 1960s was to modernise the Irish economy and provide adequate employment and income to enable Irish citizens to remain and work in the country. Beyond this, the contrast between Lemass and de Valera should not be exaggerated. Whitaker has drawn attention to the continuities between the two leaders:

> Lemass was a pragmatic nationalist, and I put the emphasis on the two words. He was a nationalist in the sense of wanting to see Ireland have a respectable place in the world, but I don't think he was opposed to Dev's traditionalist outlook. He simply had some impatience with it in so far as it might be a hindrance to change, the change he wanted. He didn't have a programme of cultural change. His aim, as indeed my own, was focussed on improving the economic and social scene.[5]

Lemass inherited a political system and an economy to which he had made a major contribution. When Lemass changed policy in the 1960s he did not cease to be a nationalist: this was a change of tactics, not an abandonment of his nationalist principles. There were also important constraints on change. Fianna Fáil's traditional nationalist support base remained intact, while Lemass' first cabinet was dominated by Fianna Fáil veterans like himself. Ireland in 1961 was still a highly stable and homogeneous society, not remarkably different from the late 1930s in social or economic terms. Furthermore, Fianna Fáil had established the status quo ante 1961 and a direct attack on its main foundations would have been rejected, even if Lemass ever considered such a challenge. In such stable societies, change will be disruptive, if the political elite does not carefully manage it. The last thing Fianna Fáil wished to do was disrupt the society, as this could challenge its political dominance. Nor were such concerns limited to Fianna Fáil; Garret FitzGerald warned of the dangers associated with change. Ireland, he urged, should avoid creating an urban proletariat, 'without roots or belief, as had developed in Britain'. Irish life was anti-family according to FitzGerald, with the public house and the café serving as community centres, when what was required was 'fully integrated people', whereas 'instead people want sport or become teddy boys'.[6] The key task for Lemass during the 1960s was to develop a modified nationalist political culture, still conservative in respect of traditional society and norms, but linked to moderate reform and economic success. What we see in Ireland during the 1960s is adaptation rather than transformation. Change takes place on terms almost exclusively dictated and directed by the government. For the most part, the changes are conservative, simultaneously reaffirming existing hierarchies of power but providing enough flexibility for the economy to respond to new challenges. Because the changes were driven almost entirely by well-established and traditional elites, this was easier to impose.[7]

There was a delicate balance to be achieved by the new government. Lemass had to persuade the public that the economy was improving but that the new departure in policy would not destabilise traditional society. He was fortunate that the economy slowly pulled out of the deep recession it had been in. Jack Lynch, the Minister for Industry and Commerce, reported at the end of 1961 that there was a new dynamic in the economy; employment was on the increase and manufacturing exports were expanding.[8] While this was good news for the government, expansion was not guaranteed and a return to previous problems could not be ruled out. In fact, relatively few policy changes had taken place between 1957 and 1961, though serious consideration continued to be given to the promotion of a more expansionist policy. As yet, Irish policy making had not developed a 'national system of innovation', identified by Mjøset as the key characteristics in postwar economic success.[9] Britain's unexpected decision to apply for membership of the EEC in 1961 added urgency to these considerations. The Irish government had little room for manoeuvre. Up to 1961, Lemass favoured bilateral trading arrangements, while the United Kingdom remained the focus for external economic policy throughout the 1950s and early 1960s. As late as January 1961, Lemass reiterated the government's view on this: 'we are neither members of the Six [EEC] nor the Seven [European Free Trade Area (EFTA)] for the very good reason that there is no overall advantage to be gained at the present time by joining either group'.[10] Nor had Ireland joined GATT by 1961.

The balance of advantage changed immediately the British decided to apply, forcing Ireland's hand, but also giving those in favour of change the opportunity to act more decisively.[11] The Irish government was caught off guard, but quickly recognised that it had no alternative but to apply, a decision also reached by Denmark. Unlike Denmark, Ireland had few advantages in 1961, as Whitaker brutally pointed out to the government:

> We have applied for membership of the EEC because it would be economic disaster for us to be outside the Community if Britain is in it. We cannot

> afford to have our advantageous position in the British market turned into one of exclusion by a tariff wall, particularly as our chief competitors would be inside this wall.[12]

Yet Ireland's problems were not easily resolved. To all intents and purposes it had become a marginal European economy with serious structural problems, a situation recognised by officials in Brussels at the time of the application. In the circumstances it would not have been considered a prospective member of the EEC if Britain had not accepted its inclusion in the application process. Despite pursuing nationalist economic policies, Ireland had become more dependent as it became more nationalist. Ireland was not diplomatically powerless in 1961, but over the next decade the state had to invest considerable resources to persuade the six EEC member states that it should be admitted to full and equal membership. More crucially the Irish government also had to clarify its priorities in respect of agriculture, industrialisation and the role of the state in Irish development. None of this was easy, but the need to do so was pressing.[13]

The decision to apply for membership galvanised the Irish government, providing a clear focus for policy making. It also introduced a constraint in terms of government intervention and choice of economic policy instruments. If Ireland was serious about membership, then it had to comply with the rules of an institution over which it had virtually no influence. This was not necessarily negative, but it did mean that more autonomous strategies could not be entertained. Lemass and Whitaker grasped the opportunity provided by the EEC to accelerate changes in the Irish economy. Lemass warned the Fianna Fáil ard fheis in January 1962 that national priorities had to change, emphasising the economic and political challenge that the EEC presented to a protectionist and isolationist Ireland: 'Henceforth our national aims must conform to the emergence, in a political as well as an economic sense, of a union of Western European States, not as a vague prospect of the distant future but as a living reality of our lives.' It was necessary to abandon economic nationalism to succeed in the application, but more generally to achieve growth and prosperity. Lemass maintained that it 'is a condition essential to our national survival' to be successful in the application. Such was the importance of achieving this end that he was prepared to abandon Ireland's opposition to joining NATO if this proved necessary to secure membership.[14] When de Gaulle vetoed the British application early in 1963, the Irish government was disappointed. However, this set-back did not change the Irish attitude to the EEC, but provided a further opportunity to promote change in the economy and to prepare the case for membership more thoroughly. Whitaker, in particular, urged that renewed efforts should be made to remove tariffs on the assumption that Ireland would become a member of the Common Market by 1970. This momentum led Ireland to accept that free trade with the United Kingdom was a first step in the direction of European integration and a sign that it was serious about liberalising the economy. The Anglo-Irish Free Trade Agreement was signed in 1965, ending Ireland's thirty-year flirtation with economic nationalism. Not long after the trade agreement came into operation Lemass emphasised the shift:

> For Irish industry, the most important fact is the coming of free trade, either at the pace set in our Agreement with Britain, or perhaps at a faster pace when EEC or EFTA membership becomes possible. There may still be some people who are hoping that something may happen to avoid this challenge and to permit us to revert to protectionism in some degree. This is to ignore the situation which is now taking shape in the world.

Lemass acknowledged that Irish industry faced serious obstacles in a free trade environment, but he and other policy makers were generally optimistic that this challenge could be met.[15]

To manage the uncertainty associated with free trade, EEC membership and economic change, Lemass made his case in nationalist terms. Remarkably, the arguments presented in favour of free trade did not differ significantly from those he had elaborated to promote economic nationalism thirty years earlier. Shortly after his election as Taoiseach, he made the link between patriotism and economic success in terms understandable to Irish nationalists:

> We cannot hope to succeed in promoting enthusiasm for national advancement, if, at the same time, we disparage and set aside the things which make up a nation. Patriotism is the produce of love of country, and of traditions, culture and characteristics of our people; and the Irish language is part of that heritage. Is there a country in the world which is striding ahead in material progress in which a lively patriotism is not the motive power which gives unity and purpose to this effort? We also need a strong patriotic urge to vitalise our economic programme. How can we generate patriotism if at the same time we discard the causes which induced it in the past?[16]

At the 1963 ard fheis he insisted that 'patriotism is still a most powerful motivating force', adding the emphasis that 'Unless we can harness patriotism to our aims, we will not succeed. The purpose of Fianna Fáil must be to bring patriotism back into fashion.' These are quite traditional sentiments for a Fianna Fáil leader, and so is the claim that only a Fianna Fáil government could secure the nation and its sovereignty in times of crisis. A defeat for Fianna Fáil, Lemass implied, was not simply an electoral defeat but would threaten the future of the state. Such an outcome 'could well mean the loss of a great deal of all that has been already achieved, and such a weakening of the whole national position, that the very possibility of maintaining our independence could be put in jeopardy.'[17]

This reassertion of the link between patriotism, Fianna Fáil and economic success was given a specific political and economic context when Lemass argued during the 1965 general election campaign that only Fianna Fáil could achieve the industrial expansion necessary to preserve Ireland's sovereignty and independence. His attack on Fine Gael demonstrated his use of nationalism as a mobilising force and as a key element in Irish political culture. He came very close to accusing the main opposition party of being unpatriotic.[18] This was a necessary tactic for Fianna Fáil because both Fine Gael and Fianna Fáil were nationalist parties and thus the room for genuine disagreement between them was actually quite small. Lemass intended his appeal to patriotism to reinforce Fianna Fáil's dominant position in the political system; to prevent an alternative coalition from emerging; to create a new nationalist consensus around economic expansion and Common Market membership; and to neutralise any potential linkage between the major interest groups and the opposition political parties by incorporating them into corporatist structures for economic growth. This strategy was remarkably successful, and by the end of the 1960s Fianna Fáil had created a wide-ranging coalition of support for its approach to economic and political development. What held it together was a nationalist consensus and the identification of Fianna Fáil with the national interest.[19]

Michael Gallagher has argued that political change was quite limited during the 1960s and 1970s and that 'Irish parties have not adapted very much mainly because they did not need to.'[20] This is an acute observation, but it ignores the nature of political adaptation in mature liberal democratic states. Without some degree of adaptation, Fianna Fáil and Fine Gael especially would have faced challenges from other parties in the system. Because it was the dominant party, the changes in Fianna Fáil are subtler than those in the Labour Party, but they are nevertheless significant. By adapting to the need for change, Fianna Fáil abandoned the policies that it had been associated with for thirty years. It captured the high ground on policy from the right and left, maintained its traditional support base and attracted new supporters among the middle classes. However, persistence remains the key characteristic of the political system as well as of the society. The three traditional parties regained their complete dominance during the 1960s, after a period of instability. By 1973 minor parties had lost most of their support and the three main parties now received 95 per cent of the vote cast, up from 84 per cent in 1958. A Gallup poll in 1961 reported that only 43 per cent considered the forthcoming election to be 'very important'. A remarkably low 22 per cent believed that it was actually important who won the election, though 53 per cent concluded that Fianna Fáil would do so. A majority agreed there was little difference between the three main parties, though Fianna Fáil supporters were more inclined to identify differences. Both Fianna Fáil and Fine Gael drew support from all social categories; but Fianna Fáil's support base was more comprehensive, confirming its position as the dominant party in the system. This was further reinforced by the 44 per cent who thought Fianna Fáil was the party most capable of handling the 'most important problems', whereas 19 per cent considered Fine Gael to be most capable of doing so.[21]

Despite this, Fianna Fáil did not do well in the 1961 election, when both Fine Gael and Labour increased their support, as was the case again in 1965. While Fianna Fáil held on to government on each of these occasions, there did seem to be a trend against it. This was further reflected in de Valera's narrow re-election as President of Ireland in 1966 and in the failure of the

Fianna Fáil-driven initiative to amend the constitution to remove proportional representation from the electoral system in 1968. Yet, suggestive though these developments were, there was no 'ideological realignment in Irish politics', as Peter Mair has suggested. There was some potential for change, but it was never realised. In the *Just Society* policy document formulated by Declan Costello, Fine Gael began to explore a Christian democratic alternative to its Catholic corporatism, clearly influenced by the progressive-sounding Pope John XXIII. To view this as a move to the left is misleading; nor did it prove popular with Fine Gael's traditional support base. Furthermore, Liam Cosgrave's election as leader of the party in 1965 did not involve a departure from Fine Gael's narrowly conservative concerns; if anything he reinforced them. It was possible that Fine Gael could have developed a more liberal political profile during the 1960s, but neither the *Just Society* nor the party's political practice supported this shift. Some liberals were attracted to the party, but their significance was limited until the end of the 1970s.[22] The Labour Party did move to the left and adopted a social democratic political programme for the 1969 election. Labour activists believed that 'The Seventies will be Socialist', but they were to be disappointed in this hope. Lemass had dismissed the Labour Party in 1966 as 'the most conservative element in our country', but in 1969 his successor, Jack Lynch, went to considerable lengths to characterise it as a divisive left-wing force bent on destroying Ireland's economic growth and its stability.[23]

Fianna Fáil won a comfortable majority in 1969, confirming its dominance over the centre of Irish politics. It did so by emphasising continuity and economic growth, while highlighting the threat from Labour to political stability. Fianna Fáil was both conservative and defensive in 1969, and this showed the limits of any reforming potential within the party. It was conservative in that it sought to secure the foundations of its political dominance put in place over the previous decade. But it also sought to defend the existing social and economic conditions against the insurgency of the Labour Party and the new politics of the 1960s. Fianna Fáil was now a force for order, similar to Richard Nixon in the United States and General de Gaulle in France after the 1968 upheavals. The primary aim in Ireland was to contain the excesses associated with the new politics and to maintain order by reflecting the cautious reformism of a moderate majority. The momentum for reform was weak in any event, as it had been largely elite driven. This is quite different to the experience of Britain or continental Europe at the same time, which drew on both elite support and popular mass movements.[24] Fianna Fáil's electoral success secured Jack Lynch's leadership for the next decade, but it also extinguished the possibility of more radical change. One of the unintended consequences of 1969 was the weakening of radical alternatives in the political system. The Labour Party had increased its vote but lost seats. As a consequence, a more cautious strategy was developed over the following three years, which led to the decision to enter a coalition with Fine Gael at the 1973 election. Various factors contributed to this, including concerns about the security of the state in 1970 and 1971; nevertheless the outcome was the pragmatic option. It was recognised that if Fianna Fáil was to be replaced, a coalition was necessary. This may have been the conservative option, but it was also a realisable aim. While this marked the end of Labour's radicalism, it also confirmed Fianna Fáil's dominance in the political system and the limited appeal of reform or radicalism.[25]

Four other factors contributed to the return to order and conservatism in Ireland by the end of the 1960s. The first was the failure to develop a national system of innovation. Lemass had assumed that it would be possible for Irish industry and agriculture to respond to free trade and generate the means for industrialisation, full employment and export growth. By 1966 it was clear to Lemass that there was no internal dynamic to achieve these ends. Although the Irish economy was performing quite well by this time, most of the growth was associated with foreign direct investment. In so far as Ireland was industrialising during the 1960s, this was a consequence of foreign investment in export-led companies attracted to Ireland by the generous package provided by the Industrial Development Authority (IDA). This was acknowledged in institutional terms when the IDA was reorganised in 1969 and was given a virtual monopoly over Irish industrial and developmental policy throughout the 1970s, becoming one of the most important institutions in the state during that time. The dependence on foreign direct investment for industrial expansion (what has been called industrialisation by invitation) had a number of consequences for Ireland. It provided the country with much-needed employment, exports and investment at a time when it would have been politically and socially costly for Ireland to provide these itself. It absolved politicians of responsibility for economic problems, as criticism could be deflected on to the uncertainties of the global economy. But, it also put paid to Lemass' hope that a vigorous outward-looking Irish entrepreneur class would be created as a result of the changes in the economy. Irish industry failed to adapt to the changing circumstances of free trade and much of native Irish industry collapsed in the face of the oil recession of the 1970s and early 1980s.[26]

Secondly, the renewed application for entry to the EEC also took on a somewhat different focus. For a nationalist party, such as Fianna Fáil, it was important to avoid distributional conflicts among the social groups composing the nation. John Whyte's analysis of the 1969 election concluded that Irish politics did not have a social basis, as was the case in most industrial states. While this was so, it did not mean that there was no conflict based on class, economic or social interests. Economic change by its very nature raises issues about who gets what and how much. During the second half of the 1960s there was considerable industrial unrest, centred on demands for improved incomes and welfare. Prior to this, the farming organisations mobilised their members in support of their demands for increased prices for their products. More generally, there was a belief that the benefits of economic growth should be shared among the population. The Labour Party unsuccessfully attempted to benefit from this unrest in 1969, but a real challenge existed. The Common Agricultural Policy was seen as a way of removing pressure from the government and transferring the subsidisation of agriculture from the Irish state to Brussels. Entry to the EEC was no longer viewed as part of a developmental strategy, but as a means to subsidise Irish farming without any cost to the state and to protect the special environment created to attract foreign direct investment. The state used considerable resources after joining the EEC to maintain this policy mix. There was little willingness on the part of the major parties to deal with change or to accept that farming had little to contribute to employment or to economic growth. Entry to the EEC was used as a mechanism to avoid conflict with the farming community, and foreign direct investment operated to divide the working class between those within foreign industry and those outside it.[27] Ireland did not gain much from membership in the medium term, though specific groups such as farmers did. Irish industry collapsed, unemployment reached its highest level on record by the beginning of the 1980s and emigration once again became a fact of life for many young people. Nor did Ireland improve its relative position within the EEC; in 1960 gross domestic product per head was 61.9 per cent of the EEC average, increasing marginally to 64.7 per cent by 1980. This is not to claim that joining the EEC was the wrong decision for Ireland, but to suggest that without an internal industrial dynamic the effect of membership would be limited despite the high expectations.[28]

The third factor contributing to conservatism was the slow pace of change at the institutional level. The most significant change came in May 1972 when the electorate endorsed the amendment to the constitution ratifying membership of the EEC. Later in the same year, the constitution was also amended to remove subsections 2 and 3 of Article 44.1 which recognised a 'special position' for the Catholic Church and recognised certain other denominations. At the same time, eligibility to vote was reduced from twenty-one to eighteen years of age. These developments, however, did not reflect a more general commitment to change, especially on controversial issues. There was considerable discussion on the possibility of introducing divorce for non-Catholics, itself a very conservative view, as suggested by the all-party Dáil Committee on the Constitution in 1967. However this and some private initiatives on the part of the Taoiseach came to nothing when it became known that senior members of the hierarchy were opposed. It is telling that Article 44 was amended after Cardinal William Conway indicated that he was not opposed to such a move on the part of the government. In fact, relations between church and state were relatively unaffected by social change during the 1960s and 1970s, despite changes in public opinion on these matters. The church successfully defended its privileged position in education and medicine and neutralised most attempts to reflect more liberal views on moral issues, such as divorce and contraception.[29] The referendum campaign on the Common Market emphasised national solidarity and the benefits to be derived from membership. The overwhelming support received (83.1 per cent) can be attributed to elite agreement on the issue, strong business and farming support and a disorganised and discredited opposition campaign. Fianna Fáil and Fine Gael successfully argued that a vote in favour was in the national interest and would contribute to Ireland's development.[30]

The fourth contributory factor was the conflict in Northern Ireland and the continuing tension between the system-maintaining conservative nationalism of Fianna Fáil (and the other political parties) and the expansionist nationalism implicit in the 1937 constitution. This latter form of nationalism was given militant expression by the republican movement. As noted earlier, nationalism took a conservative form for most of the 1960s, even in respect of Northern Ireland. Lemass promoted dialogue between unionism and nationalism for the first time, which in the short term led to an unprecedented degree of co-operation. Opinion polls in the north and the south identified a growing flexibility among unionists and nationalists, though this did not entail either giving up their respective entrenched views.[31] However, there was never enough time to consolidate the improving relationship, and the subsequent breakdown of order in 1969 undermined whatever trust existed between unionist and nationalist in Northern Ireland. In Northern Ireland the status quo ante quickly reasserted itself and the emergence of the Provisional IRA demonstrated the continuing strength of expansionist nationalism. Fianna Fáil was most affected by these events. Lemass' own position hardened as conditions deteriorated in the north in 1969.[32] More specifically, the appeal of expansionist nationalism increased within Fianna Fáil as the political situation polarised. The Arms Crisis of 1970, which led to the dismissal from government and arrest of Charles Haughey and Neil Blaney, among others, exposed serious divisions within Fianna Fáil, which were not to be resolved until the early 1990s. Although constitutional nationalism reasserted itself as the dominant form within Fianna Fáil, it remained the party most exposed to the attractions of republican militancy.[33]

When Patrick Kavanagh died in 1967, Ireland was already changing rapidly. The Ireland he had described in his 1942 masterpiece, 'The Great Hunger', was fast becoming a memory. Far removed from Kavanagh's austere rural life, John Montague's poem 'The Siege of Mullingar', published in 1972, conjures up an Ireland more relaxed, sensual and open-minded:

> In the early morning the lovers
> Lay on both sides of the canal
> Listening to Sony transistors
> To the agony of Pope John
> Yet it didn't seem strange or blasphemous
> The ground loss of death and Resurrection, as we strolled along:
> *Puritan Ireland's dead and gone,*
> *A myth of O'Connor and Ó Faoláin*[34]

Montague's poem captures the freedom and opportunity of the 1960s, the sense that something new was in the air. Personal and collective tension arose from the clash between the modern and the traditional. On television, it was possible to see bishops openly criticised; the Rolling Stones toured in 1965; the first arrests and convictions for drug offences occurred in 1967. Yet Montague's optimism was as ill-judged, as had been that of the Labour Party in 1969. Change in Ireland was curtailed by traditional views on Northern Ireland, the constitution, moral issues and the Catholic Church.

Fianna Fáil became an increasingly conservative force in Irish politics as a result of its commitment to traditional nationalism in respect of Northern Ireland, its reluctance to amend the constitution and its opposition to tolerance on moral issues. This was implicit in the 1960s, but became explicit during the 1970s and 1980s, especially after Charles Haughey became leader of the party in 1979. By the end of the 1970s, nationalism no longer provided the political or social glue for political consensus. The political parties and public opinion were increasingly divided in respect of the core values that had previously defined Ireland's traditional nationalist consensus. A liberal constituency emerged to challenge traditional views on Northern Ireland, the constitution and moral issues. Increasingly, the political system divided along conservative and liberal lines, particularly after Garret FitzGerald became leader of Fine Gael in 1977. Haughey sought to reassert a traditional nationalism which maintained old certainties, whereas FitzGerald attempted to redefine nationalism in a more open and pluralistic fashion. In retrospect, FitzGerald may have been closer to Lemass than was Haughey in this choice of strategies. During the 1980s the consensus on Northern Ireland broke down, though this was remade on terms largely dictated by Garret FitzGerald after the Anglo-Irish Agreement in 1985. Economic policy was also in dispute from the late 1970s but the FitzGerald led governments between 1981 and 1987 introduced severe neo-liberal policies. Although Haughey opposed the severity and purpose of these policies when in opposition, he was forced to accept them during the 1987 election campaign. His economic strategy after 1987, however, was to build a new consensus by encouraging co-operation among the various economic interests. This is the approach which has contributed to recent Irish economic success. Consensus was also missing on moral issues during the 1980s. Divisive referendums on abortion and divorce demonstrated the polarised nature of Irish opinion. While divorce was subsequently introduced after a referendum in November 1995, the issue of abortion remains unresolved. By the end of the 1990s Ireland had changed significantly as a consequence of these developments. Despite this, nationalism, national identity and nationalist culture remain defining characteristics of the Irish political landscape. The form in which they are expressed may differ from that of O'Connell, de Valera or Lemass, but they embody a collective identity which continues to differentiate nationalist Ireland from its British neighbours in Ireland.

NOTES AND REFERENCES

1. Why the Irish did not become British! (pages 1–28)

1. I will return to this issue briefly in ch. 7.
2. I am currently completing a book on the impact of nationalism on twentieth-century politics. See James G. Kellas, *The Politics of Nationalism and Ethnicity*, 2nd edn (London, 1998). Eric Hobsbawm, *Nations and Nationalism since 1780* (Cambridge, 1990); Ernest Gellner, *Nations and Nationalism* (Oxford, 1983); Julen Breuilly, *Nationalism and the State*, 3rd edn (Manchester, 1993); Benedict Anderson, *Imagined Communities: Reflections on the Origin and Spread of Nationalism* (London, 1983). I am grateful to Professor Kellas for discussing some of the issues central to nationalism in the modern period.
3. John R. Young, 'The Scottish Parliament and National Identity from the Union of the Crowns to the Union of the Parliaments, 1603–1707' in D. Broun, R.J. Finlay and M. Lynch (eds.), *Image and Identity: The Making and Re-making of Scotland Through the Ages* (Edinburgh, 1998), pp. 105–42; see also Linda Colley, *Britons: Forging the Nation, 1707–1837* (New Haven, 1992); S.J. Connolly, 'Varieties of Britishness: Ireland, Scotland and Wales in the Hanovarian State' in Alexander Grant and Keith J. Stringer (eds.), *Uniting the Kingdom?: The Making of British History* (London, 1995), pp. 193–207; S.J. Connolly (ed.), *Kingdoms United?: Great Britain and Ireland since 1500 – Integration and Diversity* (Dublin, 1999), for alternative approaches to this question.
4. Seymour Martin Lipset and Stein Rokkan, 'Cleavage Structures, Party Systems and Voter Alignments: An Introduction', in Seymour Martin Lipset and Stein Rokkan (eds.), *Party Systems and Voter Alignments: Cross-National Perspectives* (New York, 1967), pp. 1–64, for a classic statement of the emergence of different political cleavages in Europe; Brendan Bradshaw and John Morrill (eds.), *The British Problem, c. 1534–1707: State Formation in the Atlantic Archipelago* (Basingstoke, 1996); S.J. Connolly, *Religion, Law and Power: The Making of Protestant Ireland 1660–1760* (Oxford, 1992).
5. Quoted in Wendy Hinde, *Castlereagh* (London, 1981), p. 21; see also James Kelly, 'The Genesis of the "Protestant Ascendancy"' in Gerard O'Brien (ed.), *Parliament, Politics and People* (Dublin 1989), pp. 93–128; Thomas Bartlett, *The Fall and Rise of the Irish Nation: The Catholic Question 1690–1830* (Dublin, 1992), pp. 30–65; S.J. Connolly, *Religion, Law and Power: The Making of Protestant Ireland 1660–1760* (Oxford, 1992).
6. This is discussed in detail in Brian Girvin, 'The Act of Union, Nationalism and Religion: 1780–1850' in Jürgen Elvert (ed.), *Nordirland in Geschichte und Gegenwart/Northern Ireland: Past and Present* (Stuttgart, 1994), pp. 53–81.
7. Girvin, 'The Act of Union'; Bartlett, *The Fall and Rise of the Irish Nation*, pp. 202–67; Brian McDermott (ed.), *The Catholic Question in England and Ireland: The Papers of Denys Scully* (Dublin, 1988).

8. Mikuláš Teich and Roy Porter (eds.), *The National Question in Europe in Historical Context* (Cambridge, 1993).
9. Thomas Moore, *A Letter to the Roman Catholics of Dublin* (Dublin, 1810).
10. Theobald Wolfe Tone, *An Argument on Behalf of the Catholics of Ireland* (Belfast, 1973; original edition 1791), pp. 25–6; Marianne Elliott, *Wolfe Tone: Prophet of Irish Independence* (New Haven, 1989); Thomas Bartlett, 'The Burden of the Present: Theobald Wolfe Tone, Republican and Separatist' in David Dickson, Dáire Keogh and Kevin Whelan (eds.), *The United Irishmen: Republicanism, Radicalism and Rebellion* (Dublin, 1993), pp. 1–14.
11. Nancy J. Curtin, *The United Irishmen: Popular Politics in Ulster and Dublin 1791–1798* (Oxford, 1994), pp. 282–9.
12. Denys Scully, *An Irish Catholic's Advice to his Brethren* (Dublin, 1803), p. 50; this pamphlet provides a sustained Catholic critique of the Irish parliament. Edmund Burke shared the deep suspicion of an Irish parliament controlled by Anglicans; see Conor Cruise O'Brien, *The Great Melody: A Thematic Biography of Edmund Burke* (London, 1992).
13. David Miller, *Queen's Rebels* (Dublin, 1978); Peter Brooke, *Ulster Presbyterianism* (Dublin, 1987).
14. Brian Walker, *Dancing to History's Tune: History, Myth and Politics in Ireland* (Belfast, 1996), pp. 1–14; Graham Walker, *Intimate Strangers: Political and Cultural Interaction Between Scotland and Ulster in Modern Times* (Edinburgh, 1995), pp. 1–16.
15. Throughout the nineteenth century most unionists were Protestants and their identity, though Irish, was differentiated from Irish nationalism by its Britishness. See David Hempton, *Religion and Political Culture in Britain and Ireland from the Glorious Revolution to the Decline of Empire* (Cambridge, 1996), which unravels the complex contours of religion and Britishness among other themes; Finlay Holmes, *The Presbyterian Church in Ireland: A Popular History* (Columba Press, 1999), which provides an up-to-date assessment of many of these themes; Miller, *Queen's Rebels*, pp. 56–86; Thomas Hennessey, *Dividing Ireland: World War I and Partition* (London, 1998), pp. xi-xxi, for a discussion of the nature of British identity in Ireland.
16. Arthur Houston, *Daniel O'Connell: His Early Life and Journal, 1795-1802* (London, 1906); Scully, *An Irish Catholic's Advice to his Brethren.*
17. Daniel O'Connell to Mary O'Connell, 28 August 1803, in Maurice O'Connell (ed.) *The Correspondence of Daniel O'Connell*, 8 vols. (Dublin, 1972–80), vol. 1, p. 99 (O'Connell was a member of the Lawyers' Yeomanry Corps during this time); Charles Vane (ed.), *Memoirs and Correspondence of Viscount Castlereagh*, 12 vols. (London, 1849), vol. 4, pp. 298–313.
18. Stéphane Dion, 'The Reemergence of Secessionism: Lessons from Quebec', in Albert Breton, Gianluigi Galeotti, Pierre Salmon and Ronald Wintrobe (eds.), *Nationalism and Rationality* (Cambridge, 1995), pp. 116–42.
19. Speech at the Catholic Meeting, Royal Exchange Hall, 13 January 1800, quoted in John O'Connell (ed.), *The Life and Speeches of Daniel O'Connell, MP*, 2 vols. (Dublin, 1846), vol. 1, pp. 22–3.
20. The full speech can be found in ibid., pp. 34–52.
21. Alexis de Tocqueville, *Democracy in America*, ed. By J.P. Mayer (Garden City, New York, 1969), pp. 287–90.
22. Emmet Larkin (ed.) *Alexis de Tocqueville's Journey in Ireland: July-August 1835* (Dublin, 1990), pp. 102–3.
23. Alexis de Tocqueville, *Journeys to England and Ireland*, ed. by J.P. Mayer (London, 1958), pp. 118–96.
24. Fergus O'Ferrall, *Catholic Emancipation: Daniel O'Connell and the Birth of Irish Democracy 1820–30* (Dublin, 1985); Ravinder Kumar, *Essays in the Social History of India* (Calcutta, 1983); Dennis Dalton, *Mahatma Gandhi: Non-violent Power in Action* (New York, 1993);

see also Brian Girvin, 'Political Independence and Democratic Consolidation' in Michael Holmes and Denis Holmes (eds.), *Ireland and India: Connections, Comparisons and Contrasts* (Dublin, 1997), pp. 120–44.

25. Henry D. Inglis, *A Journey Throughout Ireland During the Spring, Summer and Autumn of 1834*, 2 vols. (London, 1834), vol. 1, pp. 24–6, 343–5, 40.
26. O'Connell to Bishop Doyle, 29 December 1827, in O'Connell (ed.), *Correspondence*, vol. 3, pp. 372–3.
27. The Irish case can be usefully compared with that of Belgium and Poland where similar adjustments were taking place. See Roger Eatwell (ed.), *European Political Cultures* (London, 1997), pp. 32–49, 122–38, 157–71, for comparative cases.
28. Girvin, 'The Act of Union', pp. 75–8; Miller, *Queen's Rebels*, pp. 58–86; see also the discussion on the nature of party competition in Ireland in the nineteenth century and its denominational character in John Coakley, 'The Evolution of Irish Party Politics' in Brian Girvin and Roland Stürm (eds.), *Politics and Society in Contemporary Ireland* (Aldershot, 1986), pp. 29–54.
29. O'Connell to Paul Cullen, 5 May 1842, in O'Connell (ed.), *Correspondence*, vol. 7, pp. 155–61.
30. Tocqueville, *Journeys to England and Ireland*, pp. 140–1, 174–8, 181–2; Eoin Burke, '"The Irishman is no lazzarone": German Travel Writers in Ireland 1828–1850', *History Ireland*, 5:3 (1997), pp. 21–5.
31. Brian Girvin, *The Right in the Twentieth Century* (London, 1994), pp. 41–5.
32. Alexis Heraclides, *The Self-Determination of Minorities in International Politics* (London, 1991). The extent to which the northern states in America were prepared to go to prevent the South from seceding reinforces the claim that secession was extremely difficult in the nineteenth century.
33. Amartya Sen, 'Individual Freedom as a Social Commitment', *New York Review of Books*, 14 June 1990, pp. 49–53, and *Poverty and Famines* (Oxford, 1981), who stresses the commitment of an independent democratic India to preventing famine, whereas the colonial administrator did not have the commitment or the pressure to do so; Michael Lynch, *A New History of Scotland* (London, 1991), pp. 370–5; T.M. Devine, *The Scottish Nation 1700–2000* (London, 1999), pp. 414–21.
34. D. George Boyce, *Nineteenth-Century Ireland: The Search for Stability* (Dublin, 1990), pp. 154–76.
35. Liam Kennedy, 'The Union of Ireland and Britain 1801–1921' in Liam Kennedy, *Colonialism, Religion and Nationalism in Ireland* (Belfast, 1996), pp. 35–74, for a broadly positive assessment of the Act of Union.
36. Boyce, *Nineteenth-Century Ireland*; K.T. Hoppen, *Elections, Politics and Society in Ireland, 1832–1885* (Oxford, 1984); Desmond Bowen, *Paul Cullen and the Shaping of Modern Irish Catholicism* (Dublin, 1983), pp. 245–81.
37. Brian Farrell (ed.), *The Irish Parliamentary Tradition* (Dublin, 1975); Alan J. Ward, *The Irish Constitutional Tradition* (Dublin, 1994).
38. In Germany and Italy, for example, the liberal state undermined its own principles by ignoring or manipulating electoral outcomes, with serious consequences for the future.
39. This dilemma continues to affect multinational states, though by the end of the twentieth century the Irish lesson had been learnt by among others Canada and the United Kingdom. It is likely that Scotland and Quebec would become independent if a majority of voters elected to support such a change. This has rarely been the case in the past; the secession of Norway from Sweden in 1905 is one of the rare examples of peaceful secession; see Raymond E. Lindgren, *Norway–Sweden: Union, Disunion, and Scandinavian Integration* (Princeton, N.J., 1959).

40. T.G. Fraser, *Partition in Ireland, India and Palestine* (London, 1984); Hennessey, *Dividing Ireland,* pp. 1–42.
41. David Martin, *A General Theory of Secularization* (Oxford, 1978), p. 109; Adrian Hastings, *The Construction of Nationhood* (Cambridge, 1997), pp. 148–84.
42. Scotland retained a number of distinct institutions after the Union, but for the purposes of this discussion it too integrated within the British state and shared in the process. Colley, *Britons,* is the most succinct account of this process; see also Lynch, *Scotland,* and the discussion in Devine, *The Scottish Nation,* pp. 231–45, 273–98.
43. The point here is not to claim that Britain had become secular during the nineteenth century, but that in comparison with Ireland it had moved beyond the politics of denomination to a large extent and had accepted a level of non-denominationalism in public policy; Hugh McLeod, *Religion and the People of Western Europe 1789–1970* (Oxford, 1981). See also Martin Conway, *Catholics in Europe 1918–1945* (London, 1997); Mark A. Noll (ed.), *Religion and American Politics: From the Colonial Period to the 1980s* (New York, 1990).
44. Tom Inglis, *Moral Monopoly: The Rise and Fall of the Catholic Church in Modern Ireland,* 2nd edn (Dublin, 1998), pp. 129–200; Emmet Larkin, *The Roman Catholic Church and the Creation of the Modern Irish State 1878–1886* (Dublin, 1975); Bowen, *Cullen;* P.S. O'Hegarty, *A History of Ireland Under the Union* (London, 1952), p. 141, claims that 'religion was a badge of nationality' during the nineteenth century, while Lawrence Geary, *The Plan of Campaign* (Cork, 1986), argues inter alia that the political culture of the Land League embodied a popular Catholicism and nationality which made the movement all the more potent; Senia Pašeta, *Before the Revolution: Nationalism, Social Change and Ireland's Catholic élite, 1879–1922* (Cork, 1999); Girvin, *The Right in the Twentieth Century,* ch. 1, discusses the various responses of conservatives to modernity.
45. Boyce, *Nineteenth-Century Ireland,* p. 130; Devine, *The Scottish Nation,* pp. 3–102; Colley, *Britons.* I have learnt a considerable amount about Scottish history and politics from discussions with James Kellas, for which I am in his debt.
46. There is no room here for a more detailed discussion of the comparative evolution of Ireland and Scotland under their respective unions and my comments here are at the most general level. The literature on Scotland under the Union is rich; see Lynch, *Scotland,* pp. 300–97; Catriona M.M. Macdonald (ed.), *Unionist Scotland 1800–1997* (Edinburgh, 1998); Callum G. Brown, *Religion and Society in Scotland since 1707* (Edinburgh, 1997), pp. 177–207.
47. Quoted in Nicholas Mansergh, *The Irish Question 1840–1921,* 3rd edn (London, 1975), pp. 96–102.
48. J.S. Mill, *Considerations on Representative Government* (1861) in John Gray (ed.), *On Liberty and Other Essays* (Oxford, 1991), pp. 433–4.
49. The literature on secession is extensive. See Margaret Moore (ed.), *National Self-Determination and Secession* (Oxford, 1998); Allen Buchanan, *Secession: The Morality of Political Divorce from Fort Sumter to Lithuania and Quebec* (Boulder, Colo., 1991). It should be noted that most contemporary writers on secession remain opposed to a general right to secede on the part of a nation from an existing state.
50. Quoted in Ulick O'Connor *Celtic Dawn* (London, 1984), pp. 165–8; see also John Hutchinson, *The Dynamics of Cultural Nationalism: The Gaelic Revival and the Creation of the Irish Nation State* (London, 1987); Tom Garvin, *Nationalist Revolutionaries* (Oxford, 1987); Pašeta, *Before the Revolution,* pp. 119–54, for a careful reassessment of opinion among the elite; Patrick Maume, *The Long Gestation: Irish Nationalist Life 1891–1918* (Dublin, 1999).
51. Tocqueville, *Journeys to England and Ireland;* John J. Horgan, *Parnell to Pearse* (Dublin, 1948), pp. 110–11.

52. Brian Walker, 'The 1885 and 1886 General Elections: A Milestone in Irish History' in Walker, *Dancing to History's Tune*, pp. 15–33.
53. David W. Miller, *Church, State and Nation in Ireland 1898–1921* (Dublin, 1973).
54. Patrick Maume, *D.P. Moran* (Dublin, 1995), pp. 19–22; Horgan, *Parnell to Pearse*, pp. 111–12.
55. Eunan O'Halpin, *The Decline of the Union: British Government in Ireland 1892–1920* (Dublin, 1987); Pašeta, *Before the Revolution*, pp. 103–18, details the extent to which the Catholic elite progressed prior to the First World War.
56. Miller, *Church, State and Nation.* Recognition of dual power was a gradual process, but probably began in the late 1860s and was openly recognised by Gladstone in the 1880s. The Conservative Party was less easy with this recognition.
57. C. Desmond Greaves, *The Irish Transport and General Workers' Union: The Formative Years, 1909–1923* (Dublin, 1982), pp. 11–50; *Sinn Féin*, 9 January 1909.
58. W.F. Mandle, *The Gaelic Athletic Association and Irish Nationalist Politics 1884–1924* (Dublin, 1987).
59. I have drawn on various sources for this discussion: Tom Garvin, 'The Politics of Language and Popular Culture in Ireland', *Irish Political Studies*, 2 (1987), pp. 49–63; Peter Murray, 'Irish Cultural Nationalism in the United Kingdom State: Politics and the Gaelic League 1900–1918', *Irish Political Studies*, 8 (1993), pp. 55–72; Michael Cronin, 'Defenders of the Nation?: The GAA and Irish Nationalist Identity', *Irish Political Studies*, 11 (1996), pp. 1–19; Garvin, *Nationalist Revolutionaries*; Joost Augusteijn, *From Public Defiance to Guerrilla Warfare* (Dublin, 1996), pp. 37–40; Patrick Maume, 'Nationalism and Partition: The Political Thought of Arthur Clery', *Irish Historical Studies* 31:122, (1998), pp. 222–40.
60. Ruth Fleischmann, *Catholic Nationalism in the Irish Revival: A Study of Canon Sheehan, 1852–1913* (Basingstoke, 1997).
61. Andy Bielenberg, 'Entrepreneurship, Power and Public Opinion in Ireland: The Career of William Martin Murphy', *Chronicon*, 2 (1998), pp. 1–35, which can be found at www.ucc.ie/chronicon/bielen.htm; see also Garvin, *Nationalist Revolutionaries*; Hutchinson, *The Dynamics of Cultural Nationalism*, for other discussions of changes in nationalist culture.
62. *Sinn Féin*, 28 January 1911, editorial on Home Rule; Pádraic H. Pearse, *Political Writings and Speeches* (Dublin, 1966), pp. 154–5.
63. Gerard O'Brien, 'The Strange Death of the Irish Language, 1780–1800' in O'Brien (ed.), *Parliament, Politics and People*, pp. 149-70; for an example of successful revival, see Matti Klinge, 'Finland: From Napoleonic Legacy to Nordic Co-operation' in Teich and Porter (eds.), *The National Question in Europe*, pp. 317–31; Reg Hindley, *The Death of the Irish Language: A Qualified Obituary* (London, 1990), pp. 3–20.
64. Canon Sheehan, *The Beauty of Summer* (Cork, 1973), pp. 24, 32–3, 50–5. The essay was originally published in Patrick A. Sheehan, *Under the Cedars and the Stars* (Dublin, 1903).
65. L. Paul-Dubois, *Contemporary Ireland* (Dublin, 1911), pp. 152–3, 160–1; the quote appears on p. 491. The original edition was published in French in 1907 as *L'Irlande Contemporaine.*
66. Conor Cruise O'Brien, 'Nationalism and the Reconquest of Ireland', *The Crane Bag*, 1:2 (1977), pp. 8–13; Monk Gibbon, 'Am I Irish?', *The Crane Bag*, 1:2, (1977), pp. 27–8; Peter Hart, 'The Protestant Experience of Revolution in Southern Ireland' in Richard English and Graham Walker (eds.), *Unionism in Modern Ireland* (Dublin, 1996), pp. 81–98. See T.M. Kettle, *The Open Secret of Ireland* (London, 1912), pp. 98–119, for a moderate nationalist critique of unionism, but one which demonstrates a fundamental lack of understanding of the movement or its strength.

2. Nationalism, Unionism and Violence (pages 29–62)

1. Pádraic H. Pearse, *Political Writings and Speeches* (Dublin, 1966), pp. 154–5; Ruth Dudley Edwards, *Patrick Pearse: The Triumph of Failure* (London, 1977).
2. *Cork Examiner* January 12, 1914 editorial.
3. Ian McBride, 'Ulster and the British Problem' in Richard English and Graham Walker (eds.), *Unionism in Modern Ireland* (Dublin, 1996), pp. 1–18; David Miller, *Queen's Rebels* (Dublin, 1978), pp. 87–120.
4. John J. Horgan, *Parnell to Pearse* (Dublin, 1948), pp. 217–18; T.M. Kettle, *The Open Secret of Ireland* (London, 1912), pp. 98–119.
5. University College Cork Archives (UCCA), O'Brien Papers, AS 85, O'Brien to H.J. Smith, 9 May 1914; AS 78, O'Grady to O'Brien, 16 March 1914.
6. Joseph V. O'Brien, *William O'Brien and the Course of Irish Politics 1881–1918* (Berkeley, Calif., 1976), pp. 185–211, for an assessment; see also Paul Bew, *Ideology and the Irish Question: Ulster Unionism and Irish Nationalism 1912–1916* (Oxford, 1994); see speech by Frank Healy, one of O'Brien's political allies, in *Cork Examiner*, 28 November 1910, at a meeting to commemorate the Manchester Martyrs.
7. 'The Partition of Ulster', *Leader*, 17 February 1906, quoted in Patrick Maume 'Nationalism and Partition: The Political Thought of Arthur Clery', *Irish Historical Studies*, 31:122 (1998), pp. 222–40, at p. 230 for quotation.
8. See the essays in English and Walker, *Unionism in Modern Ireland*; Alvin Jackson, *The Ulster Party: Irish Unionists in the House of Commons, 1884–1911* (Oxford, 1989); Peter Gibbon, *The Origins of Ulster Unionism* (Manchester, 1975).
9. *Sinn Féin*, editorial, 28 January 1911; Richard P. Davis, *Arthur Griffith and Non-Violent Sinn Féin* (Dublin, 1974), pp. 37–58.
10. National Library of Ireland (NLI), MS 18273, Horgan Papers, Martyn to John Horgan, 24 June 1907.
11. *Sinn Féin*, editorial, 3 February 1912.
12. *Sinn Féin*, 4 April 1914, 17 March 1914, 28 March 1914.
13. *Sinn Féin*, 18 April 1914, emphasis in the original.
14. *Sinn Féin*, editorial, 18 April 1914; 'Redmond and Partition', 14 March 1914; Letter by The O'Rahilly, 16 May 1914. Michael Joseph O'Rahilly (otherwise known as 'The O'Rahilly') was a Sinn Féin and Gaelic League activist. He was managing director of *An Claidheamh Soluis* and a militant member of the Irish Volunteers. He was killed during the 1916 Rebellion.
15. NLI, MS 18270, Horgan to Redmond, 21 October 1913; *Cork Examiner*, 12 January 1914; *Cork Constitution* for O'Brien's speech on partition, 4 May 1914, where he complained that the AFIL was criticised by 'men who would hand over 300,000 Irish Catholics to an Orange State, where the Orange Order would be complete masters'. Horgan, *Parnell to Pearse*, p. 252, for local elections. In the county council elected in May the IPP had twenty seats to twelve for the AFIL, a loss of seven.
16. Evelyn Long, 'The Right and British Politics, 1884–1914' (MA thesis, University College Cork, 1996).
17. Eoin MacNeill, 'The North Began', *An Claidheamh Soluis*, 1 November 1913. The journal was a Gaelic League publication. For a discussion F.X. Martin, 'MacNeill and the Foundation of the Irish Volunteers' in F.X. Martin and F.J. Byrne (eds.), *The Scholar Revolutionary: Eoin MacNeill 1867–1945* (Shannon, 1973), pp. 99–179.
18. Horgan, *Parnell to Pearse*, pp. 226–9; *Cork Examiner*, 13 December 1913; David Hogan [Frank Gallagher], *The Four Glorious Years* (Dublin, 1953), pp. 221–2.
19. Horgan, *Parnell to Pearse*, pp. 228–9, MacNeill to Horgan, 16 December 1913. The fantasy that the two Volunteer forces could unite in some unknown way seems to have

continued to affect the judgment of radical nationalists into 1914; Roger Casement mused openly on what would happen if he and Carson travelled together to Cork, though he wondered 'Would you all rise to the occasion or would you tear us limb from limb?' Casement to Horgan, 16 February 1914, in Horgan, *Parnell to Pearse*, pp. 236–9.

20. Patrick Buckland, *Ulster Unionism and the Origins of Northern Ireland 1886–1922* (Dublin, 1973); Bew, *Ideology and the Irish Question.*
21. Muldoon to Horgan, 18 December 1913, in Horgan, *Parnell to Pearse*, p. 230.
22. 'The Coming Revolution' in Pearse, *Political Writings and Speeches*, pp. 91–9; Dudley Edwards, *Patrick Pearse*, pp. 198–274, for discussion. Pearse's views on violence should be compared with those of Gandhi, who, in more difficult circumstances, refused to countenance violence against a regime which was more repressive and less representative than that faced by the Irish in 1914; John Marsden, 'Religion and the Nationalist Cause in the Thought of Patrick Pearse', *Studies*, 84 (1995), pp. 28–37, for an analysis; J.J. Lee, 'In Search of Patrick Pearse' in Máirín Ní Dhonnchadha and Theo Dorgan (eds.), *Revising the Rising* (Derry, 1991), pp. 122–38.
23. MacNeill to Horgan, 17 December 1913 in Horgan, *Parnell to Pearse*, pp. 230–1; report of meeting of the Irish Volunteers, 31 July 1914, in *Cork Free Press*, 1 August 1914.
24. Casement to Horgan, 16 February 1914, in Horgan, *Parnell to* Pearse, pp. 236-9.
25. Thomas Hennessey, *Dividing Ireland: World War I and Partition* (London, 1998), pp. 71–3.
26. Tom Garvin, 'The Rising and Irish Democracy' in Ní Dhonnchadha and Dorgan (eds.), *Revising the Rising*, pp. 21–8, at pp. 21–2 for quotation.
27. Brian Farrell (ed.), *The Irish Parliamentary Tradition* (Dublin, 1975); Alan J. Ward, *The Irish Constitutional Tradition* (Dublin, 1994), pp. 71–100.
28. Patricia Jalland, *The Liberals and Ireland* (Brighton, 1980); see also J.J. Lee, *Ireland 1912–1985: Politics and Society* (Cambridge, 1989), pp. 1–24.
29. Patrick Maume, *The Long Gestation: Irish Nationalist Life 1891–1918* (Dublin, 1999), pp. 120–46, explores the contradiction in Irish nationalist thought in respect of Ulster; Lee, *Ireland*, pp. 1–24, is extremely critical of Ulster unionism, but provides a considered assessment of its role in the crisis; see also Brian Murphy, 'The Canon of Irish Cultural History: Some Questions Concerning Roy Foster's *Modern Ireland*' in Ciaran Brady (ed.), *Interpreting Irish History: The Debate on Historical Revisionism* (Dublin, 1994), pp. 222–33.
30. McBride, 'Ulster and the British Problem'; Hennessey, *Dividing Ireland*, pp. 4–18; Lee, *Ireland*, p. 17: 'But there is one logic unionists grasped from the outset, the iron logic of violence.'
31. D.G. Boyce, *Englishmen and Irish Troubles* (London, 1972).
32. UCCA, O'Brien Papers, AS 97, Maurice Healy to O'Brien, 11 November 1914, and reply, 12 November 1914, claiming that nationalists had been 'defrauded' of an Irish regiment and were serving in 'foreign' regiments; Breandán Mac Giolla Choille (ed.), *Intelligence Notes 1913–1916* (Dublin, 1966), pp. 119–20; J.J. Walsh, *Recollections of a Rebel* (Tralee, 1944), pp. 27–33; David Fitzpatrick, *Politics and Irish Life 1913–21* (Dublin, 1977), pp. 107–8; Fergus Fitzgerald, *Memoirs of Desmond Fitzgerald* (London, 1968), pp. 46–7.
33. *Irish Times*, 4 August 1914; *Cork Free Press*, 4 August 1914; O'Brien, *William O'Brien*, p. 212, for report of pro-war meeting in Cork City Hall, 2 September 1914; O'Brien is reported as claiming that the outcome of the war would be 'genuine national unity', *Cork Free Press*, 6 August 1914; Bew, *Ideology and the Irish Question.*
34. *The Echo*, 13 March 1915, quoted in Pauline Codd, 'Recruiting and Responses to the War in Wexford' in David Fitzpatrick (ed.), *Ireland and the First World War* (Dublin, 1986), pp. 15–26; Fitzpatrick, *Politics and Irish Life*, p. 109.

35. D. George Boyce, '1916, Interpreting the Rising' in D. George Boyce and Alan O'Day (eds.), *The Making of Modern Irish History* (London, 1996), pp. 163–87; Joost Augusteijn, *From Public Defiance to Guerrilla Warfare* (Dublin, 1996), pp. 43–54, on the impact of the 1914 split on the radicals and on the difficulty encountered revitalising the Volunteers prior to 1916; Hennessey, *Dividing Ireland*, pp. 61–79; UCCA, O'Brien Papers, AS 106, O'Brien to Hugh O'Brien, n.d. but probably late 1915–early 1916 from content.
36. D.P. Moran, 'Is the Irish Nation Dying?' in D.P. Moran, *The Philosophy of Irish Ireland* (Dublin, 1905), pp. 1–10 at p. 2; Patrick Maume, *D.P. Moran* (Dublin, 1995), pp. 35–6.
37. Quoted in Garvin, *Nationalist Revolutionaries*, p. 12.
38. See de Valera speech at the time of the fiftieth anniversary of the 1916 Rising in Maurice Moynihan (ed.), *Speeches and Statements by Éamon de Valera 1917–73* (Dublin, 1995), pp. 605–7.
39. John Horgan, *Seán Lemass: The Enigmatic Patriot* (Dublin, 1997), pp. 6–12.
40. FitzGerald's articles appeared in the *Irish Times* 13, 15, 16, 17 and 18 July 1991. I am not dealing directly with the fifth article which purports to address the issue of Northern Ireland and 1916, because it does not do so. It reads more as an attempt to justify FitzGerald's role in extending the authority of the Irish Republic over Northern Ireland.
41. David Fitzpatrick, 'The Logic of Collective Sacrifice: Ireland and the British Army, 1914–1918', *The Historical Journal*, 38:4 (1995), pp. 1017–30, which notes that recruiting after the Rising was concentrated among Dublin Catholics; Hennessey, *Dividing Ireland*, pp. 80–105.
42. J.B. Lyons, *The Enigma of Tom Kettle* (Dublin, 1983).
43. NLI, Redmond Papers, MS 18270, Horgan to Redmond, 4 December 1915: 'as far as Cork is concerned O'Brien is a spent force'; Mac Giolla Choille, *Intelligence Notes*, pp. 140–50; Patrick Maume, *The Long Gestation: Irish Nationalist Life 1891–1918* (Dublin, 1999), pp. 147–78.
44. Despite this, a unionist newspaper such as the *Irish Times* emphasised loyalty to the Crown, whereas the *Freeman's Journal* or the *Cork Examiner* placed their emphasis on aspects of Irish national interest. This is not to claim that the nationalist newspapers did not express loyalty to the Crown or the state, but Irish nationalism and its interests continued to receive priority from them.
45. Albert O. Hirschman, *Shifting Involvement* (Oxford, 1982), pp. 112–13; Brian Girvin, *The Right in the Twentieth Century* (London, 1994), pp. 38–49.
46. Hirschman, *Shifting Involvement*; James DeFronzo, *Revolutions and Revolutionary Movements*, 2nd edn (Boulder, Colo., 1996), pp. 7–28.
47. 'Peace and the Gael' (December 1915); 'Ghosts' (Christmas 1915) in Pearse, *Political Writings and Speeches*, pp. 213–50.
48. 'The Sovereign People' (31 March 1916) in *Political Writings and Speeches*, pp. 335–72.
49. Tim Pat Coogan, *De Valera: Long Fellow, Long Shadow* (London, 1993), pp. 322–3; John Bowman, *De Valera and the Ulster Questions 1917–1973* (Oxford, 1982).
50. *Irish News*, 4 May 1916.
51. Bew, *Ideology and the Irish Question*, for a discussion; Mac Giolla Choille, *Intelligence Notes*, p. 147; J.J. Lee, *Ireland 1912–1985: Politics and Society* (Cambridge, 1989), pp. 24–38; Boyce, '1916, Interpreting the Rising' is critical of Lee's view.
52. NLI, Johnson Papers, MS 17116, diary; Horgan, *Seán Lemass*, p. 14.
53. James Stephens, *The Insurrection in Dublin* (Dublin and London, 1916), pp. viii–xii.
54. Hennessey, *Dividing Ireland*, pp. 125–52; Tracey R. Connolly, 'Irish Public Opinion and the Republican Movement 1916-1918' (MA thesis, University College Cork, 1995).
55. Hennessey, *Dividing Ireland*, pp. 114–58, for many other contrasts between unionist and nationalist opinion in respect of the war.

56. Dillon's speech is cited in the *Freeman's Journal*, 13 May 1916; Lynch's contribution can be found in Fitzpatrick, *Politics and Irish Life*, p. 116.
57. Connolly, 'Irish Public Opinion', pp. 51–87.
58. Quoted in ibid., pp. 83–5.
59. NLI, Redmond Papers, MS 18270, Horgan to Redmond, 4 December 1915.
60. NLI, Horgan Papers, MS 18271, Horgan to Devlin 1 July 1916, where Horgan thanks the northern nationalist leader for his sacrifice. These papers also contain a note of the resolution to accept partition temporally adopted by the IPP and prepared by Horgan for the National Directory on 3 July.
61. Chanel, 'The Interned Catholics', *Leader*, 1 July 1916.
62. UCCA, O'Brien Papers, AS 113, O'Brien to J. O'Donnell, 16 May 1916; AS 116, O'Brien to Father Madden, 20 May 1916; AS 128, O'Brien to Rev. Tom Maguire CC, 10 June 1916; AS 127 Rev. Tom Maguire CC to O'Brien, 7 June 1916.
63. UCCA, O'Brien Papers, AS 133, Michael O'Brien to O'Brien, 12 June 1916; AS 138, William M. Murphy to O'Brien, 20 June 1916; AS 140, Edmund O'Donnell (Galway) to O'Brien, 12 July 1916; AS 146–7, Lawrence Casey to O'Brien, 27 July 1916; AS 152, O'Rahilly to O'Brien, 19 August 1916; Andy Bielenberg, 'Entrepreneurship, Power and Public Opinion in Ireland: The Career of William Martin Murphy', *Chronicon*, 2 (1998), pp. 1–35, paragraphs 26–8.
64. Hogan, *The Four Glorious Years*, pp. 224–7.
65. *Cork Examiner*, 17 November 1916; UCCA, O'Brien Papers, AS 198, O'Brien to W. MacDonald, 12 December 1916; Maume, *The Long Gestation*, pp. 189–91, for a discussion of the complex background to this by-election.
66. *Cork Examiner*, editorial, 'Mr William O'Brien and West Cork', 9 November 1916.
67. Michael Laffan, *The Resurrection of Ireland: The Sinn Féin Party, 1916–1923* (Cambridge, 1999).
68. T.G. Fraser, *Partition in Ireland, India and Palestine* (London, 1984).
69. Stephens, *Insurrection in Dublin*, pp. 108–9; UCCA, O'Brien Papers, AS 203, Correspondence between Lloyd-George and O'Brien, July 1917.
70. Quoted in D. George Boyce, *Nineteenth-Century Ireland: The Search for Stability* (Dublin, 1990), p. 261; Bowman, *De Valera and the Ulster Question*, pp. 30–7; According to de Valera in 1920, 'The Irish nation is *one* nation not two . . . as homogeneous as any nation upon the earth.' Quoted in Bowman, *De Valera and the Ulster Question*, p. 38.
71. Stephens, *Insurrection in Dublin*, p. 109.
72. Michael Laffan, *The Partition of Ireland 1911–1925* (Dundalk, 1983); David W. Miller, *Church, State and Nation in Ireland 1898–1921* (Dublin, 1973), pp. 330–425; David Fitzpatrick, *The Two Irelands 1912–1939* (Oxford, 1998), pp. 63–75; Augusteijn, *From Public Defiance to Guerrilla Warfare*, pp. 55–86; F.S.L. Lyons, *John Dillon* (London, 1968).
73. NLI, Horgan Papers, MS 18273, Martyn to Horgan, 13 July 1917. Martyn was a long-time supporter of Sinn Féin and an advocate of abstention.
74. UCCA, O'Brien Papers, letter written by O'Brien to the *Times*, 26 December 1917, but not published.
75. UCCA, O'Brien Papers, AS 223, Gallagher to O'Brien, 31 December 1917; AS 226, O'Brien to Gallagher, 3 January 1918; O'Brien, *William O'Brien*, pp. 232–5, which details O'Brien's increasing belief in 1918 that Sinn Féin should be given the opportunity to represent the nation; speech by Healy at Mallow honouring the Manchester Martyrs reported in *Irish Nation*, 22 December 1917. It is not surprising that Healy supported Sinn Féin at the 1918 general election.
76. UCCA, O'Brien Papers, AS 234, Meeting of AFIL Club, Cork, 26 November 1918; AS 236, Sinn Féin to O'Brien, 27 November 1918.

77. 'Dominion Self-Government', *Cork Examiner*, 24 August 1917. See also editorials in the issues of 4, 11 and 18 September 1917.
78. Pro Patria, 'The Ulster Problem: A Way Out', *Leader*, 2 December 1916; see also William Martin Murphy's proposal to give Irish Protestants 50 per cent of the seats in a Home Rule parliament, in Bielenberg, 'Entrepreneurship, Power and Public Opinion in Ireland'; Horgan, *Parnell to Pearse*, pp. 300–1; R.B. McDowell, *The Irish Convention 1917–18* (London, 1970).
79. Coogan, *De Valera*, pp. 94–9; Augustijn, *From Public Defiance to Guerrilla Warfare*, pp. 251–334; see also de Valera speech to the Sinn Féin ard fheis, 26 October 1917, in Moynihan (ed.), *Speeches and Statements*, pp. 6–8.
80. See discussion in Boyce, '1916; Interpreting the Rising'; F.X. Martin, 'Eoin MacNeill on the 1916 Rising', *Irish Historical Studies*, 12 (1961), pp. 226–71.
81. Both quotations are in Michael Laffan, *The Resurrection of Ireland: The Sinn Féin Party, 1916-1923* (Cambridge, 1999), p. 110.
82. Arthur Mitchell and Pádraig Ó Snodaigh (eds.), *Irish Political Documents 1916–1949* (Dublin, 1985), pp. 48–9; see also Laffan, *The Resurrection of Ireland*, pp. 149–76.
83. Augustijn, *From Public Defiance to Guerrilla Warfare*, pp. 254–5, 266–7, 270; Miller, *Church, State and Nation*, pp. 397–9, 456–7, 478–9; Arthur Mitchell, *Revolutionary Government in Ireland* (Dublin, 1995), pp. 120–224; Mary Kotsonouris, *Retreat From Revolution: The Dáil Courts, 1920–24* (Dublin, 1994), pp. 17–35; Peter Hart, *The I.R.A. and Its Enemies: Violence and Community in Cork 1916–1923* (Oxford, 1998).
84. Horgan, *Parnell to Pearse*, p. 285; compare this to Garret FitzGerald's wildly pessimistic view of the environment in which the Rising took place in *Irish Times*, 13, 15, 16, 17, 18 July 1991; Walter McDonald, *Some Ethical Questions of Peace and War* (London, 1919); McDonald, who had been Prefect of the Dunboyne Establishment at Maynooth, provided a theological critique of the Rising and Sinn Féin, but was ignored by mainstream nationalism; Senia Pašeta, *Before the Revolution: Nationalism, Social Change and Ireland's Catholic Elite, 1879–1922* (Cork, 1999), pp. 103–47.
85. Coogan, *De Valera*, pp. 107–23; Miller, *Church, State and Nation*, pp. 391–426; *Cork Examiner*, 8 November 1918; compare this with de Valera's speech in 1917: 'But we are united on this — that we want complete and absolute independence. This is not the time for discussion on the best forms of government. This is the time we can get freedom. Then we can settle by the most democratic means what particular form of government we may have', quoted in Coogan, *De Valera*, p. 97. It should be noted that Irish nationalists were under an illusion as to the purpose of the Peace Conference in Paris after the war. President Wilson's 'right to self-determination' had limited application and certainly did not apply to Ireland; see Alfred Cobban, *The Nation State and National Self-Determination* (Oxford, 1945), pp. 62–9, for a useful summary of Wilson's views on this matter.
86. Horgan, *Parnell to Pearse*, pp. 329–32, emphasis added.
87. NLI, Horgan Papers, MS 18271, Horgan to Richard Hazelton MP, 23 October 1918; Horgan, *Parnell to Pearse*, pp. 345–48.
88. NLI, Horgan Papers, MS 18272, Horgan to Dillon, 11 November 1918, reporting on the meeting the previous night and enclosing the resolution, *Cork Examiner*, 11 November 1918.
89. NLI, Horgan Papers, MS 18272, Dillon to Horgan, 14 November 1918, 20 November 1918.
90. Horgan, *Parnell to Pearse*, pp. 353–4. Interestingly Frank Gallagher in Hogan, *The Four Glorious Years*, p. 306, reports that when de Valera went to negotiate with Lloyd-George on 14 July 1921 he prepared his case by reading an article by Horgan, 'Precepts and Practice in Ireland, 1914–1919', *Studies*, 8 (1919), pp. 210–22.

91. Fitzpatrick, *Politics and Irish Life*, pp. 118–24; Laffan, *The Resurrection of Ireland.*
92. Lee, *Ireland*, p. 41; Mitchell, *Revolutionary Government in Ireland*, pp. 2–16; Brian Farrell, *The Founding of Dáil Eireann: Parliament and Nation-Building* (Dublin, 1971), pp. 29–44, for a critique of the Labour decision not to field candidates.
93. Tom Garvin, *The Evolution of Irish Nationalist Politics* (Dublin, 1981), pp. 114–21; NLI, Gallagher Papers, MS 18388, Sinn Féin election leaflets 1918, where the emphasis is on achieving national unity in the face of Britain's reluctance to concede Ireland's just claims.
94. *Freeman's Journal*, 30 December 1918.
95. Emmet Larkin, *The Roman Catholic Church and the Creation of the Modern Irish State, 1878–1886* (Dublin, 1975), p. 396; Miller, *Church, State and Nation*, pp. 426–84; Mitchell, *Revolutionary Government in Ireland*, pp. 173–6.
96. Miller, *Church, State and Nation*, pp. 456–61; Mitchell, *Revolutionary Government in Ireland*, pp. 265–99; Hart, *The I.R.A. and its Enemies.*
97. Ward, *Irish Constitutional Tradition*, pp. 189–211; Tom Garvin, *1922: The Birth of Irish Democracy* (Dublin, 1996).

3. From Civil War to National Integration (pages 63–105)

1. Dermot Keogh, *Twentieth-Century Ireland: Nation and State* (Dublin, 1994), p. 17.
2. Eunan O'Halpin, *Defending Ireland: The Irish State and its Enemies since 1922* (Oxford, 1999), pp. 39–81; Tim Pat Coogan, *The IRA* (London, 1970), pp. 42–7; Conor Brady, *Guardians of the Peace* (Dublin, 1974). The Army Mutiny was a response by former members of the IRA to the demobilisation of the Free State army after the Civil War and a concern that the government would not pursue the goal of a united Ireland. The Minister for Justice, Kevin O'Higgins, played the key role in defusing the crisis, though not without armed confrontation between the two sides and the resignation of two government ministers.
3. Robert A. Dahl, 'Patterns of Opposition' in Robert A. Dahl (ed.), *Political Oppositions in Western Democracies* (New Haven, 1966), pp. 332–47, Table 11.2 on p. 342.
4. John M. Regan, *The Irish Counter-Revolution 1921–1936: Treatyite Politics and Settlement in Independent Ireland* (Dublin, 1999). Regan advances the view that there was a counter-revolution, though his reasons for this claim are not persuasive. His development of the idea of a 'treatyite settlement' is a more nuanced and subtle approach to the issue of post-1922 Irish politics, as is his recognition of the consensual basis of Irish democracy. This important book is rich in detail on this period and my criticism of it should not detract from this.
5. See Tom Garvin, *1922: The Birth of Irish Democracy* (Dublin, 1996), for discussion of the anti-democratic nature of the republican movement at the time of the Civil War.
6. Richard Sinnott, *Irish Voters Decide* (Manchester, 1995), pp. 82–7; John M. Regan, 'The Politics of Reaction: The Dynamics of Treatyite Government and Policy, 1922–33', *Irish Historical Studies*, 30:120 (1997), pp. 542–63; Regan, *The Irish Counter-Revolution*, pp. 145–62; Tim Pat Coogan, *De Valera: Long Fellow, Long Shadow* (London, 1993), pp 356–61; Michael Gallagher, 'The Pact General Election of 1922', *Irish Historical Studies*, 21:84 (1979), pp. 404–21; Michael Gallagher (ed.), *Irish Elections 1922–44: Results and Analysis* (Limerick, 1993), for the data on both elections.
7. Jeffrey Prager, *Building Democracy in Ireland* (Cambridge, 1986); David Schmitt, *The Irony of Irish Democracy: The Impact of Political Culture on Administration and Democratic Political Development in Ireland* (London and Toronto, 1973); Tom Garvin, 'Unenthusiastic Democrats: The Emergence of Irish Democracy' in Ronald J. Hill and Michael Marsh (eds.), *Modern Irish Democracy* (Dublin, 1993), pp. 9–23; the most

positive evaluation of the Irish democratic process is available in Bill Kissane, 'The Not-So-Amazing Case of Irish Democracy', *Irish Political Studies,* 10 (1995), pp. 43–68; Bill Kissane, 'Majority Rule and the Stabilisation of Democracy in the Irish Free State', *Irish Political Studies,* 13 (1998), pp. 1–24.

8. The *Daily Mail* quote can be found in Brady, *Guardians of the Peace,* pp. 90–1; for the 1925 statement, see Richard Dunphy, *The Making of Fianna Fáil Power in Ireland 1923–1948* (Oxford, 1995), p. 65 (the emphasis has been added by Dunphy); see also Garvin, *1922,* pp. 92–122; Alan J. Ward, *The Irish Constitutional Tradition* (Dublin 1994), pp. 189–211; Albert O. Hirschman, *Shifting Involvement* (Oxford, 1982), pp. 112–13.
9. A Labour TD, 'Open Letter to Eamonn De Valera', *Voice of Labour,* 17 January 1925; Dunphy, *The Making of Fianna Fáil Power,* pp. 64–5, for quotations from de Valera and Lemass expressing the continuing opposition to the existence of the state itself; for a retrospective version of this, see Todd Andrews, *Man of No Property* (Dublin and Cork, 1982); Brian Farrell, *Seán Lemass* (Dublin, 1983); for a considered, if hostile, view of de Valera's view of the new state, Coogan, *De Valera,* pp. 356–82; John Horgan, *Seán Lemass: The Enigmatic Patriot* (Dublin, 1997), pp. 21–45.
10. John H. Whyte, *Catholics in Western Europe* (Dublin, 1981); Tom Buchanan and Martin Conway (eds.), *Political Catholicism in Europe 1918–1965* (Oxford, 1996); John Cornwell, *Hitler's Pope: The Secret History of Pius XII* (London, 1999); Seymour Martin Lipset, Kyoung-Ryung Seong and John Charles Torres, 'A Comparative Analysis of the Social Requisites of Democracy', *International Social Science Quarterly,* 45:2 (1993), pp. 155–75.
11. Ayesha Jalal, *Democracy and Authoritarianism in South Asia* (Cambridge, 1995); Brian Girvin, 'Political Independence and Democratic Consolidation' in Michael Holmes and Denis Holmes (eds.), *Ireland and India: Connections, Comparisons and Contrasts* (Dublin, 1997), pp. 120–44; Derek W. Urwin, *From Ploughshare to Ballotbox: The Politics of Agrarian Defence in Europe* (Oslo, 1980), pp. 256–7.
12. Brian Farrell (ed.), *The Irish Parliamentary Tradition* (Dublin, 1973); Ward, *The Irish Constitutional Tradition,* pp. 153–211; Kissane, 'Majority Rule and the Stabilisation of Democracy'.
13. See for example Regan, 'The Politics of Reaction' and his *The Irish Counter-Revolution.* I should emphasise that I have been guilty of this negative approach in a previous study; see Brian Girvin, *Between Two Worlds: Politics and Economy in Independent Ireland* (Dublin, 1989), pp. 11–46. I now think this was a consequence of a narrowly economistic approach to the question which focused on the Department of Industry and Commerce. A more integrated analysis of the government's record provides a strongly positive conclusion; see also J.J. Lee, *Ireland 1912–1985: Politics and Society* (Cambridge, 1989), pp. 69–135, 168–74.
14. Isaiah Berlin, 'Two Concepts of Liberty' in Isiah Berlin, *Four Essays on Liberty* (Oxford, 1969), pp. 154–60; Francis Fukuyama, *Trust: The Social Virtues and the Creation of Prosperity* (New York, 1995), on how levels of trust affect economic success and political stability.
15. National Archives of Ireland (NAI), Department of the Taoiseach (DT), S. 9005, 'Constitution 1922: Historical Summary', explanatory letter by Hugh Kennedy, 11 June 1922; Arthur Griffith to Lloyd-George, 2 June 1922 where Griffith insists on the widest possible meaning of Irish sovereignty. For an appreciation of Kennedy, see Gerard Hogan, 'Irish Nationalism as a Legal Ideology', *Studies,* vol. 75 (1986), pp. 528–38. A detailed survey of the primary documents associated with this period is now available in Ronan Fanning, Michael Kennedy, Dermot Keogh and Eunan O'Halpin (eds.), *Documents on Irish Foreign Policy: Volume I 1919–1922* (Dublin, 1998), pp. 216–515. See also John Coakley, 'Competing Conceptions of Legitimacy and the

Creation of the New State', *Études Irlandaises*, 20:1 (1995), pp. 55–65, at p. 62; Basil Chubb (ed.), *A Source Book of Irish Government*, 2nd edn (Dublin, 1983), pp. 12–14.

16. Parliamentary Debates Dáil Éireann (PDDE), 16 July 1931, quoted in Nicholas Mansergh, *The Irish Free State* (London, 1934), p. 263. For a detailed discussion of the principles behind the Free State approach to this question, see D.W. Harkness, *The Restless Dominion* (London, 1969); see also Keogh, *Twentieth-Century Ireland*, pp. 22–7, 49–52; Garvin, *1922*, pp. 183–5, where he notes that Cosgrave effectively recognised a unionist veto on Northern Ireland, a recognition which was withdrawn by Fianna Fáil in 1937 and not restored until 1985; Geoffrey Hand (ed.), *Report of the Irish Boundary Commission* (Shannon, 1969).
17. Maryann G. Valiulis, *Almost a Rebellion: The Irish Army Mutiny of 1924* (Cork, 1985); O'Halpin, *Defending Ireland*, pp. 45–53.
18. Brian Girvin, *The Right in the Twentieth Century* (London, 1994), for the comparative experience. Mary E. Daly, *Industrial Development and Irish National Identity, 1922-1939* (Dublin, 1992), p. 32, has described Cumann na nGaedheal's policy constituency as a 'beer, biscuits, cars, and cattle coalition'; see also Emmet O'Connor, *A Labour History of Ireland* (Dublin, 1992); C. Desmond Greaves, *The Irish Transport and General Workers' Union: The Formative Years, 1909–23* (Dublin, 1982); Tony Fahey, 'The Agrarian Dimension in the History of the Welfare State: A Case Study' (unpublished manuscript, Economic and Social Research Institute, Dublin, January 2000).
19. J.H. Whyte, *Church and State in Modern Ireland 1923–1970* (Dublin, 1971), p. 27; see also Brendan McConvery, 'Hell-fire and Poitín: Redemptorist Missions in the Irish Free State (1922–1936),' *History Ireland*, 8:3 (2000), pp. 18–22; Michael Adams, *Censorship: The Irish Experience* (Dublin, 1968). Whyte suggests that independence gave Irish governments control over legislation, thus providing an opening for direct Catholic influence over policy. See also the important study by Patrick Murray, *Oracles of God: The Roman Catholic Church and Irish Politics, 1922–37* (Dublin, 1999).
20. NAI, DJ, 72/94A, 'Suppression of Prostitution', includes report by Commissioner Liam Ó Murchada to Minister for Justice, 26 March 1925, emphasis mine, and a later report dated 28 May 1947 reviewing the earlier campaigns by R. Hayes which summarises actions taken. See also Keogh, *Twentieth-Century Ireland*, pp. 71–3.
21. University College Dublin Archives Department (UCDA), McGilligan Papers, P35B/2, memorandums by Patrick Hogan, Minister for Agriculture, October 1923 and 25 January 1924; Girvin, *Between Two Worlds*, pp. 11–46, for discussion; for response to the report, see NAI, DT, S. 3107, memorandum by Minister for Industry and Commerce, 21 January 1924.
22. Colin Clark, *The Conditions of Economic Progress* (London, 1940); David Johnson and Liam Kennedy, 'The Two Irish Economies since 1920' in *A New History of Ireland*, vol. 7 (Oxford, forthcoming), suggest that Irish economic performance has been better than generally believed (I am grateful to the authors for generously providing me with copies of their unpublished manuscripts on this topic); Cormac Ó Gráda, *Ireland: A New Economic History* (Oxford, 1994), pp. 379–96; Andy Bielenberg and Patrick O'Mahony, 'An Expenditure Estimate of Irish National Income in 1907', *The Economic and Social Review*, 29:2 (1998), pp. 107–32.
23. Brian Girvin, 'The State and Vocational Education 1922–1960' in John Logan (ed.), *The Teachers' Union: The TUI and its Forerunners* (Dublin, 1999), pp. 62–92.
24. Brady, *Guardians of the Peace*, pp. 143–60; James Hogan, *Could Ireland Become Communist?* (Dublin, 1935); Dunphy, *The Making of Fianna Fáil Power*, pp. 74–144, 183–9.
25. Speech in Dáil Éireann, 14 October 1931, in Maurice Moynihan (ed.), *Speeches and Statements by Eamon de Valera 1917–73* (Dublin, 1980), pp. 182–8; the quotation is at p. 185.

26. UCDA, MacEntee Papers, P67/453, Letter and resolution from Wolfe Tone Cumann, TCD, to National Executive, 17 December 1935, 7 January 1936; MacEntee to Fianna Fáil National Executive, 27 January 1936.
27. Coogan, *De Valera*, p. 426.
28. Farrell, *Lemass*, pp. 11–21; Horgan, *Lemass*, pp. 21–63; Dunphy, *The Making of Fianna Fáil Power*, pp. 74–144; Fianna Fáil Archives, FF/46, E.H. Childers, 'Fianna Fáil's Four Year Social and Economic Programme', 9 April 1934, for a discussion of the groups that Fianna Fáil should appeal to.
29. The data can be found in Gallagher, *Irish Elections 1922–44*, pp. 157–85.
30. Earl of Longford and Thomas P. O'Neill, *Eamon de Valera* (London, 1970), pp. 269–71; Lee, *Ireland*, pp. 168, 217–19; see *Irish Press* editorial, 5 September 1931, for a statement of Fianna Fáil's political purpose.
31. Election Manifesto, 9 February 1932, in Moynihan (ed.), *Speeches and Statements*, pp. 189–91; UCDA, FitzGerald Papers, P80/1126l, for various responses by Cumann na nGaedheal; P80/11261, 'Election Addresses 1931', where Desmond FitzGerald goes to considerable lengths to counter this claim; Regan, *The Irish Counter-Revolution*, pp. 279–304; for the background, see Warner Moss, *Political Parties in the Irish Free State* (New York, 1933).
32. NAI, ODT, S. 8878, 'General Election 1932 — Precautions Against Disorder', Memorandum 9 February 1932; Burke to O'Hegarty, 11 February 1932; Department of Justice to Burke, 11 February 1932.
33. Brady, *Guardians of the Peace*, pp. 167–9, for details. I am grateful to Maurice Manning for bringing the details of Hogan's role to my attention.
34. Eunan O'Halpin, 'Parliamentary Party Discipline and Tactics: The Fianna Fáil Archives 1926–32', *Irish Historical Studies*, 30:120 (1997), pp. 581–90; Farrell, *Lemass*, pp. 16–21; see also Horgan, *Lemass*, and Dunphy, *The Making of Fianna Fáil Power*, for further details of Fianna Fáil's development during this period.
35. For a detailed discussion of this see Brian Girvin, 'Nationalism, Democracy and Irish Political Culture' in Brian Girvin and Roland Stürm (eds.), *Politics and Society in Contemporary Ireland* (Aldershot, 1986), pp. 3–28. Farrell, *Lemass*, pp. 11, 26–32; Girvin, *Between Two Worlds* pp. 80–7.
36. Lee, *Ireland*, p. 171; Girvin, *Between Two Worlds*; J. Anthony Gaughan, *Thomas Johnson 1872–1963* (Dublin, 1980), pp. 326–63, where the area of agreement between the two parties is outlined.
37. Moynihan (ed.), *Speeches and Statements*, pp. 134–5, 223–9, for de Valera's views; Girvin, *Between Two Worlds*, pp. 88–105; Joseph Johnston, *The Nemesis of Economic Nationalism* (London and Dublin, 1934), which is a contemporary criticism of the policies; Deirdre McMahon, *Republicans and Imperialists* (New Haven and London, 1984), provides a comprehensive and balanced account of the economic war and of the realistic options available to the government at this time; Ó Gráda, *Ireland: A New Economic History*, pp. 406–19.
38. UCDA, MacEntee Papers, P67/94(1), MacEntee to de Valera, 18 March 1932; Mansergh, *The Irish Free State*, p. 289, where he highlights the anti-liberal foundations of Fianna Fáil's economic and welfare policy.
39. Prager, *Building Democracy in Ireland*, pp. 185–92.
40. UCDA, FitzGerald Papers, P80/1121, Notes for Speakers, November 1932, for quotation. Policy in this area can be followed in UCDA, Mulcahy Papers, P7b/90(43), 30 March 1933, and UCDA, Cumann na nGaedheal Party Minutes, P39/1/3 (1932), P39/1/4 (1933).
41. UCDA, Cumann na nGaedheal Party Minutes, P39/1/3, 20 April 1932, 2 June 1932, 9 November 1932.

42. UCDA, FitzGerald Papers, P80/1111, Cosgrave to Michael Hayes, 21 September 1932; P80/1113, Cumann na nGaedheal Policy on Tariffs, 1932.
43. UCDA, Mulcahy Papers, P7b/90(31), undated memorandum in file marked March/May 1933.
44. Hogan, *Could Ireland Become Communist?*; Maurice Manning, *The Blueshirts* (Dublin, 1970), pp. 13–63; O'Halpin, *Defending Ireland*, pp. 110–21.
45. The ACA recognised that its very existence forced the government to act against the disrupters of political meetings. Subsequently it began to discuss the next stage of its development, which it described as 'non-party' but 'not non-political' and discussed the possibility of running candidates. UCDA, Blythe Papers, P24/654, 'Draft of Suggestions: ACA', probably February or March 1933.
46. J.J. Linz and A. Stepan (eds.), *The Breakdown of Democratic Regimes: Europe* (Baltimore, Md., 1978).
47. UCDA, Blythe Papers, P24/629, General Eoin O'Duffy, 'An Outline of the Political, Social and Economic Policy of Fine Gael' (Dublin, 1934), being the report of opening address at first annual ard fheis of Fine Gael, 8 February 1934; P24/649, 'A.C.A. policy', which is a brief discussion of the early dynamic behind the movement.
48. UCDA, P39/1/4, Party minutes 1933, First Meeting of the United Ireland Party, 27 September 1933.
49. Lee, *Ireland*, p. 181; Juan J. Linz, 'Some Notes Toward a Comparative Study of Fascism in Sociological Historical Perspective', in Walter Laquer (ed.), *Fascism: A Reader's Guide* (Harmondsworth, 1979), pp. 13–78.
50. Andrew Orridge, 'The Blueshirts and the "Economic War": A Study of Ireland in the Context of Dependency Theory', *Political Studies*, 31:3 (1983), pp. 351–69. The dimensions of non-parliamentary right-wing politics during the interwar years are assessed by Stanley G. Payne, *Fascism: Comparison and Definition* (Madison, Wis., 1980), pp. 7–17; Payne makes a number of distinctions between a commitment to radical right-wing politics and traditional elites embracing authoritarian methods to combat the left. In Argentina, the Catholic and nationalist right was radicalised during the 1930s; see David Rock, *Authoritarian Argentina: The Nationalist Movement, Its History and its Impact* (Berkeley, Calif., 1993), pp. 87–124.
51. The example of Finland, where the right was defeated by democratic forces, can be followed in Risto Alapuro and Erik Allardt, 'The Lapua Movement: The Threat of Rightist Takeover in Finland 1930–32' in Linz and Stepan (eds.), *The Breakdown of Democratic Regimes*, pp. 122–41.
52. UCDA, Mulcahy Papers, P7b/92(4), W.T. Cosgrave, 'Notes of Speech to National Executive', 30 August 1934.
53. Ibid.
54. For example, in November 1933 the offices of Young Ireland and the homes of O'Duffy and Blythe were raided by the police, while in December O'Duffy was arrested. In addition to this, Blueshirt militants were frequently brought before the revived Military Tribunal. UCDA, P39/1/2, 30 November 1933.
55. Interview with James Hogan in *Cork Examiner*, 3 September 1934; Hogan, it will be remembered, had in 1932 persuaded O'Duffy not to pursue plans for a coup against Fianna Fáil; Maurice Manning, *James Dillon* (Dublin, 1999), pp. 84–105.
56. UCDA, Mulcahy Papers, P7b/92(21–22), 'Special Meeting of National Executive', 21 September 1934; Adoption of resolution on resignation, 22 September 1934; Lee, *Ireland*, pp. 178–84; Paul Bew, Ellen Hazelkorn and Henry Patterson, *The Dynamics of Irish Politics* (London, 1989), pp. 48–72, provides a useful assessment of the fascist potential in the Blueshirt movement and its significance for Irish politics; Manning,

The Blueshirts, pp. 146–63; see also Mike Cronin, 'The Blueshirt movement, 1932–5: Ireland's Fascists?', *Journal of Contemporary History*, 30:2 (1996), pp. 311–32; for the most recent assessment of the movement, see Mike Cronin, *The Blueshirts and Irish Politics* (Dublin, 1997).

57. UCDA, P39/1/2, 9 November 1933: 'Draft Heads of Policy'; P24/635, Resolutions for Fine Gael Ard Fheis, 1936; P39/1/2, 16 February 1935, 12 March 1936, 16 July 1936, where the weakening of party organisation is detailed.
58. I owe this information to discussions at the James Hogan Centennial Commemorative Conference, University College Cork, 16–17 October 1998. In the archives in UCC there is a letter from veteran Fianna Fáil TD Frank Fahy to Hogan congratulating him on his attitude to the 1937 constitution; for a detailed appraisal, see Donnchadh Ó Corráin (ed.), *James Hogan: Revolutionary, Historian and Political Scientist* (Dublin, 2000).
59. NAI, DT, S. 13590, Timothy Smiddy to de Valera, 31 October 1944, 'Small Nations in the Post War World'; S. 11563, Smiddy memorandum, 'General Comments on Agricultural Policy', 4 December 1944; see also Girvin, *Between Two Worlds*, pp. 88–111; Ó Gráda, *Ireland: A New Economic History*, pp. 406–41, for discussion of these issues.
60. FF/790, 1937 election material; UCDA, Blythe Papers, P24/638, Fine Gael ard fheis resolutions 1935, which are conservative, anti-tariff, anti-taxation and pro-farmer; by 1937 in its notes for speakers the party is still conservative but it accepted the broad thrust of Fianna Fáil's policy: UCDA, FitzGerald Papers, P80/1123, notes for speakers 1937; O'Halpin, *Defending Ireland*, pp. 121–9, for a discussion of the failure of the extremes by this time.
61. *Irish Times*, 1 May 1937, reporting radio broadcast of 30 April 1937.
62. Dermot Keogh, 'The Constitutional Revolution: An Analysis of the Making of the Constitution' in Frank Litton (ed.), *The Constitution of Ireland 1937–1987* (Dublin, 1988), pp. 5, 19; Keogh, *Twentieth-Century Ireland*, pp. 96–104; see also Paul Blanshard, *The Irish and Catholic Power* (London, 1954), pp. 70–3; Jean Blanchard, *The Church in Contemporary Ireland* (Dublin, 1963), pp. 59–77; Whyte, *Church and State in Modern Ireland*, p. 56; Basil Chubb, *The Constitution and Constitutional Change in Ireland* (Dublin, 1978); Coogan, *De Valera*, pp. 486–515.
63. John Cooney, *John Charles McQuaid: Ruler of Catholic Ireland* (Dublin, 1999), pp. 94–106, which demonstrates McQuaid's anti-liberal influence on the constitution's content; Jeremiah Newman, *Studies in Political Morality* (Dublin and London, 1962), p. 407, suggests that the Irish democratic tradition was hostile to the establishment of any church by the state.
64. UCDA, De Valera Papers, 1029/1, 1935–6 handwritten note, n.d.; Keogh, 'Constitutional Revolution', p. 31, for another version. For a contrast with the Indian constitution which draws on the Irish one, see Girvin, 'Political Independence and Democratic Consolidation' pp. 120–44; *Bunreacht na hÉireann (Constitution of Ireland)*, Preamble, for the final version.
65. Murray Smith, 'The Title An Taoiseach in the 1937 Constitution', *Irish Political Studies*, 10 (1995), pp. 179–84.
66. UCDA, De Valera Papers, 1040, 1051/1; Keogh, 'Constitutional Revolution'.
67. Andrew Hastings, *The Construction of Nationhood: Ethnicity, Religion and Nationalism* (Cambridge, 1997); Conor Cruise O'Brien, *God Land: Reflections on Religion and Nationalism* (Cambridge, Mass., 1988); Cooney, *McQuaid*, discusses this interaction in the framing of the Irish constitution.
68. The detail of these articles have been discussed in various places; see Tom Inglis, *Moral Monopoly: The Rise and Fall of the Catholic Church in Modern Ireland*, 2nd edn (Dublin,

1998), pp. 65–76; Brian Farrell (ed.), *De Valera's Constitution and Ours* (Dublin, 1988).

69. Coogan, *De Valera*, pp. 486–500, for discussion; Eamon de Valera, *National Discipline and the Majority Rule* (Dublin, 1936), for a selection of de Valera's speeches which emphasise majoritarian sentiments and themes; Brady, *Guardians of the Peace*, pp. 178–90, illustrates the anti-liberal and authoritarian aspects of Fianna Fáil.
70. UCDA, MacEntee Papers, P67/115, memorandum on abdication crisis, n.d. but from content late 1936; Coogan, *De Valera*, pp. 499–500; 'Q. Whether it would be proper, from the point of view of the Catholic Church, that a Catholic Aide-de-Camp should be present in attendance on the President in a non-Catholic Church.
R. It would not be proper; particularly in this country where the danger of a grave scandal would be always present.' Heinrich Böll, *Irish Journal* (New York, 1967), which is a translation of the 1957 German edition.
71. Michael McInerney, 'The Gerry Boland Story', *Irish Times*, 11 October 1968; NAI, DT, S. 9715, for draft dated 16 March 1937; Keogh, 'Constitutional Revolution'; Coogan, *De Valera*, pp. 498–500; Cooney, *McQuaid*, pp. 94–106.
72. *Irish Catholic*, 1 May 1937; NAI, DT, S. 9715; S. 97748, 'Progressive Development of the Constitution'; *Irish Independent*, 30 December 1937, radio talk by de Valera on previous evening; Cardinal Joseph McRory endorsed the new constitution quite fulsomely as 'a great Christian document', *Irish Press*, 3 January 1938; Donal Barrington, *The Church, the State and the Constitution* (Dublin, 1959), pp. 1–7; Kees van Kersbergen, *Social Capitalism: A Study of Christian Democracy and the Welfare State*, (London, 1995), pp. 177–85, 219-28; Girvin, *The Right in the Twentieth Century*, pp. 94–110.
73. Barrington, *The Church, the State and the Constitution*; Newman, *Studies in Political Morality*.
74. George L. Mosse, *The Image of Man: The Creation of Modern Masculinity* (Oxford, 1996); Inglis, *Moral Monopoly*, pp. 159–200.
75. Kieran Allen, *Fianna Fáil and Irish Labour, 1926 to the Present* (London, 1997), pp. 58–60; Eoin O'Leary, 'The Irish National Teachers' Organisation and the Marriage Bar for Women National Teachers, 1933–1958', *Saothar*, 12 (1987), pp. 47–52; for background to this decision, see NAI, DT, S. 6231A.
76. NAI, DT, S. 9278, 'Women: Constitutional and Economic Position in Dáil Eireann', correspondence September 1936 to January 1937; Report of meeting with de Valera, 29 January 1937; S. 9880, J.J. Walsh to de Valera, 15 May 1937; Macardle to de Valera, 21 May 1937, which also included a draft amendment; Coogan, *De Valera*, p. 497, for McQuaid; Cooney, *McQuaid*, pp. 102–3.
77. FF/342, National Executive Minutes, 6 September 1937, 13 September 1937.
78. Moynihan (ed.), *Speeches and Statements*, pp. 330–44, for the entire speech.
79. Ibid., pp. 331, 333.
80. FF/342, National Executive Minutes, 1 February 1937, 8 November 1937.
81. FF/439, Party Minutes, 13 July 1938.
82. NAI, DT, S. 10463, 'Constitution 1937: Attitude of British Government' for memoranda.
83. Dennis Kennedy, *The Widening Gulf: Northern Attitudes to the Independent Irish State, 1919-49* (Belfast, 1988); Bowman, *De Valera and the Ulster Question*.
84. NAI, DT, S. 10631, for agreement; S. 10633, Industry and Commerce minute, June 1939, noting that Ireland had been the main beneficiary from the agreements on agriculture, trade and finance; Public Record Office, London (PRO), BT11/2834, Sir W.B. Brown to J. Leydon, 25 April 1938, confirming the arrangements between the two states; NAI, DT, S. 10389 Annex, 'Transfer of Ports, Financial and Trade Agreements: Conference in London', minutes of ministerial conference, 17 January 1938; S. 10389A, Cab. 8/28, 23 November 1937, for Irish decisions on negotiations.
85. NAI, DT, S. 10389 Annex, minutes of ministerial conference, 17 January 1938.

86. UCDA, McEntee Papers, P67/179, MacEntee to Margaret MacEntee, Friday morning on notepaper but n.d.; P67/155, MacEntee to de Valera, 17 February 1938, emphasis added.
87. UCDA, MacEntee Papers, P67/155, MacEntee to de Valera, 17 February 1938; FF/439, 31 January 1938, 30 June 1938, 25 October 1938.
88. UCDA, MacEntee Papers, P67/155, MacEntee to de Valera, 17 February 1938; Bowman, *De Valera and the Ulster Question*, pp. 160–70; McMahon, *Republicans and Imperialists*, pp. 242–7; Coogan, *De Valera*, pp. 516–20.
89. The relationship between size, dependency and democracy has not, to my knowledge, been explored in a systematic way in the scholarly literature. My use here has been influenced by the work of Albert O. Hirschman, *Essays in Trespassing: Economics to Politics and Beyond* (Cambridge, 1981), pp. 27–33; see also the discussion on the concept of democratic peace in Michael E. Brown, Sean M. Lynn-Jones and Steven E. Miller (eds.), *Debating the Democratic Peace* (Cambridge, Mass., 1996); Mary E. Daly, 'Integration or Diversity? Anglo-Irish Economic Relations, 1922–39', in S.J. Connolly (ed.), *Kingdoms United?: Great Britain and Ireland since 1500 — Integration and Diversity* (Dublin, 1999), pp. 169–80.
90. FF/790, '1937 Election'; FF/46, E.H. Childers, 'Fianna Fáil Four Year Social and Economic Programme', 9 April 1934.
91. Sinnott, *Irish Voters Decide*, p. 220. This was Fine Gael's first election and comparisons have been made with the predecessor parties that combined to form the new organisation.
92. FF/439, Parliamentary Party Minutes, 7 March 1938.
93. FF/791, 'General Election Report 1938', 17 June 1938.
94. John H. Whyte, 'Ireland: Politics without Social Bases' in Richard Rose (ed.), *Electoral Behaviour: A Comparative Handbook* (New York, 1974), pp. 619–51. Whyte's influential study was based on data from the late 1960s and early 1970s, but the system it describes had its origins in the 1930s.
95. Joseph Lee and Gearóid Ó Tuathaigh, *The Age of de Valera* (Dublin, 1982), p. 129; NAI, DT, S. 9627, 'Emigration', Dáil reply by de Valera, 17 February 1937; UCDA, FitzGerald Papers, P80/1123, which contains Fine Gael criticism of policy; Enda Delaney, *Demography, State and Society: Irish Migration to Britain, 1921–1971* (Liverpool, 2000), pp. 36–111.
96. NAI, Department of Finance (DF), F200/21/38, 'Comparison of Northern Ireland and Eire', 19 October 1938.
97. NAI, DF, F200/21/38, draft statement by de Valera, 20 October 1938; McMahon, *Republicans and Imperialists* on the trade discussions; David Johnson, *The Interwar Economy in Ireland* (Dublin, 1985), pp. 21–35; 39–42.
98. NAI, DT, S. 11563A, 'National Income', Smiddy to de Valera, 15 June 1943; further memorandum, March 1944; NLI, MS 924, Commission on Vocational Organisation, question 6445, Evidence from Senator Douglas, Boyne Linen company; NAI, DF, F200/21/38, draft statement by de Valera, 20 October 1938.
99. Girvin, *Between Two Worlds*, pp. 123–30; NAI, DT, S. 11018, 'Irish Industries: Standards of Efficiency', 24 November 1938.
100. NAI, DT, S. 10620, Per Jacobson to de Valera, 25 March 1938, which refers to conversation with de Valera the previous evening; UCDA, MacEntee Papers, P67/153, notes on economic situation, November 1937, with accompanying minutes by MacEntee.
101. UCDA, MacEntee Papers, P67/117, 'Parity with Sterling', n.d. but mid 1930s from internal evidence; NAI, DT, S. 11169A, 'Irish Banking System: Link with Sterling', 16 January 1940. See Ronan Fanning, *The Irish Department of Finance 1922–1958* (Dublin, 1978).

102. NAI, DT, S. 11563A, 'National Income', Smiddy to de Valera, 4 December 1944.
103. NLI, MS 923, Evidence of J. Kelly, Manager and Secretary of ACC, questions 4424–54; Browne's intervention is at 4428.
104. NAI, DT, S. 11563A, Smiddy, 'General Comments on Agricultural Policy', 4 December 1944; NAI, DF, F200/20/38, McElligott to Lyons, 21 October 1938; Lyons to McElligott, 17 November 1938; memorandum by Seán Ó Muineacháin for Taoiseach, 16 January 1939.
105. NAI, DT, S. 13590, Smiddy to de Valera, 31 October 1944, 'Small Nations in the Post War World'; Damien Hannan, *Displacement and Development: Class, Kinship and Social Change in Irish Rural Communities* (Dublin, 1979).
106. UCDA, Mulcahy Papers, P7A/210, notes on defence conference, 11 March 1940.
107. Lee, *Ireland,* pp. 283–4, for discussion.
108. UCDA, MacEntee Papers, P67/133, memorandum, 20 April 1939; MacEntee to de Valera, 30 April 1939; Coogan, *De Valera,* pp. 697–8, reports that Maurice Moynihan had no knowledge of this threat to resign.
109. Rona Fitzgerald and Brian Girvin, 'Political Culture, Growth and the Conditions for Success in the Irish Economy' in Brian Nolan, Philip J. O'Connell and Christopher T. Whelan (eds.), *Bust to Boom?: The Irish Experience of Growth and Inequality* (Dublin, 2000), pp. 268–85.
110. UCDA, MacEntee Papers, P67/195, MacEntee to de Valera, 16 January 1939.
111. O'Halpin, *Defending Ireland,* pp. 151–99; Theo Farrell, 'Professionalization and Suicidal Defence Planning by the Irish Army, 1921–1941', *Journal of Strategic Studies,* 21:3 (1997), pp. 67–85.
112. NAI, DJ, S51/39, contains letter by Walsh to *Sunday Independent,* 16 April 1939. It may be a coincidence, but the IRA held a General Army Convention to prepare for the bombing campaign in Britain at around the same time as this letter was written; see J. Bowyer Bell, *The Secret Army* (London, 1972), pp. 175–201; for insights into the mentality of the IRA volunteer, see Brendan Behan, *Borstal Boy* (London, 1958).
113. UCDA, MacEntee Papers, P67/118, MacEntee to de Valera, 20 January 1937. How much this letter was a straw in the wind or had a more political intention is difficult to judge given de Valera's obstinacy on foreign policy and defence issues.
114. UCDA, MacEntee Papers, P67/210, Seamus O'Neill to MacEntee and MacEntee reply, n.d. but probably mid 1940 according to archivist.
115. Michael Walzer, *Just and Unjust Wars,* 2nd edn (New York, 1992), pp. 233–50, provides a powerful defence of the right to be neutral in wartime and offers a critical commentary on this.
116. NAI, DT, S. 10967, 'Irish Citizens in Great Britain, Liability for Conscription', de Valera in Dáil, 2 November 1938; *Irish Press,* 18 May 1939; PDDE, vol. 77, cols. 267–72, 500–82 (27 September 1939), for the government's positions.
117. NAI, Department of Foreign Affairs (DFA), P70, 'British Threat to Enforce Conscription in Six Counties, 1939-1941', 26 April 1939 Dulanty to Chamberlain. See also headline in *Irish Press,* 28 April 1939, which reiterates this position as if it was an objective analysis.
118. FF/342, 13 February 1939.
119. NAI, DFA, P70, Dulanty to Dublin, 27 April 1939; see also Dennis Kennedy, *The Widening Gulf: Northern Attitudes to the Independent Irish State, 1919–49* (Belfast, 1988), pp. 217–40; Brian Barton, *Northern Ireland during the Second World War* (Belfast, 1996).
120. NAI, DFA, P70, Dulanty to Dublin, 3 May 1939.
121. Quoted in Dermot Keogh, *Ireland and Europe 1919–1989* (Cork, 1990), pp. 143–4.

122. Ibid., pp. 140–2; National Archives, Washington DC, RG59, General Records of State Department, Gray to Hull, 24 October 1944.
123. UCDA, FitzGerald Papers, P80/1118C4, memorandum by Mulcahy on co-operation with de Valera; Mulcahy Papers, P7A/210, note by Mulcahy, 1 January 1940; FitzGerald Papers, P80/1119C4, memorandum by W.T. Cosgrave, 15 November 1940, complaining of de Valera's refusal to consult the opposition despite a possible threat of invasion. See W. David Clinton, 'The National Interest: Normative Foundations', *The Review of Politics*, 48:4 (1986), pp. 495–519, for a useful discussion of how the concept has been and might be used. For a detailed discussion of some of these themes, see Brian Girvin, 'Politics in Wartime: Governing, Neutrality and Elections', in Brian Girvin and Geoff Roberts (eds.), *Ireland in the Second World War: Politics, Society and Remembrance* (Dublin, 2000), pp. 24–46.
124. 'Silent Night', *Bell*, 6:6 (1943); Donal Ó Drisceoil, *Censorship in Ireland 1939–1945: Neutrality, Politics and Society* (Cork, 1996), for the most comprehensive assessment; PRO, DO, 130/28 XC164899, Elizabeth Bowen, Notes on Éire, 12 July 1942, 31 July 1942.
125. Lee, *Ireland*, pp. 244–50; Keogh, *Ireland and Europe*, pp. 130–8; Keogh, *Twentieth-Century Ireland*, pp. 113–20; Robert Fisk, *In Time of War: Ireland, Ulster and the Price of Neutrality 1939–45* (London, 1983), p. 194, reports that Gerry Boland expected Britain to win the war, even in 1940, when others including Aiken and de Valera did not; MacEntee seems to have been in favour of the Allies, but there is little evidence that he was active in that respect; Waltzer, *Just and Unjust Wars*, pp. 245–50, discusses the decision of Britain to infringe Norwegian neutrality in 1940.
126. UCDA, Mulcahy Papers, P7/C/112, notes on interview with de Valera 1 July 1940; PRO, PREM, 3/131/1, MacDonald memorandum, 21–2 June 1940; Fisk, *In Time of War*, p. 198; de Valera's indifference as to outcome can be appreciated in a study of his wartime speeches, Eamon de Valera, *Ireland's Stand: Being a Selection of Speeches of Eamon de Valera During the War (1939–1945)* (Dublin, 1946).
127. Fisk, *In Time of War*, p. 201; Lee, *Ireland*, p. 248; Keogh, *Ireland and Europe*, pp. 130–40; Cornelius O'Leary, 'Professor Lee's Ireland' (unpublished manuscript in author's possession).
128. Fisk, *In Time of War*, pp. 201–2; Brian Barton, 'Northern Ireland: The Impact of War, 1939–1945' in Girvin and Roberts (eds.), *Ireland and the Second World War*, pp. 47–75.
129. UCDA, Mulcahy Papers, P7A/210, The A Summary, 5 July 1940; Fisk, *In Time of War*, pp. 203–4.
130. Fisk, *In Time of War*, pp. 212–16; see also Geoffrey Roberts, 'The British Offer to End Partition, June 1940', *History Ireland*, 9:1 (2001), pp. 5–6, where he discusses new information contained in file NAI DT 2001/1/6/500 (S. 18565).
131. UCDA, Mulcahy Papers, P7A/210, report of meeting between de Valera and Sir Emerson Herdman, 5 or 6 July 1940. Herdman was a director of Great Northern Railways and a unionist senator in Northern Ireland.
132. NAI, DFA, P70, Report by High Commissioner, 12 August 1942.
133. Raymond J. Raymond, 'David Gray, the Aiken Mission and Irish Neutrality, 1940–41', *Diplomatic History*, 9 (1985), pp. 55–71; Joseph L. Rosenberg, 'The 1941 Mission of Frank Aiken to the United States: An American Perspective', *Irish Historical Studies*, 22:88 (1980), pp. 162–77; the claim can be found in Moynihan (ed.), *Speeches and Statements*, p. 459.
134. NAI, DFA, P70, 'Conscription in Northern Ireland', notes of meeting between Dulanty and Churchill, 22 May 1941, 26 May 1941, 27 May 1941.
135. Manning, *James Dillon*, pp. 151–77, for an assessment of the one Irish politician who actively supported entering the war.

136. PRO, DO, 130/28 XC164899, 'Notes on Eire', 9 February 1942, 20 February 1942, 31 July 1942.
137. This view draws on the recollections of veterans collected by the Irish Volunteers Project, University College Cork, of which I was the co-director with Dr Geoff Roberts. I am grateful to Tina Neylon for carrying out interviews with veterans. See also Brian Girvin and Geoff Roberts (eds.), *Ireland in the Second World War.*

4. Building a Moral Community (pages 106–35)

1. Tom Buchanan and Martin Conway (eds.), *Political Catholicism in Europe 1918–1968* (Oxford, 1996), for important examples of how Catholic moral communities were attempted.
2. NAI, DT, S. 9853, 'Rights of Free Speech', Dáil reply, 2 June 1937.
3. Stephen Holmes, *The Anatomy of Antiliberalism* (Cambridge, Mass., 1993), for a critique; Amitai Etzioni, *The Spirit of Community* (London, 1995); Frank McCourt, *Angela's Ashes* (London, 1996).
4. NAI, DT, S. 12506, S.A. Roche to M. Ó Muimhneacháin, 13 September 1940.
5. FF/343, National Executives Minutes, 30 July 1945.
6. FF/440, Parliamentary Party Minutes, 11 June 1941.
7. FF/440, Parliamentary Party Minutes, 4 November 1943, 19 October 1944.
8. UCDA, Mulcahy Papers, P7C/153, Mulcahy note, 7 November 1949 and correspondence.
9. UCDA, Mulcahy Papers, P7C/155, note to Mulcahy, 7 April 1948.
10. *Statistical Abstract of Ireland 1960* (Dublin, 1960), Tables 49–51, p. 58; see also *Statistical Abstract of Ireland, 1966* (Dublin, 1966), Tables 46–8, p. 55; UCDA, Mulcahy Papers, P7C/155, Department of Lands, 'Migration of People of Great Blasket Island to Mainland', 21 December 1948.
11. UCDA, Mulcahy Papers, P7C/152/48, note prepared for Minister, 20 November 1948. In 1943 the Governing Body of University College Cork agreed that senior administrative posts would be filled by Irish speakers; UCCA, Governing Body Minutes, 28 September 1943. Parallel lectureships also were set up, one teaching through English, the other Irish. During the following decade this rule was progressively extended to more and more of the non-academic staff; see Brian Girvin, 'The Presidency of Alfred O'Rahilly, 1943–54' (unpublished manuscript, available from author). From time to time this had consequences for those applying for senior academic posts within UCC; Jack Whyte, *Minority Report: The Protestant Community in the Irish Republic* (Dublin, 1975).
12. Richard Doherty, 'Irish Heroes of the Second World War' in Brian Girvin and Geoff Roberts (eds.), *Ireland and the Second World War* (Dublin, 1999), pp. 91–106, for a re-evaluation of the evidence for the number. The Dominions Office estimated that approximately 150,000 Irish citizens went to Britain during the Second World War, including both war workers and those who joined the armed forces; PRO, DO, 35/1229/WX132/59, Note prepared for Secretary of State, 19 September 1945.
13. NAI, DT, S. 3370C, Department of Justice note on 1945 parade; *Irish Times*, 9 November 1945; PDDE, vol. 98, cols. 1240–8 (15 November 1945). NAI, DT, S. 3370B for exchanges between 1932 and 1939; PRO, DO, 35/1230/4374 contains considerable correspondence and estimates on the numbers who might have fought. Studies undertaken by the Volunteers Project in University College Cork between 1995 and 1998 under the direction of Brian Girvin and Geoff Roberts revealed that of those who were interviewed by the project all of them simultaneously supported Irish neutrality and the Allied war effort; Girvin and Roberts (eds.), *Ireland and the Second World War.* The hostility to James Dillon for his support for the Allied war effort reflects further the refusal

of most Irish politicians to come to terms with the significance or the consequences of the war; see Maurice Manning, *James Dillon* (Dublin, 1999), pp. 151–77.

14. PDDE, vol. 91, cols. 569–72 (9 July 1943) and vol. 105, col. 371 (27 March 1947).
15. PRO, FO, 800/310, notes on Éire, 9 November 1940; NAI, DT, S. 11007A, 'Admission of Aliens', Memorandum by Department of Justice, 24 September 1945; Dermot Keogh, *Jews in Twentieth-Century Ireland: Refugees, Anti-Semitism and the Holocaust* (Cork, 1998); Mícheál Mac Gréil, *Prejudice and Tolerance in Ireland* (Dublin, 1977), pp. 332–47; this is the first and most objective analysis of this phenomenon in Ireland.
16. NAI, Department of Industry and Commerce (DIC), Departmental Minutes, No. 11, 25 October 1945; No. 13, 1 November 1945; FF/440, party meeting, 16 October 1944, which includes motion by deputies Killilea and Beegan on land question; UCDA, MacEntee Papers, P67/363, Burke to MacEntee, 10 June 1943.
17. G.M. Goulding, *George Gavan Duffy 1882–1951: A Legal Biography* (Dublin, 1982), pp. 127–42, for a discussion of the case; J.H. Whyte, *Church and State in Modern Ireland 1923–1970* (Dublin, 1971), does not discuss this issue, but does offer an opinion on Gavan Duffy's influence, pp. 167–73.
18. UCDA, MacEntee Papers, P67/298, Childers to MacEntee (1945); P67/298, Childers to MacEntee, 11 December 1948.
19. *Irish Times*, 16 March 1946; Jeremiah Newman, *Studies in Political Morality* (Dublin and London, 1962), pp. 331–4, cites this speech as evidence that Protestants had full civil rights in the Irish Republic.
20. NAI, DT, S. 12952A, 'Marriage in Ireland, Constitutional and Ecclesiastical Position', which contains correspondence on various issues related to this; see note by M. Ó Muimhneacháin, 22 October 1940, on Taoiseach's intention to legislate; note by O'Donoghue, Attorney General's Office, 17 September 1942.
21. *Irish Press*, 11 December 1945; *Standard*, 7 May 1937; W. Conway, 'Marriage in Ireland: Church and State', *Irish Ecclesiastical Record*, 5th Series, 68 (1946), pp. 361–6; Whyte, *Church and State*, p. 55, identified only three cases of bigamy before the courts between 1937 and 1964.
22. Whyte, *Church and State*, pp. 170–1, discusses the decision; see also Eoin de Bhaldraithe, 'Mixed Marriages and Irish Politics: The Effect of *Ne Temere*', *Studies*, 77 (1988), pp. 284–99, for a discussion of the background to the regulation and its continuing importance in Ireland; John Cooney, *John Charles McQuaid: Ruler of Catholic Ireland* (Dublin, 1999), pp. 245–6; Gerard Hogan, 'A Fresh Look at Tilson's Case', *Irish Jurist*, 33 (1998), pp. 311–32, for the most careful assessment of this issue to date.
23. *Re Corcoran* (1952) 86 Irish Law Times Report, 49–73. See Hogan, 'A Fresh Look at Tilson's Case'.
24. The only member of the Supreme Court to dissent from the conclusion was a Protestant.
25. Hogan, 'A Fresh Look at Tilson's Case' for discussion; Cooney, *McQuaid*, pp. 245–6, notes correspondence between Joseph Walshe, the Irish Ambassador to the Vatican, and McQuaid dealing with the High Court decision. Walshe was certainly of the opinion that the decision was a consequence of Article 44.
26. In general, Catholics and non-Catholics attended different schools and universities, went to different hospitals if sick and rarely socialised.
27. *Statistical Abstract of Ireland 1966*, Table 42, p. 53. Those describing themselves as 'other religion' or 'no statement' however increased by 58.9 per cent between 1936 and 1961. This is the category that does not include Catholics, Protestants or Jews, though the actual numbers are small. This is an area which requires further analysis.
28. NAI, DT, S. 13438A, 'Necessitous Families: Assistance in Kind', Department of Finance memorandum, 29 February 1944; Department of Local Government and Public

Health, 6 March 1944; James Deeny, *To Cure and to Care* (Dublin, 1989), pp. 85–6; I have unfortunately been unable to trace Deeny's original report in the files of the Department of the Taoiseach or the Department of Health.

29. NAI, DFA, P99, Papal Nuncio to External Affairs, 7 April 1945, enclosing Bishop Cohalan's letter; Deeny to J.P. Walshe, 29 May 1945; Walshe to Taoiseach, 12 June 1945, reporting on meeting with nuncio on previous day and the agreement reached. Deeny, *To Cure and to Care*, p. 85, for his account; Deeny identifies the bishop as Cornelius Lucey, but this is a mistake.
30. Deeny, *To Cure and to Care*, pp. 147–9; *Statistical Abstract of Ireland 1945* (Dublin, 1945), for data on births; Pauline Jackson, 'Outside the Jurisdiction: Irishwomen Seeking Abortion' in Chris Curtin, Pauline Jackson and Barbara O'Connor (eds.), *Gender in Irish Society* (Galway, 1987), pp. 203–23; some of the consequences of the treatment of unmarried mothers can be found in Mike Milotte, *Banished Babies: The Secret History of Ireland's Baby Export Business* (Dublin, 1997); Commission on Emigration and other Population Problems, *Reports*, (Dublin, 1954), paragraphs 242–7, pp. 112–13, and Appendix IV, 'Arrangements by Public Assistance Authorities for the Accommodation of Unmarried Mothers and their Children', Department of Health, pp. 263–5.
31. NAI, DT, S. 11582E, 'The Problem of Irish Girls Emigrating to England', by Elizabeth Fitzgerald, 25 August 1953; *Statistical Abstract of Ireland 1960*, Table 16, p. 27. In 1952 illegitimate births were 2.5 per cent of total, while by 1959 this had dropped to 1.59 per cent; Cormac Ó Gráda, *A Rocky Road: The Irish Economy since the 1920s* (Manchester, 1997), pp. 202–3; Nuala O'Faolain suggests that the culture of fear surrounding pregnancy outside marriage had not declined by the early 1960s: 'You lost everything if you became pregnant outside marriage'; Nuala O'Faolain, *Are You Somebody?* (Dublin, 1996), p. 87; NAI, DFA, 402/218/A, draft prepared for Dáil reply to Frank Sherwin, December 1960; *Sunday Review*, 1 June 1958, reports views of the County Medical Officer of Health for London on the nationality of the pregnant girls; *Irish Times*, 16 December 1960, raised the issue which in turn led to Sherwin raising the issue in the Dáil; NAI, DFA, 402/218/1, C.K. Murphy to W. Fay, 8 July 1953, 17 July 1953, Fay to Murphy, 20 July 1953.
32. Milotte, *Banished Babies*, pp. 40–1, 60–5; Milotte shows that section 39 of the act was included after a recommendation by the Episcopal Committee, 3 January 1952. This book is a more detailed study of the controversy over adoption highlighted in Milotte's television documentary broadcast on RTÉ, 20 June 1996; see also Whyte, *Church and State*, pp. 183–93; Cooney, *McQuaid*, pp. 296–7.
33. Commission on Vocational Organisation, *Report* (Dublin, 1944); PRO, DO, 130/28 XC164899, 'Notes on Eire', 31 July 1942, written by Elizabeth Bowen.
34. Whyte, *Church and State*, pp. 113–19; for the departmental critique of the report see NAI, DT, S. 13552, 'Commission on Vocational Organisation: Departmental Views on Report' (January to March 1945); S. 12753A–B.
35. A comprehensive study of vocationalism is now available: Don O'Leary, *Vocationalism and Social Catholicism in Twentieth-Century Ireland* (Dublin, 1999).
36. Reported in *Cork Examiner*, 20 February 1940.
37. NAI, DT, S. 13552, 'Commission on Vocational Organisation: Departmental Views on the Report': Industry and Commerce, 13 January 1945; Agriculture, March 1945; Lands, 8 January 1945; Finance, 'Further Observations', January 1945. The report was criticised by some of the most formidable Fianna Fáil ministers including Lemass, Seán T. Ó Ceallaigh (later to be President), Seán Moylan and James Ryan.
38. Brian Girvin, *The Right in the Twentieth Century* (London, 1994), pp. 94–104; John Cornwell, *Hitler's Pope: The Secret History of Pius XII* (London, 1999); Whyte, *Church and State*, pp. 96–119, 156–95.

39. The detailed argument can be followed in NAI, DT, S. 13552 and S. 12753A–B.
40. Whyte, *Church and State*, pp. 118–19; Lucey's remarks can be found in a book review on Salazar in *Irish Ecclesiastical Record*, 5th Series, 63 (1944), pp. 213–14.
41. James Hogan, *Election and Representation* (Cork and Oxford, 1945), pp. 206–38; James Hogan, *Modern Democracy* (Cork, 1938), for his earlier and more sympathetic views on corporatism; Brian Girvin, 'Nationalism, Catholicism and Democracy: Hogan's intellectual evolution' in Donnchadh Ó Corráin (ed.), *James Hogan: Revolutionary, Historian and Political Scientist* (Dublin, 2001), pp. 163–76.
42. Whyte, *Church and State*, p. 79; quoted in Cooney, *McQuaid*, p. 258; see also John Horgan, *Noël Browne: Passionate Outsider* (Dublin, 2000), pp. 133–8.
43. Brian Girvin, *Between Two Worlds: Politics and Economy in Independent Ireland* (Dublin, 1989), pp. 116–21.
44. Ian McCabe, *A Diplomatic History of Ireland 1948–49* (Dublin, 1991), pp. 82–96, 117–33. The shift in opinion can be appreciated in Fine Gael's acceptance of the Republic and the recognition by James Dillon that this was inevitable; see Manning, *James Dillon*, pp. 242–5.
45. NAI, DT, S. 9756A, 'Position of the Catholic Church'; Westmeath County Council passed a motion to this effect, 28 January 1950; Dermot Keogh and Finín O'Driscoll, 'Ireland' in Buchanan and Conway (eds.), *Political Catholicism in Europe*, pp. 275–300.
46. NAI, DT, S. 12891B, 'A Report on School Leaving Age', June 1947. A note prepared for Derrig's successor in the Inter-Party government, Richard Mulcahy, concluded in similar fashion that 'The primary system is undenominational in theory but denominational in practice'; UCDA, Mulcahy Papers, P7C/66, 'Notes on the Education System in Republic of Ireland', n.d. but is included with material dated 1949.
47. Cornelius Lucey, 'Making the School System of Ireland Catholic', *Irish Ecclesiastical Record*, 5th Series, 52 (1938), pp. 405–17; Lucey admitted that 'Our present system is not fundamentally vicious. It is not even fundamentally defective. But it is by no means perfect as to its legal form.' To remedy this, a Council of Education on guild lines was proposed. The Commission on Vocational Education recommended that such a council be set up and the second Inter-Party government adopted this.
48. Martin Brennan, 'Vocational Schools', *Irish Ecclesiastical Record*, 5th Series, 57 (1941), pp. 113–27; F. McNamara, 'Reply', *The Vocational Education Bulletin;* 22 (April 1941), pp. 3–6.
49. Séamas Ó Buachalla, *Education Policy in Twentieth-Century Ireland* (Dublin, 1988), p. 269; the claim is made on the basis of private information reported in the book.
50. Private correspondence John Logan to Brian Girvin, 30 November 1992 (I am grateful to John Logan for providing me with this and other information on the document and related matters); Memorandum V.40 (1942) in my possession; NAI, DT, S. 12753A–B for a detailed rebuttal of the Commission on Vocational Organisation by the Department of Education.
51. Logan to Girvin, 30 November 1992, with the information on the film; the film itself is available from the Irish Film Institute, Dublin, and is entitled 'Rural Vocational Education' (I am grateful to Dr John Logan for my copy of the film).
52. Ó Buachalla, *Education Policy*, p. 265; UCDA, Mulcahy Papers, P7C/66, Report on ECA visit to vocational schools, 4 November 1949; memorandum, P.E. Ó Suilleabháin to Mulcahy, 27 October 1949.
53. NAI, DT, S. 12891B, 'Note on Continuation Schools', J.P. Hackett, 18 July 1947.
54. NAI, DT, S. 15101B/61, memorandum for government, 25 January 1951; UCDA, Mulcahy Papers, P7C/154, 30 June 1954, Report of meeting between Minister for Education and Brother White, Dingle Christian Brothers School, who complained that the local vocational school was encroaching on the catchment area for Catholic

secondary schools; for a fuller discussion of the plight of vocational education, see John Logan (ed.), *The Teachers' Union: The TUI and its Forerunners 1899–1994* (Dublin, 1999).

55. Charles Lindblom, *Politics and Markets* (New York, 1977), pp. 170–88.
56. Whyte, *Church and State*, pp. 363–4.
57. This is not to say that a causal relationship could not exist. I have been unable to discover comprehensive documentary evidence in the existing archives and when I enquired was told that no such material existed.
58. Whyte, *Church and State*, pp. 365–6.
59. Congress of Irish Unions, *Annual Report 1951* (Dublin, 1951), pp. 126–7, where the Mother and Child controversy is debated; Manning, *James Dillon*, pp. 296–302, which discusses clerical opposition to the proposed establishment of an Agricultural Institute.
60. There is a huge literature on Gramsci and the concept of hegemony. His prison notebooks remain the best source of his later ideas, Antonio Gramsci, *Selections From Prison Notebooks* (London, 1971). Gramsci's use of hegemony is a more nuanced approach to power in modern society than one usually finds in Marxist thinking. I use it here to demonstrate that an organisation without visible coercive power can achieve considerable influence because public opinion and the political culture accept its role and right to exercise such power. I do not have a view on whether this oppressed the Irish Catholic nationalist people, though the evidence for the period 1922 to *c.* 1966 suggests that they were not oppressed.
61. NAI, DT, S. 12891B, 'Interim Report of the Departmental Committee to Examine the Educational System', 31 August 1946; UCDA, Mulcahy Papers, P7C/159, Speech by Mulcahy, 27 March 1951; Brian Titley, *Church, State and the Control of Schools in Ireland, 1900–1944* (Kingston and Montreal, 1983).
62. PDDE, vol. 125, col. 784 (12 April 1951).
63. This was most evident during the Mother and Child controversy, but, as David McCullagh, *A Makeshift Majority: The First Inter-Party Government, 1948–57* (Dublin, 1998), pp. 198–202, shows, it is apparent throughout the Inter-Party administration. Government ministers William Norton, Joseph Blowick, Richard Mulcahy and Seán Mac Eoin were members of the Knights of St Columbanus. Lemass had at one time been a member and so had MacEntee; Evelyn Bolster, *The Knights of Saint Columbanus* (Dublin, 1979), identifies the members.
64. Alexander J. Humphreys, *New Dubliners: Urbanization and the Irish Family* (London, 1966), pp. 28–9, 37–8, 103–7, 156–9, 219–20, 231–2; Heinrich, Böll, *Irish Journal* (New York, 1967), for a more impressionistic view; Jean Blanchard, *The Church in Contemporary Ireland* (Dublin, 1963), pp. 30–5, provides evidence for a parish in south Dublin which confirms the high participation rates. He also estimated that about 30 per cent of the parishioners received communion at least once a week, this latter finding being based on participant observation by the author while a diplomat in Dublin during the 1950s. Nor had these patterns broken down in the 1960s; Conor Ward, 'Ireland' in Hans Mol (ed.), *Western Religion: A Country by Country Sociological Inquiry* (The Hague, 1972), pp. 295–303, reports that during the 1960s church-going in rural areas was still at 100 per cent, but in urban areas it was 'slightly less' than this.
65. In addition to *Studies* and the *Standard* some of the better known magazines include *Catholic Digest, Far East, Redemptorist Record, Hibernia* and *Irish Ecclesiastical Record.* For details of circulation of some of these, see *Official Handbook of Audit Bureau of Circulation, 1948* (London, 1948).
66. NAI, DT, S. 15593, 'Irish Farmers Association', which provides an insight into Hayes' influence and notes that he continued to display a picture of Mussolini in his home during the 1950s; Stephen Rynne, *Father John Hayes, Leader of Muintir na Tíre* (Dublin, 1960).

67. Blanchard, *The Church in Contemporary Ireland*, p. 30; Jack Gannon, *Catholic Power, Culture and the Constitution of Ireland* (Belfast, 1972), pp. 53–63; the Corish statement can be found in Michael Gallagher, *The Irish Labour Party in Transition 1957–82* (Dublin, 1982), p. 42, a study which also provides additional evidence for this view. When James Larkin died the former communist had reconciled with the church and had rosary beads wrapped around his hands; Cooney, *McQuaid*, pp. 211–12.
68. For coverage of the Mindszenty demonstration, see reports in the *Irish Press* and *Irish Independent*, especially; on the more general issue of communism, see the provincial press, especially the *Cork Examiner*. Despite this anti-communism, the public often made fine distinctions between the proper spheres of the political and the non-political. For example, over 20,000 Dublin football fans attended an Ireland–Yugoslavia match in 1955 even though Archbishop McQuaid had denounced it. That they did so despite fierce criticism by Catholic lay groups demonstrates the importance of the distinction drawn. See Cooney, *McQuaid*, pp. 310–15.
69. I have relied on Butler's own account of the incident, Hubert Butler, *Escape From the Anthill* (Mullingar, 1986), pp. 270–82, which reprints the original essay written in 1956; see also appendix, 'Statement to the Committee and Members of the Kilkenny Archaeological Society', pp. 339–42. A contemporary observer of the Butler incident and its repercussions is Paul Blanshard, *The Irish and Catholic Power* (London, 1954), pp. 190–5. For the Fethard-on-Sea boycott, see Dermot Keogh, *Twentieth-Century Ireland: Nation and State* (Dublin, 1994), pp. 240–1; Whyte, *Church and State*, pp. 322–5; both authors claim that de Valera opposed the boycott, and this is strictly true. However, his speech openly accepts the right of the Catholic Church to demand certain terms before permitting a Catholic to marry a Protestant, and this had been given some legal support in the Tilson case; Maurice Moynihan (ed.), *Speeches and Statements by Éamon de Valera 1917–73* (Dublin, 1980), p. 580, for de Valera's response, 4 July 1957.
70. Bruce Francis Biever, *Religion, Culture and Values: A Cross-Cultural Analysis of Motivational Factors in Native Irish and American Irish Catholicism* (New York, 1976).
71. Ó Buachalla, *Education Policy*, pp. 99–100; Patrick Duffy, *The Lay Teacher* (Dublin, 1966), pp. 87–8; see also appendix which contains documentation concerning the dispute sent to the Vatican, 20 October 1956, pp. 125–54; Tom Inglis, *Moral Monopoly: The Rise and Fall of the Catholic Church in Modern Ireland*, 2nd edn (Dublin, 1998), for a discussion of the church in the 1950s.
72. *Irish Times*, 12 April 1951; Blanshard, *The Irish and Catholic Power*, pp. 205–43.
73. *Kilkenny People*, 1 May 1954; see also John D. Sheridan, 'Mr Blanshard Rides Again', *Irish Ecclesiastical Record*, 5th Series, 84 (1955), pp. 1–10. Blanchard's earlier book *Freedom and Catholic Power* had already been received unfavourably by Catholic opinion in both Ireland and the United States. More recently, Whyte, *Church and State*, pp. 79, 294, 369, noted Blanshard's critique, but did not address this in detail. Dermot Keogh, *History Ireland*, 8:3 (2000), pp. 53–55, simply repeats MacBride's position that Blanshard was anti-Catholic without addressing the detail of the criticism.
74. Blanshard, *The Irish and Catholic Power*, pp. 67, 289–90.
75. Donal Barrington, *The Church, the State and the Constitution* (Dublin, 1959), p. 7.
76. Ibid., pp. 8–13; Barrington enumerates the various ways in which the constitution, the legal system and certain institutional arrangements meet the requirements of the Catholic Church, noting also that 'the articles in the Constitution dealing with fundamental rights are almost a synopsis of Catholic teaching on the matter. Some slight anomalies remain in the ordinary law, but these will pass with time' (p. 10). A very similar conclusion is drawn by Blanchard, *The Church in Contemporary Ireland*, pp. 59–77; see also Vincent Grogan, 'The Constitution and the Natural Law', *Christus Rex*,

8 (1954), pp. 201–18, for an analysis which makes the case for the Thomist and natural law basis of the constitution.

77. Blanchard, *The Church in Contemporary Ireland,* p. 69; Newman, *Studies in Political Morality,* pp. 331–429, for the complete discussion; Peter Berger, *The Social Reality of Religion,* rev. edn (Harmondsworth, 1973); Colleen McDannell, *Material Christianity: Religion and Popular Culture in America* (New Haven, 1995), for a revisionist view of the relationship between the sacred and the secular.
78. The controversy and its consequences has been treated in detail in a number of sources: Whyte, *Church and State,* pp. 215–35; Keogh, *Twentieth-Century Ireland,* pp. 219–23; J.J. Lee, *Ireland 1912–1985: Politics and Society* (Cambridge, 1989), pp. 313–17; Noël Browne, *Against the Tide* (Dublin, 1986); Eamonn McKee, 'Church–State Relations and the Development of Irish Health Policy: The Mother and Child Scheme, 1944–53', *Irish Historical Studies,* 25:98 (1986), pp. 159–94; Tim Pat Coogan, *De Valera: Long Fellow, Long Shadow* (London, 1993), pp. 647–54; John Horgan, *Seán Lemass: The Enigmatic Patriot* (Dublin, 1997), pp. 150–52; McCullagh, *A Makeshift Majority,* pp. 198–232; Horgan, *Browne,* pp. 120–49.
79. Horgan, *Lemass,* p. 151; Cooney, *McQuaid,* pp. 252–76.
80. Whyte, *Church and State,* p. 235; Keogh, *Twentieth-Century Ireland,* p. 213; Dermot Keogh, 'The Role of the Catholic Church in the Republic of Ireland 1922–1995' in Forum for Peace and Reconciliation, *Building Trust in Ireland* (Belfast, 1996), pp. 85–214, the discussion on the Mother and Child case is at pp. 130–5.
81. White, *Church and State,* pp. 302–61; NAI, DT, 96/6/364, 'Marriage in Ireland', which contains exchange between Lemass and Brian Lenihan on prospects for divorce in Ireland.
82. Browne, *Against the Tide,* pp. 141–72; Deeny, *To Cure and to Care,* pp. 174–8; McKee, 'Church–State Relations'; Ruth Barrington, *Health, Medicine and Politics in Ireland, 1900–1970* (Dublin, 1987).
83. Coogan, *De Valera,* pp. 647–55; Cooney, *McQuaid,* pp. 252–76.
84. Blanchard, *The Church in Contemporary Ireland,* pp. 29, 102; Biever, *Religion, Culture and Values*; this work involved a comparative study of Dublin and Chicago and was carried out under the auspices of the National Committee for Religion in Higher Education of the United States of America. It was submitted as a PhD thesis to the University of Pennsylvania in 1965. I have used the 1976 published version of the thesis, as I have been unable to obtain the original data sets. I would like to thank Andrew M. Greeley SJ and Robert A. Wild SJ, both of whom provided me with assistance in my search for these data.
85. Biever, *Religion, Culture and Values,* Table 17, p. 419, pp. 409–18 for individual views reported; see also John A. O'Brien (ed.), *The Vanishing Irish: The Enigma of the Modern World* (New York, 1953), for other contributions to this debate; Humphreys, *New Dubliners,* quotes one of his respondents as saying 'I think there is something wrong with sex and nothing will ever change me', pp. 120–1, 138–40, for this and other examples; Inglis, *Moral Monopoly,* pp. 138–9, 188–90, also discusses attitudes to sexuality.
86. Biever adopts a scale of 1–5, where 1 is the most positive endorsement of the proposition and 5 is a rejection. I have collapsed 1–2 as agreement and 4–5 as disagreement, with 3 as neutral.
87. Biever, *Religion, Culture and Values,* pp. 480–3; *Statistical Abstract of Ireland 1968* (Dublin, 1968); *Statistical Abstract of Ireland 1968.* In proposition 64, 'I think the pleasure sensations connection with sex are good things', are reported in the table as 19.2 per cent agree and 73.3 per cent disagree. In the text at p. 479 Biever reads these data as the majority of respondents affirming the pleasure principle and the minority rejecting it. This is open to question, as is other material contained in the discussion on sexuality.

88. Biever, *Religion, Culture and Values*, pp. 486–8.
89. Ibid., pp. 428–34, emphasis added.
90. Ibid., Tables 23 and 25, pp. 473, 469.
91. Ibid., pp. 314–15.
92. Ibid., Table 10, pp. 368–70.
93. Ibid., Table 16, p. 400; for interviews and comments, see pp. 398–9.
94. For a highly critical view of the idealised version of the 1950s and early 1960s, see O'Faolain, *Are You Somebody?*, pp. 276–83.
95. Biever, *Religion, Culture and Values*, pp. 232, 519–21; John Whyte, *Dáil Deputies* (Dublin, 1965), p. 25.

5. Emigration and the Failure of Rural Ireland, 1945–1961 (pages 136–68)

1. Maurice Moynihan (ed.), *Speeches and Statements by Eamon de Valera 1917–73* (Dublin, 1980), pp. 466–8; Daniel Corkery, *Synge and Anglo-Irish Literature* (Cork, 1931); Hilaire Belloc, *The Servile State* (London, 1912), p. 189; Tom Garvin, *Nationalist Revolutionaries* (Oxford, 1987) for the importance of the rural motif in nationalist thinking.
2. Patrick Kavanagh, 'The Great Hunger' (1942) in *Collected Poems* (New York, 1964), pp. 34–55; Damien F. Hannan, *Displacement and Development: Class, Kinship and Social Change in Irish Rural Communities* (Dublin, 1979), provides a valuable account and assessment of the nature of small farm communities in western Ireland; Tony Fahey, 'The Agrarian Dimension in the History of the Welfare State: A Case Study' (unpublished paper, Economic and Social Research Institute, Dublin, 2000). I am indebted to Dr Fahey for providing me with a copy of his paper prior to publication.
3. Derek Urwin, *From Ploughshare to Ballotbox: The Politics of Agrarian Defence in Europe* (Oslo, 1980); Brian Girvin, *The Right in the Twentieth Century* (London, 1994); Richard T. Griffiths and Brian Girvin (eds.), *The Green Pool and the Origins of the Common Agricultural Policy* (London, 1995), for a discussion of these forces.
4. United Nations European Commission for Europe, *Economic Survey of Europe in 1951* (Geneva, 1952); Richard T. Griffiths and Brian Girvin, 'Introduction: The Origins of the Common Agricultural Policy' in Griffiths and Girvin (eds.), *The Green Pool*, pp. vii–xl; Kieran Kennedy, Thomas Giblin and Deirdre McHugh, *The Economic Development of Ireland in the Twentieth Century* (London, 1988), p. 212.
5. NAI, DT, S. 14134A, 'British Financial Crisis', for material on the importance of the British market for Irish agriculture and exports; Maurice Manning, *James Dillon: A Biography* (Dublin, 1999), pp. 235–8, for the 1948 trade agreement; Raymond Crotty, *Irish Agricultural Production* (Cork, 1966), p. 178; *Statistical Abstract of Ireland 1931* (Dublin, 1931) and *Statistical Abstract of Ireland 1962* (Dublin, 1962) for the data.
6. NAI, DT, S. 13590, 'Small Nations in the Post War World', Smiddy to de Valera, 31 October 1944. Smiddy's career was a particularly interesting one. A former Professor of Economics in University College Cork, he played an active role as a diplomat for the Irish Free State, as well as chairing the Fiscal Inquiry Committee and the Tariff Commission. He became a director of the Central Bank in 1943 and was Chairman of the Commission of Inquiry into Post-Emergency Agricultural Policy as well as acting as adviser to de Valera. Although Smiddy was probably the most influential economist during the first twenty years of the state's existence, de Valera's view of the relationship was rather reserved; see Moynihan (ed.), *Speeches and Statements*, pp. 562–3.
7. NAI, DT, S. 10620, 'Per Jacobson: Letter on Economic Situation', Jacobson to de Valera, 25 March 1938, where the discussion between the two men is summarised.
8. Lars Mjøset, *The Irish Economy in a Comparative Institutional Perspective* (Dublin, 1992), p. 35. See also Brian Girvin, 'Why did Ireland not benefit from the Marshall Plan?: A

Comparative Approach' in Mary Browne, Till Geiger and Michael Kennedy (eds.), *Ireland and the Marshall Plan* (Dublin, forthcoming). Australia and Argentina were wealthy and agrarian in 1914.

9. Brian Girvin, 'Political Culture, Political Independence and Economic Success in Ireland' in *Irish Political Studies,* 12 (1997), pp. 48–77; Griffiths and Girvin (eds.), *The Green Pool,* for a discussion of these forces.
10. This has been extensively documented; see J.J. Lee, *Ireland 1912–1985: Politics and Society* (Cambridge, 1989), for discussion; Girvin, 'Political Culture'; Mjøset, *The Irish Economy in a Comparative Institutional Perspective.*
11. I am grateful to Johnny Larson for alerting me to the difficulties encountered by Denmark in its transition and for providing me with copies of his studies of Danish policy towards Europe during the 1950s and 1960s. Thorsten B. Olesen (ed.), *Interdependence Versus Integration: Denmark, Scandinavia and Western Europe 1945–1960* (Odense, 1995).
12. Michael Gallagher, *Electoral Support for Irish Political Parties 1927–1973* (London, 1976), pp. 53–5; Tony Varley, 'Farmers against Nationalists: The Rise and Fall of Clann na Talmhan' in Raymond Gillespie and Gerard Moran (eds.), *Galway: History and Society* (Dublin, 1995), pp. 589–622; voting percentages have been rounded up.
13. FF/440, Parliamentary Party Minutes, 16 October 1944.
14. NAI,DT, S. 11563A, 'General Comments on Agricultural Policy', Smiddy to Department of the Taoiseach, 9 December 1944; S. 12888, 'Post War Planning: Agriculture', for discussion on this and other related issues; Kennedy et al., *The Economic Development of Ireland,* pp. 202–3; Commission of Inquiry into Banking, Currency and Credit, *Reports* (Dublin, 1938).
15. NAI, DT, S. 11563A, 'General Comments on Agricultural Policy'; James J. Byrne, 'The Interrelation of Agriculture and Industry in the Development of the Irish Economy', *Studies,* 43 (1954), pp. 299–316.
16. Alan S. Milward, *The European Rescue of the Nation State* (London, 1992); Griffiths and Girvin, 'Introduction', in Griffiths and Girvin (eds.), *The Green Pool,* pp. vii–xl; Vibeke M. Sørensen, '"Free Trade" versus Regulated Markets: Danish Agricultural Organizations and the Green Pool, 1950–1954' in Griffiths and Girvin (eds.), *The Green Pool,* pp. 203–22; Richard T. Griffiths (ed.), *The Netherlands and the Integration of Europe 1945–1957* (Amsterdam, 1990).
17. *Irish Press,* 28 March 1945, for Lemass speech; UCDA, MacEntee Papers, P67/273, Department of Local Government and Public Health memorandum, 15 April 1945; P67/264, Department of Finance memorandum on full employment, 8 June 1945; 'Observations of M/Ag on memorandum on Full Employment', 1945. See also Brian Girvin, *Between Two Worlds: Politics and Economy in Independent Ireland* (Dublin, 1989), for discussion on Lemass' original proposals; John Horgan, *Seán Lemass: The Enigmatic Patriot* (Dublin, 1997), for the most recent observations on this; Crotty, *Irish Agricultural Production,* pp. 158–91.
18. UCDA, MacEntee Papers, P67/282, Aodh de Blacam, 'Rural Depopulation: Memorandum to Taoiseach and members of the National Executive', 4 December 1946. For a discussion of de Blacam, see Patrick Maume, 'Anti-Machiavel: Three Ulster Nationalists in the Age of De Valera', *Irish Political Studies,* 14 (1999), pp. 43–63.
19. UCDA, MacEntee Papers, P67/282, MacEntee reply to de Blacam, n.d.
20. UCDA, MacEntee Papers, P67/271, 'Economic and Social Aspects of Land Policy' n.d. but early 1945 from context; P67/282, 'Regarding Inducement to Marriage and flight from the Land' by Canon Malachy MacBranain, PP, to MacEntee, arguing that land division contributes to prosperous neighborhoods and happy families.

21. Manning, *James Dillon*, pp. 235–41; NAI, DT, S. 14134A–G, 'British Financial Crisis 1947'; S. 14042C, 'Trade Discussions June 1948'.
22. NAI, DT, S. 15290A/1, 'Inter-departmental ERP Committee', meeting no. 52, 24 November 1948; the committee had representatives of the Departments of Agriculture, External Affairs, Industry and Commerce, and Finance.
23. NAI, DIC, E26/1/8, 'Report of Foreign Trade Committee on the Anglo-Irish Trade Agreements 1938 and 1948', 20 July 1951.
24. NAI, DIC, E26/1/8, Foreign Trade Committee meeting, 21 August 1951; Boland (Ambassador) to Department of External Affairs, 15 November 1951, reporting on meeting with new Minister for Food; Report on Export of Pressed Meat to the $ area, 1952.
25. PRO, CAB, 134/842, Economic Policy Committee, 11 June 1952; CAB, 134/844, EA (52) 81, Memorandum by Minister of Food, 9 June 1952; Cmd. 8877, New annex to 1948 Trade Agreement; MAF, 40/448, for details of negotiations with Ireland.
26. NAI, DT, S. 14042F, 'Trade with Britain', 4 October 1952.
27. NAI, DT, S. 15011A, Minutes of Interdepartmental European Recovery Programme, 27 February 1953; Department of Agriculture memorandum, 4 March 1953; Brian Girvin, 'Irish Agricultural Policy, Economic Nationalism and the Possibility of Market Integration in Europe' in Griffiths and Girvin (eds.), *The Green Pool*, pp. 239–59.
28. NAI, DT, S. 14042/I, 'Trade with Britain', Department of Agriculture memorandum, 11 January 1954; Cabinet decision on strategy, 1 March 1954; Report of ministerial meeting in London, 4 March 1954 and 14 April 1954.
29. NAI, DT, S. 15062C, 'Progress Reports: Department of Agriculture', December 1955; PRO, MAF, 40/47, Cairncross to Perrin, Agriculture, 22 January 1956.
30. See the contributions to Griffiths and Girvin (eds.), *The Green Pool*, especially Fernando Guirao, 'Spain and the Green Pool: Challenge and Response, 1950–1955', pp. 261–88.
31. Fahey, 'The Agrarian Dimension in the History of the Welfare State'.
32. NAI, DT, S. 14197, 'Farming Community: Benefits Received at the Expense of the Exchequer', Department of Finance memorandum for Taoiseach, 23 December 1947; *Irish Independent*, 24 January 1949, for Inter-Party government achievements in agricultural sector; for comparison, see Mjøset, *The Irish Economy in a Comparative Institutional Perspective*; see also Manning, *James Dillon*, pp. 229–41.
33. UCDA, MacEntee Papers, P67/282, 'Rural Depopulation', 4 December 1946; P67/290, 'Comparison of Tax Levels UK/Ireland'; P67/289, MacEntee on standard of living, 8 September 1947; NAI, DFA, P81, Departmental memorandum, 3 December 1945; NAI, DT, S. 14186, 'Twenty-Six Counties and Northern Ireland: Contrast of Conditions, 1947'; *Sunday Times*, 16 November 1947; PDDE, vol. 108, col. 2135 (20 November 1947); PDDE, vol. 109, cols. 1–6 (26 November 1947); *Belfast Telegraph*, 8 December 1947.
34. The Church of Scotland expressed grave concern at the increase in the number of Catholic immigrants during the 1950s, a point I owe to my colleague James Kellas; T.W. Freeman, 'Emigration from Rural Ireland', *Journal of the Statistical and Social Inquiry Society of Ireland*, 17 (1944–5), pp. 404–22, for an early assessment; Enda Delaney, *Demography, State and Society: Irish Migration to Britain, 1921–1971* (Liverpool, 2000), pp. 160–225, for the most recent evaluation.
35. NAI, DFA, 402/21, 'New Travel Permits', 15 April 1946.
36. NAI, DT, S. 11582B, 'Irish Labour', Cabinet decision G.C. 4/116, 2 November 1945; Industry and Commerce, 'Emigration to Employment', 21 June 1946 and 22 June 1946; Taoiseach to McQuaid, 25 June 1946. Rev J. McCarthy, 'Morality of a State Ban on the Emigration of Minors', *Irish Ecclesiastical Record*, 5th Series, 71 (1949), pp. 269–72, claimed that it was 'morally inadmissible' for the state to ban the emigration of young

people as this would 'conflict with parental rights'. S. 11582B, Department of Social Welfare, 'Growth of Emigration Control', 22 July 1947.
37. Delaney, *Demography, State and Society*, pp. 160–221.
38. NAI, DT, S. 11582B, External Affairs 402/21, 2 April 1947 and 30 August 1947.
39. Federation of Irish Manufacturers, Council Minute Books, 15 November 1946; 19 December 1947; Annual General Meeting, 11 February 1948, for the President's speech.
40. NAI, DT, S. 13965A, 'Wage Policy', 23 November 1946; *Connaught Tribune*, 16 November 1946.
41. NAI, DT, S. 11582B, External Affairs 'Memorandum for Government on Emigration', 30 August 1947.
42. *Irish Press*, 8 October 1947, for the bishops' statement which is titled 'Bishops Warning on Dangers of Emigration'; NAI, DT, S. 15398A, 'Emigration: View of the Hierarchy'; Department of Social Welfare, 'Restriction on Emigration to Employment', 15 December 1947; de Valera to Ryan, 23 December 1947; Department of Social Welfare, 'Functions and Utility of the British Liaison Office in Dublin', 9 January 1948; Minister for Justice (Gerry Boland) to Department of Social Welfare including Garda report, 27 January 1948; draft memorandum, Department of the Taoiseach, January 1948.
43. NAI, DT, S. 15398A, de Valera to Staunton, 16 February 1948; Commission on Emigration and other Population Problems, *Reports* (Dublin, 1954), Table 11, pp. 20, 33–4.
44. NAI, DT, S. 15398A, de Valera to Staunton, 16 February 1948; see also the sentiments expressed above by de Blacam.
45. Commission on Emigration, *Reports*, pp. 134–43.
46. NAI, DT, S. 11582B, Department of External Affairs, 'Emigration', 30 December 1947. It should be noted that de Valera was both Taoiseach and Minister for External Affairs during this period of office. At the 1951 census there were 965 females for every 1,000 males in Ireland; in rural Ireland the ratio was 868:1,000 but in urban Ireland it was 1,120:1000.
47. Data taken from Commission on Emigration, *Reports,* Table 3, p. 283.
48. NAI, DT, S. 11582B, Department of External Affairs, 'Emigration', 30 December 1947.
49. Data available to the Commission on Emigration for those who transferred national health insurance to UK 1939–48 showed that 75,555 did so, but that 49,651 transferred back to Ireland subsequently, accounting for 66 per cent of the total, *Reports*, p. 128; James B. Wolf, '"Withholding Their Due": The Dispute between Ireland and Great Britain over Unemployment Insurance Payments to Conditionally Landed Irish Wartime Volunteer Workers', *Saothar*, 21 (1996), pp. 39–45.
50. Entry to employment was often restricted by non-economic considerations. An individual required an introduction to an employer, sometimes provided by a priest but more often by a trade union official or a relative already in the firm. For certain types of employment, such as Fords in Cork or most of the semi-state jobs, there was a long waiting list.
51. NAI, DT, S. 11582B, Department of External Affairs, 'Emigration', 30 December 1947.
52. *Irish Press*, 4 December 1948.
53. NAI, DT, S. 14149A/1, 'Emigration and Rural Depopulation'; Eithne MacDermott, *Clann na Poblachta* (Cork, 1998), pp. 32–4, notes the absence of a policy statement on agriculture in 1948.
54. *Irish Press*, 14 June 1948.
55. NAI, DT, S. 14310A, Aodh de Blacam, 'Emigration: Cause and Cure', 23 March 1948.
56. NAI, DT, S. 14249A/2, 'Emigration and Rural Depopulation', W.A. Honohan to Taoiseach, 28 August 1951, emphasis in the original.
57. *Irish Independent*, 7 July 1950, 2 August 1950.

58. PDDE, vol. 120, cols. 477–9 (18 April 1950); *Irish Press*, 15 August 1950; *Irish Catholic*, 'The Celt is Still Going', editorial, 21 June 1951.
59. *Irish Times*, 15 August 1951; Central Statistics Office, *Irish Statistical Survey 1950–51* (Dublin, 1952); NAI, DT, S. 13808B, 'National Expenditure'; S. 11582C, R.C. Geary to Ó Nualláin, 11 July 1951.
60. PDDE, vol. 126, cols. 2016–17 (19 July 1951).
61. *Kerryman*, 31 January 1953, for the report, quoted in John A. O'Brien, 'The Vanishing Irish' in John A. O'Brien (ed.), *The Vanishing Irish: The Enigma of the Modern World* (New York, 1953), pp. 11–41; the quote from Bishop Lucey and the report can be found at pp. 35–6.
62. NAI, DT, S. 15135, 'Employment Opportunities in Ireland, 1951–53', Agnes Rynne to de Valera, 28 September 1951; Inter-Departmental Committee on Availability of Employment, 31 October 1951, and Interim Report, 15 December 1951, for analysis of employment.
63. NAI, DT, S. 11582C, F.H. Boland to External Affairs, 23 July 1951; Maurice Foley, 'Some notes on the situation of Irish workers in Birmingham'; Note on de Valera decision to make speech, 22 August 1951; External Affairs to Secretary of State for Commonwealth Relations complaining of the 'objectionable and degrading conditions' for Irish workers in Birmingham, 28 August 1951; Report of speech on emigration by de Valera, 29 August 1951.
64. NAI, DT, S. 11582C–D for details of the controversy. The Irish media fully reported the controversy and there are numerous features and letters on the topic in the *Irish Times*, *Irish Press* and *Irish Independent*. Maureen Hartigan, 'Irish Emigration 1931–1961' (MA thesis, University College Cork, 1990).
65. NAI, DT, S. 13101C/1, 'Full Employment', Industry and Commerce to Taoiseach, 28 July 1953.
66. NAI, DT, S. 13831C, 'Ways in which British Policy had been Detrimental to Ireland's Economic Interests', 7 February 1952, paragraph 4 of report.
67. NAI, DT, S. 11582D, Irish Womens Workers' Union delegation to Taoiseach, 4 December 1951; Boland to External Affairs, 11 November 1952, 29 January 1953; PDDE, vol. 127, cols. 3–4 (31 October 1951).
68. NAI, DT, S. 11582D, Boland to Secretary, External Affairs, 11 November 1952.
69. NAI, DT, S. 11582E, Boland to Aiken, 16 November 1952, on meeting to discuss the situation of Irish women in England; Memorandum by Elizabeth Fitzgerald, 'The Problem of Irish Girls Emigrating to England', 19 July 1953; MacEntee note on this, 1 July 1953; the *Standard*, under a heading 'Parents Blamed for Exiles Misfortunes', claimed that Irish parents had little concern for those in England but simply wanted a share of their earnings; Heinrich Böll, *Irish Journal* (New York, 1967), pp. 3–6.
70. NAI, DT, S. 11582F, Taoiseach to External Affairs, 1 January 1954; External Affairs to Taoiseach, 6 January 1954; 'Irish Community Trust Fund', Taoiseach to Aiken, 7 January 1957.
71. NAI, DT, S. 11582F, de Valera to Private Secretary to Minister for External Affairs, 7 January 1954; Tim Pat Coogan, *De Valera: Long Fellow, Long Shadow* (London, 1993), pp. 664–6.
72. NAI, DT, S. 11582F, Boland to Fay, 30 January 1954.
73. NAI, DT, S. 11582F, Nunan, External Affairs, to Moynihan, Department of the Taoiseach, 9 December 1954; Cabinet note, 10 May 1955; see also memorandum by B.W. Haveman, 3 December 1954, outlining the active emigration policy pursued by the Dutch government.
74. *Irish Independent*, 10 May 1955, for Bishop Lucey; *Irish Independent*, 11 July 1955, for

pastoral letter. Archbishop McQuaid held a meeting with officials prior to the pastoral; NAI, DT, S. 11582, for details of meeting, 10 May 1955.

75. NAI, DT, S. 14249B, G.C. 7/8, 2 July 1954; *Irish Independent*, 13 July 1954.
76. All references are from Commission on Emigration, *Reports*.
77. O'Brien (ed.), *The Vanishing Irish*; *Irish Press* and *Irish Independent*, 10 May 1954, for reports on the conference; R.C. Geary, 'Some Population Questions', *Studies*, 43 (1954), pp. 168–76; Enda Delaney, 'State, Politics and Demography: The Case of Irish Emigration, 1921–71', *Irish Political Studies*, 13 (1998), pp. 25–50.
78. The following chapters from *The Vanishing Irish* are of particular interest: John A. O'Brien, 'The Vanishing Irish', pp. 11–41; Maura Laverty, 'Woman-shy Irishmen', pp. 50–9; Sean O'Faolain, 'Love Among the Irish', pp. 111–22; Bryan MacMahon, 'Getting on the High Road Again', pp. 208–25. Tom Inglis, *Moral Monopoly: The Rise and Fall of the Catholic Church in Modern Ireland*, 2nd edn (Dublin, 1998), pp. 178–200, provides a persuasive discussion of the historical origins of the role of the mother in this respect; Robert E. Kennedy, Jr, *The Irish: Emigration, Marriage, and Fertility* (Berkeley, Calif., 1973), pp. 139–72.
79. PDDE, vol. 148, cols. 464–92 (16 February 1955).
80. Böll, *Irish Journal*, pp. 52, 94–5.
81. NAI, DT, S. 14249B, Department of Lands memorandum, 30 June 1956; Department of Health, 25 October 1955; Department of Industry and Commerce, October 1955; Department of Justice, 28 June 1956; S. 14249C, Department of Agriculture 3 July 1956.
82. NAI, DT, S. 14249B, for Blowick's and Department of Lands' memorandum, 30 June 1956.
83. NAI, DT, S. 14249D, G.C. 7/129, 6 July 1956. There is a note in the file dated 1968 which states: 'It is not clear, however, what action, if any, had been taken pursuant to this decision prior to the termination of the Seventh (Inter-Party) Government in March 1957.'
84. Gary Murphy, 'The Politics of Economic Realignment, Ireland 1948–1964' (PhD thesis, Dublin City University, 1996), pp. 83–5.
85. *Irish Times*, 27 April 1959.
86. FF/79, which includes a letter from Dominic Mockler, Secretary of Coachford Comhairle Ceanntair, Co. Cork, who commends one of FitzGerald's articles on emigration, suggesting that 'Perhaps some use could be made of the last few paragraphs as the views of a distinguished independent commentator.'
87. NAI, DT, S. 16325B, Speech by Seán Lemass to Dublin Chamber of Commerce, 25 October 1960.

6. Conservative Nationalism and the Fear of Change, 1945–1961 (pages 169–200)

1. Jean-Dominique Lafay, 'Conservative Nationalism and Democratic Institutions' in Albert Breton, Gianluigi Galeotti, Pierre Salmon and Ronald Weintrobe (eds.), *Nationalism and Rationality* (Cambridge, 1995), pp. 159–72.
2. S.M. Lipset and S. Rokkan, 'Cleavage Structures, Party Systems and Voter Alignment' in S.M. Lipset and S. Rokkan (eds.), *Party Systems and Voter Alignment* (New York, 1967), pp. 1–64; John H. Whyte, 'Ireland: Politics without Social Bases' in Richard Rose (ed.), *Electoral Behaviour: A Comparative Handbook* (New York, 1974), pp. 619–51; Brian Girvin, 'Political Independence and Democratic Consolidation' in Michael Holmes and Denis Holmes (eds.), *Ireland and India: Connections, Comparisons and Contrasts* (Dublin, 1997), pp. 120–44.
3. James Hogan, *Election and Representation* (Cork, 1945), pp. 26–36; Lafay, 'Conservative Nationalism'.

4. UCDA, MacEntee Papers, P67/465, 'Notes on Republic', 1948; see also Tim Pat Coogan, *De Valera: Long Fellow, Long Shadow* (London, 1993), pp. 640–6, for de Valera's views on this issue. Basil Chubb, *The Constitution and Constitutional Change in Ireland*, rev. edn (Dublin, 1978). The original edition of this study, published in 1963, was titled *The Constitution of Ireland* and was an analysis of the stabilising force of the constitution. The third edition in 1970 retained the stable framework, but by the late 1970s it was necessary to rethink the nature of the constitution as reflected in the revised title. Committee on the Constitution, *Report* (Dublin, 1967), discusses the context for referendums and related issues.
5. UCDA, Aiken Papers, P104/5836, 23 February 1953; for similar sentiments expressed by protectionist businessman J.J. Walsh, see *Sunday Independent*, 28 July 1946.
6. PRO, DO 35/2088/WX101/104, Conversation with de Valera, 6 July 1945.
7. PRO, DO, 35/2087WX101/102, meeting with McQuaid, 4 July 1945. However a note on the file in the Dominions Office included a comment by Mrs Cameron that McQuaid's view was not in line with previous actions of the Catholic Church in Ireland, which 'fosters anti-British feeling and cultivates isolation as a safeguard against the contagion of non-Catholic culture'; DO, 35/1228/WX101/101, Report of meeting between Maffey and the Italian Minister, Baron Gonfalonieri, 25 June 1945.
8. PRO, PREM, 8/1222 part 1, 'Eire and Northern Ireland', memorandum by Lord President of the Council C. P. (46) 381, 16 October 1946; DO, 35/5205, 29 September 1953, Report by W.C. Hankinson.
9. PRO, DO, 35/1229/WX110/3, Note on de Valera's broadcast, 16 May 1945; de Valera replyied to Churchill in a radio broadcast on 16 May 1945, which can be found in Maurice Moynihan (ed.), *Speeches and Statements by Eamon de Valera 1917–73* (Dublin, 1980), pp. 474–6. For uncritical examinations of the exchange, see Earl of Longford and Thomas P. O'Neill, *Eamon de Valera* (London, 1970), pp. 413–14; Coogan, *De Valera*, pp. 609–13. For a somewhat more balanced analysis, see Dermot Keogh, *Twentieth-Century Ireland: Nation and State* (Dublin, 1994), pp. 157–61; Dermot Keogh, 'Eamon de Valera and Hitler: An Examination of International Reaction to the Visit to the German Minister, May 1945', *Irish Studies in International Affairs*, 3:1 (1989), pp. 69–92.
10. Keogh, *Twentieth-Century Ireland*, p. 161; Michael Kennedy and Joseph Morrison Skelly (eds.), *Irish Foreign Policy, 1919–1966: From Independence to Internationalism* (Dublin, 2000), for various assessments; Eithne MacDermott, *Clann na Poblachta* (Cork, 1998), pp. 1–26.
11. NAI, DT, S. 12891B, 'Report on Raising the School Age Prepared for the Minister', June 1947.
12. NAI, DT, S. 14106A, 'Economic Reconstruction of Europe 1947', Report on Lemass visit to the Netherlands, 10 July 1947. I am indebted to my colleagues in the Denmark, Ireland and Netherlands project on small states for information on Denmark and the Netherlands during this period; for a comparison with Spain, see Jean Grugel and Tim Rees, *Franco's Spain* (London, 1997), pp. 109–17, 128–42; Lars Mjøset, *The Irish Economy in a Comparative Institutional Perspective* (Dublin, 1992), pp. 152–93, 262–71.
13. Radio broadcast, 17 March 1943, in Moynihan (ed.), *Speeches and Statements*, pp. 466–9; Derek W. Urwin, *From Ploughshare to Ballotbox: The Politics of Agrarian Defence in Europe* (Oslo, 1980), pp. 159–274, for an analysis of general themes related to rural life and politics in Europe during the interwar period; Ernest Gellner, *Plough, Sword and Book* (London, 1991), pp. 224–60.
14. Ireland did become a member of the OEEC, but it was a reluctant member through the 1950s. The literature on this topic is immense and controversial. See Richard T.

Griffiths, 'The National and International Ramifications of Post-War Europe' in Thorsten B. Olesen (ed.), *Interdependence Versus Integration: Denmark, Scandinavia and Western Europe 1945–1960* (Odense, 1995), pp. 24–39, in addition to other contributions to this volume; Alan S. Milward, et al., *The Frontiers of National Sovereignty* (London, 1993), for a critical review of the alternatives. Ireland did become a member of the OEEC, and participated in the Marshall Plan, but remained uneasy concerning the liberal economic order being promoted.

15. NAI, DT, S. 13590, 'Small Nations in the Post War World', for invitation and preparation; for reports of the debate see *Irish Times* and *Irish Press*, 2 November 1944, from which this account is taken. The other contributors included Jan Masaryk, Arnold Toynbee and D.L. Kerr, the Vice-Chancellor of Queen's University Belfast.
16. PRO, DO, 35/3924/X2631/17, meeting between Secretary of State at the Dominions Office and de Valera, 4 November 1947. De Valera's views recorded here and the alacrity with which he led the anti-partitionist campaign in 1948–9, when out of office, raise the question of how far Fianna Fáil was prepared to accept the IRA if it was acting in Northern Ireland but not within or against the Republic.
17. Paul Bew and Henry Patterson, *Seán Lemass and the Making of Modern Ireland 1945–66* (Dublin, 1982), pp. 39–40; PRO, PREM 8/1222 part 1, 16 October 1947, Lord Rugby [formerly Sir John Maffey] interview with de Valera. See also Coogan, *De Valera*; John Horgan, *Seán Lemass: The Enigmatic Patriot* (Dublin, 1997), for the internal politics of Fianna Fáil at the end of the war.
18. PRO, PREM, 8/1222 part 1, note by Sir John Maffey, 3 August 1946.
19. In correspondence, Dr Gary Murphy has suggested to me that the Department of External Affairs was more innovative than this discussion suggests. This point is well taken; nevertheless such activism if not innovation is rarely translated into policy.
20. PRO, PREM, 8/1222 part 1, note by Sir John Maffey, 3 August 1946.
21. NAI, DT, S. 14002, Minister for External Affairs to British Embassy, 23 January 1947, refers to cabinet meeting of 22 January, where decision was taken; memorandum on above, 25 October 1947, reiterates the same argument. See also Brian Barton, 'Relations between Westminster and Stormont during the Attlee Premiership', *Irish Political Studies*, 7 (1992), pp. 1–20.
22. John Bowman, *De Valera and the Ulster Question 1917–1973* (Oxford, 1982), pp. 262–73.
23. PRO, PREM, 11/1409 C. I. (56) 5, 18 September 1956, 'Immigration from the Irish Republic', which discusses among other matters the British policy in respect of the Republic in 1948–9; NLI, MS, 22848, Shane Leslie Papers, O'Kelly to Leslie, 9 May 1949.
24. PRO, PREM, 8/1222 part 2, Conversation between the United Kingdom Representative to the Republic of Ireland and the Irish Republican Minister for External Affairs, 6 May 1950 (report dated 16 June, Sir Gilbert Laithwaite to Sir Percival Liesching).
25. PRO, DO, 35/3988, Conversation between Lord Pakenham and Mr de Valera and Mr Aiken, 2 May 1952; PREM, 11/923, '1955 Ireland', Conversation between F.H. Boland and Sir G. Laithwaite, 22 February 1955.
26. FF/42, 'Anti-Partition Committee', Feehan to Hon. Secretary, Fianna Fáil, 20 January 1955; Feehan had been a Fianna Fáil candidate at the 1951 and 1954 general elections for Dublin North West.
27. FF/42, memorandum from Tomás Ó Cléirigh Cumann, Dublin North East constituency, n.d. but probably early 1955.
28. FF/42, memorandum prepared by Lemass, 5 March 1955; Horgan, *Lemass*, pp. 168–74; see also Michael Kennedy, *Division and Consensus: The Politics of Cross-Border Relations in Ireland, 1925–1969* (Dublin, 2000), pp. 148–216, for the most comprehensive assessment available.

29. FF/42, Lemass to de Valera, 6 April 1955; de Valera to Lemass, 7 April 1955.
30. PRO, DO, 35/5205, Report from Dublin Embassy to London, 5 October 1953.
31. FF/277, Resolution by Seán Mac Diarmada Cumann, Dublin North East Constituency, n.d. but early 1957 from content; FF/274 for Lemass circular, 23 January 1957.
32. The three seats were Kerry South, Longford–Westmeath and Monaghan, while the fourth seat was in Sligo–Leitrim.
33. *Irish Press*, 20 November 1957; Reply in Dáil Eireann, 17 July 1958, both reproduced in Moynihan (ed.), *Speeches and Statements*, pp. 581–8.
34. NAI, DFA, P203/2, London discussions, 21 October 1957; 3 March 1958; 4 July 1957; DT, S. 16220, Study promoted by Department of the Taoiseach, 2 February 1957; replies, 1 July 1957; see also S. 9361F–G; report in *Irish Press*, 30 January 1958, of Seanad motion and de Valera's response.
35. NAI, DFA, P203/2, Lemass meeting in London, 13 July 1959; Horgan, *Lemass*, pp. 252–71, traces the development of Lemass' policy in respect of Northern Ireland; Kennedy, *Division and Consensus*, pp. 175–217, for the most recent assessment of Lemass' shift in policy.
36. Hogan, *Election and Representation*, p. 32.
37. *Irish Times*, 13 October 1947; Horgan, *Lemass*, p. 131–4; David McCullagh, *A Makeshift Majority: The First Inter-Party Government, 1948–51* (Dublin, 1998), pp. 7–42; Peter Mair, *The Changing Irish Party System* (London, 1987), pp. 51–5; Richard Sinnott, *Irish Voters Decide* (Manchester, 1995), pp. 131–4.
38. FF/793, 'General Election Report 1944'.
39. The by-election was unusual because it was a result of the resignation from the Dáil of William Dwyer, an independent candidate who had topped the poll in 1944. Fianna Fáil's share of the vote actually increased at the by-election, whereas during the general election it had lagged behind the party's average vote elsewhere in Munster and in Ireland generally.
40. UCDA, Cumann na nGaedheal/Fine Gael General Purposes Committee, P39/1/2, 14 November 1945. At the Clare by-election held on 4 December 1945, the Fine Gael candidate received 27.8 per cent of the vote, losing decisively to the Fianna Fáil candidate who received 72.2 per cent. Fine Gael did not nominate candidates at by-elections in Kerry South (won by Fianna Fáil) and Wexford (won by the Labour Party).
41. Hogan, *Election and Representation*, pp. 33–6, for an interesting discussion of this outcome and correspondence with leading figures in Fine Gael on the subject.
42. Michael Gallagher, *Electoral Support for Irish Political Parties, 1927–1973* (London, 1976), pp. 55–8; MacDermott, *Clann na Poblachta*, pp. 13–41, 59–62.
43. Sinnott, *Irish Voters Decide*, p. 104, discusses a 'three pronged attack on Fianna Fáil from the left', though he does conclude that this attack was weak and unsuccessful. Likewise, J.J. Lee, *Ireland 1912–1985: Politics and Society* (Cambridge, 1989), p. 318, points to the failure 'of an opening to the left in post-war Ireland', but does not clarify what this means; Kieran Allen, *Fianna Fáil and Irish Labour, 1926 to the Present* (London, 1997), pp. 88–94, is more sceptical of the political parties, but emphasises the radical potential of mass mobilisation.
44. PRO, DO, 35/3926/X2631/19, Rugby interview with de Valera, 16 October 1947; UCDA, MacEntee Papers, P67/289, 8 September 1947; P67/290, Statistics on tax levels in 'Budget 1947'; Hugh Shearman, 'Ulster's Success and Eire's Failure', *Belfast Telegraph*, 8 December 1947; NAI, DT, S. 14186, 'Twenty Six Counties and Northern Ireland: Contrast of Conditions, 1947', for details of exchanges. De Valera continued to be reluctant to increase taxation, even at the height of the 1950s depression; PRO, DO, 35/5210, report by British Ambassador of meeting with de Valera, 8 April 1957.

45. NAI, DT, S. 14134A, 'British Financial Crisis 1947', Memorandum, Minister for Finance to Taoiseach, 27 August 1947; Memorandum, Minister for Industry and Commerce to Taoiseach, 27 August 1947; S. 14186, note to Taoiseach, 13 November 1948.
46. UCDA, MacEntee Papers, P67/299, Childers to MacEntee, n.d. but from context written shortly after the 1948 election; Childers to Mullins, 10 February 1948; McCullagh, *A Makeshift Majority*, pp. 7–42.
47. I use this term advisedly because both Fianna Fáil and the NLP adopted interventionist and social policies for nationalist reasons.
48. McCullagh, *A Makeshift Majority*, pp. 29, 35–6; Horgan, *Lemass*, p. 141.
49. NAI, DT, S. 13700, 'Congress of Irish Unions', memorandum 13 July 1945 on decision to recognise the CIU; Dublin Trades Union Council to Taoiseach, 27 June 1946; reply from Industry and Commerce, 4 July 1946; see also NAI, DIC, TIW 971 for other files on this issue. The material in these files confirms the view that the Fianna Fáil government was ready to promote the interests of the CIU to the disadvantage of the ITUC and directly to prolong the split. See also Charles McCarthy, *Trade Unions in Ireland 1894–1960* (Dublin, 1977).
50. McCullagh, *A Makeshift Majority*, pp. 7–42; Allen, *Fianna Fáil and Irish Labour*, pp. 88–99.
51. *Cork Examiner*, 12, 21, 22 January 1948, for the exchanges; James Hickey, one of the founding members of the NLP and a TD for Cork City, was close to O'Rahilly, as was the Cork branch of the ITGWU; see also NLI, William O'Brien Papers, MS 13960, for correspondence.
52. Calculated from Michael Gallagher, *Irish Elections 1922–44: Results and Analysis* (Limerick, 1993), pp. 272, 302; Dáil Eireann, *Copies of the Public Notices of the Results of the Elections and of the Transfers of Votes in Respect of the General Election 1948, General Election 1951, Bye-Elections 1944–1952* (Dublin, 1953).
53. NAI, DT, S. 1396A, 'Cost of Living', 27 November 1946, for cabinet decision; a Finance memorandum identified a number of problems associated with this decision, 19 November 1946.
54. NAI, DT, S. 1396A, 'Observations by Minister for Agriculture', 6 January 1947.
55. NAI, DT, S. 1395A, Cab. G.C. 4/289, 2 October 1947, 'decision on prices and wages'; MacDermott, *Clann na Poblachta*, pp. 48–67; McCullagh, *A Makeshift Majority*, pp. 26–7.
56. UCDA, MacEntee Papers, P67/293, Childers to MacEntee, n.d. but late 1947 from context.
57. FF/73, Report of meeting and statement, 25 April 1946; Letter to Mullins, 14 June 1946; John Cooney, *John Charles McQuaid: Ruler of Catholic Ireland* (Dublin, 1999), pp. 210–11, on the strike.
58. NAI, DT, S. 14224, General Election 1948: Election Literature issued by various parties; FF/73 for communist accusation, 13 January 1948.
59. UCDA, MacEntee Papers, P67/372 on by-election 1947; P67/373–4 for election itself; P67/381 contains an exchange between Alfred O'Rahilly and MacEntee on the election; *Cork Examiner*, 12, 21, 22 January 1948.
60. UCDA, MacEntee Papers, P67/375 for MacEntee's refutation.
61. FF/794, '1948 Election Material', National Executive statement, 'In Times of Peace and War', December 1947.
62. UCDA, MacEntee Papers, P67/299, Childers to MacEntee, n.d. but from context February 1948; Note on education with letter to Mullins, 10 February 1948.
63. UCDA, MacEntee Papers, P67/466, Hon, Secretary's report, 8 June 1948.
64. Horgan, *Lemass*, pp. 135–48. Coogan, *De Valera*, pp. 638–46.
65. *Irish Times*, 28 October 1947 and 4 November 1947 for policy statements; McCullagh, *A Makeshift Majority*, pp. 7–42, for a detailed discussion of the election campaign and

the policies of the respective parties, including Clann na Poblachta; see also Kevin Rafter, *The Clann: The Story of Clann na Poblachta* (Cork, 1996), pp. 31–8, for a discussion of Clann policies.

66. *Irish Times*, 2 February 1948.
67. *Irish Times*, 18 February 1948, for statement and programme.
68. Ronan Fanning, *The Irish Department of Finance 1922–1958* (Dublin, 1978), pp. 442–56.
69. Ibid., pp. 359–61; Lee, *Ireland*, pp. 199–201.
70. Conor Cruise O'Brien, *Memoir: My Life and Themes* (Dublin, 1998), pp. 133–60, for a detailed description of working with MacBride; MacDermott, *Clann na Poblachta*, provides a critical assessment of the party and MacBride in particular.
71. James Deeny, *To Cure and to Care* (Dublin, 1989), pp. 164–74; for other assessments see McCullagh, *A Makeshift Majority*, pp. 198–232; John Horgan, *Noël Browne: Passionate Outsider* (Dublin, 2000), pp. 59–119.
72. Noël Browne, *Against the Tide* (Dublin, 1986), pp. 100–3; Browne also claims that the republican inner core around MacBride intended to use the social reformers such as Browne and Jack McQuillan to have former IRA members elected, but that this backfired; Sinnott, *Irish Voters Decide*, p. 63; MacDermott, *Clann na Poblachta*, pp. 1–26.
73. Peter Mair, *The Changing Irish Party System* (New York, 1987), pp. 51–3.
74. Tony Varley and Peter Moser, 'Clann na Talmhan: Ireland's Last Farmers' Party', *History Ireland*, 3:2 (1995), pp. 39–43.
75. Calculated from Gallagher, *Irish Elections 1922–44*; Dáil Eireann, *Copies of the Public Notices of the Results of the Elections and of the Transfers of Votes in Respect of the General Election 1948, General Election 1951, Bye-Elections 1944–1952.*
76. For an alternative view, see Sinnott, *Irish Voters Decide*, p. 289.
77. Browne's decision to join Fianna Fáil in 1953 is, I believe, a product of this, as well as of William Norton's view that 'he would never sit around a table' with Browne; see Browne, *Against the Tide*, pp. 220–4.
78. Sinnott, *Irish Voters Decide*, pp. 289–90, 145–7.
79. Keogh, *Twentieth-Century Ireland*, pp. 185–213; MacDermott, *Clann na Poblachta*, pp. 133–67; McCullagh, *A Makeshift Majority*, pp. 233–63, for assessments of the Inter-Party government.
80. NAI, DT, S. 13241A, 'National Government', *Irish Press*, 13 May 1943, which reported the Tánaiste's refusal to provide time to discuss a proposal for a national government; PDDE, vol. 86, col. 354 (26 March 1942), for Fianna Fáil claim; *Irish Press*, 15 May 1944.
81. NAI, DT, S. 14900, 'The Inter-Party System of Government', de Valera to H. Warren Hutchinson, 11 June 1951.
82. PDDE, vol. 127, cols. 1110–12 (21 November 1951), for de Valera reply; NAI, DT, S. 12295A, 'Economic Council', for further details; Moynihan (ed.), *Speeches and Statements*, pp. 545–62, for full speech.
83. FF/344, National Executive Minutes, 28 November 1949, 23 January 1950; Horgan, *Lemass*, pp. 135–48.
84. NAI, DT, S. 15042A, 'Statement of Government Policy, June 1951'; de Valera press conference reported in *Irish Press*, 5 June 1951.
85. NAI, DT, S. 15713, 'Inter-party Government 1954'; *Irish Independent*, 1 June 1954.
86. UCDA, MacEntee Papers, P67/223, *Irish Times*, 27 April 1954, 'Mr Costello Outlines Fine Gael's Financial Policy'; MacEntee, 'Directional Control of Total Investments', n.d.
87. FF/792, Tommy Mullins, Reflections on Cork by-election, 3 March 1954.
88. *Irish Press*, 30 May 1951, quoted in Mair, *The Changing Irish Party System*, p. 51.
89. FF/68, 'East Limerick By-Election 1952', which contains election material; O'Malley to

Breen, 30 June 1952. The campaign can be followed in the *Limerick Leader*, June 1952, especially 27 and 28 June 1952.

90. FF/277, 'Dublin North East', Circular on reorganisation, 2 September 1952; Lemass to Charles Haughey, 4 November 1954.
91. FF/277, Lemass to Kevin Boland, Charles Haughey and others, 8 September 1954.
92. FF/280, 'Comhairle Ceanntair Atha Cliath', Lemass to Andreas O'Keefe, SC, 20 September 1954; further notes by Lemass, late 1954 to early 1955.
93. FF/344, Minutes for meeting, 24 November 1952. Alderman Breathnach did not stand at the 1954 general election, but he did not resign his seat.
94. FF/344, National Executive Minutes, 11 November 1953; FF/281, Dublin South East, correspondence on communist charge; Lynch to Lemass, 7 February 1957.
95. Browne, *Against the Tide*, p. 221; see also pp. 220–6, on Browne's experiences in Fianna Fáil; Horgan, *Browne*, pp. 150–86.
96. FF/277, 'Dublin North East', Joe O'Neill, Hon. Secretary, North East Comhairle Ceanntair, report of meeting, 10 December 1954.
97. FF/277, Colley to Lemass, 20 May 1955; Hon. Secretary report by Charles Haughey for AGM of Cumann, 13 January 1956; Horgan, *Lemass*, p. 161. Horgan claims that Colley did not resign, but the evidence from the secretary's report suggests that he did not play an active role in the campaign and that this weakened Fianna Fáil in the area.
98. FF/277, Report from East Wall Cumann to Lemass, 10 January 1955; Haughey to Lemass, 28 July 1956.
99. FF/277, Haughey to Lemass, 22 January 1957.
100. FF/281, 'Dublin South East', Boland to Lemass, 28 February 1956.
101. FF/281, Boland to Lemass, 28 February 1956; FF/275, 'Dublin South West', Seán Monks Cumann, Ballyfermot, to Lemass, 14 January 1955; Lemass reply, 19 January 1955, and further exchanges; FF/305, 'Donegal West', correspondence on constituents' requests; FF/290, 'Tipperary', W.J. Ryan to Lemass, 22 September 1955; Lemass reply, 22 September 1955; Lemass to Breen, 27 September 1955; Ryan was secretary of a Fianna Fáil cumann in Tipperary.
102. FF/266, Lenihan to Lemass, 5 March 1956; Lemass to Lenihan, 9 June 1956.
103. FF/281, Lamb to MacEntee, 13 February 1957; Lemass to MacEntee, 15 February 1957.
104. FF/441, Parliamentary Party Minutes, 26 November 1952, 14 January 1953, 22 July 1953, 27 January 1954; see discussion in Gary Murphy, 'The Politics of Economic Realignment Ireland, 1948–1964', (PhD thesis, Dublin City University, 1996), p. 51.
105. FF/344, National Executive Minutes, 27 July 1953.
106. Horgan, *Lemass*, pp. 164–8; Lee, *Ireland*, pp. The British Ambassador reported in 1957 that de Valera was greatly concerned at the state of the economy, but was opposed to any new injection of money into the system; PRO, DO, 35/5210, 10 April 1957.
107. FF/344, 26 September 1955; Browne, *Against the Tide*, pp. 225–6.
108. See Horgan, *Lemass*, pp. 174–86, for an evaluation of this period.

7. Back to the Future (pages 201–12)

1. I use the word conservative with some caution here. It refers to the conserving nature of stable nationalist states and not to specific policy stances, which may not be conservative.
2. *Economic Development* (Dublin, 1958), p. 5; Lars Mjøset, *The Irish Economy in a Comparative Institutional Perspective* (Dublin, 1992), p. 5; *Statistical Abstract of Ireland 1964* (Dublin, 1964), pp. 20–6.
3. Colin Clark, *The Conditions of Economic Progress*, 3rd edn (London, 1957), pp. 44–50, 65–9; United Nations Economic Commission for Europe, *Economic Survey of Europe in*

1948 (Geneva, 1949), p. 235; David Johnson and Liam Kennedy, 'The Two Irish Economies since 1920' in *A New History of Ireland*, vol. 7 (Oxford, forthcoming). I am grateful to Till Geiger for alerting me to the UN data and to David Johnson for providing me with copies of the unpublished chapter noted here. Data for EC comparison in National Economic and Social Council, *Ireland in the European Community: Performance, Prospects and Strategy* (Dublin, 1989), pp. 116–18.

4. John Horgan, *Seán Lemass: The Enigmatic Patriot* (Dublin, 1997), pp. 189–251; Tim Pat Coogan, *De Valera: Long Fellow, Long Shadow* (London, 1993), pp. 647–89.
5. Quoted in John F. McCarthy, 'Ireland's Turnaround: Whitaker and the 1958 Plan for Economic Development' in John F. McCarthy (ed.), *Planning Ireland's Future: The Legacy of T.K. Whitaker* (Dublin, 1990), p. 53.
6. Garret FitzGerald, *Irish Times*, 26 January 1961.
7. Brian Girvin, *The Right in the Twentieth Century* (London, 1994), pp. 190–206, which discusses how conservatives can direct change to their advantage.
8. NAI, DT, S. 11987E/61, 'Establishment of Industries/Underdevelopment', Lynch to Lemass, 29 December 1961.
9. Mjøset, *The Irish Economy in a Comparative Institutional Perspective*, pp. 5–22.
10. NAI, DT, S. 17064A, Taoiseach's address to National Export Conference, 16 January 1961.
11. Richard T. Griffiths and Stuart Ward (eds.), *Courting the Common Market: The First Attempt to Enlarge the European Community 1961–1963* (London, 1996).
12. NAI, DT, S. 16877X/62, Whitaker to Minister for Finance, 5 January 1962.
13. PRO, PREM, 11/4320, Lemass meeting with Heath to discuss collapse of application, 18 March 1963. Lemass is reported as believing that 'it was in the interests both of Britain and the Republic to keep tariff cuts on a bilateral basis'; 'Ireland, the United Kingdom and the Common Market', notes on proposed visit by Lemass to London, 10 June 1961; for a fuller discussion of the reasoning behind the Irish decision to apply, see Brian Girvin, 'Irish Economic Development and the Politics of EEC Entry' in Griffiths and Ward (eds.), *Courting the Common Market*, pp. 247–62.
14. NAI, DT, S. 16877Y/62, Presidential address by Lemass to Fianna Fáil Ard Fheis, 16 January 1962.
15. NAI, DT, S. 17120C/95, Speech to Junior Chamber of Commerce of Ireland, Galway, 30 April 1966; Girvin, 'Irish Economic Development and the Politics of EEC Entry'; Horgan, *Lemass*, pp. 213–51.
16. Speech reported in *Irish Press*, 11 November 1959.
17. NAI, DT, S. 9361K/63, Lemass speech to Fianna Fáil Ard Fheis, 19 May 1963.
18. NAI, DT, 96/6/682, Election speech by Lemass, 2 April 1965.
19. John H. Whyte, 'Ireland: Politics without Social Bases' in Richard Rose, (ed.), *Electoral Behaviour: A Comparative Handbook* (New York, 1974), pp. 619–51.
20. Michael Gallagher, 'Societal Change and Party Adaptation in the Republic of Ireland 1960–1981', *European Journal of Political Research*, 9:3 (1981), pp. 269–95.
21. FF/79, Vivion de Valera to Lemass, 22 November 1961, with copy of Gallup report prepared by Dr Henry Durant and William Gregory.
22. Peter Mair, *The Changing Irish Party System* (New York, 1987), pp. 184–9; Garret FitzGerald, *All in a Life* (Dublin, 1991), pp. 68–73, 298.
23. Michael Gallagher, *The Irish Labour Party in Transition 1957–82* (Manchester, 1982), pp. 67–103.
24. Arthur Marwick, *The Sixties* (Oxford, 1998).
25. Stephen Collins, *The Power Game: Fianna Fáil since Lemass* (Dublin, 2000), pp. 27–99; Justin O'Brien, *The Arms Trial* (Dublin, 2000).

26. Brian Girvin, *Between Two Worlds: Politics and Economy in Independent Ireland* (Dublin, 1989), pp. 202–11; Telesis, *A Review of Industrial Policy* (Dublin, 1982).
27. Gary Murphy, 'The Politics of Economic Realignment, Ireland 1948–1964' (PhD thesis Dublin City University, 1996), pp. 156–98; Rona Fitzgerald and Brian Girvin, 'Political Culture, Growth and the Conditions for Success in the Irish Economy' in Brian Nolan, Philip J. O'Connell and Christopher T. Whelan (eds.), *Bust to Boom?: The Irish Experience of Growth and Inequality* (Dublin, 2000), pp. 268–85; Damian F. Hannan and Patrick Commins, 'The Significance of Small-Scale Landholders in Ireland's Socio-Economic Transformation' in J.H. Goldthorpe and C.T. Whelan (eds.), *The Development of Industrial Society in Ireland* (Oxford, 1992), pp. 79–104. See also Jack Lynch's assurance to the Dáil in 1967 that membership would not involve the taxpayer in any additional support for farmers, PDDE, vol. 230, cols. 755–6 (25 July 1967).
28. National Economic and Social Council, *Ireland in the European Community*, p. 117.
29. J.H. Whyte, *Church and State in Modern Ireland 1923–1970* (Dublin, 1971), pp. 350, 388–90; NAI, DT, 96/6/364, 'Marriage in Ireland', Lemass to Lenihan, 25 September 1965; Lenihan to Lemass, 17 February 1966.
30. John Coakley, 'Public Opinion and the European Communities', in David Coombs (ed.), *Ireland and the European Communities: Ten Years of Membership* (Dublin, 1983), pp. 43–67.
31. Michael Kennedy, *Division and Consensus: The Politics of Cross-Border Relations in Ireland, 1925–1969* (Dublin, 2000), pp. 230–331; opinion polls in the *Irish Press*, 16–19 April 1968, and the *Belfast Telegraph*, 16–17 April 1968, show a softening of opinion.
32. Horgan, *Lemass*, pp. 342–3.
33. Collins, *The Power Game.*
34. From John Montague, 'The Siege of Mullingar', in John Montague, *Collected Poems* (Oldcastle, Co. Meath, 1995), p. 67.

Bibliography

Primary Sources

National Archives of Ireland, Dublin (NAI)
Department of Finance (DF)
Department of Foreign Affairs (DFA)
Department of Health (DH)
Department of Industry and Commerce (DIC)
Department of Justice (DJ)
Department of the Taoiseach (DT)

University College Dublin Archives Department (UCDA)
Frank Aiken Papers
Ernest Blythe Papers
Cumann na nGaedheal/Fine Gael Party Minutes
Eamon de Valera Papers
Desmond FitzGerald Papers
Seán MacEntee Papers
Patrick McGilligan Papers
Richard Mulcahy Papers

National Library of Ireland, Dublin (NLI)
Commission on Vocational Organisation: Evidence and Minutes to the Commission
Frank Gallagher Papers
J.J. Horgan Papers
Thomas Johnson Papers
Shane Leslie Papers
William O'Brien Papers
Redmond Papers

Public Record Office, London (PRO)
Cabinet Office (CAB)
Dominion Office (DO)
Foreign Office (FO)
Ministry of Agriculture and Fisheries (MAF)
Prime Ministers' Office (PREM)

University College Cork (UCCA)
William O'Brien Papers

National Archives, Washington DC
General Records of the State Department

Irish Business and Employers Confederation, Dublin
Federation of Irish Manufacturers: Council Minutes Books

Fianna Fáil Head Office, Dublin
Fianna Fáil Archives (FF)

Printed Sources

Adams, M., *Censorship: The Irish Experience* (Dublin, 1968)
Alapuro, R., and Allardt, E., 'The Lapua Movement: The Threat of Rightist Takeover in Finland 1930–32' in Linz and Stepan (eds.), *The Breakdown of Democratic Regimes*, pp. 122–41
Allen, K., *Fianna Fáil and Irish Labour, 1926 to the Present* (London, 1997)
Anderson, B., *Imagined Communities: Reflections on the Origin and Spread of Nationalism* (London, 1983)
Andrews, T., *Man of No Property* (Dublin and Cork, 1982)
Augusteijn, J., *From Public Defiance to Guerrilla Warfare* (Dublin, 1996)
Barrington, D., *The Church, the State and the Constitution* (Dublin, 1959)
Barrington, R., *Health, Medicine and Politics in Ireland, 1900–1970* (Dublin, 1987)
Bartlett, T., *The Fall and Rise of the Irish Nation: The Catholic Question 1690–1830* (Dublin, 1992)
—— 'The Burden of the Present: Theobald Wolfe Tone, Republican and Separatist' in D. Dickson, D. Keogh and K. Whelan (eds.), *The United Irishmen: Republicanism, Radicalism and Rebellion* (Dublin, 1993)
Barton, B., 'Northern Ireland: The Impact of War, 1939–1945' in Girvin and Roberts (eds.), *Ireland and the Second World War*, pp. 47–75
—— 'Relations between Westminster and Stormont during the Attlee Premiership', *Irish Political Studies*, 7 (1992), pp. 1–20
Behan, B., *Borstal Boy* (London, 1958)
Belloc, H., *The Servile State* (London, 1912)
Berger, P., *The Social Reality of Religion*, rev. edn (Harmondsworth, 1973)
Berlin, I., 'Two Concepts of Liberty' in I. Berlin, *Four Essays on Liberty* (Oxford, 1969), pp. 154–60.
Bew, P., *Ideology and the Irish Question: Ulster Unionism and Irish Nationalism 1912–1916* (Oxford, 1994)
—— Hazelkorn, E. and Patterson, H., *The Dynamics of Irish Politics* (London, 1989)
Bielenberg, A., 'Entrepreneurship, Power and Public Opinion in Ireland: The Career of William Martin Murphy', *Chronicon*, 2 (1998), pp. 1–35, which can be found at *www.ucc.ie/chronicon/bielen.htm*
—— and O'Mahony, P., 'An Expenditure Estimate of Irish National Income in 1907', in *The Economic and Social Review*, 29:2 (1998), pp. 107–32
Biever, B.F., *Religion, Culture and Values: A Cross-Cultural Analysis of Motivational Factors in Native Irish and American Irish Catholicism* (New York, 1976)
Blanchard, J., *The Church in Contemporary Ireland* (Dublin, 1963)
Blanshard, P., *The Irish and Catholic Power* (London, 1954)

Böll, H., *Irish Journal* (New York, 1967)
Bolster, E., *The Knights of Saint Columbanus*, (Dublin, 1979)
Bowen, D., *Paul Cullen and the Shaping of Modern Irish Catholicism*, (Dublin, 1983)
Bowman, J., *De Valera and the Ulster Questions 1917–1973* (Oxford, 1982)
Bowyer Bell, J., *The Secret Army* (London, 1972)
Boyce, D.G., *Englishmen and Irish Troubles* (London, 1972)
—— *Nineteenth-Century Ireland: The Search for Stability* (Dublin, 1990)
—— '1916, Interpreting the Rising' in D.G. Boyce and A. O'Day (eds.), *The Making of Modern Irish History* (London, 1996), pp. 163–87
Bradshaw, B. and Morrill, J. (eds.), *The British Problem, c.1534–1707: State Formation in the Atlantic Archipelago* (Basingstoke, 1996)
Brady, C., *Guardians of the Peace* (Dublin, 1974)
Breuilly, J., *Nationalism and the State*, 3rd edn (Manchester, 1993)
Brooke, P., *Ulster Presbyterianism* (Dublin, 1987)
Broun, D., Finlay R.J. and Lynch, M. (eds.), *Image and Identity: The Making and Re-making of Scotland Through the Ages* (Edinburgh, 1998)
Brown, C.G., *Religion and Society in Scotland since 1707* (Edinburgh, 1997)
Brown, M.E., Lynn-Jones, S.M. and Miller, S.E. (eds.), *Debating the Democratic Peace* (Cambridge, Mass., 1996)
Browne, N., *Against the Tide* (Dublin, 1986)
Buchanan, A., *Secession: The Morality of Political Divorce from Fort Sumter to Lithuania and Quebec* (Boulder, Colo., 1991)
Buchanan, T. and Conway, M. (eds.), *Political Catholicism in Europe 1918–1965* (Oxford, 1996)
Buckland, P., *Ulster Unionism and the Origins of Northern Ireland 1886–1922* (Dublin, 1973)
Burke, E., '"The Irishman is no lazzarone': German Travel Writers in Ireland 1828–1850', *History Ireland*, 5:3 (1997), pp. 21–5
Butler, H., *Escape from the Anthill* (Mullingar, 1986)
Byrne, J.J., 'The Interrelation of Agriculture and Industry in the Development of the Irish Economy', *Studies*, 43 (1954), pp. 299–316
Chubb, B., *The Constitution and Constitutional Change in Ireland*, 3rd edn (Dublin, 1978)
—— *A Source Book of Irish Government*, 2nd edn (Dublin, 1983)
Clark, C., *The Conditions of Economic Progress*, 3rd edn (London, 1957)
Clinton, W.D., 'The National Interest: Normative Foundations', *Review of Politics*, 48:4 (1986), pp. 495–519
Coakley, J., 'Competing Conceptions of Legitimacy and the Creation of the New State', *Études Irlandaises*, 20:1 (1995), pp. 55–62
—— 'Public Opinion and the European Communities' in D. Coombes (ed.), *Ireland and the European Communities: Ten Years of Membership* (Dublin, 1983), pp. 43–67
—— 'The Evolution of Irish Party Politics' in Girvin and Sturm (eds.), *Politics and Society in Contemporary Ireland*, pp. 29–54
Cobban, A., *The Nation State and National Self-Determination* (Oxford, 1945)
Codd, P., 'Recruiting and Responses to the War in Wexford' in D. Fitzpatrick (ed.), *Ireland and the First World War* (Dublin, 1986)
Colley, L., *Britons: Forging the Nation, 1707–1837* (New Haven, 1992)
Collins, S., *The Power Game: Fianna Fáil since Lemass* (Dublin, 2000)
Commission of Inquiry into Banking, Currency and Credit, *Reports* (Dublin, 1938)
Commission on Emigration and other Population Problems, *Reports* (Dublin, 1954)
Commission on Vocational Organisation, *Report* (Dublin, 1944)
Committee on the Constitution, *Report* (Dublin 1967)

Connolly, S.J., *Religion, Law and Power: The Making of Protestant Ireland 1660–1760* (Oxford, 1992)
—— 'Varieties of Britishness: Ireland, Scotland and Wales in the Hanovarian State' in A. Grant and K.J. Stringer (eds.), *Uniting the Kingdom?: The Making of British History* (London, 1995)
—— (ed.), *Kingdoms United?: Great Britain and Ireland since 1500 — Integration and Diversity* (Dublin, 1999)
Connolly, T.R., 'Irish Public Opinion and the Republican Movement 1916–1918' (MA thesis, University College Cork, 1995)
Conway, M., *Catholics in Europe 1918–1945* (London, 1997)
Conway, W., 'Marriage in Ireland: Church and State', *Irish Ecclesiastical Record,* 5th Series, 68 (1946), pp. 361–6
Coogan, T.P., *De Valera: Long Fellow, Long Shadow* (London, 1993)
—— *The IRA* (London, 1970)
Cooney, J., *John Charles McQuaid: Ruler of Catholic Ireland* (Dublin, 1999)
Corkery, D., *Synge and Anglo-Irish Literature* (Cork, 1931)
Cornwell, J., *Hitler's Pope: The Secret History of Pius XII* (London, 1999)
Cronin, M., *The Blueshirts and Irish Politics* (Dublin, 1997)
—— 'Defenders of the Nation?: The GAA and Irish Nationalist Identity', *Irish Political Studies,* 11 (1996), pp. 1–19
—— 'The Blueshirt Movement, 1932–5: Ireland's Fascists?', *Journal of Contemporary History,* 30:2 (1996), pp. 311–32
Crotty, R., *Irish Agricultural Production* (Cork, 1966)
Curtin, N.J., *The United Irishmen: Popular Politics in Ulster and Dublin 1791–1798* (Oxford, 1994)
Dahl, R.A., 'Patterns of Opposition' in R.A. Dahl (ed.), *Political Oppositions in Western Democracies* (New Haven, 1966), pp. 332–47
Dalton, D., *Mahatma Gandhi: Non-Violent Power in Action* (New York, 1993)
Daly, M.E., *Industrial Development and Irish National Identity, 1922–1939* (Dublin, 1992)
—— 'Integration or Diversity?: Anglo-Irish Economic Relations, 1922–39' in Connolly (ed.), *Kingdoms United?,* pp. 169–80
Davis, R.P., *Arthur Griffith and Non-Violent Sinn Féin* (Dublin, 1974)
de Bhaldraithe, E., 'Mixed Marriages and Irish Politics: The Effect of *Ne Temere*', *Studies,* 77 (1988), pp. 284–99
Deeny, J., *To Cure and to Care* (Dublin, 1989)
DeFronzo, J., *Revolutions and Revolutionary Movements,* 2nd edn (Boulder, Colo., 1996)
Delaney, E., *Demography, State and Society: Irish Migration to Britain, 1921–1971* (Liverpool, 2000)
—— 'State, Politics and Demography: The Case of Irish Emigration, 1921–71', *Irish Political Studies,* 13 (1998), pp. 25–50
de Valera, E., *Ireland's Stand: Being a Selection of Speeches of Eamon de Valera During the War (1939–1945)* (Dublin, 1946)
—— *National Discipline and the Majority Rule* (Dublin, 1936)
Devine, T.M., *The Scottish Nation 1700–2000* (London, 1999)
Dion, S., 'The Reemergence of Secessionism: Lessons from Quebec' in A. Breton, G. Galeotti, P. Salmon and R. Wintrobe (eds.), *Nationalism and Rationality* (Cambridge, 1995), pp. 116–42
Doherty, R., 'Irish Heroes of the Second World War' in Girvin and Roberts (eds.), *Ireland and the Second World War,* pp. 91–106
Dudley Edwards, R., *Patrick Pearse: The Triumph of Failure* (London, 1977)

Duffy, P., *The Lay Teacher* (Dublin, 1966)
Dunphy, R., *The Making of Fianna Fáil Power in Ireland 1923–1948* (Oxford, 1995)
Eatwell, R., (ed.), *European Political Cultures* (London, 1997)
Economic Development (Dublin, 1958)
Elliott, M., *Wolfe Tone: Prophet of Irish Independence* (New Haven, 1989)
Etzioni, A., *The Spirit of Community* (London, 1995)
Fahey, T., 'The Agrarian Dimension in the History of the Welfare State: A Case Study' (unpublished manuscript, Dublin, January 2000)
Fanning, R., *The Irish Department of Finance 1922–1958* (Dublin, 1978)
—— Kennedy, M., Keogh, D. and O'Halpin, E., (eds.) *Documents on Irish Foreign Policy: Volume I, 1919–1922* (Dublin, 1998)
Farrell, B., *Seán Lemass* (Dublin, 1983)
—— *The Founding of Dáil Eireann: Parliament and Nation-Building* (Dublin, 1971)
—— (ed.), *De Valera's Constitution and Ours* (Dublin, 1988)
—— (ed.), *The Irish Parliamentary Tradition* (Dublin, 1975)
Farrell, T., 'Professionalization and Suicidal Defence Planning by the Irish Army, 1921–1941', *Journal of Strategic Studies*, 21:3 (1997), pp. 67–85
Fisk, R., *In Time of War: Ireland, Ulster and the Price of Neutrality 1939–45* (London, 1983)
Fitzgerald, F., *Memoirs of Desmond Fitzgerald* (London, 1968)
FitzGerald, G., *All in a Life* (Dublin, 1991)
Fitzgerald, R. and Girvin, B., 'Political Culture, Growth and the Conditions for Success in the Irish Economy' in B. Nolan, P.J. O'Connell and C.T. Whelan (eds.), *Bust to Boom?: The Irish Experience of Growth and Inequality* (Dublin, 2000), pp. 268–85
Fitzpatrick, D., *Politics and Irish Life 1913–21* (Dublin, 1977)
—— *The Two Irelands 1912–1939* (Oxford, 1998)
—— 'The Logic of Collective Sacrifice: Ireland and the British Army, 1914–1918', *The Historical Journal*, 38:4 (1995), pp. 1017–30
Fleischmann, R., *Catholic Nationalism in the Irish Revival: A Study of Canon Sheehan, 1852–1913* (Basingstoke, 1997)
Fraser, T.G., *Partition in Ireland, India and Palestine* (London, 1984)
Freeman, T.W., 'Emigration from Rural Ireland', *Journal of the Statistical and Social Inquiry Society of Ireland*, 17 (1944–5), pp. 404–22
Fukuyama, F., *Trust: The Social Virtues and the Creation of Prosperity* (New York, 1995)
Gallagher, M., *Electoral Support for Irish Political Parties 1927–1973* (London, 1976)
—— *The Irish Labour Party in Transition 1957–82* (Dublin, 1982)
—— 'Societal Change and Party Adaptation in the Republic of Ireland 1960–1981', *European Journal of Political Research*, 9:3 (1981), pp. 269–95
—— 'The Pact General Election of 1922', *Irish Historical Studies*, 21:84 (1979), pp. 404–21
—— (ed.), *Irish Elections 1922–44: Results and Analysis* (Limerick, 1993)
Gannon, J., *Catholic Power, Culture and the Constitution of Ireland* (Belfast, 1972)
Garvin, T., *Nationalist Revolutionaries* (Oxford, 1987)
—— *1922: The Birth of Irish Democracy* (Dublin, 1996)
—— *The Evolution of Irish Nationalist Politics* (Dublin, 1981)
—— 'The Politics of Language and Popular Culture in Ireland', *Irish Political Studies*, 2 (1987), pp. 49–63
—— 'The Rising and Irish Democracy' in Ní Dhonnchadha and Dorgan (eds.), *Revising the Rising*, pp. 21–8
—— 'Unenthusiastic Democrats: The Emergence of Irish Democracy' in R.J. Hill and M. Marsh (eds.), *Modern Irish Democracy* (Dublin, 1993)
Gaughan, J.A., *Thomas Johnson 1872–1963* (Dublin, 1980)

Geary, L., *The Plan of Campaign* (Cork, 1986)
Geary, R.C., 'Some Population Questions', *Studies*, 43 (1954), pp. 168–76
Gellner, E., *Nations and Nationalism* (Oxford, 1983)
—— *Plough, Sword and Book* (London, 1991)
Gibbon, M., 'Am I Irish?', *The Crane Bag*, 1:2 (1977), pp. 27–8
Gibbon, P., *The Origins of Ulster Unionism* (Manchester, 1975)
Girvin, B., *Between Two Worlds: Politics and Economy in Independent Ireland* (Dublin, 1989)
—— *The Right in the Twentieth Century* (London, 1994)
—— and Roberts, G. (eds.), *Ireland and the Second World War: Politics, Society and Remembrance* (Dublin, 2000)
—— and Stürm, R. (eds.), *Politics and Society in Contemporary Ireland* (Aldershot, 1986)
—— 'Irish Agricultural Policy, Economic Nationalism and the Possibility of Market Integration in Europe' in Griffiths and Girvin (eds.), *The Green Pool*, pp. 239–59
—— 'Irish Economic Development and the Politics of EEC Entry' in Griffiths and Ward (eds.), *Courting the Common Market*, pp. 247–62
—— 'Nationalism, Catholicism and Democracy: Hogan's Intellectual Evolution' in Ó Corráin (ed.), *James Hogan*, pp. 163–76
—— 'Nationalism, Democracy and Irish Political Culture' in Girvin and Stürm (eds.), *Politics and Society in Contemporary Ireland*, pp. 3–28
—— 'Political Culture, Political Independence and Economic Success in Ireland', *Irish Political Studies*, 12 (1997), pp. 48–77
—— 'Political Independence and Democratic Consolidation' in M. Holmes and D. Holmes (eds.), *Ireland and India: Connections, Comparisons and Contrasts* (Dublin, 1997), pp. 120–44
—— 'Politics in Wartime: Governing, Neutrality and Elections' in Girvin and Roberts (eds.), *Ireland and the Second World War*, pp. 24–46
—— 'The Act of Union, Nationalism and Religion: 1780–1850' in J. Elvert (ed.), *Nordirland in Geschichte und Gegenwart/Northern Ireland: Past and Present* (Stuttgart, 1994)
—— 'The State and Vocational Education 1922–1960' in Logan (ed.), *Teachers' Union*, pp. 62–92
—— 'Why did Ireland not benefit from the Marshall Plan?: A Comparative Approach' in M. Browne, T. Geiger and M. Kennedy (eds.), *Ireland and the Marshall Plan* (Dublin, forthcoming)
Goulding, G.M., *George Gavan Duffy 1882–1951: A Legal Biography* (Dublin, 1982)
Gramsci, A., *Selections From Prison Notebooks* (London, 1971)
Greaves, C.D., *The Irish Transport and General Workers' Union: The Formative Years, 1909–1923* (Dublin, 1982)
Griffiths, R.T., 'The National and International Ramifications of Post-War Europe' in Olesen (ed.), *Interdependence Versus Integration*, pp. 24–39
—— and Girvin, B., 'Introduction: The Origins of the Common Agricultural Policy', in Griffiths and Girvin (eds.), *The Green Pool*, pp. vii–xl
—— (ed.), *The Netherlands and the Integration of Europe 1945–1957* (Amsterdam, 1990)
—— and Girvin, B. (eds.), *The Green Pool and the Origins of the Common Agricultural Policy* (London, 1995)
—— and Ward, S. (eds.), *Courting the Common Market: The First Attempt to Enlarge the European Community 1961–1963* (London, 1996)
Grugel, J. and Rees, T., *Franco's Spain* (London, 1997)
Guirao, F., 'Spain and the Green Pool: Challenge and Response, 1950–1955' in Griffiths and Girvin (eds.), *The Green Pool*, pp. 261–88
Hand, G. (ed.), *Report of the Irish Boundary Commission* (Shannon, 1969)

Hannan, D.F., *Displacement and Development: Class, Kinship and Social Change in Irish Rural Communities* (Dublin, 1979)
—— and Commins, P., 'The Significance of Small-Scale Landholders in Ireland's Socio-Economic Transformation' in J.H. Goldthorpe and C.T. Whelan (eds.), *The Development of Industrial Society in Ireland* (Oxford, 1992), pp. 79–104
Harkness, D.W., *The Restless Dominion* (London, 1969)
Hart, P., *The I.R.A. and Its Enemies: Violence and Community in Cork 1916–1923* (Oxford, 1998)
—— 'The Protestant Experience of Revolution in Southern Ireland' in R. English and G. Walker (eds.), *Unionism in Modern Ireland* (Dublin, 1996), pp. 81–98
Hartigan, M., 'Irish Emigration 1931–1961', (MA thesis, University College Cork, 1990)
Hastings, A., *The Construction of Nationhood: Ethnicity, Religion and Nationalism* (Cambridge, 1997)
Hempton, D., *Religion and Political Culture in Britain and Ireland from the Glorious Revolution to the Decline of Empire* (Cambridge, 1996)
Hennessey, T., *Dividing Ireland: World War I and Partition* (London, 1998)
Heraclides, A., *The Self-Determination of Minorities in International Politics* (London, 1991)
Hinde, W., *Castlereagh* (London, 1981)
Hindley, R., *The Death of the Irish Language: A Qualified Obituary* (London, 1990)
Hirschman, A.O., *Essays in Trespassing: Economics to Politics and Beyond* (Cambridge, 1981)
—— *Shifting Involvement* (Oxford, 1982)
Hobsbawm, E., *Nations and Nationalism since 1780* (Cambridge, 1990)
Hogan, D. [Frank Gallagher], *The Four Glorious Years* (Dublin, 1953)
Hogan, G., 'A Fresh Look at Tilson's Case', *Irish Jurist*, 33 (1998), pp. 311–32
—— 'Irish Nationalism as a Legal Ideology', *Studies*, 75 (1986), pp. 528–38
Hogan, J., *Could Ireland Become Communist?* (Dublin, 1935)
—— *Election and Representation* (Cork and Oxford, 1945)
—— *Modern Democracy* (Cork, 1938)
Holmes, F., *The Presbyterian Church in Ireland: A Popular History* (Columba Press, 1999)
Holmes, S., *The Anatomy of Antiliberalism* (Cambridge, Mass., 1993)
Hoppen, K.T., *Elections, Politics and Society in Ireland, 1832–1885* (Oxford, 1984)
Horgan, J., *Noël Browne: Passionate Outsider* (Dublin, 2000)
—— *Seán Lemass: The Enigmatic Patriot* (Dublin, 1997)
Horgan, J.J., *Parnell to Pearse* (Dublin, 1948)
Houston, A., *Daniel O'Connell: His Early Life and Journal, 1795–1802* (London, 1906)
Humphreys, A.J., *New Dubliners: Urbanization and the Irish Family* (London, 1966)
Hutchinson, J., *The Dynamics of Cultural Nationalism: The Gaelic Revival and the Creation of the Irish Nation State* (London, 1987)
Inglis, H.D., *A Journey Throughout Ireland During the Spring, Summer and Autumn of 1834*, 2 vols. (London, 1834)
Inglis, T., *Moral Monopoly: The Rise and Fall of the Catholic Church in Modern Ireland*, 2nd edn (Dublin, 1998)
Jackson, A., *The Ulster Party: Irish Unionists in the House of Commons, 1884–1911* (Oxford, 1989)
Jackson, P., 'Outside the Jurisdiction: Irishwomen Seeking Abortion' in C. Curtin, P. Jackson and B. O'Connor (eds.), *Gender in Irish Society* (Galway, 1987)
Jalal, A., *Democracy and Authoritarianism in South Asia* (Cambridge, 1995)
Jalland, P., *The Liberals and Ireland* (Brighton, 1980)
Johnson, D., *The Interwar Economy in Ireland* (Dublin, 1985)
—— and Kennedy, L., 'The Two Irish Economies since 1920' in *A New History of Ireland*, vol. 7 (Oxford, forthcoming)

Johnston, J., *The Nemesis of Economic Nationalism* (London and Dublin, 1934)

Kavanagh, P., *Collected Poems* (New York, 1964)

Kellas, J.G., *The Politics of Nationalism and Ethnicity*, 2nd edn (London, 1998)

Kelly, J., 'The Genesis of the "Protestant Ascendancy', in G. O'Brien (ed.), *Parliament, Politics and People* (Dublin, 1989), pp. 93–128

Kennedy, D., *The Widening Gulf: Northern Attitudes to the Independent Irish State, 1919–49* (Belfast, 1988)

Kennedy, K., Giblin, T. and McHugh, D., *The Economic Development of Ireland in the Twentieth Century* (London, 1988)

Kennedy, L., 'The Union of Ireland and Britain 1801–1921' in L. Kennedy, *Colonialism, Religion and Nationalism in Ireland* (Belfast, 1996), pp. 35–74

Kennedy, M., *Division and Consensus: The Politics of Cross-Border Relations in Ireland, 1925–1969* (Dublin, 2000)

—— and Skelly, J.M. (eds.), *Irish Foreign Policy, 1919–1966: From Independence to Internationalism* (Dublin, 2000)

Kennedy, R.E. Jr, *The Irish: Emigration, Marriage, and Fertility* (Berkeley, Calif., 1973)

Keogh, D., *Ireland and Europe 1919–1989* (Cork, 1990)

—— *Jews in Twentieth-Century Ireland: Refugees, Anti-Semitism and the Holocaust* (Cork, 1998)

—— *Twentieth Century Ireland: Nation and State* (Dublin, 1994)

—— 'Eamon de Valera and Hitler: An Examination of International Reaction to the Visit to the German Minister, May 1945', *Irish Studies in International Affairs*, 3:1 (1989), pp. 69–92

—— 'The Constitutional Revolution: An Analysis of the Making of the Constitution' in F. Litton (ed.), *The Constitution of Ireland 1937–1987* (Dublin, 1988)

—— 'The Role of the Catholic Church in the Republic of Ireland 1922–1995' in Forum for Peace and Reconciliation, *Building Trust in Ireland* (Belfast, 1996), pp. 85–214

—— and O'Driscoll, F., 'Ireland' in Buchanan and Conway, *Political Catholicism in Europe*, pp. 275–300

Kersbergen, K.V., *Social Capitalism: A Study of Christian Democracy and the Welfare State* (London, 1995)

Kettle, T.M., *The Open Secret of Ireland* (London, 1912)

Kissane, B., 'Majority Rule and the Stabilisation of Democracy in the Irish Free State', *Irish Political Studies*, 13 (1998), pp. 1–24

—— 'The Not-So-Amazing Case of Irish Democracy', *Irish Political Studies*, 10 (1995), pp. 43–68

Klinge, M., 'Finland: From Napoleonic Legacy to Nordic Co-operation' in Teich and Porter, *The National Question*, pp. 317–31

Kotsonouris, M., *Retreat From Revolution: The Dáil Courts, 1920–24* (Dublin, 1994)

Kumar, R., *Essays in the Social History of India* (Calcutta, 1983)

Lafay, J.-D., 'Conservative Nationalism and Democratic Institutions' in A. Breton, G. Galeotti, P. Salmon and R. Weintrobe (eds.), *Nationalism and Rationality* (Cambridge, 1995), pp. 159–72

Laffan, M., *The Partition of Ireland 1911–1925* (Dundalk, 1983)

—— *The Resurrection of Ireland: The Sinn Féin Party, 1916–1923* (Cambridge, 1999)

Larkin, E., *The Roman Catholic Church and the Creation of the Modern Irish State 1878–1886* (Dublin, 1975)

—— (ed.), *Alexis de Tocqueville's Journey in Ireland: July–August 1835* (Dublin, 1990)

Lee, J.J., *Ireland 1912–1985: Politics and Society* (Cambridge, 1989)

—— 'Aspects of Corporatist Thought in Ireland: The Commission on Vocational Organisation, 1939–43' in A. Cosgrove and D. McCartney (eds.), *Studies in Irish History Presented to R. Dudley Edwards* (Dublin, 1979), pp. 324–46

—— 'In Search of Patrick Pearse' in Ní Dhonnchadha and Dorgan (eds.), *Revising the Rising*, pp. 122–38
—— and Ó Tuathaigh, G., *The Age of de Valera* (Dublin, 1982)
Lindblom, C., *Politics and Markets* (New York, 1977)
Lindgren, R.E., *Norway–Sweden: Union, Disunion, and Scandinavian Integration* (Princeton, N.J., 1959)
Linz, J.J., 'Some Notes Toward a Comparative Study of Fascism in Sociological Historical Perspective' in Walter Laquer (ed.), *Fascism: A Reader's Guide* (Harmondsworth, 1979), pp. 13–78
—— and Stepan, A. (eds.), *The Breakdown of Democratic Regimes: Europe* (Baltimore, Md., 1978)
Lipset, S.M. and Rokkan, S., 'Cleavage Structures, Party Systems and Voter Alignment' in S.M. Lipset and S. Rokkan (eds.), *Party Systems and Voter Alignment* (New York, 1967), pp. 1–64
—— Seong, K.-R. and Torres, J.C., 'A Comparative Analysis of the Social Requisites of Democracy', *International Social Science Quarterly*, 45:2 (1993), pp. 155–75
Logan, J. (ed.), *Teachers' Union: The TUI and its Forerunners 1899–1994* (Dublin, 1999)
Longford, Earl of and O'Neill, T.P., *Eamon de Valera* (London, 1970)
Lucey, C., 'Making the School System of Ireland Catholic', *Irish Ecclesiastical Record*, 5th Series, 52 (1938), pp. 405–17
Lynch, M., *Scotland: A New History* (London, 1991)
Lyons, F.S.L., *John Dillon* (London, 1968)
Lyons, J.B., *The Enigma of Tom Kettle* (Dublin, 1983)
McBride, I., 'Ulster and the British Problem' in Richard English and Graham Walker (eds.), *Unionism in Modern Ireland* (Dublin, 1996), pp. 1–18
McCabe, I., *A Diplomatic History of Ireland 1948–49* (Dublin, 1991)
McCarthy, C., *Trade Unions in Ireland 1894–1960* (Dublin, 1977)
McCarthy, Rev J., 'Morality of a State Ban on the Emigration of Minors', *Irish Ecclesiastical Record*, 5th Series, 71 (1949), pp. 269–72
McCarthy, J.F., 'Ireland's Turnaround: Whitaker and the 1958 Plan for Economic Development' in J.F. McCarthy (ed.), *Planning Ireland's Future: The Legacy of T.K. Whitaker* (Dublin, 1990)
McConvery, B., 'Hell-fire and Poitín: Redemptorist Missions in the Irish Free State (1922–1936), *History Ireland*, 8:3 (2000), pp. 18–22
McCourt, F., *Angela's Ashes* (London, 1996)
McCullagh, D., *A Makeshift Majority: The First Inter-Party Government, 1948–51* (Dublin, 1998)
McDannell, C., *Material Christianity: Religion and Popular Culture in America* (New Haven, 1995)
McDermott, B. (ed.), *The Catholic Question in England and Ireland: The Papers of Denys Scully* (Dublin, 1988)
MacDermott, E., *Clann na Poblachta* (Cork, 1998)
Macdonald, C.M.M. (ed.), *Unionist Scotland 1800–1997* (Edinburgh, 1998)
McDonald, W., *Some Ethical Questions of Peace and War* (London, 1919)
McDowell, R.B., *The Irish Convention 1917–18* (London, 1970)
Mac Giolla Choille, B. (ed.), *Intelligence Notes 1913–1916* (Dublin, 1966)
Mac Gréil, M., *Prejudice and Tolerance in Ireland* (Dublin, 1977)
McInerney, M., 'The Gerry Boland Story', *Irish Times*, 11 October 1968
McKee, E., 'Church-State Relations and the Development of Irish Health Policy: The Mother and Child Scheme, 1944–53', *Irish Historical Studies*, 25:98 (1986), pp. 159–94
McLeod, H., *Religion and the People of Western Europe 1789–1970* (Oxford, 1981)

McMahon, D., *Republicans and Imperialists* (New Haven and London, 1984)
Mair, P., *The Changing Irish Party System* (New York, 1987)
Mandle, W.F., *The Gaelic Athletic Association and Irish Nationalist Politics 1884–1924* (Dublin, 1987)
Manning, M., *James Dillon* (Dublin, 1999)
—— *The Blueshirts* (Dublin, 1970)
Mansergh, N., *The Irish Free State* (London, 1934)
—— *The Irish Question 1840–1921*, 3rd edn (London, 1975)
Marsden, J., 'Religion and the Nationalist Cause in the Thought of Patrick Pearse', *Studies*, 84 (1995), pp. 28–37
Martin, D., *A General Theory of Secularization* (Oxford, 1978)
Martin, F.X., 'Eoin MacNeill on the 1916 Rising', *Irish Historical Studies*, 12 (1961), pp. 226–71
—— 'MacNeill and the Foundation of the Irish Volunteers' in F.X. Martin and F.J. Byrne (eds.), *The Scholar Revolutionary: Eoin MacNeill 1867–1945* (Shannon, 1973), pp. 99–179
Marwick, A., *The Sixties* (Oxford, 1998)
Maume, P., *D.P. Moran* (Dublin, 1995)
—— 'Anti-Machiavel: Three Ulster Nationalists in the Age of De Valera', *Irish Political Studies*, 14 (1999), pp. 43–63
—— Nationalism and Partition: The Political Thought of Arthur Clery', *Irish Historical Studies*, 31:122 (1998), pp. 222–40
—— *The Long Gestation: Irish Nationalist Life 1891–1918* (Dublin, 1999)
Mill, J.S., *Considerations on Representative Government* (1861) in J. Gray (ed.), *On Liberty and Other Essays* (Oxford, 1991)
Miller, D.W., *Church, State and Nation in Ireland 1898–1921* (Dublin, 1973)
—— *Queen's Rebels* (Dublin, 1978)
Milotte, M., *Banished Babies: The Secret History of Ireland's Baby Export Business* (Dublin, 1997)
Milward, A.S., *The European Rescue of the Nation State* (London, 1992)
—— Lynch, F.B., Romero, F., Ranieri, R. and Sørensen, V., *The Frontiers of National Sovereignty* (London, 1993)
Mitchell, A., *Revolutionary Government in Ireland* (Dublin, 1995)
Mjøset, L., *The Irish Economy in a Comparative Institutional Perspective* (Dublin, 1992)
Montague, J., *Collected Poems* (Oldcastle, Co. Meath, 1995)
Moore, M. (ed.), *National Self-Determination and Secession* (Oxford, 1998)
Moore, T., *A Letter to the Roman Catholics of Dublin* (Dublin, 1810)
Moran, D.P., 'Is the Irish Nation Dying?' in D.P. Moran, *The Philosophy of Irish Ireland* (Dublin, 1905), pp. 1–10
Moss, W., *Political Parties in the Irish Free State* (New York, 1933)
Mosse, G.L., *The Image of Man: The Creation of Modern Masculinity* (Oxford, 1996)
Moynihan, M. (ed.), *Speeches and Statements by Eamon de Valera 1917–73* (Dublin, 1980)
Murphy, G., 'The Politics of Economic Realignment, Ireland 1948–1964' (PhD thesis, Dublin City University, 1996)
Murray, P., 'Irish Cultural Nationalism in the United Kingdom State: Politics and the Gaelic League 1900–1918', *Irish Political Studies*, 8 (1993), pp. 55–72
—— *Oracles of God: The Roman Catholic Church and Irish Politics, 1922–37* (Dublin, 1999)
National Economic and Social Council, *Ireland in the European Community: Performance, Prospects and Strategy* (Dublin, 1989)
Newman, J., *Studies in Political Morality* (Dublin and London, 1962)
Ní Donnchadha, M. and Dorgan, T. (eds.), *Revising the Rising* (Derry, 1991)
Noll, Mark A. (ed.), *Religion and American Politics: From the Colonial Period to the 1980s* (New York, 1990)

O'Brien, C.C., *God Land: Reflections on Religion and Nationalism* (Cambridge, Mass., 1988)
—— *Memoir: My Life and Themes* (Dublin, 1998)
—— *The Great Melody: A Thematic Biography of Edmund Burke* (London, 1992)
—— 'Nationalism and the Reconquest of Ireland', *The Crane Bag*, 1:2 (1977), pp. 8–13
O'Brien, G., 'The Strange Death of the Irish Language, 1780–1800' in G. O'Brien (ed.), *Parliament, Politics and People* (Dublin, 1989), pp. 149–70
O'Brien, J., *The Arms Trial* (Dublin, 2000)
O'Brien, J.A. (ed.), *The Vanishing Irish: The Enigma of the Modern World* (New York, 1953)
O'Brien, J.V., *William O'Brien and the Course of Irish Politics 1881–1918* (Berkeley, Calif., 1976)
Ó Buachalla, S., *Education Policy in Twentieth-Century Ireland* (Dublin, 1988)
O'Connell, J. (ed.), *The Life and Speeches of Daniel O'Connell, MP*, 2 vols. (Dublin, 1846)
O'Connell, M. (ed.), *The Correspondence of Daniel O'Connell*, 8 vols. (Dublin, 1972–80)
O'Connor, E., *A Labour History of Ireland* (Dublin, 1992)
O'Connor, U., *Celtic Dawn* (London, 1984)
Ó Corráin, D. (ed.), *James Hogan: Revolutionary, Historian and Political Scientist* (Dublin, 2000)
Ó Drisceoil, D., *Censorship in Ireland 1939–1945: Neutrality, Politics and Society* (Cork, 1996)
O'Faolain, N., *Are You Somebody?* (Dublin, 1996)
O'Ferrall, F., *Catholic Emancipation: Daniel O'Connell and the Birth of Irish Democracy 1820–30*, (Dublin, 1985)
Ó Gráda, C., *A Rocky Road: The Irish Economy since the 1920s* (Manchester, 1997)
—— *Ireland: A New Economic History* (Oxford, 1994)
O'Halpin, E., *Defending Ireland: The Irish State and its Enemies since 1922* (Oxford, 1999)
—— *The Decline of the Union: British Government in Ireland 1892–1920* (Dublin, 1987)
—— 'Parliamentary Party Discipline and Tactics: The Fianna Fáil Archives 1926–32', *Irish Historical Studies*, 30:120 (1997), pp. 581–90
O'Hegarty, P.S., *A History of Ireland Under the Union* (London, 1952)
O'Leary, C., 'Professor Lee's Ireland' (unpublished manuscript in author's possession)
O'Leary, D., *Vocationalism and Social Catholicism in Twentieth-Century Ireland* (Dublin, 1999)
O'Leary, E., 'The Irish National Teachers' Organisation and the Marriage Bar for Women National Teachers, 1933–1958', *Saothar*, 12 (1987), pp. 47–52
Olesen, T.B. (ed.), *Interdependence Versus Integration: Denmark, Scandinavia and Western Europe 1945–1960* (Odense, 1995)
Orridge, A., 'The Blueshirts and the "Economic War": A Study of Ireland in the Context of Dependency Theory', *Political Studies*, 31:3 (1983), pp. 351–69
Pašeta, S., *Before the Revolution: Nationalism, Social Change and Ireland's Catholic Élite, 1879–1922* (Cork, 1999)
Paul-Dubois, L., *Contemporary Ireland* (Dublin, 1911)
Payne, S.G., *Fascism: Comparison and Definition* (Madison, Wis., 1980)
Pearse, P.H., *Political Writings and Speeches* (Dublin, 1966)
Prager, J., *Building Democracy in Ireland* (Cambridge, 1986)
Rafter, K., *The Clann: The Story of Clann na Poblachta* (Cork, 1996)
Raymond, R.J., 'David Gray, the Aiken Mission and Irish Neutrality, 1940–41', *Diplomatic History*, 9 (1985), pp. 55–71
Regan, J.M., *The Irish Counter-Revolution 1921–1936: Treatyite Politics and Settlement in Independent Ireland* (Dublin, 1999)
—— 'The Politics of Reaction: The Dynamics of Treatyite Government and Policy, 1922–33', *Irish Historical Studies*, 30:120 (1997), pp. 542–63
Roberts, G., 'The British Offer to End Partition, June 1940', *History Ireland*, 9:1 (2001), pp. 5–6

Rock, D., *Authoritarian Argentina: The Nationalist Movement, its History and its Impact* (Berkeley, Calif., 1993)

Rosenberg, J.L., 'The 1941 Mission of Frank Aiken to the United States: An American Perspective', *Irish Historical Studies*, 22:88 (1980), pp. 162–77

Rynne, S., *Father John Hayes, Leader of Muintir na Tíre* (Dublin, 1960)

Schmitt, D., *The Irony of Irish Democracy: The Impact of Political Culture on Administration and Democratic Political Development in Ireland* (London and Toronto, 1973)

Scully, D., *An Irish Catholic's Advice to his Brethren* (Dublin, 1803)

Sen, A., *Poverty and Famines* (Oxford, 1981)

—— 'Individual Freedom as a Social Commitment', *New York Review of Books*, 14 June 1990

Sheehan, Canon P.A., *The Beauty of Summer* (Cork, 1973); originally published in *Under the Cedars and the Stars* (Dublin, 1903)

Sinnott, R., *Irish Voters Decide* (Manchester, 1995)

Smith, M., 'The Title An Taoiseach in the 1937 Constitution', *Irish Political Studies*, 10 (1995), pp. 179–84

Sørensen, V.M., '"Free Trade" versus Regulated Markets: Danish Agricultural Organizations and the Green Pool, 1950–1954' in Griffiths and Girvin (eds.), *The Green Pool*, pp. 203–22

Stephens, J., *The Insurrection in Dublin* (Dublin and London, 1916)

Teich, M. and Porter, R. (eds.), *The National Question in Europe in Historical Context* (Cambridge, 1993)

Telesis, *A Review of Industrial Policy* (Dublin, 1982)

Titley, B., *Church, State and the Control of Schools in Ireland, 1900–1944* (Kingston and Montreal, 1983)

Tocqueville, A. de, *Democracy in America*, ed. by J.P. Mayer (Garden City, New York, 1969)

—— *Journeys to England and Ireland*, ed. by J.P. Mayer (London, 1958)

Tone, T.W., *An Argument on Behalf of the Catholics of Ireland* (Belfast, 1973; original edition 1791)

United Nations Economic Commission for Europe, *Economic Survey of Europe in 1948* (Geneva, 1949)

—— *Economic Survey of Europe in 1951* (Geneva, 1952)

Urwin, D.W., *From Ploughshare to Ballotbox: The Politics of Agrarian Defence in Europe* (Oslo, 1980)

Valiulis, M.G., *Almost a Rebellion: The Irish Army Mutiny of 1924* (Cork, 1985)

Vane, C. (ed.), *Memoirs and Correspondence of Viscount Castlereagh*, 12 vols. (London, 1849)

Varley, T., 'Farmers against Nationalists: The Rise and Fall of Clann na Talmhan in Galway' in R. Gillespie and G. Moran (eds.), *Galway: History and Society* (Dublin, 1995), pp. 589–622

—— and Moser, P., 'Clann na Talmhan: Ireland's Last Farmers' Party', *History Ireland*, 3:2 (1995), pp. 39–43

Walker, B., 'The 1885 and 1886 General Elections: A Milestone in Irish History' in Walker, *Dancing to History's Tune*, pp. 15–33

—— *Dancing to History's Tune: History, Myth and Politics in Ireland* (Belfast, 1996)

Walker, G., *Intimate Strangers: Political and Cultural Interaction Between Scotland and Ulster in Modern Times* (Edinburgh, 1995)

Walsh, J.J., *Recollections of a Rebel* (Tralee, 1944)

Walzer, M., *Just and Unjust Wars*, 2nd edn (New York, 1992)

Ward, A.J., *The Irish Constitutional Tradition* (Dublin, 1994)

Ward, C., 'Ireland' in H. Mol (ed.), *Western Religion: A Country by Country Sociological Inquiry* (The Hague, 1972)

White, J., *Minority Report: The Protestant Community in the Irish Republic* (Dublin, 1975)

Whyte, J.H., *Catholics in Western Europe* (Dublin, 1981)
—— *Church and State in Modern Ireland 1923–1970* (Dublin, 1971)
—— *Dáil Deputies* (Dublin, 1965)
—— 'Ireland: Politics without Social Bases' in R. Rose (ed.), *Electoral Behaviour: A Comparative Handbook* (New York, 1974), pp. 619–51
Wolf, J.B., '"Withholding Their Due": The Dispute between Ireland and Great Britain over Unemployment Insurance Payments to Conditionally Landed Irish Wartime Volunteer Workers', *Saothar*, 21 (1996), pp. 39–45
Young, J.R., 'The Scottish Parliament and National Identity from the Union of the Crowns to the Union of the Parliaments, 1603–1707' in Broun, Finlay and Lynch (eds.), *Image and Identity*, pp. 105–42

INDEX